Doing the Work
of Comparative Theology

Doing the Work
of Comparative Theology

Veli-Matti Kärkkäinen

WILLIAM B. EERDMANS PUBLISHING COMPANY
GRAND RAPIDS, MICHIGAN

Wm. B. Eerdmans Publishing Co.
4035 Park East Court SE, Grand Rapids, Michigan 49546
www.eerdmans.com

26 25 24 23 22 21 20   1 2 3 4 5 6 7

ISBN 978-0-8028-7466-5

Library of Congress Cataloging-in-Publication Data

Names: Kärkkäinen, Veli-Matti, author.
Title: Doing the work of comparative theology / Veli-Matti Kärkkäinen.
Description: Grand Rapids: Wm. B. Eerdmans Publishing Co., 2020. |
   Includes bibliographical references and index. | Summary: "This text in
   comparative theology correlates and compares Christian with those of
   four other living faiths, Islam, Judaism, Buddhism, and Hinduism"—
   Provided by publisher.
Identifiers: LCCN 2019026126 | ISBN 9780802874665 (paperback)
Subjects: LCSH: Christianity and other religions.
Classification: LCC BR127 .K3735 2020 | DDC 261.2—dc23
LC record available at https://lccn.loc.gov/2019026126

Contents

Preface

This book introduces the idea, task, and ways of doing comparative theology. This fairly recent theological subdiscipline—usually grouped under systematic theology—provides a platform for focused and limited detailed comparisons of beliefs, doctrines, and teachings among faith traditions. Christian comparative theology approaches these interfaith exercises from the standpoint of its own scriptural, theological, and ecclesiastical traditions. This primer conducts comparative exercises focused on main Christian doctrinal beliefs vis-à-vis Jewish, Islamic, Buddhist, and Hindu teachings.

This text is based on sections of my five-volume series titled A Constructive Christian Theology for the Pluralistic World (2013–2017): *Christ and Reconciliation* (2013), *Trinity and Revelation* (2014), *Creation and Humanity* (2015), *Spirit and Salvation* (2016), and *Community and Hope* (2017). To communicate and make this highly technical and complex theology available to theology students and other interested readers, the current textbook aims for clarity, simplicity, and user-friendliness without in any way sacrificing accuracy.

I dedicate this volume to the "so great a cloud of" students from five continents, men and women from all Christian traditions: those at Fuller Theological Seminary, a "theological laboratory" to learn from and in which to engage in global diversity and plurality, and also my students, past and present, in Thailand and Finland—and beyond.

As with so many other books, I owe greater gratitude than I am able to express to my Fuller Theological Seminary editor, Susan Carlson Wood. Suffice it to say that her impeccable editorial skills have again helped transform my

"Finnish English" into American English! My doctoral student Viktor Toth checked the accuracy of all references and also compiled the indexes.

Since this textbook is based on the five-volume constructive theology series, I also wish to take this opportunity to thank once again all of my research assistants who over many years collaborated in this project, all of them doctoral students at Fuller's Center for Advanced Theological Studies: Getachew Kiros, Leulseged Tesfaye, Naoki Inoue, Amy Chilton Thompson, David Hunsicker, Dan Brockway, Joshua Muthalali, Christopher O'Brian, Jongseock Shin, and Viktor Toth. They helped find sources, finished the meticulous checking of the accuracy of all references, and compiled indexes. Without the help of these doctoral students, representing four continents, the writing process would have taken much longer.

Abbreviations

A&D	*Angels and Demons: Perspectives and Practice in Diverse Religious Traditions.* Edited by Peter G. Riddell and Beverly Smith Riddell. Nottingham, UK: Apollos, 2007.
CD	Karl Barth, *Church Dogmatics.* Edited by Geoffrey William Bromiley and Thomas Forsyth Torrance. Translated by G. W. Bromiley. 14 vols. Edinburgh: T&T Clark, 1956–1975. (Online edition by Alexander Street Press, 1975.)
CCCIT	*The Cambridge Companion to Classical Islamic Theology.* Edited by Tim Winter. Cambridge: Cambridge University Press, 2008, online edition.
DEHF	*Divine Emptiness and Historical Fullness: A Buddhist-Jewish-Christian Conversation with Masao Abe.* Edited by Christopher Ives. Valley Forge, PA: Trinity, 1995.
DIRW	*Death and Immortality in the Religions of the World.* Edited by Paul Badham and Linda Badham. New York: Paragon House, 1987.
EJ	*Encyclopedia Judaica.* Edited by Michael Berenbaum and Fred Skolnik. 17 vols. 2nd ed. Detroit: Macmillan Reference, USA, 2007. Available at http://www.bjeindy.org/resources/library/encyclopediajudaica/.
ER	*Encyclopedia of Religion.* Edited by Lindsay Jones. 15 vols. 2nd ed. Detroit: Macmillan Reference, USA; Gale, Cengage Learning, 2005.

HRC	*Handbook of Religious Conversion.* Edited by H. Newton Malony and Samuel Southard. Birmingham, AL: Religious Education Press, 1992.
I&E	*Islam and Ecology: A Bestowed Trust.* Edited by Richard C. Foltz, Frederick M. Denny, and Azizan Baharuddin. Cambridge, MA: Harvard University Press, 2003.
ISHCP	*Islam and Science: Historic and Contemporary Perspectives.* Edited by Muzaffar Iqbal. 3 vols. Surrey, UK: Ashgate, 2012.
	ISHCP 1: Studies in the Islam and Science Nexus
	ISHCP 2: Contemporary Issues in Islam and Science
	ISHCP 3: New Perspectives on the History of Islamic Science
JBC	*Jesus beyond Christianity: The Classic Texts.* Edited by Gregory A. Barker and Stephen E. Gregg. Oxford: Oxford University Press, 2010.
JWF	*Jesus in the World's Faiths: Leading Thinkers from Five Religions Reflect on His Meaning.* Edited by Gregory A. Barker. Maryknoll, NY: Orbis, 2008.
OHE	*Oxford Handbook of Eschatology.* Edited by Jerry L. Walls. New York: Oxford University Press, 2009, online edition.
OHM	*The Oxford Handbook of Millennialism.* Edited by Catherine Wessinger. New York: Oxford University Press, 2011, online edition.
OHRD	*The Oxford Handbook of Religious Diversity.* Edited by Chad Meister. Oxford: Oxford University Press, 2010.
OHRS	*The Oxford Handbook of Religion and Science.* Edited by Philip Clayton. Associate editor, Zachary Simpson. Oxford: Oxford University Press, 2006.
Pannenberg, *ST*	Wolfhart Pannenberg. *Systematic Theology.* Translated by Geoffrey W. Bromiley. 3 vols. Grand Rapids: Eerdmans, 1991, 1994, 1998.
RCP	*Repentance: A Comparative Perspective.* Edited by Amitai Etzioni and David E. Carney. Lanham, MD: Rowman & Littlefield, 1997.
SBE	*Sacred Books of the East.* Translated by Max Müller. 50 vols. Oxford: Oxford University Press, 1879–1910. Available at www.sacred-texts.com.

| SRPW | *Science and Religion in a Post-colonial World: Interfaith Perspectives.* Edited by Zainal Abidin Bagir. Adelaide: ATF, 2005. |
| TRV | *Teaching Religion and Violence.* Edited by Brian K. Pennington. Oxford: Oxford University Press, 2012. |

Bible references, unless otherwise indicated, are from the Revised Standard Version of the Bible, copyright 1952 [2nd edition, 1971] by the Division of Christian Education of the National Council of the Churches of Christ in the United States of America. Used by permission. All rights reserved.

Unless otherwise indicated, contemporary Roman Catholic documents, documents of Vatican II, papal encyclicals, and similar works are quoted from the official Vatican website: www.vatican.va. This includes also dialogue documents with Lutherans, Reformed, Anglicans, Methodists, and Pentecostals.

Contemporary World Council of Churches documents are quoted from their official website: http://www.oikoumene.org/, unless otherwise indicated.

Mishnah texts are from eMishnah.com (2008) at http://www.emishnah .com/Yoma.html.

The Qur'anic references, unless otherwise indicated, are from *The Holy Qur'ān: A New English Translation of Its Meanings* © 2008 Royal Aal al-Bayt Institute for Islamic Thought, Amman, Jordan. This version of the Qur'ān is also available online at http://altafsir.com.

Hadith texts are from the Hadith Collection website: http://www .hadithcollection.com/ (2009–).

Bhagavad Gita texts, unless otherwise noted, are from the translation by Ramanand Prasad, EAWC Anthology, 1988. Available at http://eawc.evansville .edu/anthology/gita.htm.

All other Hindu texts, unless otherwise indicated, are from the Sacred Texts website: http://www.sacred-texts.com/hin/index.htm.

Buddhist texts, unless otherwise indicated, are from "Tipitaka: The Pali Canon," edited by John T. Bullitt. *Access to Insight*, May 10, 2011. http://www .accesstoinsight.org/tipitaka/index.html.

INTRODUCTION:
What Is Comparative Theology?
Why Do We Need It?

Orientation: Why Do We Need Comparative Theology?

The simple answer to this question is that we need comparative theology because the world in which we live in the beginning of the third millennium is deeply and widely religious! Indeed, to the surprise of the "prophets of secularism," what had been expected to become a religionless world with the progress of modernity has become even more religious. At the global level, religions are not only holding their own but are also flourishing and (in some cases) growing in numbers. Religious plurality no longer characterizes only certain locations and continents but is now a reality over the whole globe, including the Global North.[1]

Just think of the statistics: currently about a third of the world's population belongs to the Christian church (2.4 billion) and about a quarter is comprised of Muslims (1.6 billion). The 1 billion Hindus make up about 15 percent, followed by Buddhists at half that number. Jews number fewer than 15 million, and over 400 million belong to various kinds of "folk religions." Only about 15 percent (1 billion) label themselves religiously unaffiliated (even though the majority of them entertain some kind of religious-type beliefs and practices).[2]

1. See Charles L. Cohen and Ronald L. Numbers, eds., *Gods in America: Religious Pluralism in the United States* (New York: Oxford University Press, 2013).

2. Pew Research Center, *The Global Religious Landscape*, December 18, 2012, http://www.pewforum.org/2012/12/18/global-religious-landscape-exec/. See also the massive resource of Stanley D. Brunn, ed., *The Changing World Religion Map: Sacred Places, Identities, Practices, and Politics*, 5 vols. (Dordrecht and New York: Springer, 2015).

This means that our world is currently more religious than ever—even if forms of secularism are also flourishing, though numbers-wise much more modestly.

Religions are growing and flourishing, and they are in constant interaction with each other. Whereas Hinduism and Buddhism are mainly regional (Asian) religions, Christians are by far the most evenly distributed around the globe. Roughly equal numbers of Christians live in Europe (26 percent), Latin America and the Caribbean (24 percent), and sub-Saharan Africa (24 percent). Muslims are also fairly evenly spread out, although a majority (over 60 percent) live in Pacific Asia, and the rest in Africa and the Middle East. And although three-quarters of the adherents of the world's religions live in a majority position in their own context—Hindus most consistently so in India—religions are not isolated from each other. Adherents of religions meet each other in homes and at work, on the streets and in markets, as well as at schools and in worship places.

This reality shows why we need ministers, other religious leaders, laypersons, academicians, and students who know something about other faiths and who are able to compare notes. The statistical analysis above should be a clarion call for Christian theology to seriously engage other religions' views, teachings, and doctrines.[3] That Christian theologians seem not to be interested in that should not be made a pretext for Christian oblivion. There are of course reasons for that oblivion; beyond the lack of awareness, for instance, the task of acquiring enough learning even in the basics of other faiths is daunting for the theologian.[4] That, however, should not be an excuse but rather an invitation for expanding scholarship.

Because of the overwhelming continuing presence and force of religious plurality and forms of religious pluralisms (ideologies and interpretations of how to deal with the fact of plurality), the ambitious and noble challenge for all Christian theologians calls them to work toward a truly comparative theological mode in an authentic dialogue with the teachings, doctrines, and insights of other faiths. Willingness to do that takes the theologian out of the safe zone of her own tradition and makes her vulnerable, but at the same time it opens up whole new ways of engaging the complex world around her.[5]

3. See the important reflections and suggestions in Douglas John Hall, *Thinking the Faith: Christian Theology in a North American Context* (Minneapolis: Fortress, 1991), 208–9.

4. See Timothy C. Tennent, *Theology in the Context of World Christianity: How the Global Church Is Influencing the Way We Think about and Discuss Theology* (Grand Rapids: Zondervan, 2007), 55.

5. Francis X. Clooney, SJ, *Comparative Theology: Deep Learning across Religious Borders* (West Sussex, UK: Wiley-Blackwell, 2010), 7.

Comparative Theology and Related Disciplines in the Interfaith Engagement

There are three interrelated yet distinct disciplines that facilitate an interfaith engagement: religious studies/comparative religion, theology of religions, and comparative theology. Let us first define each of the three and then focus on the topic of this book, comparative theology.[6]

First, comparative religion is a subset of the larger domain of religious studies. Religious studies employs various subdisciplines and approaches in investigating the phenomenon, spread, spiritual life, practices, teachings, and other facets of living religions. Comparative religion focuses—as the name indicates—on a scientific comparison of religions' doctrines, teachings, and practices. While it may be and often is interdisciplinary in that it deals with many aspects of religion, a major component of comparative religion examines doctrines and teachings. Comparative religion seeks to do its work from a neutral, noncommitted point of view.

Second, Christian theology of religions, as the name indicates, is a confessional Christian discipline. It seeks to reflect critically and sympathetically on the theological meaning of religions in the economy of God. Its goal is to "account theologically for the meaning and value of other religions. Christian theology of religions attempts to think theologically about what it means for Christians to live with people of other faiths and about the relationship of Christianity to other religions."[7]

Since theology of religions operates usually at a fairly general level, third, yet another discipline is needed: "comparative theology." Gleaning resources not only from Christian theology and theology of religions but also from comparative religion, it investigates "ideas, words, images and acts, historical developments—as found in two or more traditions or strands of tradition."[8] Complementing theology of religions' more generic approach, comparative theology makes every effort to consider in detail specific topics in religious traditions.

Whereas comparative religion seeks to be "neutral" on faith commitments and look "objectively" at the features of religious traditions, and typically does

---

6. A useful discussion is Clooney, *Comparative Theology*, 8–16.

7. Veli-Matti Kärkkäinen, *An Introduction to the Theology of Religions: Biblical, Historical, and Contemporary Perspectives* (Downers Grove, IL: InterVarsity Press, 2003), 20.

8. Clooney, *Comparative Theology*, 9. For historical precedents, see chap. 2, and for a survey of some leading contemporary comparative theologians, see chap. 3.

3

not allow for the reality of gods/deities of religions, *comparative theology*, in contrast, "marks acts of faith seeking understanding which are rooted in a particular faith tradition but which, from that foundation, venture into learning from one or more other faith traditions."[9] Comparative theology is robustly Christian theology; it is committed to its traditions and contemporary expressions.[10]

The confessional nature of comparative theology, however, does not therefore disqualify it as an academic discipline. It acknowledges that it is "tied to specific communities of faith [but] without being trapped by these communities."[11] As any other academic discipline, it also exercises proper critical assessment.

What are the benefits of comparative theology? We can list the following three as a summary statement:

> First, Christians can and should learn something about non-Christian religious traditions for the sake of the religious other; in fact, both the license and the imperative to do so rest on a biblical foundation. Second, Christians can and should expect to learn something about God in the course of that exploration, and the basis for such a belief can be found in who God has revealed Godself to be and how Christians have traditionally understood that divine self-revelation. Third, Christians can and should expect that their understanding of their own faith tradition will be stretched and challenged, but at the same time deepened and strengthened through such interreligious dialogue.[12]

Is Comparative Theology Feasible?

Even a casual acquaintance with world religions raises the question of whether comparing notes on theological issues is an appropriate and useful way of assessing religions. Just think of the foundational doctrine of God. Whereas Judaism and Islam certainly affirm belief in God akin enough to Christian theology, neither Hinduism nor Buddhism intuitively appears to be a candi-

---

9. Clooney, *Comparative Theology*, 10.

10. See further, James Fredericks, "A Universal Religious Experience? Comparative Theology as an Alternative to a Theology of Religions," *Horizons* 22, no. 1 (1995): 67–87.

11. J. Wentzel Van Huyssteen, *Alone in the World? Human Uniqueness in Science and Theology* (Grand Rapids: Eerdmans, 2006), 12.

12. Kristin Johnston Largen, *Baby Krishna, Infant Christ: A Comparative Theology of Salvation* (Maryknoll, NY: Orbis, 2011), 9.

date for comparison. Whether Hinduism represents monotheism (belief in one deity) or polytheism (belief in a number of deities), its conception of the deity or the ultimate reality differs vastly from that of the Semitic faiths. In Buddhism's case, the gap is even wider, as in its original Theravada form it makes a marked effort to turn away from the focus on any deity, and even in its current major form, Mahayana, the question of the ultimate reality is utterly complex. Many other such complicating examples could be listed. So, how feasible is it to even attempt this kind of dialogical comparison?

A growing number of comparative theologians hold the opinion that notwithstanding these radical challenges, a dialogue attempted cautiously and with a discerning mind is indeed possible. This confidence is funded by the conviction that "there is a tradition at the very heart of [many living] . . . faiths which is held common. It is not that precisely the same doctrines are believed, but that the same tendencies of thought and devotion exist, and are expressed within rather diverse patterns of thought, characteristic of the faiths in question." That said, "religions generate infinite differences."[13] Hence, comparative theology does not seek to brush aside or undermine deep dynamic tension concerning religions and their claims for truth; in the spirit of hospitality, these differences are brought to the dialogue table. In other words, properly done, comparative theology does not attempt to reach an agreement at any cost. Attempting to water down or deny real differences among religions, as typical forms of religious pluralism seek to do, is a failing exercise on more than one account. In this context, just consider how useless and uninteresting a task it would be to compare two items that are supposed to be alike!

Comparison for a Better Understanding

A key to doing comparative theology and practicing proper dialogue is to find and carefully read sacred scriptures and other authoritative texts on the chosen topic. Indeed, honing the skills of reading theological texts from other traditions is of utmost importance for anyone wishing to become a comparative theologian. Careful reading takes time, is often cumbersome and challenging, and is never far from making forced or mistaken conclusions.[14]

13. Keith Ward, *Images of Eternity: Concepts of God in Five Religious Traditions* (London: Darton, Longman & Todd, 1987), 1.

14. For guidance in reading for comparative theology work, see Clooney, *Comparative Theology*, chap. 4.

Any reading of religious texts and any interfaith conversation bring to the fore the question of the conditions for understanding between two different horizons and perspectives. The German hermeneutical philosopher H.-G. Gadamer reminds us that all true "understanding is ultimately self-understanding."[15] Rather than external, understanding is an "internal" process that also shapes us. Knowledge in the humanities in particular is a process not between "subject" and "object" but rather between two "subjects" whose horizons of (self-)understanding cohere and mutually influence each other. In relation to interfaith dialogue, this means that, on the one hand, I as a Christian should not—and cannot—imagine putting aside my convictions, and that, on the other hand, those very convictions are in the process of being reshaped, sometimes even radically altered.[16] "In understanding we are drawn into an event of truth and arrive, as it were, too late, if we want to know what we are supposed to believe."[17]

Ultimately, with careful reading and a desire for proper mutual understanding, comparative theology aims at truthfulness about beliefs and doctrines, as much as that is possible for the human mind. In the words of F. X. Clooney, "Dialogue must permanently shape the whole theological environment, but dialogue is not the primary goal of theology, which still has to do with the articulation of the truths one believes and the realization of a fuller knowledge of God (insofar as that is possible by way of theology). Both within traditions and across religious boundaries, truth does matter, conflicts among claims about reality remain significant possibilities, and making a case for the truth remains a key part of the theologian's task."[18]

Comparison for the Sake of the Truth

Of course, pursuing the question of the truth of God in our pluralistic world may strike one not only as a hybrid sort of task but also as something easily

15. Hans-Georg Gadamer, *Truth and Method*, trans. Joel Weinsheimer and Donald G. Marshall, 2nd rev. ed. (New York: Continuum, 2006 [1960]), 251, emphasis removed. For reminding me of Gadamer's importance to interfaith conversation, I wish to acknowledge Kristin Johnston Sutton, "Salvation after Nagarjuna: A Reevaluation of Wolfhart Pannenberg's Soteriology in Light of a Buddhist Cosmology" (PhD diss., Graduate Theological Union, 2002), 2–16.

16. See Sutton, "Salvation after Nagarjuna," 4–5.

17. Gadamer, *Truth and Method*, 484; for understanding as an event, see also xxii, 157, 478.

18. Francis X. Clooney, *Hindu God, Christian God: How Reason Helps Break Down the Boundaries between Religions* (Oxford: Oxford University Press, 2001), 173.

leading to violence and oppression. How could any theologian (of any faith tradition) claim such a task? Before dismissing the question, let us remember the obvious yet all-too-often-neglected necessary connection between monotheism—whether Islamic, Jewish, or Christian—and the assumption of the location of truth (and beauty and goodness, among other virtues) in the one and same God. The English philosopher of religion R. Trigg reminds us that "Christianity and Islam both believe that they have a universal message. If there is one God, one would expect that He would be regarded as the God of all people, and not just some." Consequently, there is an assumption of "only one world, one version of reality": "Monotheism can have no truck with relativism, or alternative gods. Beliefs may construct gods, but those who believe in one God cannot allow for other parallel deities, even in the sense that other people have their gods while monotheists look to their one deity. Monotheism must not only imply the falsity of all other alleged gods, but, if it is true to itself, it has to proclaim it to all, loud and clear. Otherwise, by definition, it is not monotheism, or even realism."[19]

Consequently, we should seriously critique the common tendency to assume that since there are so many religions and ideologies with competing truth claims, none of them can be true and, therefore, relativism is the only way out—the view according to which "each group must live by their own truth, but there is no overarching 'truth' that all should recognize."[20] Should relativism be adopted, it would mean that religious commitments, similarly to, say, personal tastes, are merely subjective choices but have no role to play in the public arena.[21] That argument fails in light of the fact that "religions that only express the personal attitudes of the believer cannot claim any truth that can be rationally assessed. Faith then is merely an idiosyncrasy that some have and some do not."[22]

The very fact that we continue speaking of *different* religions indicates that they are something bigger than just one person's—or even a group's—personal "tastes." There is a necessary intersubjective side to religion—as there

---

19. Roger Trigg, *Religious Diversity: Philosophical and Political Dimensions* (Cambridge: Cambridge University Press, 2014), 115.

20. Trigg, *Religious Diversity*, 2.

21. Trigg, *Religious Diversity*, 15–18. A strong appeal to the subjective nature of religions is presented by the Italian philosopher Gianni Vattimo, *A Farewell to Truth*, trans. William McCuaig (New York: Columbia University Press, 2011); for a critique, see Trigg, *Religious Diversity*, 26–27.

22. Trigg, *Religious Diversity*, 23. This has also been the persistent argument throughout Pannenberg's theological career; see, e.g., chap. 1 in *ST* 1.

is also to secularism, as far as that is thoughtfully and rationally defended. Indeed, "total subjectivism brings the threat of nihilism."[23]

Common sense tells us that the content of faith matters. Just think of everyday nonreligious life: the content matters with regard to the kind of doctor or car mechanic we put our faith in. I agree with Trigg's argument that "all faith has to be faith in something or somebody. There is no such thing as undirected faith."[24]

Nor does doubt or uncertainty, that is, the difficulty or even seeming impossibility of establishing the basis of one's beliefs, constitute relativism.[25] It just makes the pursuit of truth a lifelong, communal, and painstaking task for all. Only if one is an ontological nonrealist, that is, if one holds that all there is, is a result of human construction, could a link between doubt and relativism be made. Most of us, however, are realists (of some sort), which simply means that "reality is independent of all our knowledge and not a construction out of human knowledge." As a result, the jump from epistemology (how we know) to ontology (how things are) cannot be taken for granted.[26]

A Hospitable Dialogue

That kind of comparative task in the search of the truth can only be attempted in the spirit of hospitality. The postcolonialist feminist Mayra Rivera reminds us that we "constantly fail to encounter the other as Other. Time and again we ignore or deny the singularity of the Other—we don't see even when the face stands in front of us. We still need, it seems, 'eyes to see and ears to hear'—and bodies capable of embracing without grasping."[27]

What makes hospitality such a fitting metaphor for interfaith relations is that it "involves invitation, response and engagement."[28] True hospitality

---

23. Trigg, *Religious Diversity*, 23.

24. Trigg, *Religious Diversity*, 18. See further, Roger Trigg, *Rationality and Religion: Does Faith Need Reason?* (Oxford: Blackwell, 1998); Harold A. Netland, *Christianity and Religious Diversity: Clarifying Christian Commitments in a Globalizing Age* (Grand Rapids: Baker Academic, 2015), chap. 7.

25. For thoughtful reflections, see Netland, *Christianity and Religious Diversity*, chap. 6.

26. Trigg, *Religious Diversity*, 23–30 (27); Trigg uses the term "antirealism" for what I call here nonrealism.

27. Mayra Rivera, *The Touch of Transcendence: A Postcolonial Theology of God* (Louisville: Westminster John Knox, 2007), 118.

28. George Newlands and Allen Smith, *Hospitable God: The Transformative Dream* (Surrey, UK: Ashgate, 2010), 32.

helps us avoid "bearing false witness."[29] Hospitality reaches out, makes room, facilitates dialogue. Even more: "Hospitality is important to all the great world religions today."[30] Hence, there is a common denominator. Even though it is true, as mentioned, that often religions may not appear to be hospitable, it is just as true that all living faiths seek hospitality and dream of it.[31]

But even though hospitality is a common denominator—in terms of invitation for mutual engagement—it also represents complexity. "It is hard to underestimate the complexity of the task of religious conversation and dialogue, with its interaction of the global and local, the pluralist, the inclusive and the exclusivist strands, the fluctuations between essentialist and changing elements."[32] Only careful attention to the details of investigation, respectful honoring of the otherness of other traditions and their representatives, as well as bold but humble arguing for one's deepest convictions make such a multifaceted enterprise feasible.[33]

Indeed, plurality and diversity of religions itself is not the problem. On the contrary, ultimately it is the case that "for a religious person, to *accept* disagreement is to see it as within the providence of God"—even disagreement due to diversity of religious beliefs and convictions. Religions are not here without God's permission and allowance. The continuing challenge, particularly for the staunch monotheist, is how to reconcile the existence of one's own deeply felt (God-given?) beliefs with different, often opposite, kinds of convictions.[34]

Ultimately, comparative theology itself becomes an act of hospitality, giving and receiving gifts. This kind of hospitable dialogue is a "relationship where both parties are recognized by each other as someone not determined by the conditions of one's own horizon, but rather as an Other, a relationship that is not part of the world and the concrete expectations (or anticipations) of the Other. Hence, in such a relationship one is invited into the world of the Other by means of an open invitation."[35]

---

29. See John J. Thatamanil, *The Immanent Divine: God, Creation, and the Human Predicament; An East-West Conversation* (Minneapolis: Fortress, 2006), xii.

30. Newlands and Smith, *Hospitable God*, 32.

31. Newlands and Smith, *Hospitable God*, 33.

32. Newlands and Smith, *Hospitable God*, 37.

33. See Reid B. Locklin, "A More Comparative Ecclesiology? Bringing Comparative Theology to the Ecclesiological Table," in *Comparative Ecclesiology: Critical Investigations*, ed. Gerard Mannion (London: T&T Clark, 2008), 125–49.

34. Keith Ward, *Religion and Community* (Oxford: Oxford University Press, 1999), 25.

35. Jan-Olav Henriksen, *Desire, Gift, and Recognition: Christology and Postmodern Philosophy* (Grand Rapids: Eerdmans, 2009), 44–45.

Borrowing from the biblical scholar Walter Brueggemann, I make the term "other" a verb to remind us of the importance of seeing the religious other not as a counterobject but rather as a partner in "othering," which is "the risky, demanding, dynamic process of relating to one that is not us."[36] What matters is the capacity to listen to the distinctive testimony of the other, to patiently wait upon the other, and to make a safe space for him or her.

The contemporary secular mind-set often mistakenly confuses tolerance with lack of commitment to any belief or opinion. That is to misunderstand the meaning of the word "tolerance." Deriving from the Latin word meaning "to bear a burden," tolerance is something we need to allow real differences. Tolerance means patient and painstaking sharing, listening, and comparing notes—as well as the willingness to respectfully and lovingly make space for continuing differences.[37]

To foster tolerance and heal conflicts between religions, in collaboration with representatives of other faiths of good will, Christians should do their best to help governments and other authorities to secure a safe, noncoercive place for adherents of religions to present their testimonies without fear. The late missionary bishop Lesslie Newbigin reminds us that while for Christians the gospel is a "public truth," it has nothing to do with a desire to return to the Christendom model in which the state seeks to enforce beliefs.[38] That should be unacceptable to all religions. In a truly pluralist society, decision for beliefs can never be a matter of power-based enforcement. When Christians, Muslims, Hindus, Buddhists, Sikhs, Confucians, and followers of other faiths can without fear and threat meet each other in a free "marketplace" of beliefs and ideologies, genuine missionary encounters are also possible.[39]

On the Nature and Approach of This Primer

This guide to doing comparative theology differs from (almost all) other similar primers in that, rather than merely listing a number of guidelines and

36. Walter Brueggemann, *The Covenanted Self: Explorations in Law and Covenant* (Minneapolis: Augsburg Fortress, 1999), 1.

37. A highly useful discussion is Harold A. Netland, *Encountering Religious Pluralism: The Challenge to Christian Faith and Mission* (Downers Grove, IL: InterVarsity Press, 2001), chap. 4.

38. For details, see Veli-Matti Kärkkäinen, "The Church in the Post-Christian Society between Modernity and Late Modernity: L. Newbigin's Post-critical Missional Ecclesiology," in *Theology in Missionary Perspective: Lesslie Newbigin's Legacy*, ed. Mark T. B. Laing and Paul Weston (Eugene, OR: Pickwick, 2013), 125–54.

39. See the WCC document "Religious Plurality and Christian SelfUnderstanding," #27.

then discussing in detail how they could be applied to the comparative task, it majors in doing the actual comparative theological work. In this way, this book complements primers that focus on methodological explanations such as the book by the leading comparative theologian Francis X. Clooney, SJ, *Comparative Theology: Deep Learning across Religious Borders* (2010). The approach of my book comes closest to former Oxford University philosopher-theologian Keith Ward's comparative exercises in the doctrine of God, creation, humanity, and revelation (although his are not designed primarily for classroom use).[40]

In this book I attempt to demonstrate in practice how a Christian theologian might engage in detailed comparative work with other faith traditions. The book engages four living faiths—Judaism, Islam, Hinduism, and Buddhism—with regard to specific, focused topics of interest. Hence, it facilitates dialogue with not only the other two Abrahamic traditions but also two main Asiatic faiths.

The outline of the book follows Christian tradition, manifesting that comparative theology is a confessional exercise. The book is divided into ten chapters, each of which provides a brief presentation of a basic Christian doctrine or belief, from the doctrine of revelation and the triune God, to creation, to Christology and atonement, to pneumatology and salvation, all the way to the church and eschatology.[41]

Each chapter begins with a short and nontechnical presentation of the chosen doctrine's main outline and beliefs in Christian theology, noting both shared commonalities and defining differences among various theological traditions. Thereafter, each of the four faith traditions is engaged following this basic template: first, a careful exposition of the chosen doctrine's main affirmations and beliefs based on the sacred scripture, authoritative tradition, and (where necessary) the thought of some leading modern teachers. In the second moment, a careful and hospitable Christian engagement follows by highlighting potential common affirmations and important differences. This template allows those readers with no or limited knowledge of these four faith traditions' teachings and beliefs to first get basic instruction and only thereafter engage the comparative task.

Just a brief glance at the contents page reveals that not all chapters have been allotted equal amounts of space. The first two chapters, on revelation and

---

40. Keith Ward, *Images of Eternity: Concepts of God in Five Religious Traditions* (London: Darton, Longman & Todd, 1987); *Religion and Community* (Oxford: Oxford University Press, 1999); *Religion and Human Nature* (Oxford: Clarendon, 1998); *Religion and Revelation: A Theology of Revelation in the World's Religions* (Oxford: Clarendon, 1994).

41. Were this an exercise, say, in Islamic comparative theology, then the book would be divided following Islam's main doctrinal and belief template.

the doctrine of God, respectively, are significantly longer than the others—particularly so with chapter 1. This is intentional, and the reason is obvious: the conversation on all doctrinal topics among living faith traditions is rooted in their scriptural and other authoritative written traditions as well as in their conception of the divine. Hence, an informed comparison of notes regarding, say, the doctrine of creation or salvation or "consummation" has to refer back all the time to these two formative theological topics, namely, revelation and the deity.

The materials in this primer come with adaptations and additions from my five-volume series titled A Constructive Christian Theology for the Pluralistic World (2013–2017): *Christ and Reconciliation* (2013), *Trinity and Revelation* (2014), *Creation and Humanity* (2015), *Spirit and Salvation* (2016), and *Community and Hope* (2017). To communicate and make this highly technical and complex theology accessible to theology students and other interested readers, the current textbook aims for clarity, simplicity, and user-friendliness without in any way sacrificing accuracy. For technical discussions and meticulous documentation, the interested reader is referred to that multivolume work.

1 | Revelation and Scripture among Religions

Revelation and Scripture in Christian Tradition

In Christian understanding, God's revelation comes in many forms, most foundationally in the Word made flesh, the incarnated Son of God, as inscripted in the Bible, the written Word (special revelation). A less full manifestation of revelation can be found in nature and history and in humanity, having been created in God's image (general revelation). Briefly put: while divine in origin, Christian revelation is historical, embedded in history, and also progressive, as it unfolds slowly amidst the people of God.

To use theological language, revelation is a Trinitarian process: out of his abundant love the Father reaches out to humanity in order to establish a fellowship, by sending his Son to be one of us, to die and be raised to new life, in the power of the Spirit. This same Spirit is also believed to have inspired the Scripture and to continuously make it lively.

All Christian churches consider the Bible, whose first part (in Christian parlance), the Old Testament, is shared with the Jewish mother faith, as authoritative and as a special channel of revelation. Whereas up until the Enlightenment the Bible was universally believed to be an inerrant (at least in substance) divine revelation, in modernity, alongside the rise of historical-critical study, a massive revision emerged among scholars leading to the (in)famous "conservative" (fundamentalist) and "liberal" divide. While the former camp still maintains the Bible's divine origin and authority, the latter considers Scripture a humanly produced, uniquely inspiring religious text. Between these two extremes lie all kinds of variations.

Notwithstanding all the disputes concerning the nature of Scripture as revelation and the nature of its inspiration, all Christians agree that in some real sense the Bible is God's word in human words. In other words, it has neither come directly from God, as in dictation, nor is it merely humans talking to each other about human experiences of the sacred.

The great dispute at the time of the Protestant Reformation in the sixteenth century related to the relationship between revelation in written Scripture and its continuing growth in church tradition. It took hundreds of years for the churches on both sides of the divide to come to understand that this is not an either-or matter but rather a both-and. While it is an ecumenical consensus that the Scripture is the highest norm of faith and practice, it is also acknowledged that the formation and final ratification of the Bible as Scripture are a matter of the community of faith seeking to discern the nature and function of the Bible. Hence, the Bible is primarily a book of and for the Christian community and should be read and interpreted there even if—thanks to the Reformation—it has also been put into the hands of the individual Christian.

A vibrant twentieth-century debate concerned the relationship between special and natural revelation. While few would juxtapose them, there are understandably varying ways to relate them and to assess the value and benefits of revelation "outside" the incarnated, living Word and written Word.

The Challenge and Complexity of Interfaith Engagement of Scriptures

Putting Christian Scripture and doctrine of revelation into mutual dialogue with other living faiths is an enormous challenge. To begin with, the reservoir of sacred scriptures is amazingly huge among religions—illustrated by Max Müller's classic, *Sacred Books of the East*, in fifty hefty volumes; yet even that "library" misses noteworthy portions of scriptures from various parts of Asia!

Whereas until recent decades religious studies as an academic discipline used to downplay the importance of *written* scriptures for the study of religions, giving preference to nontextual elements such as ritual, myth, and symbols, more recently a new appreciation of the importance of written scriptures to the study and knowledge of religions has emerged. That is not to undermine the importance of other elements such as folk religiosity, arts, and ritual, but rather to acknowledge that basically all living faiths are either based on or have been shaped in the presence of authoritative scriptures. There are virtually no living religions without sacred scriptures.

While most religions have either canonical or otherwise determined "primary" scripture (Torah, Qur'an, Bible, Vedas, Tipitaka), they also have a huge secondary literature that typically is believed to be based on and to derive its (relative) authority from the primary revelation. Hence the Jews have the extensive Talmud, the "Oral Torah"; the Muslims have the huge collection of Hadiths; the main way to study the Vedas is the growing commentary literature in Vedic Hinduism and the whole *smrti* tradition for the rest of the Hindus. The Christian church has accumulated a massive secondary literature of creedal and other definitive traditions. An important theological task not only for Christians but also for Jews, Hindus, and Muslims is to discern the relationship between the "canonical" and "extracanonical" texts, to use the Christian parlance.

Having underscored the presence and twofold nature of scriptures among all religions, we also need to add some nuancing. First of all, religions such as Judaism, Islam, and Christianity have a clearly defined and closed canon. In many others, most profoundly in Buddhism, especially in Mahayana traditions, there is hardly any notion of a "closed canon." Hinduism lies somewhere in between, as it has the twofold structure of primary, most authoritative scriptures, the Vedas (*shruti*), and the secondary *smrti* collections of various types of materials, from epics to songs to folklore, and so forth. Even the collection of Vedas, let alone the rest of the Hindu scriptures, is immense. Hence, in a typical household in India, a small part of an important epic in the *smrti* collection, the Bhagavad Gita, may be the only scripture available.

Scriptures also play different roles in various religions. Whereas Judaism, Christianity, and Islam can be rightly called "religions of the book" because of the necessary and authoritative role played by the written canonical scripture, in Hinduism the spoken word is primary. The Vedas, even though found in written form in Sanskrit, are considered divine speech, and hence the written form is inferior to the oral reciting and hearing. Furthermore, whereas almost all religions of the world regard their scriptures as inspired and of divine origin, that is not the case with all traditions. Buddhism has no concept of divine inspiration. One could also, perhaps somewhat ironically, point to liberal Protestantism in Christianity, according to which the Bible is primarily an invaluable human sharing of responses to religious experiences.

Finally, the nature and function of scripture among various traditions vary greatly. For the typical Muslim, the Qur'anic revelation is truly verbatim and relates to all aspects of life. Typical contemporary Jews and Christians consider Scripture the ultimate authority, even though, apart from fundamentalists, they consider its principles and thoughts to be the inspired guide to faith and practice. For most Buddhists, scripture's main role and authority lie in its capacity to convey Buddha's enlightenment and precepts. It is the scripture's "object" rather than the scripture as such that is highly venerated and authoritative. In Hinduism, Brahmins study Vedas as the divinely originated religious (and in many traditions, philosophical) authority, whereas for most Hindus, scriptural content comes in the form of folklore, rituals, artistic forms, and the general cultural environment in India.

With these diversities in mind, we should be mindful of the danger of generalizations and assumptions. The Christian theologian sees the interfaith exchange between scriptures and notions of revelation among other living faiths through the lens of his or her own tradition. The Muslim scholar would do the same, and so forth. This is not to block dialogue but rather to serve as a reminder to be mindful.

The Christian comparativist should also mind the current one-sided focus on written Scripture and the eclipse of the oral mode. This is ironic in that the First Testament, shared by the Jewish tradition, builds essentially on the role of oral transmission of scriptural content. Even the New Testament is essentially based on oral traditions, epistles read aloud in the congregation, and speeches. In keeping with the times, Jesus and the apostles, as Jews, memorized and recited Scriptures daily. The early church also did that, as the Gospels were not yet written and were circulating in oral form. In the Islamic tradition, oral memorization and recital of scripture took on even greater importance. "Indeed, spiritual merit in Islam is said to be measured by the thoroughness of one's oral knowledge of the scripture. According to the tradition, on the day of resurrection everyone will be called upon to rise up and recite the Qur'an." Examples from other living faith traditions could be easily compiled.[1]

Yet another bias or liability that the Christian theologian should keep in mind is the post-Enlightenment emphasis on propositional, cognitive, and doctrinal language over the poetic, mystical, and intuitive. The theologian Keith Ward's observation is right on target: "The language of religion is like the language of poetry; and it is a major heresy of post-Enlightenment rationalism to try to turn poetry into pseudo-science, to turn the images of religion, whose function is to evoke eternity, into mundane descriptions of improbable facts."[2]

---

1. Harold Coward, introduction to *Experiencing Scripture in World Religions*, ed. H. Coward (Maryknoll, NY: Orbis, 2000), 1–14 (5).

2. Keith Ward, *Images of Eternity: Concepts of God in Five Religious Traditions* (London: Darton, Longman & Todd, 1987), 3.

Some recent approaches in systematic and constructive theology may turn out to be helpful in capturing a more holistic view of scriptures not only in Christian but also in other faith traditions. These include approaches such as discussed in Kevin Vanhoozer's *Drama of Doctrine*, which seeks to reenvision the Christian story as drama, and in William A. Dyrness's *Poetic Theology*, which builds on the intuition that since religion—and knowledge of God—comes to us in so many forms, the category of the "poetic" in the most inclusive sense, going back to the Aristotelian notion of "making," is needed along with the more traditional discursive approach.

Having now clarified some conditions and desiderata regarding comparative work focused on Scripture and revelation, we will engage Hindu, Buddhist, Islamic, and Jewish traditions. As mentioned in the introduction, for the sake of readers who most likely are not well versed in any other tradition's scriptures and views of revelation, before we begin comparative exercises, basic knowledge and data will be provided.

Hindu Scriptures and Authority in a Christian Perspective

The Matrix of Hindu Scriptures

A Plentiful and Pluriform Scriptural Heritage

The notion of scripture in Hinduism is pluriform and inclusive in nature. "No other living tradition can claim scriptures as numerous or as ancient as Hinduism."[3] Hindu scriptures are commonly divided into two categories. First, there are the Vedas, which are called the *shruti* ("what is heard"), received directly by the *rishis*, "seers." This is the foundational, primary scripture, honored by all Hindu traditions. Then there are the secondary scriptures, the *smrti* ("what is remembered"), which are considered to be humanly authored and come in the forms of epics, narratives, and folklore. Basically all forms of Hinduism consider the ancient Vedas as the scripture par excellence. Indeed, it can be said that what keeps Hinduism together and allows meaningful discussion of Hinduism as a unified—albeit extremely diversified—tradition is the common belief in the Vedas as foundational, authoritative, divine revelation.

3. Klaus Klostermaier, *A Survey of Hinduism*, 3rd ed. (Albany: State University of New York Press, 2010), 45.

The Vedic literature is by and large unknown to most Hindus apart from the higher castes (especially Brahmins). Instead, most Hindus get their scriptural teaching from various epics, religious folklore called the Puranas (to be introduced below). Furthermore, unlike in contemporary Christianity, religious and religiously inspired art such as music, dance, and paintings is often taken as revelatory in nature. To this list one should add an important caveat related to the most foundational Hindu concept of *dharma*. Variously translated as "righteousness," "duty," and "ethics/morality," it denotes common human virtues such as generosity, compassion, and abstaining from violence. In addition to this *dharma*, which is common to all humanity, there is every human person's own *dharma* that leads to liberation. Now, where is this *dharma* to be found? It is found in the Vedas and epics, but also in the practices and behavior of good people and in promptings and insights of one's mind and conscience.[4]

The Vedic Literature

The Vedas originated beginning around 1500 BCE. Each of the four collections (Rig Veda, Sama Veda, Yajur Veda, and Atharva Veda) has four parts: Samhitas, hymns to various deities; Brahmanas, rules for Vedic rituals; Aranyakas, "forest" discussions, symbolic and philosophical reflections on the rituals; and, for the purposes of theological discourse, the most important, the Upanishads. The last collection's name comes from "sitting near [the teacher]" and contains the developing philosophic-theological reflection on the divine and the world. The Upanishads were composed around 600 BCE or later.[5]

The theologies based on the Upanishads, called Vedanta, embody much of Hinduism as seen in the West.[6] A few qualifications, however, will assist those not well versed in Indian traditions. First, Vedanta is merely one of the six main schools or traditions of Hinduism,[7] even though it is by far the best

---

4. See Vasudha Narayanan, "Hinduism," in *Eastern Religions: Origins, Beliefs, Practices, Holy Texts, Sacred Places*, ed. Michael D. Coogan (Oxford: Oxford University Press, 2005), 41–49, 62–63.

5. While tradition numbers 108 Upanishads, about 10 have become prominent because of extensive commentary literature written by *advaita* (nondualist) interpreters of various subschools.

6. Vedanta is also known as "Later" (Uttara) Mimamsa, related to the important text that its representatives comment on extensively, the Uttara Mimamsa Sutras, better known in the West as Brahma Sutras, by Badarayana, of the fifth century CE.

7. The six orthodox traditions are Nyaya, Vaisesika, Samkhya, Yoga, Purva Mimamsa,

known. Second, philosophical in nature, based on the Vedas, it is not necessarily the Hindu religion of common folks. It is the philosophically oriented and often abstract account of the faith of India known to Hindu "theologians." Third, very importantly, even the Vedanta school has several quite widely different subtraditions. For the purposes of this conversation—to be amplified in chapter 2 on the doctrine of God—the most important is the divide between the advaitic, nondualistic (literally, "not-two"), monistic tradition and the moderately dualistic tradition.

Sacred Stories and Narratives as Scripture of the Common Folks

As said, other scriptures, apart from the Vedas, belong to the realm of *smrti*, "remembered" literature, among which the two most important and widely used are Ramayana, a story of Rama, depicted as an incarnation of Vishnu in later tradition, and Mahabharata ("Great Epic"),[8] part of which is the Bhagavad Gita, the most important single writing of scripture among all Hindus. Indeed, this "Sacred Song" is the "Bible" of most Hindus and can be found in virtually every home.

As epics, both of these narrative collections portray an exciting story with many turns—in Mahabharata, of the war between two families (the Kauravas and Pandavas), and in Bhagavad Gita, of Arjuna of the Pandava family, who consults his cousin Krishna about the wisdom of fighting against the family. Krishna is a major Hindu figure who in later tradition, like Rama, but more importantly than Rama, is depicted as one of the main *avataras* of the deity Vishnu. The Hindu devotional literature (*bhakti*) is immense, and it appears in many languages.

Unlike Vedas, the epics are believed to have human authors. But even then, their inspired nature is not denied, although their authority is lower than that of the Vedas. Ironically, this "second-class" form of inspired scriptures has played a far more significant role in the actual lives of Hindu communities and individuals than the Vedas, for the reasons mentioned, including the common person's very limited access to the most authoritative sources.

---

and Vedanta. Buddhism and Jainism, as well as the Hindu tradition of Caravakas, reject the Vedas and hence are not considered orthodox. For a basic discussion of the revelatory meaning of the Vedas, see George Chemparathy, "The Veda as Revelation," *Journal of Dharma* 7, no. 3 (1982): 253–74.

8. Mahabharata is huge—more than one hundred thousand verses, making it the world's longest poem.

The Centrality of Oral Scripture

Scripture comes first and foremost in oral form for Hindus, whether in daily recitation or in the ritual or repetition of mantras or *japa*, a single word or a brief verse from scripture, either audibly or silently; its main goal is liberation rather than accumulation of information. This fact, however, does not undermine careful study and analysis of the text and debate about its meaning. The well-known verse from *Laws of Manu* (12:103) is often invoked as an example of the need to ascertain as carefully as possible the exact meaning of the scriptural text: "(Even forgetful) students of the (sacred) books are more distinguished than the ignorant, those who remember them surpass the (forgetful) students, those who possess a knowledge (of the meaning) are more distinguished than those who (only) remember (the words), men who follow (the teaching of the texts) surpass those who (merely) know (their meaning)."[9]

We can see the profound importance of the Vedas even in contemporary Hinduism from the continuing inquiry into their meaning, including the renewed interest in modern times, beginning from the Hindu renewals of the nineteenth century, which were, ironically, prompted by the modern Christian missionary movement. The Hindu intellectual Ram Mohun Roy's (d. 1833) translation of the Upanishads into Bengali and English was an effort similar in many ways to the Protestant Reformers' desire to get the Bible into the hands of the common folk. According to the famed Hinduologist Julius Lipner, Roy is to be credited with "restoring the Vedas to public consciousness in modern India, both as an object of study and as a source of religious inspiration."[10]

Competing Hermeneutics

While all six Hindu traditions consider study and knowledge of scripture the necessary source of theology, two traditions excel in Vedic exegesis: the ritualistic, nontheistic Purva Mimamsa and all Vedanta schools (which, as mentioned, focus on the study of the Upanishads).[11] Profound hermeneutical differences exist between these two main traditions devoted to the study of the

9. "The Laws of Manu," circa 1500 BCE, trans. G. Buhler, in *Indian History Sourcebook*, https://sourcebooks.fordham.edu/india/manu-full.asp.

10. Julius J. Lipner, *Hindus: Their Religious Beliefs and Practices* (London: Routledge, 1994), 66.

11. As mentioned, much of Vedantic theologians' focus is devoted to commenting on the fifth century CE Brahma Sutras (originally Uttara Mimamsa Sutras) attributed to Badarayana.

Vedas; this observation is useful for Christian students who are often bewildered by the internal divisions of their own tradition. Since Purva Mimamsa is oriented toward ritual and is nontheistic,[12] it regards the Vedas' main purpose as guiding in the right ritual. Hence, the Vedas in this hermeneutic are not looked upon as guides for how to live in the world or, perhaps surprisingly to outsiders, even as information about the deities or immortality (even if deities are generally considered to be worthy of proper worship).[13] It is not surprising, then, that this school gives precedence to the first three parts of each Veda (Samhitas, Brahmanas, and Aranyakas), all of which are ritually oriented and contain hymns to the deities.

The Vedanta schools, also known as the "Later" (Uttara) Mimamsa, in contrast, extensively and painstakingly engage the task of commenting on the Upanishads, in which they see the revelation of the Ultimate or Absolute, Brahman, as the main theme. Usually Vedanta theologians begin with and concentrate on attentive commentary of Brahma Sutra, including the careful consideration of the nature and works of the deities. But even within this tradition, there are significant divisions between those who are strictly monistic, the nondualist *advaita* school represented most famously by Sankara of the eighth century, and the qualified nondualist (*visistadvaita*) school of Ramanuja of the eleventh century. In the discussion of God, creation, and some themes related to human nature, these complex discussions between the two main Vedanta schools will be presented and engaged from a Christian perspective.

Suffice it to add one important related note here, to be expanded below in the chapter on salvation: in addition to the Upanishads, Sankara's followers consult diligently the above-mentioned Brahma Sutra and Bhagavad Gita,[14] the latter of which presents the threefold path of *jnana yoga* (knowledge/insight), *bhakti yoga* (devotion), and *karma yoga* (ritual action). The ultimate "salvific" vision present in the Bhagavad Gita is some kind of unity of these three main yoga schools, aiming at union with the Absolute.

What about Hindu tradition's scripture and understanding of revelation in relation to Christian faith?

---

12. This not to say that this tradition is atheistic or even antitheistic after Western logic, but rather that it is something similar to Theravada Buddhism, which grants the existence of the deities but considers their existence more or less irrelevant for pursuing the goal of liberation.

13. See further, Francis X. Clooney, *Hindu God, Christian God: How Reason Helps Break Down the Boundaries between Religions* (Oxford: Oxford University Press, 2001), 18–19.

14. These three primary texts are often referred to as Prasthana Trayi, the triple foundation of the Vedanta.

Hindu and Christian Views of Scripture: Parallels and Differences

The Nature and Power of the Sacred Language and Ritual

An important indication of the depth of scholarship and the use of reason's best resources in India is the millennia-long investigation into the nature and functions of religious language, a topic dear also to past and recent Christian theologians. Indeed, the Vedas themselves speak of the nature of language and words used in these texts. An entire hymn in Rig Veda (71 of book 10) is devoted to the discussion of the origin of language.

Very importantly, in the Vedas, language is not only closely connected with the divine but also directly identified with Brahman,[15] as Brihadaranyaka Upanishad puts it (4.1.2) by stating that "speech (*vâk*) is Brahman." The Christian reader of this Upanishadic passage is of course reminded of the first verse of John's Gospel: "In the beginning was the Word, and the Word was with God, and the Word was God." The difference between the two traditions is that, in Vedic teaching, words (plural) are manifestations of Brahman, while in the Christian view the Word, which became embodied in one particular human person, Jesus of Nazareth (John 1:14), is equated with God.

A further parallel might be made between the eternal Veda and the biblical statement in John's Gospel of the Logos, particularly in that the Vedic word *vak* is believed to have creative power "through which the entire creation is brought forth in each cycle."[16] This resonates with Saint John's statement that "all things were made through" the Logos (1:3). The leading advaitic commentator from the eighth century, Sankara, teaches that "Scripture declares in different places that the word precedes the creation."[17]

Christian theology could also reflect on the potential promise of the close link between ritual and language. "The meaningfulness of *mantras* is not of the merely intellectual kind, it is meaning which has power (*śakti*). *Mantras* have the power to remove ignorance (*avidyā*), reveal truth (*dharma*), and realize release (*mokṣa*)."[18] While Christian theology hardly wishes to go as far as

---

15. As will be discussed in detail in the following chapter and elsewhere, Brahman is the "Ultimate," the "Absolute"—the God in Christian parlance.

16. Anantanand Rambachan, "Hinduism," in Coward, *Experiencing Scripture in World Religions*, 92.

17. Sankara, Vedanta-Sutras 1.3.28; *SBE* 34:203 (the whole of this section, 201–11, is devoted to this topic).

18. Harold Coward, *Sacred Word and Sacred Text: Scripture in World Religions* (Maryknoll, NY: Orbis, 1988), 115. Even mightier than any single mantra is the chanting of "Om." While

to use mantras in a semimagical way, which often happens particularly in folk piety, there certainly are some parallels between the Hindu view and the best of Christian sacramental understanding of the words in liturgy and sacraments. According to a Christian sacramental understanding, words uttered by human beings in such settings bring about what they promise. The history of Christian theology reminds us of various ways of trying to explain how that happens, and that has led to deep divisions among Christians. However, beyond and beneath those debates there is an intuition—shared with Hindus—that certain words are creative, powerful, and "sacramental" since they are linked with the divine and divine actions.

Scriptural Inspiration

Christian and Hindu understandings of "inspiration" differ markedly from each other. In Christian understanding the divine inspiration of Scripture, even as a genuinely "human" word, is miraculous. That is not, however, the Hindu view of the coming into existence of the Vedas. The reception by the "seers" of the Vedic revelation as oral speech originating in eternity was a matter of "the progressive purifying of consciousness through the disciplines of yoga, [which] had simply removed the mental obstructions to the revelation of the Divine Word." Hence, "in this Vedic idea of revelation there is no suggestion of the miraculous or supernatural."[19]

On the other hand, there is nothing like the long struggle of the prophets and other biblical authors with God in real historical events or the notion of progressive revelation developing and clarifying incrementally over the course of history. Differently from the Vedas, the sense of the "noncanonical" Bhagavad Gita idea of revelation comes much closer to the Christian idea of incarnation, as it contains the story of the incarnation of Vishnu, Krishna. Coupled with a strong *bhakti*-devotional orientation and a personalized God, popular Hindu piety based on that celebrated narrative shares similarities with Christian tradition.

Related to the distinctive idea of revelation as Vedas, the words and sentences "function only as the 'ladder' to raise one to the direct, intuitive experi-

different Hindu schools debate whether Om is Brahman itself or a near verbal expression of Brahman, in all Hindu traditions it is the most sacred sound, and in it are contained all other mantras. The classic description of Om is in Chandogya Upanishad 1.1.1–3, 7, 9 (*SBE* 1).

19. Coward, *Sacred Word*, 106.

ence of the complete Divine Word. Once the full enlightenment experience is achieved, the 'ladder of scripture' is no longer needed." Rightly, Coward notes here a profound difference between Hinduism and the three "traditions of the book": "The very idea that scripture can be transcended is heresy to Jews, Christians, and Muslims. For them the obstructions of human limitations are such that even the most saintly person would get only part-way up the ladder; Scripture (Torah, Bible, or Qur'an) could never be transcended in the sense that most Hindus accept."[20]

Scriptural Authority

Regardless of the difference in the understanding of inspiration, both Hinduism and Christianity build on scriptural authority. According to the noted Hindu scholar and statesman Sarvepalli Radhakrishnan, an important characteristic of Indian philosophy is "its so-called acceptance of authority." He goes on to explain: "Although the systems of Indian philosophy vary in the degree to which they are specifically related to the ancient *śruti*, not one of the systems— orthodox or unorthodox, except the Cārvāka—openly stands in violation of the accepted intuitive insights of its ancient seers, whether it be the Hindu seers of the Upaniṣads, the intuitive experience of the Buddha, or the similarly intuitive wisdom of Mahāvīra, the founder of Jainism, as we have it today."[21]

A contemporary Christian may mistakenly assume that with the rise of highly rational, philosophical views of the divine developed among Vedanta traditions (to be engaged in the following chapter), the authority of the Vedas is replaced with a typical post-Enlightenment historical-critical attitude. Nothing could be more off the mark. With all their rational powers, even the philosophically oriented Vedanta scholars build solidly on the divine revelation.[22]

The affirmation of Vedic authority is so central to Hinduism as a religious tradition—at least in principle—that those who did not subscribe to it, such as adherents of Buddhism and Jainism, early deviations from Hinduism, were

20. Coward, *Sacred Word*, 106. See also Arvind Sharma, *Classical Hindu Thought: An Introduction* (Oxford: Oxford University Press, 2000), 33.

21. Sir Sarvepalli Radhakrishnan, "The Nature of Hinduism," in *The Ways of Religion*, ed. Roger Eastman (New York: Harper & Row, 1975), 13; see also Lipner, *Hindus*, chap. 2. Also known as Lokayata, Carvaka is a Hindu tradition that embraces skepticism and some sort of epistemological indifference, and hence does not consider the Vedas or any other similar work as authoritative.

22. Ward, *Images of Eternity*, 5.

named *nastikas*, those who said "there is no such thing" (as Vedic authority). Hence, they were considered "heretics" and under destructive influences.[23]

Post-Enlightenment Christianity, which has rejected all notions of authority not only in the Christian religion but also, by implication, among other faiths, is yet to reflect critically and constructively on the significance of authority in most living faiths of the contemporary world. This is a task for both intra-Christian and interfaith investigation.

Scriptural Infallibility

As explained above, because of their divine origin and eternal nature, the Vedas are taken to be infallible, free from all error. Says Sankara: "Brahman is the source, i.e. the cause of the great body of Scripture."[24] Hence, scripture is both a necessary and a sufficient source of the knowledge of Brahman.[25] It is highly significant that not only among the Vedanta theologians and others who are theistic but also among the ritualistically oriented nontheistic Mimamsa tradition the infallibility of the Vedas is defended and taken for granted.[26]

One can also say with full justification that all orthodox Hindu traditions stick with a strong doctrine of verbal revelation.[27] Materially, they affirm a similar kind of doctrine of the infallibility of sacred scripture as affirmed by classical Christianity and Judaism, as well as Islam. "So one common theme of these traditions is the existence of a revealed, propositional text which communicates truths unknowable by the human mind or reason alone. Orthodox Vedanta is just as dogmatic in making this claim as any orthodox Jew or Muslim"[28] or, I would like to add, any conservative Christian. Rightly, therefore, Ward concludes, "In that sense, Vedanta is not really quite as tolerant or as capable of adapting itself to include other religious traditions as is sometimes thought."[29] Here again, we have a challenge and continuing

23. Lipner, *Hindus*, 27.

24. Sankara, Vedanta-Sutras 1.1.3; *SBE* 34:20.

25. Sankara, Vedanta-Sutras 1.1.4; *SBE* 34:22–23.

26. For comments, see Clooney, *Hindu God, Christian God*, 18–19.

27. Only in revisionist forms of Hinduism is verbal inspiration replaced with some kind of personal experience of enlightenment. For a highly useful and nuanced discussion, see Julius J. Lipner, *The Face of Truth: A Study of Meaning and Metaphysics in the Vedāntic Theology of Rāmanujā* (London: Macmillan, 1986), chaps. 1 and 2.

28. Ward, *Images of Eternity*, 6.

29. Ward, *Images of Eternity*, 6.

task for post-Enlightenment Christian theology, which tends to eschew any notions of "authority."

Scripture and the Knowledge of God

Similarly to Abrahamic traditions, Hindus believe that the ultimate and most authoritative way to the knowledge of God is through the scripture. But what kind of knowledge is in view in the Hindu understanding of scripture? The word *veda* derives from the Sanskrit root *vid*, "to know." The knowledge in mind, however, is neither the Western Enlightenment–based "objective" knowledge nor even the biblical (Old Testament) *hokhma* (wisdom), which has as the ultimate goal the "fear of the Lord," and related to that, guidance to right(eous) living in this life. Even when Indian philosophers highly value the use of reason, as demonstrated by the complicated and complex debates among Vedanta scholars, "intuition is accepted as the only method through which the ultimate can be known."[30]

The Vedic knowledge has everything to do with the ultimate goal of the "salvific" vision of *moksa*, "liberation." Behind the need for liberation as *moksa* is *avidya*, "ignorance," lack of true knowledge. This ignorance has to do with the true nature of the self (*atman*), the Absolute (Brahman), and the world (*jagat*). Even the Upanishads, the most philosophically oriented part of each Veda, do not seek detached abstract knowledge but rather have as their main goal liberation from ignorance. Etymologically, the Sanskrit term derives from "to remove" or "to destroy," thus implying the removal of ignorance through right knowledge.[31]

For this kind of goal, mere intellectual knowledge is not enough. In the words of Radhakrishnan, "Reason is not useless or fallacious, but it is insufficient. To know reality one must have an actual experience of it. One does not merely *know* the truth in Indian philosophy; one *realizes* it. The word which most aptly describes philosophy in India is *darśana* . . . meaning 'to see.'"[32]

In Christian understanding, Scripture's ultimate goal is to lead men and women into salvific knowledge of and personal fellowship with the personal

---

30. Radhakrishnan, "The Nature of Hinduism," 12.

31. See further, Rambachan, "Hinduism," 86–89. Two famous examples of dialogues between the teacher and student illustrate well the ultimate goal of attaining knowledge: Chandogya Upanishad, chap. 7, and Brihadaranyaka Upanishad, chap. 2.

32. Radhakrishnan, "The Nature of Hinduism," 12–13.

triune God who has revealed himself in the Word become flesh, in the power of the Holy Spirit. Rather than an insight into the way of liberation from false attachment or ignorance—even though both of these goals have meaning for Christians as well—faith as trust and assent is the main goal. Subsequently, scriptural teaching is necessary for continuing cultivation of Christian values, mind-set, and virtues.

What about Liberation?

A significant difference between Abrahamic and Asiatic traditions comes to the fore when we further probe into the "practical" effects of the scriptural teaching. Not only among the so-called Christian liberation theologians whose main focus targets the sociopolitical, economic, gender, and other such liberative issues, but also more widely in Christian understanding, Scripture's role is also to cultivate a proper lifestyle. Liberation is not only about one's own salvation but also about neighborly love at all levels of society. In this respect, Asiatic traditions—as will be detailed in discussions of salvation and eschatology—seem to point to a completely different orientation. In those traditions, scripture's main goal seems to fall on insight leading to detachment.

Despite its eschatological goal, in the Christian tradition liberation integrally embraces sociopolitical and ethical dimensions. "In the Semitic tradition a succession of prophets was possessed by the Word of God, who was experienced as absolute moral demand, judge of all human conduct. Their visions were of a personal God who demanded justice and mercy."[33] Not so in Indian traditions. Detachment from the world rather than a robust, embodied engagement of the divine with earthly realities is the dominant vision, and there simply is no prophetic tradition of preaching justice and judgment; there are only seers and hearers of the eternal voice of the divine. Nor is there a historical purpose or goal that—as in the Christian expectation of the righteous rule of God—summons men and women to "seek first his kingdom."[34]

This dramatic difference of orientation between the Semitic and Asiatic traditions has to do with both historical and theological considerations. In terms of historical context, the Judeo-Christian view of revelation derives the category of historical promise pointing to eschatological consummation from

33. Keith Ward, *Religion and Revelation: A Theology of Revelation in the World's Religions* (Oxford: Clarendon, 1994), 134.

34. Ward, *Religion and Revelation*, 135.

its originally nomadic lifestyle, an experience of life as the way to "home." In the birthplaces of the Vedas, the historical situation was much different: the Vedic religion was born among the "noble" ones, the Aryans, who were indeed conquerors, rather than herdsmen or slaves.[35] Christian theology of history can imagine that the nomadic origins of the people of God were divinely willed and sanctioned for the coming into existence of the biblical history–oriented, eschatologically loaded, promise theology.

The marked difference between Semitic and Asiatic "theologies of history" means that whereas the former sees the historical arena as the domain in which God is working out his divine purposes by also inviting men and women to live justly, "Indian thought tended to see history as the arena of the working-out of the consequences of human actions, through a series of rebirths."[36] For Abrahamic believers, history progresses toward God's ultimate consummation; in India, history is but eternal repetition. Christian revelation is historical, based on historical events, and is "on the way" to eschatological fulfillment in the coming of God's kingdom. Second, Christian Scripture is confessed to be humanly authored, as discussed above, and therefore bears the kinds of limitations stemming from finite human work. It is God's Word in human words.

All this is not of course to argue—naively—that therefore Indian philosophy and religious teaching lacks moral aspects. It does not. But Scripture's nature and function with regard to ethics and earthly improvement differ vastly with regard to their ultimate goal, as explained above.

What about Tolerance toward the Other?

What about Hinduism's relation to other religious traditions and their holy scriptures? Is Hinduism all-inclusive? Does it embrace all other traditions in its belief that beyond all notions of the divine there is one Brahman and that "the various religions and their scriptures are simply different secondary revelations of the one Divine Reality—*Brahman*"?[37] Not really—or, to be more precise, the seemingly inclusive attitude toward other traditions among the Hindus must be greatly qualified and put in perspective.

---

35. See further, Ward, *Religion and Revelation*, 135–36.

36. Ward, *Religion and Revelation*, 136; see also 135.

37. Coward, *Sacred Word*, 129; see further, Harold Coward, *Pluralism: Challenge to World Religions* (Maryknoll, NY: Orbis, 1985), chap. 4.

As already implied, there are deep—and in many ways, irreconcilable—internal differences among the main Hindu schools and traditions.[38] Fierce and animated intra-Hindu debates about the proper interpretation of the Vedas remind one of the continuing ecumenical divisions of the Christian church—and among other religious communities as well! Furthermore, the adoption of the authority of the Vedas anathematized the early significant dissenters: Buddhists and Jainists.

The Canadian religion scholar H. Coward summarizes well this complex matter: "Because it [Hinduism] asserts that the Vedas are the most perfect revelation of *Brahman*, Hinduism sees its scripture as providing the criterion against which all other scriptures must be tested. Thus the Hindu tolerance of other religions is directly proportionate to their congruence with the Vedas. There is no doubt that for the Hindu there is only one Divine, as revealed by the Hindu scriptures, and that any other revelation (e.g., Torah, New Testament, or Qur'an) is seen as a secondary manifestation to be verified against the Hindu Veda."[39]

The possibility and nature of a Hindu "theology of religions" will be discussed in the last chapter. Here it suffices to say that in orthodox Hinduism, by and large the "canonical" scriptural tradition serves the same function it does in most living faiths, that is, it builds boundaries between "us" and "others." This is the identity-forming function of tradition, in this case, scriptural tradition.

Revelation and Scripture in Buddhism

The Dhamma *and Its Proliferation*

The Rise of Sacred Literature Following Buddha's Enlightenment

While it is true that "Buddhism is, in one sense, a religion without revelation . . . [as] there is no active communication from a God in most forms of Buddhism," it is also true that "there is certainly an authoritative teaching in

---

38. Ward (*Images of Eternity*, 6) lists examples of mutual condemnations between Sankara and Ramanuja, and then in relation to Buddhists; similarly, Clooney (*Hindu God, Christian God*, 143–46) accumulates a list of textual examples from Kumarila Bhatta, an eighth-century Mimamsa theologian, against Buddhists and in support of their exclusion.

39. Coward, *Sacred Word*, 129.

Buddhism, derived from the enlightened insight of Gautama."[40] Ironically, among all religions, Buddhism, with its multiple denominations, has produced the largest mass of sacred texts in various languages.[41]

It makes sense to speak of scripture in Buddhism as long as one keeps in mind some distinctive features that mark it off from other, more "typical" religious traditions. The Buddhist scripture is focused on the founder, the Gautama who became Buddha as a result of his enlightenment. In this respect, there is some parallelism with the New Testament's focus on Jesus of Nazareth—although very importantly, without any notion of Buddha being the "savior." Rather than savior, the Buddha serves as the embodiment and grand example of the goal attained, namely, the enlightenment that leads to release (nirvana).[42] That said, the Buddhist schools debate whether the content of Buddha's enlightenment can ever be put into words, since Gautama experienced it in silence under the Boddhi Tree.[43]

A particularly important and defining piece of writing for all Buddhist schools is the first sermon of Gautama (also called Sakyamuni), "First Turning of the Wheel of *Dhamma*."[44] Therein the enlightened Buddha explained his theology under the four Noble Truths as a way to overcome *dukkha* (often somewhat mistakenly translated as "vanity"), a theme to be explained in detail in the forthcoming chapters.

The summa of Buddhist doctrine, *dhamma* (Pali; *dharma* in Sanskrit), which is variously translated as "law," "teaching," or "principle(s)," contains, in addition to the Noble Truths, the Eightfold Path, the summary of the means toward the goal of final "release" and several related concepts concerning the nature of reality and human nature. In sum: to be a Buddhist means taking "refuge" in Buddha, *dhamma*, and *sangha* (community, particularly monastic community in Theravada schools). These serve as aids in one's pursuit of "salvation."

---

40. Ward, *Religion and Revelation*, 58; Coward, *Sacred Word*, 138.

41. For example, the Chinese Buddhist canon would require more than five hundred thousand pages if translated into Western languages! See Coward, *Sacred Word*, 138.

42. "If the Buddha is to be called a 'saviour' at all, it is only in the sense that he discovered and showed the Path to Liberation, Nirvana. But we must tread the Path ourselves." Walpola Rahula, *What the Buddha Taught*, rev. ed. (New York: Grove, 1974), 1–2.

43. Malcolm David Eckel, "Buddhism," in Coogan, *Eastern Religions*, 143.

44. Also known as "Setting the Wheel of *Dhamma* in Motion."

Any Divine Inspiration?

Since Buddhism at large is not a theistic religion in the sense of the three Semitic religions and Hinduism, the focus of its scripture is geared toward helping the human in the pursuit of enlightenment. The nontheistic nature of Buddhism, however, does not mean that it is therefore atheistic. All forms of Buddhism, even the most traditional Theravada tradition, acknowledge deities and divine beings. But the deities are not the focus of either revelation or spiritual pursuit. But even that statement calls for a qualification. In what nowadays is the largest Buddhist tradition (with a number of schools), the Mahayana, divine beings play a more profound role. In the Lotus Sutra, the "Bible" of many Mahayana faithful, one is struck with its way of speaking of Buddha in divine terms, of the authority of his sayings, and his "salvific" works.[45] Importantly, one subfamily of the Mahayana movement, Pure Land Buddhism, not only acknowledges god but also looks upon god as "savior."[46]

Not surprisingly, the Buddhist tradition does not speak with one voice. Yet, as a whole and in light of its original (Theravada) vision, any talk about *divinely* revealed, inspired holy scripture—after Hindu or Semitic religions—is foreign to Buddhism, notwithstanding a huge collection of sacred writings.

The Diversification and "Canonization" of Scripture

Following the approximately forty-five-year teaching career of Buddha, each of the early schools developed rich scriptural collections; unfortunately, only the Pali-language Tipitaka ("Three Baskets") was preserved, and that is the "canonical" scripture of the oldest and most traditional Theravada school.[47]

45. Read only, for example, Saddharma-Pundarika (Lotus Sutra), chap. 24 (in *SBE* 21:n.p.; a few pages in English), which strongly echoes not only the Vedic teaching but also teachings of many theistic religions concerning divinely given revelation, as authoritative message, which leads to salvation. Here the savior Buddha is named Avalokitesvara, known as Amitabha in the Japanese (and some Chinese) Pure Land traditions.

46. The role of Amitabha Buddha as "savior" is discussed in the context of Christology, salvation, and eschatology.

47. Of the rapid divisions and proliferation of Buddhism from its beginnings onward, a profound example is the rise of about eighteen different schools (*nikaya*) during the first century after the death of Gautama. Of those, the only one surviving is Theravada. Hence, its scriptural canon is defining for all later developments. Theravada tradition is concentrated in Cambodia, Laos, Myanmar, Sri Lanka, and Thailand.

According to written Buddhist history, after Buddha's death the First Buddhist Council (486 BCE) was invoked to recite the teachings of the Enlightened One. The council established criteria and procedures for the memorization of Buddha's words. Only after about five hundred years was the canonical collection now known as Tipitaka put into writing. As in Hinduism, oral tradition is highly appreciated in Buddhism, even though most schools also highly revere the canonical writings.

According to tradition, Tipitaka was written down in 29 BCE in Sri Lanka under King Vattagamani. Sutta Pitaka contains mainly doctrinal discourses, which appear in shorter poems and longer narratives. Some of those narratives related to earlier lives of Buddha. A separate, huge collection of former incarnations of Buddha, often numbered around five hundred, is called Jataka, and in English is published in no fewer than six volumes! While noncanonical, this collection is highly popular, and samples of it circulate widely among Buddhist laypeople. The second "basket" of Tipitaka is the Vinaya Pitaka, which is mainly about (monastic) rules of conduct and discipline. Many of the Buddhist moral principles can be found here, often illustrated with narratives and stories. Abhidhamma Pitaka is the most systematic form of Buddhist thought and beliefs.

The important early Buddhist teacher of the fifth century CE, Buddhaghosa, collected and translated important commentaries on canonical texts. His own most important contribution is Visuddhimagga, "The Path to Purification," a highly significant guide particularly to religious practices among the Theravadans. Like the Hindu Vedas, it is inaccessible to most faithful adherents, and very few have the luxury to study widely the extensive canonical collection of more than forty volumes. Instead, a small portion from the canonical text, called Dhammapada, is close to what we may call the "Buddhist Bible." It is drawn from Sutta Pitaka's Khuddaka Nikaya ("Minor Collection"). Basically it is a slim anthology of verses, which for the Jewish-Christian writer brings to mind the Old Testament Proverbs, that crystallizes much of the core teaching of the Buddha and Buddhism.[48] Buddhaghosa's celebrated commentary on Dhammapada is an important source of Buddhist theology.

---

48. A little more than four hundred verses, in English translation it takes only about 150 pages and hence—similarly to catechisms in Christian tradition—serves well the purposes of lay education and teaching.

The Rise of Mahayana Tradition and Its Scriptures

Around the beginning of the common era, the most significant split occurred, giving birth to the Mahayana school.[49] This branch developed a rich and variegated treasure of scriptures as well as a competing hermeneutics alongside the older tradition. Significantly, the Mahayana tradition claimed to build on Buddha's own teaching—thus representing the mentality of some Christian "back to the Bible" restorationist movements—with the alleged "Second Turning of the Wheel of *Dhamma*." This sermon was believed to be hidden for a while and then rediscovered by this renewal movement—again, a development not unknown in other religious traditions.

Mahayana advocates a much more open access to the pursuit of nirvana for all men and women, not only to a few religious.[50] It also developed the theological interpretation of Buddha into the significant notion of trikaya, "three bodies," three interrelated ways to access the manifestation and knowledge of Buddha, to be explained in chapter 5, on Christology.

The development and dissemination of Mahayana tradition throughout various Asian locations are closely related to the proliferation of sacred literature. As early as the second century CE, the earliest texts were translated into Chinese. During the second half of the first millennium CE, the Chinese Tripitaka (Sanskrit translation of the Pali name Tipitaka) was codified into Chinese writing, and the Tibetan collection of sacred writings, a couple of hundred years after. In both of these locations, the monastic connection is evident.

While no canonization is in place here, a "canon within the canon," to use Christian parlance, evolved quite early. Both the Chinese and Tibetan collections of sutras include a section called "Perfection of Wisdom" (Prajnaparamita), an essential Mahayana teaching about Bodhisattvas (the Enlightened Ones) and the principle of "emptiness" (sunyata). Once this core text expanded to become huge—over one hundred thousand lines—it was condensed into short texts such as the Diamond Sutra and the Heart Sutra, the best-known parts of the Sanskrit "canon." Alongside these two collections of sutras, the Lotus Sutra functions in much of East Asia as an accessible, lim-

---

49. Mahayana is currently present in India, Vietnam, Tibet (mainly in the form of Tantric Buddhism or Vajrayana), China, Taiwan, Korea, and Japan, among other locations. That tradition is also the most familiar form of Buddhism in the Global North.

50. Whereas in Theravada, the *arahant*, enlightened one, wishes to "cross the river" and extinguish in nirvana all desires, thus reaching personal salvation, in Mahayana, the enlightened Boddhisattvas postpone their own final bliss for the sake of helping others. See chaps. 8 and 10 for details of the Buddhist teaching on "salvation."

ited collection of key Mahayana teachings. Quite distinct from the Mahayana tradition, the Tibetan Tantric or Vajranaya school produced large collections of sacred writings as well, including Mahavairochana Tantra, "the Tantra of the Great Vairochana."

While Mahayana and all other Buddhist schools consider Tipitaka to be founding scriptures, Mahayana has produced a number of significant sutras that are rejected by most Theravadans. While the production of rich sacred literature is the hallmark of Mahayana, no canon has been formulated.[51] Hence, when speaking of the Buddhist "canon," one must keep in mind that there is no fixed pan-Buddhist canon even though Tipitaka is greatly appreciated by all, and that only in the Theravada school can the written Tipitaka be said to function as canonical writing.[52]

The Function and Authority of Scripture in Buddhist and Christian Traditions

Pursuing the Experience of Enlightenment

Why is it that, in light of what has just been explained, Buddhism has produced such huge amounts of sacred literature? "Perhaps Buddhists have more scripture than others because, in their view, scriptural words do not have a special status such as the *qur'ans* of Islam or the *vāk* of Hinduism. For the Buddhist, words, even most scriptural words, are not divine but merely conventional—created by humans for the purpose of solving practical problems in everyday life."[53]

Consider the well-known fact that, unlike, say, most Vedanta theologians to whom metaphysical and "abstract" philosophical questions are important, Buddha himself on various occasions sought to avoid speculation and to just focus on the "practical" issues.[54] What bothered the young nobleman was not

---

51. See Richard H. Robinson and Willard L. Johnson, *The Buddhist Religion: An Historical Introduction* (Belmont, CA: Wadsworth, 1997), 84.

52. For a highly useful and accessible presentation of the sacred writings in various Buddhist schools, see Eckel, "Buddhism," 143–52.

53. Coward, *Sacred Word*, 138.

54. In this context, one is reminded of Buddha's parable of the house on fire (Aggi-Vacchagotta Sutta: To Vacchagotta on Fire, #72 of Majjhima Nikaya) as a way of shifting interest in metaphysical speculations about the infinite/finite nature of reality to practical matters of rescue. His famous parable of a man wounded by a poisoned arrow makes the same

only the sometimes-speculative approach to the scriptures among the Brahmins, but particularly the fact that, lacking direct experience of Brahman, the students of the Vedas had to rely solely on the authority of the "seers," the human recipients of the eternal divine voices. That is why in Gautama's reasoning the Vedas could not be accepted as revelation.[55]

Gautama sought to escape the need to pursue and allegedly reach the defining personal experience only by way of the Vedic teaching. Unlike gnosticism or similar movements that consider the experience of the few "enlightened" unattainable by the masses, in Gautama's vision and in the understanding of most of his followers, that is not the case, particularly in the Mahayana school. Rightly, Lewis Lancaster observes:

> While the followers of the Buddha considered that his words possessed special power, the idea that the teaching arose from insights achieved in a special state of yogic development, a state open and available to all who have the ability and the desire to exert the tremendous effort needed to achieve it, meant that the words based on the experience need not be considered as unique or limited to one person in one time. Indeed, the Buddhists held that Sākayamuni was but one of a line of Buddhas who have appeared in this world system to expound the Dharma, and that there will be others to follow.[56]

A Sympathetic Critical Christian Engagement

Some observations and critical questions emerge from the perspective of Christian tradition particularly with regard to the role of "authority" in revelation and faith. First of all, a sympathetic Christian critic would remind Buddha's followers that in the absence of the experience of the enlightenment—even among those who still earnestly pursue it—the only way to obtain guidance

---

point (Cula-Malunkyovada Sutta: The Shorter Instructions to Malunkya, #63 of Majjhima Nikaya). Furthermore, Buddha's comparison between teaching and a raft to cross over the river not only makes the point evident among many Hindu theologians that scripture only has an intermediary agency (having reached its goal, it can be left behind) but also radicalizes it (Alagaddupama Sutta: The Snake Simile, #22 of Majjhima Nikaya).

55. See further, Coward, *Sacred Word*, 139–40.

56. Lewis Lancaster, "Buddhist Literature: Its Canon, Scribes, and Editors," in *The Critical Study of Sacred Texts*, ed. Wendy Doniger O'Flaherty, Berkeley Religious Studies Series 2 (Berkeley, CA: Graduate Theological Union, 1979), 215, quoted in Coward, *Sacred Word*, 140.

is to trust the authority, namely, the report of Buddha. It seems to me that all religious—as well as philosophical and metaphysical—explanations always build to some extent on authority and tradition, even the post-Enlightenment Christian, allegedly "contra-authority" viewpoints. A contingent, finite, and fallible human person or even humanity as a whole "is not an island." Second, the Buddhist belief that even Gautama represented a continuity of religious insights, albeit in a dramatically "new" way, seems to suggest that even his experience of enlightenment is not so novel that it would not be building on tradition and authority.

Third, a sympathetic observer of the Buddhist approach to scripture may note yet another irony or dynamic tension. Reginald A. Ray puts it well:

> Throughout its history, Buddhist tradition has maintained a paradoxical attitude towards its sacred texts. On the one hand, those texts have themselves been the objects of the utmost veneration; and life, limb, and more have been sacrificed to ensure their unaltered preservation and correct understanding. At the same time, Buddhism avers that the sacred text has, in and of itself, no particular value. Its worth depends entirely on what is done with it, and at best, the sacred text is never more than an aid that must be abandoned by each individual at a certain point on his journey toward the Buddhist goal of enlightenment. Thus in Buddhism, the sacred text is an answer to spiritual longing, and also no answer at all, or rather an "answer" in the way it points beyond and, in fact, away from itself.[57]

This twofold, dynamic attitude toward the scripture is best illustrated in the famous "Discourse on the Great Decease," which recounts the death of Gautama. On the one hand, it urges the disciple Ananda to be the "lamp" and "refuge" unto himself, and on the other hand, it tells him that the *dhamma* is the lamp and refuge![58]

In Buddhist texts one never hears the saying "Thus said Buddha"—as is customary in the Christian canon, "Thus said the Lord." Buddhist texts, on the contrary, at times begin with an epithet, "Thus I have heard," and it is most often Gautama himself who is the hearer. And even when the Theravada

---

57. Reginald A. Ray, "Buddhism: Sacred Text Written and Realized," in *The Holy Book in Comparative Perspective*, ed. Frederick M. Denny and Rodney L. Taylor (Columbia: University of South Carolina Press, 1985), 148.

58. Mahaparinibbana Sutta 1.33 (#16 of Digha Nikaya). See further, Ray, "Buddhism," 148–88.

tradition claims to preserve the "words" of Gautama, it always comes with the theological assumption that "the *dharma* transcends all words and the capability of language."[59] As Eva K. Neumaier correctly observes: "On the one hand, Buddhists have compiled hundreds of volumes of 'canonical' Buddha words while, on the other hand, maintaining that all words are, at best, only approximations of the truth, and at worst, altogether useless."[60]

What about Belief and Doubt?

A Distinctive Account of "Doubt"

So, what do Buddhists believe are the "authority" and defining function of scripture? While there certainly are doctrines in Buddhism, rather than "believing the doctrines" as described in the tightly formulated canons of Semitic religions and Vedic Hinduism, the main function and authority of scripture in all Buddhist schools are to serve as an aid to accessing Buddha's experience of the Awakening, and hence, to provide an opportunity for each Buddhist to tread that path.

True, Buddha's teaching speaks of doubt as one of the five hindrances[61] to an understanding of the truth and to spiritual progress. But the "doubt" spoken of by the Buddha is not a sinful attitude, as is often understood in Semitic traditions in terms of being unwilling to submit to and embrace divinely revealed truth. Walpola Rahula puts it brilliantly:

> Doubt . . . is not a "sin," because there are no articles of faith in Buddhism. In fact there is no "sin" in Buddhism, as sin is understood in some religions. The root of all evil is ignorance . . . and false views. . . . It is an undeniable fact that as long as there is doubt, perplexity, wavering, no progress is possible. It is also equally undeniable that there must be doubt as long as one does not understand or see clearly. But in order to progress further it is also absolutely necessary to get rid of doubt. To get rid of doubt one has to see clearly.[62]

59. Eva K. Neumaier, "The Dilemma of Authoritative Utterance in Buddhism," in Coward, *Experiencing Scripture in World Religions*, 138.

60. Neumaier, "Dilemma of Authoritative Utterance," 138–39.

61. The other four hindrances are usually listed as sensuous lust, ill-will, physical and mental languor, and restlessness and worry. See Rahula, *What the Buddha Taught*, 3.

62. Rahula, *What the Buddha Taught*, 3.

Hence, Buddha also always encouraged his disciples to test every teaching, even his own, in order to attain full conviction.[63] Considering ignorance as the root of evil is of course a shared conviction with Hinduism, even though the role of scripture differs vastly between the two traditions: Vedas are believed to be eternal divine voices, whereas Tipitaka is an authoritative access to Buddha's experience and teachings.

"Seeing" Rather Than Believing

The key to Buddhist pursuit of removing ignorance—based on the attachment to *dukkha*—is insight, or perhaps what Rahula calls "seeing":

> Almost all religions are built on faith—rather "blind" faith it would seem. But in Buddhism emphasis is laid on "seeing," knowing, understanding, and not on faith, or belief. In Buddhist texts there is a word *saddhā* (Skt. *Āraddhā*) which is usually translated as "faith" or "belief." But *saddhā* is not "faith," as such, but rather "confidence" born out of conviction. In popular Buddhism and also in ordinary usage in the texts the word *saddhā*, it must be admitted, has an element of "faith" in the sense that it signifies devotion to the Buddha, the *Dhamma* (Teaching) and the *Sangha* (The Order).[64]

The valid point in Rahula's explanation is the shift away from a "blind" or merely intellectual belief, a concept foreign to Buddhist pursuit of enlightenment. However, in Christian tradition, "faith" has little to do with "blind" or merely intellectual grasping either!

Highlighting the importance of "seeing" and insight helps put the role of Buddhist scripture in proper perspective. We do this not to circumvent the cognitive or even doctrinal nature of the sacred literature as much as to point to the specifically human-centered orientation of all Buddhist schools, particularly Theravada.

---

63. See Vimamsaka Sutta ("The Examination"), #47 of Majjhima Nikaya. It can be found in English at http://www.buddhasutra.com/files/vimamsaka_sutta.htm. Ukkacita-Sutta ("Bombast"), Anguttara Nikaya 2.46, similarly makes a distinction between two kinds of people: those who listen attentively and critically to the *dhamma*, and those who listen uncritically to other teachings.

64. Rahula, *What the Buddha Taught*, 8.

Gospel and *Dhamma*

A certain parallelism was noted above between the Hindu understanding of the Vedas as eternal, creative words and the Christian idea of the Word/ Logos. What about Buddhism in this regard? Note this saying in Samyutta Nikaya: "Enough, Vakkali! What is there to see in this vile body? He who sees Dhamma, Vakkali, sees me; he who sees me sees Dhamma. Truly seeing Dhamma, one sees me; seeing me one sees Dhamma."[65] A Christian observer is tempted to see some parallels here with the idea of the living Word of God. Although the partial yet important parallelism between Hinduism and Christian tradition appears more pointed in that for both traditions the "Word" is eternal and divine, establishing the parallelism between Buddhism and Christian theologies seems to me a stretch of the imagination. The differences are too dramatic, not only because of Buddhism's ambivalence about theistic notions but also because of its approach to scripture and "revelation" as expounded above. This is not to deny scripture's centrality to the Buddhist pursuit of "salvific" insight; it is merely to highlight the vastly different view of revelation and the role of the divine (or lack of) therein.

Other significant differences exist between Christian faith and Buddhism when it comes to revelation. Since these have been noted above, including some relevant comments in the discussion of Hinduism, let it suffice to list them briefly here: the detachment of revelation from the historical process; the lack of any notion of inspiration of the sacred text; and a very different linking of the sacred words/scripture to the "founder" of the faith than in Christian tradition—Jesus not only speaks authoritatively but *is* the *eternal* Word made *flesh*.

This is not to say that Christian tradition couldn't learn from Buddhism. Buddhism's strength, which ironically is also its weakness in Christian estimation, is the focus on "human responsibility . . . and a practice leading to personal fulfillment while shedding all the myths of authoritative obedience which existed in the Brahmanical tradition." That said, as K. Ward helpfully reminds us, "it would be a terrible misunderstanding to take Buddhism simply as a humanist protest against religious authoritarianism, against a moralism which subjugates human freedom in the name of God."[66] Totally unlike atheistic or other forms of "secular" ethics, for Buddhism—as a *religious* tradition— the fulfillment points to transcendence, ultimate release.

---

65. Vakkali Sutta, in Samyutta Nikaya, 22.87.
66. Ward, *Religion and Revelation*, 160–61.

How do Christian and Buddhist notions of authority relate to each other? Two points are in order. First of all, both traditions build on authority. Second, they do this so differently that their views conflict dramatically. The Buddhist conviction about its view's correctness is based on the teachings of the Buddhas, in whose lives, most profoundly in the life of the Gautama Buddha, the insight gained led to fulfillment. But since no Buddhas are living physically with us now, the account of these Buddhas' enlightenment must be taken by faith. The same goes for Christians, who build on the words of Jesus Christ that are available only through the writings of the early witnesses.

Scripture and the Relation to the Religious Other

How does Tipitaka take other religious traditions and their scriptures? Estimates vary. The noted Buddhist expert Walpola Rahula—in my understanding—somewhat naively praises the absolute open-mindedness of Buddhist tradition in relation to all other living faiths.[67] I fear that a study of the history may not yield so rosy a picture. Be that as it may, others take a more moderate stance. Like Hinduism, Buddhism is firmly anchored in the conviction that the final and fullest revelation came through Buddha and that this is the criterion for the value of other claims to revelation.

It seems to me the famed comparative theologian H. G. Coward is right when, specifically comparing the Tipitaka to other living faiths' scriptures, he names the Buddhist attitude "critical tolerance":

> Critical in the sense that any removal of moral freedom and responsibility in these [other] scriptures will be rejected. Tolerant in that so long as moral responsibility is safeguarded, other teachings contained in these [other] scriptures such as, for example, belief in God—teachings that the *Tripiṭaka* rejects—will be put up with. The approach of the Buddha to other scriptures is to superimpose his teaching over the other scripture. So long as the main points of the Buddhist teaching, or *Dharma*, can be found (i.e., belief in survival after death, moral values, freedom, responsibility, and the noninevitability of salvation or release) then other unacceptable aspects such as free grace from God can be tolerated.[68]

67. Rahula, *What the Buddha Taught*, 5 particularly.
68. Coward, *Sacred Word*, 157.

While this is not necessarily a contradictory assessment, Coward is a bit more reserved. For him—and the present author agrees—it hardly makes sense to claim that the human-centered (rightly understood), "nontheistic" approach adopted in the Tipitaka is speaking the same truth as the fully theistic Judeo-Christian Bible (and Islam's Qur'an): "The teachings of the *Tripiṭaka* are clearly different from the Christianity of St. Paul, the devotional Hinduism of the *Bhagavad-Gītā*, or the Qur'an. The scriptures of these last three teach that it is God's grace that makes possible religious attainment, whereas, for the Buddhist *Tripiṭaka* it is human effort, not supernatural intervention, that is effective."[69]

The Qur'an and the Bible as Vehicles of Divine Revelation

Islamic Canon and Sacred Texts

Unlike Hinduism and Buddhism, in which the canon is either vast or hardly defined, but similar to Judeo-Christian traditions, Islam has a clearly defined canon, the Qur'an. Linked to later exposition and expansion of the Qur'anic materials, a huge and vast Hadith tradition also exists, which consists of the sayings of the Prophet and other sages. The sayings and actions of Muhammad narrated in the Hadith are not believed to be revealed, although they are inspired.[70] By the ninth century, as many as six hundred thousand Hadiths had been recorded, which were then condensed into about twenty-five thousand. By far the most important is the Hadith of Bukkhari; significant also are the Hadiths of Muslim, of Sunan Abu-Dawud, and of Malik's Muwatta.

Understandably, Islamic tradition has brought about commentary literature, similar to that of other living faiths. The Sunni exegesis during the first Islamic centuries became especially famous for its meticulous and tedious work. Along with the mainline Sunni and Shi'ite schools, the mystical Sufi schools have produced an amazingly diverse devotional and mystical literary and poetic treasury.

Of all living faiths, there is probably none for which the holy scripture plays a more profound role. "Out of the Qur'an arises the Islamic community,

---

69. Coward, *Sacred Word*, 157.

70. For details of this highly nuanced doctrinal view, see Ward, *Religion and Revelation*, 174–75.

its law, literature, art, and religion. Perhaps more than any other religious community, Muslims are a 'people of the Book.'"[71]

The Qur'an does not do away with earlier revelations—the Jewish First Testament and the Christian Second Testament—but rather considers itself their fulfillment and correction. Similar to how Hindus view the Vedas, most Muslims consider the Qur'an the eternal speech of God.[72] Again, like Hinduism, the oral scripture is the primary mode. What is interesting is that the term *Qur'an* in Arabic means both "recitation" and "reading," thus embracing both oral and written aspects.

Muhammad's Critical Role as the Recipient of Revelation

Unlike in Hinduism, whose *rishis* (seers) merely "hear" the eternal speech in the Vedas, passively, by virtue of having been cultivated spiritually to tap into the divine, the recipient in Islam, the Prophet Muhammad, is more than just a passive recipient. Hence, the usual nomenclature of the "messenger" probably says too little of the role of the Prophet.[73] Coward puts it well: "God is the speaker of the revelation, the angel Gabriel is the intermediary agent, and Muhammad is the recipient. Not a passive recipient, however, for God's word acts by its own energy and makes Muhammad the instrument, the 'sent-doer,' by which all people are warned by God and called to respond."[74] A mediator—the angel Gabriel, or at times, the Holy Spirit (Q 16:102), or the Trustworthy Spirit (26:193)—is needed because of the categorical separation between the transcendence of God and the immanence of humanity.

Unlike in the Bible, in which most of the divine speech comes in human forms, often embedded in the struggles of human life and in the events of history, and which often contains substantial narratives about key figures such as prophets and apostles, in the Islamic Qur'an "there is no notion of an inspi-

---

71. Coward, *Sacred Word*, 81. A massive contemporary source is *The Blackwell Companion to the Qur'ān*, ed. Andrew Rippin (Malden, MA: Blackwell, 2006).

72. This is the official standpoint of the major tradition of Islam, the Sunni theology. The minority Shi'ite school teaches that the Qur'an was created in time (that statement, however, does not make the Qur'anic word less authoritative). See Moojan Momen, *An Introduction to Shi'i Islam* (New Haven: Yale University Press, 1985), 176.

73. Coward, *Sacred Word*, 82.

74. Coward, *Sacred Word*, 82.

ration from God that is then clothed and uttered in the best words a human mind can create. In the Qur'an, Muhammad receives a direct, fully composed revelation from God, which he then recites to others."[75]

While progressive contemporary scholars, mainly based in the West, acknowledge the personal, religious, sociohistorical, and similar contextual factors in the formation of the canon,[76] orthodox Islam regards the Arabic Qur'an as the direct, authoritative speech of God conveyed through the Prophet. In that sense, Muhammad's role is critical and unique (Q 42:7, 17, 52). Unlike the Christian understanding of the formation of the canon as a centuries-long divine-human synergy, orthodox Islam rests on the firm conviction that the formation and closing of the Qur'anic canon were a divine act through Muhammad. Indeed, there is an old tradition according to which the Qur'an is but a copy of a "Guarded Tablet" in heaven (85:22).[77]

The belief that the revelation of the Qur'an came to Muhammad directly from God does not mean that it all came at one time. According to Q 17:106, "We have revealed it by [successive] revelation." Hadith traditions give vivid accounts of various ways the reception of revelation took place, including through dramatic emotional states.[78] However, theologically, unlike the experiences of the Old Testament prophets or the New Testament apostle Paul, these emotional and personal struggles were not part of the revelation and revelatory process in Islamic understanding.

The Strict Infallibility of the Qur'an

Although the sacred texts of the living faiths were conveyed originally in particular languages—Vedas in Sanskrit, Tipitaka in Pali, Torah in Hebrew, the New Testament in Greek—the Qur'an insists that its original language, Arabic,

---

75. Coward, *Sacred Word*, 82. An important Qur'anic explanation of the "sending down" of the divine revelation on the "Night of Destiny" is in 53:5–11. For more on the divine origin and authority of scripture, see 16:102; 26:192–95; 42:7. Whether Muhammad was illiterate or not is a debated question because of the ambiguity of interpretation of 7:158 ("uninstructed," in other renderings "unlettered" or similar).

76. So Abdulaziz Abdulhussein Sachedina, *The Islamic Roots of Democratic Pluralism* (New York: Oxford University Press, 2001), 45–46.

77. Hanna Kassis, "The Qur'an," in Coward, *Experiencing Scripture in World Religions*, 72–73.

78. See Sahih of Bukhari 1, #2 and #3.

is also its only "revelatory" language.[79] The Qur'an can only exist in Arabic; all translations fall short of full revelation.[80]

The form of Arabic used in the Qur'an is of the tribe of Quraysh, that of Muhammad. Interestingly, stylistically it is identical with none of the known bodies of Arabic. Even the Arabic of the Hadiths is different from that of the Qur'an. "The uniqueness of the language of the Qur'an has become a dominant element in Muslim orthodoxy."[81]

As with the Vedas and Tipitaka, the oral form of (the Arabic) Qur'an is the most foundational and most authentic revelation. Beginning from Muhammad, who was commanded by the angel to commit revelation to memory and who then recited it to the first disciples, there has been an unbroken line of reciters of the Qur'an. Islam holds a firm belief that great blessings come from this recital, not only in this life but also in the life to come. "The Qur'an is uttered to call others to it, to expiate sins, to protect against punishment, and to ensure blessings in paradise."[82]

Like the New Testament, the Qur'an defines its main and ultimate goal as the salvation of humankind. It also often refers to itself as the guide (14:1; 2:185; among others). An extreme view of the infallibility of the Qur'anic revelation and words is affirmed by all orthodox Muslim traditions. Sura 11, which speaks of Muhammad's task as prophet, opens with this affirmation: "(This is) a Scripture the revelations whereof are perfected and then expounded. (It cometh) from One Wise, Informed" (11:1, Marmaduke Pickthall trans.). According to 2:2, "That Book, in it there is no doubt" (see also 5:15–16; 5:48).

The Qur'anic view of scripture is understandably strongly propositional. That said, part of the Islamic doctrine of scripture has to do with its "sacramental" nature, to use the Christian vocabulary. The Arabic term *ayat*, which also means "verse" (of the sura), carries the meaning of "sign"—to be more precise, a divine or divinely sanctioned sign. Consider Jesus's miracles as "signs" (named as such in the Gospel of John, and understood as such in the Synoptics) as a material parallel.[83]

---

79. Q 42:7: "And thus have We revealed to you an Arabic Qur'ān." So also 12:2; 13:37; 16:103; 20:113; 26:195; 39:28.

80. Hence Rana Kabbani (*A Letter to Christendom* [London: Virago, 2003], 34) bluntly says that a translated text is a different text.

81. Kassis, "The Qur'an," 70.

82. Coward, *Sacred Word*, 85–86.

83. There is a belief that the "verses" and "chapters" were placed in a certain order by Muhammad himself. The "verses" can be identified auditively by rhyme and rhythm. See Kassis, "The Qur'an," 70–71.

The Right Interpretation

Not surprisingly, the Islamic tradition has paid close attention to careful and authoritative exegesis (*tafsir*) of the Qur'an. Indeed, because the Qur'an lays the foundation for and regulates all aspects of life and society, more is at stake in the hermeneutics of scripture in Islam than with most other traditions.[84] As mentioned, in early times the Sunni school excelled in a most detailed exegesis. The tenth-century Abu Ja'far Muhammad at-Tabari and the twelfth-century Fakhr ad-Diin ar-Razi are often lifted up as most brilliant commentators. While the former established the procedure of citing all relevant Hadith comments with regard to the Qur'anic passage under exegesis, the latter also helped move exegesis in a philosophical and rationalistic direction.

The main difference between the Sunni and Shi'ite schools[85] is that the latter regards the imams as also inspired (and perhaps even infallible), a claim strongly rejected by the Sunni. Indeed, the Shi'ite school has a strictly regulated theology of succession, which maintains that while all Muslims may understand the scripture at the basic level, the authoritative interpretation comes only from the imams who are considered to be standing in the line of Ali, the legitimate successor of the Prophet. Hence, this line of "apostolic succession" goes all the way to Muhammad via Ali.

It does not take much imagination for a Christian to see parallels with Christian tradition's deeply divisive debates about the episcopal succession and its relation to a rightful magisterium, the church's teaching office. Indeed, there is the notion not only of continuing inspiration but also (at least in some sense) of infallibility attached to the office of the imam, as Ali and his successors have received the "inner knowledge" of Muhammad. Again, reflecting some aspects of Christian tradition, it is not the differing exegetical techniques that make the difference but rather the deeply differing notion of succession and authority. The way of doing exegesis varies only in the Sufi traditions, with their immersion in mystical materials and their use of Greek philosophical materials.[86]

---

84. Ahmad von Denffer, *Ulūm al-Qur'ān: An Introduction to the Sciences of the Qur'ān* (Leicester: Islamic Foundation, 1983), 123. An important part of the exegesis negotiates the universal and limited applicability of passages (say, polygamy) in light of the "occasions of revelation" principle; for succinct comments, see Clinton Bennett, *Understanding Christian-Muslim Relations: Past and Present* (London: Continuum, 2008), 41–42.

85. A detailed account of the division of Islam into these main schools (with an endless diversity of subcategories) is the theme of chap. 9 on the community.

86. For a useful account of Islamic exegesis, see Coward, *Sacred Word*, 94–101.

Because of the nature of the Qur'an's divine origin—void of historical contextual factors and absolutely infallible—it is understandable that orthodox Muslim traditions reject the kind of historical-critical study that has been the hallmark of the Christian—and more recently Jewish—study of Scriptures for a long time now. This is not to say that no such inquiry into the Qur'an exists; rather, it means that it is marginal and rejected by the "curia" and the masses of the faithful.

Qur'an as the Fulfillment and Correction

What is the relationship of the Qur'an to other scriptures? This is a dynamic and complex question that calls for a nuanced reflection. Well known is the statement in Q 42:15 that clearly bespeaks universality: "I believe in whatever Book God has revealed."[87] The Holy Qur'an makes it clear that the divine revelation as guide is available to all nations (Q 35:24). Hence, the current "A Common Word"[88] project between Muslims and Christians took its inspiration from Q 3:64: "Say: 'O People of the Scripture! Come now to a word agreed upon between us and you, that we worship none but God.'"

To balance and complicate this openness and universality, there is an equally important principle of sufficiency and completeness in the Qur'an. The passage from Q 43:3–4 puts this dynamic in perspective: "Lo! We have made it an Arabic Qur'ān that perhaps you may understand. And it is indeed in the Mother Book, [which is] with Us [and it is] indeed exalted." Whereas the former verse states that the Arabic Qur'an, this particular book, is the vehicle for understanding divine revelation, the latter verse seems to be referring to a "Mother Book" (also mentioned in 13:39)—a universal treasure of divine revelation of which even the Qur'an is a part. If so, this means that all the sacred books of the religions derive from the same divine origin. That would again bespeak universality.

On the other hand, Islamic theology of revelation also includes the determined insistence on the supremacy and finality of the Qur'anic revelation. Sura 5:44–48 makes this clear by presenting the Jewish Torah and the Christian New Testament as stepping-stones to the final revelation given in the Qur'an. Not only does the Qur'an provide fulfillment; it also provides

---

87. Even the context of this passage speaks for a unity of divine revelation (42:13–14).

88. For the project, see the official website of A Common Word at http://www.acommon word.com/.

correction and criteria. It is in light of the Qur'an that the value of other revelations is assessed. The obvious problem posed by this interpretation is that whereas it seems to fit well Judeo-Christian Scriptures, it has a hard time negotiating other faith traditions' revelations. I am not aware of any satisfactory solutions to this problem.[89]

The Dynamic of the Christian-Muslim Engagement of Scripture

The Muslim Charge of Christian "Alteration" of Scripture

A major challenge to a common reading of Christian and Muslim scriptures is the prevalent Muslim charge of *tahrif*, usually translated as "alteration." Early in Muslim history, *tahrif* was devised as a powerful counter-Christian tool. The term *tahrif* is used in more than one sense. At its most basic level, it refers to problems of textual variants and, hence, the lack of the authentic original. It may also denote deliberate altering of the text—the most typical charge being that Ezra altered the Old Testament text. But it can also simply mean a misguided interpretation of the texts.

A brilliant form of *tahrif* accusation, going back all the way to the important fourteenth-century Muslim apologist Ibn Taymiyyah's massive rebuttal of Christianity in response to the Christian writings of Paul of Antioch, is that perhaps the New Testament is like Hadith rather than scripture.[90] In light of Islamic tradition, this makes sense, as the New Testament contains not only sayings of Jesus but also his activities, not unlike the Hadith of Islam. The current *tahrif* criticism of the Bible uses skillfully—and selectively—the insights of (Christian) historical-critical study in rebutting the truthfulness and reliability of the text.

The dilemma of Muslim-Christian views of revelation does not have to do with the differences but rather with the deep affinity between these two traditions. Both claim a strictly defined canon and both appeal to one God as its source and provider. Yet they differ dramatically concerning which one of the books is the ultimate revelation. Adding to the complexity of this question

---

89. For thoughtful and important reflections, see Basit Koshul, "Affirming the Self through Accepting the Other," in *Scriptures in Dialogue: Christians and Muslims Studying the Bible and the Qur'an Together*, ed. Michael Ipgrave (London: Church House Publishing, 2004), 111–19; also, Coward, *Pluralism*, 55–59.

90. Bennett, *Understanding Christian-Muslim Relations*, 124–26 particularly.

are the dramatic differences in understanding of the category of revelation in general and of the other party's revelation in particular. Clinton Bennett succinctly lays out this complexity—which, of course, is an urgent invitation to continuing careful dialogue:

> In many respects, the conservative Christian view of the Bible as infallible and as inspired word for word is closer to how Muslims view the Qur'an than to the liberal Christian view of the Bible as a potentially fallible, human response to experience of the divine. On the Muslim right, the Bible is regarded as so corrupt that it no longer has any value. On the Christian left, an attempt is made to understand how the Qur'an can be accepted as "revelation." One difficulty is that Christians who deconstruct the Bible are likely to transfer this approach to the Qur'an as well, which is unacceptable, even to more liberal Muslims. Yet despite each side's view of the Other's scripture, Christians and Muslims from both the "right" and "left" cite from the Other's scripture to support their views. Christians have their favourite Qur'anic passages while Muslims have favourite Bible passages. More often than not, when Christians and Muslims use each other's scriptures, they do so in a manner that ignores or refutes how Christians and Muslims understand the passages concerned.[91]

The "Word of God Incarnate" and the "Word as Written"

Amidst these many challenges, a potentially fruitful common theme between these two cousin religions' views of revelation comes to the fore with regard to the theme mentioned in two comparative exercises above: the importance of the "Word" (of God). As is routinely—and correctly—remarked, it is not the Prophet but rather the book that is the closest parallel to Christ, the center of Christianity. Unlike Christian faith, which is determined by belief in Christ, Islam is not based on Muhammad but rather on the Qur'an and Allah. Neither Christ nor Muhammad in Islamic interpretation is divine; only God is. Hence, it is in Christ's role as the living Word of God in relation to the divine revelation of the Qur'an that the deepest commonalities are to be investigated.[92]

---

91. Bennett, *Understanding Christian-Muslim Relations*, 16.

92. Hence, the heading "The 'Christ of Islam' Is the Koran," in Josef Imbach, *Three Faces of Jesus: How Jews, Christians, and Muslims See Him*, trans. Jane Wilde (Springfield, IL: Templegate Publishers, 1992), 87. See further, Smail Balić, "The Image of Jesus in Contemporary

Rightly it has been noted that whereas Jesus in Christian tradition is the "Word made flesh," the Qur'an in Islam is the divine word "inlibrate."[93]

There are surprisingly deep similarities among the accounts in the Qur'an of the power of its word and Old Testament claims about the word of the Lord and New Testament statements about Christ as the creative word. Consider Q 59:21: "Had We sent down this Qur'an upon a mountain, you would have surely seen it humbled, rent asunder by the fear of God. And such similitudes do We strike for mankind, that perhaps they may reflect." Again, just as the word of the Lord has many functions in the Bible, whether for encouragement or healing or miraculous acts, the Islamic tradition speaks of the living words of the Qur'an:

> In addition to its destructive power, the words of the Qur'an are also a positive source for healing and tranquility. According to tradition when the Qur'an is recited divine tranquility (*sakīnah*) descends, mercy covers the reciters, angels draw near to them, and God remembers them. Tradition also tells how one of the companions of Muhammad came to him and reported seeing something like lamps between heaven and earth as he recited while riding horseback during the night. Muhammad is reported to have said that the lights were angels descended to hear the recitation of the Qur'an. For the pious Muslim, then, the chanted words of the Qur'an have the numinous power to cause destruction, to bring mercy, to provide protection, to give knowledge, and to evoke miraculous signs.[94]

The noted Muslim scholar Mahmoud Ayoub makes the startling claim that the Islamic notion to "live in the Qur'an" as it is faithfully and piously recited is a very close parallel to the New Testament idea of being "in Christ."[95] There is, however, also a significant difference here, aptly noticed by Ayoub, that whereas in the beginning of the Gospel of John the Word is not only with God but *is* God, "no one has asserted that the Qur'an is God."[96] In terms of the

---

Islamic Theology," in *We Believe in One God*, ed. A. M. Schimmel and Abdoldjavad Falaturi (London: Burns & Oates, 1979), 1; see 1–8.

93. Vincent Cornell, "Listening to God through the Qur'an," in Ipgrave, *Scriptures in Dialogue*, 37.

94. Coward, *Sacred Word*, 86, based on Mahmoud Ayoub, *The Qur'an and Its Interpreters*, vol. 1 (Albany: State University of New York Press, 1984), 8–9 particularly.

95. Ayoub, *The Qur'an*, 11; I am indebted to Coward, *Sacred Word*, 86.

96. Mahmoud Ayoub, "The Word of God in Islam," in *Orthodox Christians and Muslims*, ed. Nomikos Michael Vaporis (Brookline, MA: Holy Cross Orthodox Press, 1986), 73.

dialogue among Islam, Christianity, and Judaism, one topic well worth careful consideration is whether not only the Qur'an and the Word but also the Jewish Torah would function as parallels, a topic to which we turn below.[97]

The Bible between the Jews and Christians

Salient Features of Jewish Theology of Revelation

The Scripture as the Call to Obedient and Loving Covenant

It might strike one as odd to discuss the Jewish view of Scripture last, after the more foreign traditions from Asia and even Islam. There are two reasons for this choice. First, unlike some other topics, such as Christology and the Trinity, which are plagued with deep and irreconcilable conflicts discussed under those loci, Christian and Jewish traditions hold more in common when it comes to Scripture. Second, because the Christian Bible is partly Jewish, a number of common convictions, as well as differences from other traditions, have already been treated.

Differently from Hinduism and Islam with their belief in more or less direct mediation of revelation, in "the first book of the Hebrew Bible, Judaism has its historical origins in the act of obedience."[98] The origins of the Hebrew people lie in the response of faith of the forefather Abram (later named Abraham), who obediently set out on a journey to the promised land (Gen. 12:1–3). As the later history of the First Testament narrates it, this "missionary call" was meant to bring blessing not only to the family of Israel but also to the whole world. Hence, the universal scope of this particular and local revelation.

In light of these preliminary observations, several interrelated aspects can be discerned in the Jewish understanding of revelation in addition to its deep embeddedness in history and the matrix of human experiences. Its focus is on ethical and moral obedience. This is to say that even if other living faiths maintain a connection between moral conduct and religious practice, they do not establish it in the integral way that Judaism does[99] (and of course,

---

97. "Torah and Christ are both seen, respectively, as Word of God." Michael S. Kogan, *Opening the Covenant: A Jewish Theology of Christianity* (Oxford: Oxford University Press, 2008), 31.

98. John Corrigan et al., *Jews, Christians, Muslims: A Comparative Introduction to Monotheistic Religions*, 2nd ed. (Upper Saddle River, NJ: Prentice Hall, 2012), 3.

99. Ward, *Religion and Revelation*, 111–33.

by implication, Christianity). Furthermore, because revelation comes in the unfolding of history, it looks into history, to the future, for fulfillment.

That said, its orientation to Yahweh's final intervention, the most significant sign and manifestation of which is the arrival of the Messiah, does not mean that therefore Jewish faith is otherworldly. It is not. Indeed, one of the most significant differences between the Jewish view and the Christian view of revelation is that the latter is deeply eschatologically oriented, and hence its revelational category of promise is also eschatological, whereas Judaism's is much more this-worldly.

The focus on this-worldly needs and concerns, however, has nothing to do with the ethos of Christian classical liberalism, which made Jesus merely a convenient ethical teacher. Judaism's this-worldly orientation is fully and absolutely based in Yahweh, the creator, almighty ruler, and personal Father of all. Israel is to submit in love and covenant faithfulness to the One who loves and is faithful. Part of the revelation is also the readiness—albeit at times quite reluctant—to become the object of Yahweh's fatherly rebuke when ethical standards and covenant faithfulness are lacking. Rightly it can be noted that the First Testament is "surely the most self-critical body of literature any people has ever produced . . . [and] has ultimately only one hero: God."[100]

As much as there is emphasis on obedience, based on the covenant, Jewish revelation is propositional in nature. On the one hand, according to ancient tradition—although not supported by recent Jewish historical academic study—Moses basically received the law by divine "dictation." On the other hand, what he received—the detailed lists of commands, exhortations, laws, and practices conveyed by Yahweh—can only be appreciated as cognitive, propositional statements. How different is the content of the Hebrew Bible's law code from the style and content of, say, the Rig Veda of Hinduism!

The Jewish Canon

The center and most sacred part of the Jewish canon, Tanak,[101] is Torah ("teaching," "instruction"). In written form it is the "Five Books of Moses." An important counterpart is the Oral Torah, which came to full flourishing with the emergence of rabbinic Judaism beginning around the start of the

---

100. Kogan, *Opening the Covenant*, 7.

101. Tanak is an acronym formed from the first letters of the three sections of Scripture: Torah, Nevi'im, and Ketuvim.

common era, but which was believed to have been revealed to Moses along with the written Torah.

The two other parts of the canon, albeit not as sacred, are Nevi'im (prophetic books) and Ketuvim ("Writings").[102] A significant portion of the second part, the prophetic books, is composed of writings that could be better labeled "historical books" (Joshua, Judges, 1–2 Samuel, 1–2 Kings). In the Jewish theological outlook, however, they are rightly located, since Yahweh is the Lord of history, and hence, the post-Enlightenment separation of "secular" and "sacred" history is a foreign idea. Similarly, the last book of the Hebrew Bible (which, incidentally, in the Christian Old Testament is placed after 1–2 Kings), the two-volume Chronicles, is placed at the end of the canon because it ends on a hopeful note of the release from the exile. It is a book of promise, pointing toward future fulfillment. It is fittingly placed in the collection that is mainly about wisdom and religious poetry and parable.

If "prophetic Judaism" (the Judaism until the beginning of the common era) brought about the Hebrew Bible as we have it now, rabbinic Judaism (religion and theology of our common era) produced the huge and varied collections of the so-called Oral Torah; the nomenclature "oral," of course, has to be taken in a qualified sense here. While it was put into written form in Mishnahs (and commented on in Talmuds), the first transmission of this material from Yahweh to Moses is believed to have been oral. While not canonical in the sense of Torah (and the rest of the Hebrew Bible), it is irreplaceable in that it helps make the written Torah living and applicable to ever-new situations. Hence, the importance of midrash, the meticulous examination of the written text to find its right and true meaning.

Scripture in the Defining of Rabbinic Judaism

Rabbinic Judaism became the dominant form of the religion following the devastation caused by the destruction of the Second Temple in 70 CE, which of course meant yet another loss of the land and more importantly the temple, the earthly locus and guarantee of God's presence. Not surprisingly, rabbinic Judaism was not a uniform movement; it consisted of several factions, such as the Pharisees and Sadducees, both of which held Torah as the canonical

---

102. See the important remarks in Jonathan Rosenbaum, "Judaism: Torah and Tradition," in *The Holy Book in Comparative Perspective*, ed. Frederick M. Denny and Rodney L. Taylor (Columbia: University of South Carolina Press, 1985), 12–17.

Scripture but had opposite views concerning the value of extrascriptural tradition. The Sadducees took only the received text of the written Scripture as authoritative, as it had been entrusted to the priesthood, and consequently they regarded any tradition whose source was not in the written Scripture as human invention.

The Pharisees, who became the mainstream of rabbinic Judaism after 70 CE, did not think the canonical status of the written Scripture excluded the later developing tradition. Through painstaking study of the Law (Torah) and the rest of the canon, they uncovered meanings not apparent at a cursory reading. For the Pharisees—and indeed, for rabbinic Judaism at large—revelation is thus "progressive," unlike traditional prophetic Judaism, which believes in the reception by Moses of Yahweh's revelation; if the term "progressive revelation" is too much, then we should speak at least of "progressive interpretation of revelation" in rabbinicism.[103]

This huge Oral Torah is classified under the general categories of halakah, ritual and legal practices and traditions, and haggadah, with its focus on homiletics, ethics, exegesis, and theology. The first major work that also became foundational to the Oral Torah is the Mishnah, compiled in the second century CE. Huge collections of Talmudic tractates—the most important of which are the Babylonian and Palestinian—emerged as commentaries on the Mishnah over several centuries. The Babylonian Talmud, completed in the sixth century CE, is the most important of these works and an indispensable resource for everything Jewish.[104]

Later Developments

In medieval times revisionist movements arose, such as Karaism, which questioned and basically rejected the rabbinic notion of Jewish tradition. Another one, kabbalism, did not reject either rabbinic tradition or the Oral Torah, but rather filled it with new meanings, often highly speculative and imaginative.

As important as prophetic and rabbinic Judaism is to that religion, in the contemporary world there are a number of nonorthodox movements, from the Reform movements of the mid-nineteenth century to various liberal schools of our era. While all these movements, in some sense or another, consider

---

103. See Coward, *Sacred Word*, 13.

104. For a highly accessible discussion, see Eliezer Segal, "Judaism," in Coward, *Experiencing Scripture in World Religions*, 15–33.

Torah the canonical Scripture, they disagree widely about how to deal with the rules (*mitzvoth*) of Torah in the contemporary world. Should they be taken "literally," as the unchanging will of God for all ages? Are they supposed to be considered principles with different applications?

How to Deal with the Religious Other

To locate the Jewish tradition in the multifaith matrix, it is helpful to follow Keith Ward's characterization. He identifies Judaism as "seminal" and "intermediate." It is seminal in its functioning as the basis for two other faiths, Christianity and Islam, and it is intermediate because it is a local or tribal tradition. However—and this is significant for Christian considerations—its view of revelation is universal in that it speaks of Yahweh as the creator and God of all men and women and the whole of creation.[105]

When it comes to the relation of the two peoples of God who share the same Torah as their Scripture, we have to begin with the sad and long track record of Christian anti-Semitism. As early as the second century CE, Marcion wanted the Christian church to reject the Old Testament as canonical Scripture. "In the period from the fourth to the sixteenth century no fewer than 106 popes and 92 Church councils issued anti-Jewish laws and regulations."[106] While anti-Semitism in all its forms is to be rejected, the Christian challenge still remains as long as the church wishes to stay faithful to its canonical Scriptures of both Testaments. This challenge is so eloquently and ironically described by the contemporary Jewish scholar Michael S. Kogan: How is it possible "to be faithful to the New Testament command to witness for Christ to all peoples and to convert all nations, while, at the same time, affirming the ongoing validity of the covenant between God and Israel via Abraham and Moses[?] Can the church have it both ways?"[107]

The Jewish conviction of being the elected people is based on Torah, which speaks of the covenant struck between Yahweh and Israel. However, if the people of God do not adhere to the covenant, its benefits may be lost. On the other hand, from as early as the third century CE, rabbinic Judaism has appealed to the Noachic covenant as a means for offering the "way of salva-

---

105. Ward, *Religion and Revelation*, 111–12.

106. Pinchas Lapide, *Israelis, Jews, and Jesus*, trans. Peter Heinegg (Garden City, NY: Doubleday, 1979), 81.

107. Kogan, *Opening the Covenant*, xii.

tion" to non-Jews.[108] This admission is not a matter of compromising Israel's covenant status; it is rather to act in light of the universally oriented revelation. Kogan poses the challenge to his Jewish counterparts aptly: "Are Jews really ready and willing to affirm that God, the God of Israel and of all humanity, was involved in the life of Jesus, in the founding of the Christian faith, in its growth and spread across much of the world, and in its central place in the hearts of hundreds of millions of their fellow beings?" His conviction is that the response of yes is inevitable from the perspective of the universal nature of revelation in his faith.[109] Only when mutual trust is being established could this mutual, painstaking dialogue and common Scripture reading enrich relationships within the same family of faith.

After these four comparative exercises, a proper way to end this chapter is to look at the promise of the emerging practice of common reading of scriptures, often called "scriptural reasoning," among adherents of different faith traditions.

Common Scripture Reading as a Form of Interfaith Theologizing

The previous comparative exercises have helped us discern continuities among religions, such as the centrality of scripture in all living faiths and its authoritative nature even when its origin and inspiration may be differently negotiated. Similarly, a number of defining differences have come to the surface, most profoundly the deep historical embeddedness of Judeo-Christian revelation in radical contrast to the Islamic and the two Asiatic traditions. Unless one is satisfied with the naive pluralistic denial of differences that hardly does justice to any tradition, even to one's own, a careful consideration of the theological implications of real conflicts is called for.

It seems to me that Keith Ward's response to this dilemma is as good as any: "Apparently, God has not given an unambiguous revelation and preserved it unequivocally from error. God has permitted many alleged competing revelations to have currency in the modern world."[110] Isn't that a reason to maintain modesty and humility, without rejecting proper confidence, about

108. According to the Noachic covenant, gentiles, provided they keep the seven laws described in the Oral Torah (which are claimed to be based on the teaching of Genesis even though there is no direct reference to it), may be saved. The seven laws are described in the Tosefta (tractate Avodah Zarah 9.4).

109. Kogan, *Opening the Covenant*, xiii.

110. Ward, *Religion and Revelation*, 174.

the truth of revelation in Christ? Isn't that a reason to continue careful reflection on how to best understand the complicated relationship between the divine and human elements in the inspiration of Scripture and formation of the canon?

As Christian theology continues constructing an adequate theology of revelation and Scripture, it also is well served by inviting scholars and practitioners from other faith traditions into a common reading of scriptures—every tradition's own scriptures. This is an act of hospitality: "we" are opening our Scriptures for others to read, and "they" are opening theirs. We are not only talking about how similar or different our theologies of revelation are; we are learning from and contributing to each other by reading together.

One of the theologically most promising initiatives in this respect is called "scriptural reasoning." It is actually a loose network of various types of international and interfaith enterprises that aims at helping scholars and clergy study sacred scriptures together.[111] It was started at the turn of the millennium among Jewish, Christian, and Islamic representatives and has so far concentrated heavily on monotheistic faiths for the simple reason that they share much in common.[112] It is likely that soon scriptural reasoning will be tried among other religions as well. The strength and promise of these kinds of interfaith enterprises are that they not only study *about* scriptures but they also study *scriptures* together.

Having considered in some detail some key aspects of four living faith traditions' views of scripture and revelation in relation to Christian understanding, we move naturally to similar exercises regarding God and deities.

---

111. For basics, see David F. Ford and C. C. Pecknold, eds., *The Promise of Scriptural Reasoning* (Oxford: Blackwell, 2006). A highly useful, continuously updated database is the website of *Journal of Scriptural Reasoning*, http://jsr.shanti.virginia.edu/. Other noteworthy current works include David Cheetham et al., eds., *Interreligious Hermeneutics in Pluralistic Europe: Between Texts and People* (Amsterdam and New York: Rodopi, 2011); Steven Kepnes and Basit Bilal Koshul, eds., *Scripture, Reason, and the Contemporary Islam-West Encounter: Studying the "Other," Understanding the "Self"* (Hampshire, UK: Palgrave Macmillan, 2007).

112. For basic guidelines, see Steven Kepnes, "A Handbook for Scriptural Reasoning," *Modern Theology* 22, no. 3 (2006): 367–83; David F. Ford, "An Interfaith Wisdom: Scriptural Reasoning between Jews, Christians and Muslims," *Modern Theology* 22, no. 3 (2006): 345–66.

2 | The Triune God among Religions

The Doctrine of the Triune God in Christian Tradition

Rooted in the uncompromising belief in one God of the mother faith, Judaism, Christianity constructed a Trinitarian monotheism, belief in one God as three "persons," Father, Son, and Spirit. Although the move from the Old Testament to the New without any preparatory notes to the reader may seem jarring, with God-talk as Father, Son, and Spirit now pervasive, recent research has also shown that the *idea* of diversity in the one God of the Old Testament, Yahweh, is not totally unknown. Alongside (and under) Yahweh, semipersonifications such as the "word," "spirit," "name," and even "glory" seem to hint at some kind of plurality in the one Godhead. This is not to try to soften the difference between the Jewish and Christian confessions of one God but rather to point to a potential avenue for a better understanding.

In addition to the Trinitarian nature of monotheism added to the Old Testament theology of God, the New Testament expands the theme of fatherhood. It plays a far more pervasive role in the New Testament. The God of Abraham, Isaac, and Jacob is the Father of Jesus Christ, and by definition the father of all. This filial relationship shapes the God-world relationship everywhere in Christian tradition.

While it took centuries for Christian tradition to clarify the relations between Father, Son, and Spirit, a consensus emerged according to which each of them is fully God, and that the Father, Son, and Spirit as one is fully God. Continuing oscillation between the heretical notions of modalism (that there are no distinctions of persons, merely "modes" or names) and tritheism (that there are three deities) has characterized much of the history of the doctrine of the Trinity.

An important effort to express the inseparable unity of the three persons while also allowing distinctions is the Trinitarian "rule" that the works of the Trinity "outwardly" (in relation to the world) are indistinguishable, whereas "inwardly" (in relation to the eternal relationship between the three) the three should be distinguished. In other words, the first part of this rule helps protect unity whereas its second part protects the distinct persons.

Alongside the narrative, testimonial, and metaphorical story of God of the Bible, in a critical dialogue with the best of pagan philosophies (particularly Hellenistic in patristic times and Aristotelian in medieval times), a fairly neat theology of God's essence and attributes was worked out. It led to precise definitions of God's features such as aseity (that God exists of Godself), immutability (that God does not change), impassibility (that God does not suffer), as well as omniscience, omnipotence, and omnipresence. In hindsight, this way to conceive of God was named "classical theism." During the twentieth century, a massive criticism against liabilities of classical theism emerged, with complaints that it made God too distant and disengaged, made God a virtual tyrant as an omnipotent Being, made God incapable of sharing the sufferings of the world, and so forth.

As an antithesis to the alleged liabilities of classical theism, what can be named "panentheism" arose. Unlike pantheism, which equates God and the world (a position impossible for any Abrahamic faith), panentheism brings God and world into a closer, more intimate mutual relationship—but in a way that God is still much "bigger" and "stronger" than the world. We can put it this way: whereas God is everywhere in creation, not everything in creation is God. Much of contemporary debate about the doctrine of God centers on how to best relate God and world to each other, negotiating between these two templates. Another vital issue has to with how to negotiate the implications of male terminology related to Father and Son as well as the wider issues of liberation and equality.

The Task of the Comparative Study of God

Neither atheism, the flat denial of God's existence, nor agnosticism, an informed and reasonable doubt, was found in Christian or other faith traditions' history prior to the Enlightenment. The "atheists" of the past, say, the famed Socrates, did not deny the reality of gods; he rather wanted to shift attention to matters of this world and human wisdom. Here we see a material similarity with original Buddhist thought, which is nontheistic in its attempt to move away from Vedic Hinduism's concentration of deities at the expense of this-worldly ethical pursuit. It took until the nineteenth century in modern Europe to produce the first great atheists whose goal was to defeat the meaningfulness and rationality of all God-talk. But not so among religions of the world. Belief in deities is widespread and universal.

Comparative theology works carefully, assessing, comparing, and reflecting on the ways living faiths embrace notions of the divine. In that work, the comparativist has to exercise utmost care in not ignoring or flattening potential deep differences; this is particularly important with regard to the nontheistic (original) Theravada tradition.

The order and selection of faith traditions to be engaged in this chapter differ from the previous one. The most extreme monotheism of Islam will be engaged first; thereafter, going to the other extreme, the apparently polytheistic Hinduism will be invited for dialogue, to be followed by Buddhist traditions.

There will be no separate focused investigation of Christian-Jewish dialogue because the most burning issue related to Trinity, namely, Christology, is discussed in a separate chapter, and the somewhat parallel problems related to the unity of God are investigated in relation to Islam. Furthermore, throughout this investigation, where relevant, Judaism, as the closest monotheistic religion to Christianity, sharing part of the same Scripture, will be engaged in relation to other faiths.

The chapter ends with a focused comparative look at the widely debated issue of whether religion and belief in God/deities necessarily leads to violence. This is a concern for all living faiths—as well as secular ideologies!

Allah and the Triune God

Strict Monotheism

While it is deeply similar to older monotheistic "cousin" faiths, Judaism and Christianity,[1] "no religious community puts more emphasis on the absolute oneness of God than does Islam."[2] It is affirmed everywhere in Islamic theol-

---

1. See further, Hans Köchler, ed., *The Concept of Monotheism in Islam and Christianity* (Vienna: Wilhelm Braumüller, 1982); Lucinda Mosher and David Marshall, eds., *Monotheism and Its Complexities: Christian and Muslim Perspectives* (Washington, DC: Georgetown University Press, 2018).

2. John B. Carman, *Majesty and Meekness: A Comparative Study of Contrast and Harmony in the Concept of God* (Grand Rapids: Eerdmans, 1994), 323.

ogy. The short sura 112 of the Qur'an puts it succinctly, taking notice also of the fallacy of the Christian confession of the Trinity:

> Say: "He is God, One.
> God, the Self-Sufficient, Besought of all.
> He neither begot, nor was begotten.
> Nor is there anyone equal to Him."

Hence, the basic Muslim confession of *shahada*: "There is no god but God, and Muhammad is the apostle of God." So robust is the belief in the unity of God that for some Muslim philosophers and mystics the principle of unity also applies to reality itself.

The Qur'an absolutely and unequivocally affirms the oneness of God. According to the leading medieval authority, al-Ghazali, that "God is one" means, on the one hand, "the negation of anything other than He and the affirmation of His essence." On the other hand, oneness means the denial of plurality in God: "He does not accept divisibility, i.e., He has no quantity, neither definition nor magnitude. It also means that He has no equal in rank and absolutely no equal in any manner." As in Christian tradition, the unity also includes the unity of God's existence and essence.[3]

An essential aspect of the divine unity is Allah's distinction from all else. The common statement "God is great" (*Allah akbar*) means not only that but also that "God is greater" than anything else. Hence, the biggest sin is *shirk*, associating anything with Allah.[4]

Importantly, *shirk* means literally "ingratitude," in other words, "that there is only one divine Creator who should be thanked and praised; no other being is to be given the thanks due only to God."[5] In that light it is understandable that, unlike modern forms of Christianity, the Muslim faith encompasses all of life. "Faith does not concern a sector of life—no, the whole of life is *islam* [submission]."[6] Hence, the Five Pillars of Islam (profession of faith, prayers, almsgiving, fasting, and pilgrimage) shape all of life.

---

3. In Abu Zayd, *Al-Ghazali on Divine Predicates and Their Properties* (Lahore: Sh. Muhammad Ashraft, 1970), x–xi, at x (available at: http://ghazali.org/books/abu-zayd.pdf). For an authoritative contemporary presentation, see Muhammad 'Abduh, *The Theology of Unity*, trans. Ishaq Musa'ad and Kenneth Cragg (London: Allen & Unwin, 1966).

4. There are numerous Qur'anic condemnations of *shirk*, although it is not quite clear what that "tremendous sin" (4.48) consists of.

5. Carman, *Majesty and Meekness*, 323.

6. Hendrik Vroom, *No Other Gods: Christian Belief in Dialogue with Buddhism, Hinduism, and Islam* (Grand Rapids: Eerdmans, 1996), 84.

God's Names and Attributes

The Importance of the Divine Name(s)

One of the most well-known ways in Islamic theology to imagine God is the listing of the 99 Beautiful Names of God.[7] Interestingly, there is no unanimity concerning whether Allah belongs to that number or is the 100th one. Be that as it may, that foundational name is attached to a number of other designations, for example, *al-Malik* (the King), *al-Salam* (the Peace), and *al-Muhaymin* (the Vigilant).[8]

The naming of the divine is more important for Islamic theology than for Christian theology.[9] Illustrative here is the beginning of each Qur'anic sura (save one, that is, 9) with the description of God as the "Compassionate, the Merciful."[10]

While there is hardly a classified typology of attributes in Islamic traditions—although many contemporary Islamic theologians familiar with Christian tradition find the classification into "communicable" and "incommunicable"[11] attributes meaningful—traditionally thirteen attributes mentioned in sura 59:22–24 feature first on the list. The most well-known listing of attributes, as presented by al-Ghazali, includes knowing, powerful, living, willing, hearing, seeing, and speaking,[12] followed by four "properties": existence, eternity, unity, and knowability. Unlike the attributes, which "are not [God's] essence," these four properties are part of God's essence, whereas the seven attributes are "superadded to the essence."[13] Like some aspects of Christian theology of God that take a paradoxical approach, Islam also knows polarities such as "Creator of Life" and "Creator of Death."[14] Luther's theology of the cross comes to mind here.

---

7. While the Qur'an does not specify ninety-nine names (indeed, more than ninety-nine names and designations of God can be found therein), early in Islamic theology the number ninety-nine came to be used. The Qur'an merely mentions: "And to God belong the Most Beautiful Names" (7:180). The list of ninety-nine names is given definitively in the established commentaries on sura 17:110. See Samuel M. Zwemer, *The Moslem Doctrine of God: An Essay on the Character and Attributes of Allah according to the Koran and Orthodox Tradition* (New York: American Tract Society, 1905), chap. 3.

8. Carman, *Majesty and Meekness*, 327.

9. William Montgomery Watt, *Islam and Christianity Today: A Contribution to Dialogue* (London: Routledge & Kegan Paul, 1983), 47–48.

10. See Kenneth Cragg, "Al-Rahman al-Rahim," *Muslim World* 43 (1953): 235–36.

11. For such a listing, see Carman, *Majesty and Meekness*, 329 n. 14.

12. For details, see Zayd, *Al-Ghazali on Divine Predicates*, 1–63, 65–101, at 65.

13. Zayd, *Al-Ghazali on Divine Predicates*, 65–101, at 65.

14. Carman, *Majesty and Meekness*, 326–27, at 327.

The Dynamic of Divine Immanence and Transcendence

As in the Bible, there are occasionally anthropomorphic metaphors of Allah such as the "face of God" (Q 2:115; 92:20) or the "hand(s) of God" (48:10; 5:64), although in general Islam is very cautious about picturing Allah. While Muslim theology is not in general favorably disposed toward personal characteristics of Allah, such characteristics are sometimes employed to highlight the absolute distinction between the Creator and creature. Al-Ghazali may at times say that "God is more tender to his servants than a mother to her suckling-child," attributing this statement to the Prophet Muhammad.[15]

Muslim theology of God includes the built-in dynamic between the absolute transcendence of God, because of his incomparability and uniqueness, and his presence and rulership in the world, which is a call for total obedience.[16] Unlike Christian theologians in general and classical panentheists in particular, Muslims "tend to speak of God's presence in terms of 'presence with' rather than 'presence in.'"[17] In his transcendence and incomparability, argues al-Ghazali, God is "infinitely" great, meaning that no comparison is possible, as that would put God among other beings[18]—an argument well known also in Christian theology.

As for major themes in the Qur'an's teaching about Allah, along with transcendence and mercy, the following predominate: first, God as creator and origin of everything; second, the divine unity, mentioned above; and, third, the dual emphasis on Allah's omnipotence and benevolence.[19] Furthermore, the theme of Allah's justice and judgment looms large in the Qur'an, and of course—as in Christian and Jewish tradition—they must be linked with mercy.[20] Echoing the Christian teaching, al-Ghazali reminds us that "My

---

15. Al-Ghazali, *The Alchemy of Happiness*, trans. Claud Field (1909), chap. 2, p. 35; available at sacred-texts.com.

16. For a useful discussion, see Lewis E. Winkler, *Contemporary Muslim and Christian Responses to Religious Plurality: Wolfhart Pannenberg in Dialogue with Abdulaziz Sachedina* (Eugene, OR: Pickwick, 2011), 270–75.

17. Michael Nazir-Ali, *Frontiers in Muslim-Christian Encounter* (Oxford: Regnum, 1987), 21.

18. Al-Ghazali, *The Niche for Lights* [*Mishkat al-Anwarâ*], trans. W. H. T. Gairdner (1924), 1.6; available at sacred-texts.com.

19. Louis Gardet, "Allāh," in *The Encyclopedia of Islam*, ed. H. A. R. Gibb et al., new ed. (Leiden: Brill, 1979), 1:40.

20. For an important discussion of love, mercy, and justice in relation to Allah, see Miroslav Volf, *Allah: A Christian Response* (New York: HarperCollins, 2011), chaps. 8; 9.

mercy is greater than My wrath," but that is not a pretext for complacency, as if, "Well, whatever we do, God is merciful."[21]

As in Christianity, in Islam there is a dynamic, at times tense, relationship between divine determinism and human freedom, although, in principle, Islam teaches that humans have been granted freedom and thus responsibility. It is axiomatic that "God would be neither just nor good if He punished people for acts for which they were not responsible," in light of the fact that humans have been given the capacity to choose between wrong and right.[22] That said, there is no denying some kind of view of divine predestination, based on Allah's omniscience and omnipotence. But that has to be understood in a way not negating human responsibility.

Islamic "Classical Theism"

Early Muslim theology's relation to pagan philosophy was not much different from that of Christian tradition. A great appreciation and liberal borrowing from the greatest masters of antiquity, including Plato and Aristotle, are evident, but at times there were reminders of the inadequacy of philosophy alone, apart from Qur'anic authority, to establish divine truths.[23] As early as in the ninth-century work of the famous philosopher-theologian al-Farabi, we see significant Platonic and Aristotelian influences. His listing of the attributes of God, under the rubric "Metaphysical Theology," could have easily come from a typical Christian manual: simplicity, infinity, immutability, unity, intelligence, "God Knows All Things through Knowledge of Himself," "God Is Truth," "God Is Life."[24]

In fact, as did Christian tradition, Islam moved toward "classical theism" early on. For example, Muslim theologians engaged "proofs" for the existence of God using the same kinds of arguments Jews and Christians were employing, and they occasionally borrowed from pagan sources such as Aristotle.

Muslim theologians began making lists of attributes of God similar to those in Christian classical theism. "A Short Creed by al-Ashari" reads like a

---

21. Al-Ghazali, *The Alchemy of Happiness*, chap. 2, pp. 35 and 45, respectively.

22. Andrew Rippin and Jan Knappert, *Textual Sources for the Study of Islam* (Totowa, NJ: Barnes & Noble Books, 1986), 18.

23. The classic work here is that of al-Ghazali, *The Incoherence of the Philosophers* (Provo, UT: Brigham Young University Press, 1997).

24. Robert Hammond, *The Philosophy of Alfarabi and Its Influence on Medieval Thought* (New York: Hobson Book Press, 1947), 22–29; for a detailed linking of the attributes with Plato and Aristotle, see Zayd, *Al-Ghazali on Divine Predicates*, xiii–xx.

Christian scholastic formulation (although, of course, it rebuts its Trinitarian claims): "We believe . . . that God is One God, Single, One, Eternal; beside Him no God exists; He has taken to Himself no wife (*sahiba*), nor child (*walad*)."[25] The creed lists basic beliefs in God as creator, as powerful, as providing, and as eschatological consummator.

Interestingly, not unlike what occurred in Christian history, a continuing debate went on between the traditionalists, who wished to retain the verbatim biblical account (the Asharites), and the rationalists (the Mu'tazilites), who were drawn to systematic explanations, which in many ways paralleled Christian scholasticism.[26] The rise of "orthodox" *kalam* theology, a form of Islamic scholasticism, of the majority Sunni denomination, was the culmination of this development (authoritatively defined in the masterful work of the tenth-century al-Ashari).

Similarly to Christian scholastics, defining medieval Islamic teachers conducted sophisticated debates about, for example, how to understand the attributes of God in relation to God's essence. Whereas the Mu'tazilites were willing to attach the attributes not to the essence of God but rather to his actions, the Asharites—as well as al-Ghazali (a leading Sunni himself as well)—linked some attributes to the essence and others to his actions.[27] Furthermore, Muslim theologians of old delved deeply into debate about God language, for example, how to best understand the anthropomorphisms present in the Qur'an.[28]

Islamic philosophers also entertained the question of whether there is a relationship between human knowledge of self and the knowledge of God, an idea well established in Christian tradition. Understandably, this is a delicate topic for Islamic tradition. That said, al-Ghazali boldly states at the beginning of *The Alchemy of Happiness*: "Knowledge of self is the key to the knowledge of God, according to the saying: 'He who knows himself knows God' and, as it is written in the Koran, 'We will show them Our signs in the world and *in themselves*, that the truth may be manifest to them.'"[29] This is quite a bold statement coming from the defining Muslim teacher.

---

25. In Duncan B. MacDonald, *Development of Muslim Theology, Jurisprudence, and Constitutional Theory* (New York: Scribner's Sons, 1903), 294. Available at www.sacred-texts.com.

26. For an important discussion, see Richard M. Frank, *Beings and Their Attributes: The Teachings of the Basrian School of the Mu'tazila in the Classical Period* (Albany: State University of New York Press, 1978).

27. See further, Nader el-Bizri, "God: Essence and Attributes," in *CCCIT*, 121–40.

28. See further, Zayd, *Al-Ghazali on Divine Predicates*, viii.

29. Al-Ghazali, *The Alchemy of Happiness*, chap. 1, 19. The first citation is attributed to Muhammad.

The Unity of God and Christian Confession of Trinity

As has become clear, Qur'anic teaching categorically rejects any notion of threeness of God, including Jesus's incarnation and divinity (4:171); indeed, the Trinitarian confession is nothing less than blasphemy (5:72–76). A foundational reason for the strict rebuttal of the Christian doctrine of the Trinity includes the absolute exaltedness of Allah and the sheer absurdity of the idea of God having a child by a woman.[30]

As mentioned, the major reason for the categorical rejection of the Trinity in Islamic theology is that it represents *shirk*, associating with Allah something other. Jesus's sonship obviously represents *shirk* to Islam; from the Christian perspective, though, the Qur'anic statement that gives praise to God who does not take up a son to himself (17:111; 19:35; 19:92; 25:2) does not correctly express our christological doctrine. Literally taken, that statement expresses rather adoptionism, an early heresy according to which Jesus of Nazareth at some point of his life was made divine. Furthermore, often behind the Muslim charge of *shirk* is another early heretical notion called Arianism, which taught that Christ was almost as divine as the Father but not quite. That heretical notion, however, was strictly ruled out by the early creeds.

Christian theology—from the point of view of Christian doctrine—resists the charge of *shirk* with its Trinitarian monotheism and its christological doctrines of incarnation and deity (to be explained in detail below in chapter 5). Consider the Athanasian Creed, one of the earliest creeds: "That we worship one God in Trinity, and Trinity in Unity; Neither confounding the persons nor dividing the substance. For there is one person of the Father, another of the Son, and another of the Holy Spirit. But the Godhead of the Father, of the Son, and of the Holy Spirit is all one, the glory equal, the majesty coeternal."[31] Rightly, the medieval Catholic cardinal Nicholas of Cusa, who widely engaged Islam, reminds us that even for Christians the oneness of God is prior to the plurality,[32] and that the three "persons" make one God![33]

---

30. See further, Geoffrey Parrinder, *Jesus in the Qur'an* (London: Sheldon; Oxford: Oneworld, 1995), 126–41.

31. In *Historic Creeds and Confessions*, ed. Rick Brannan, 56; available at www.ccel.org.

32. Nicholas of Cusa, *De pace fidei*, ##15, 23, in *De Pace Fidei and Cribratio Alkorani: Translation and Analysis*, ed. and trans. Jasper Hopkins, 2nd ed. (Minneapolis: Arthur J. Banning, 1994), http://jasper-hopkins.info/DePace12-2000.pdf; Nicholas of Cusa, *De docta ignorantia*, #14, in *Selected Spiritual Writings*, trans. H. Lawrence Bond (Mahwah, NJ: Paulist, 1997).

33. See Volf, *Allah*, 53–54, for detailed listing of passages from Nicholas of Cusa in

Christian theologians can also remind their Muslim counterparts that Islamic monotheism does not preclude Allah's "association" with the divine word of God, the Qur'an, implying that *shirk* has to be understood in a more nuanced manner. The same with God's love, a theme common to both traditions. In an argument materially similar to Muslim theology, Nicholas asserted that when the Bible tells us that God is love, it means that there must be an internal distinction in the one Godhead to allow for the "lover" to show love to "another"[34]—an argument presented by other Christian theologians as well.

What about incarnation? Isn't that necessarily a statement about plurality in the Christian understanding of God: one God "up there in heaven" and the other one "down here on earth"? Christian tradition negotiates that dilemma with the Trinitarian "rule" explained in the beginning of this chapter, namely, that all works of the Trinity are undivided and that the mutual love between Father, Son, and Spirit allows for distinctions of persons but not plurality of deities. Consider the prologue to John's Gospel, which speaks of the Word (*Logos*) that became flesh (1:14) as not only being *with* God but also *being* God (1:1). Similarly, consider the Johannine Jesus's saying that "the Father is in me and I am in the Father" (10:38).[35] Hence, Christianity affirms that "in worshipping Jesus one does not worship another than God; one simply worships God," as difficult as that statement is in light of its christological ramifications, namely, that Jesus, the human person, is considered to be divine.[36] Nor is Christian theology or the Bible ever affirming what the Qur'an claims to be a Christian statement: "Behold, God is the Christ, son of Mary" (Q 5:72).[37] Christian faith, rather, says that Christ is God.

What if Muslim and Christian theologians took these affirmations of the unity of God from the Christian side as guidelines when working toward a common understanding without artificially ignoring the differences?

---

response to the classic Qur'anic passages of affirming the oneness of God and rebutting the (Christian) doctrine of Trinity (5:73, 116; 23:91).

34. Nicholas of Cusa, *Cribratio Alkorani*, #108, in *De Pace Fidei and Cribratio Alkorani*.

35. See further, Volf, *Allah*, 138.

36. Keith Ward, *Religion and Revelation: A Theology of Revelation in the World's Religions* (Oxford: Clarendon, 1994), 179.

37. See further, Nancy Roberts, "Trinity vs. Monotheism: A False Dichotomy?," *Muslim World* 101 (January 2011): 90.

Do Muslims and Christians Believe in the Same God?

What Is at Stake?

Against common Christian intuitions, it is not untypical at all for a Muslim theologian to assume that these two traditions worship the same God. Consider the conservative American-based Muslim theologian Seyyed Hossein Nasr's comment:

> There are already those on the Christian side who assert that the Christian God is not the same as Allah, who is an Arabic lunar deity or something like that. Such people who usually combine sheer ignorance with bigotry should attend a Sunday mass in Arabic in Bethlehem, Beirut, Amman, or Cairo and hear what Arabic term the Christians of these cities use for the Christian God. Nor is God simply to be identified with one member of the Christian Trinity, one part of three divinities that some Muslims believe wrongly that Christians worship. Allah, or God, is none other than the One God of Abraham, Isaac, Ishmael, Moses, Jesus, and Muhammad.[38]

Now, what is at stake in this debate? Briefly put, both peace and theological integrity. Why? Because more than half of the world's population are Christians and Muslims![39]

While this practical reason alone would warrant rigorous and widespread common work on this topic, a deep and foundational theological issue is also at stake. The question at hand has to do with more than just interfaith hospitality; in the words of the Jewish theologian Jon D. Levenson, "no monotheist can ever accuse anyone—certainly not another monotheist—of worshiping *another* God, only (at most) of improperly identifying the one God that both seek to serve."[40]

---

38. Seyyed Hossein Nasr, "The Word of God: The Bridge between Him, You, and Us," in *A Common Word: Muslims and Christians on Loving God and Neighbor*, ed. Miroslav Volf and Prince Ghazi bin Muhammad bin Talal (Grand Rapids: Eerdmans, 2010), 115.

39. Volf, *Allah*, 1. See also "A Common Word between Us and You."

40. Jon D. Levenson, "Do Christians and Muslims Worship the Same God?," *Christian Century* 121, no. 8 (April 20, 2004): 32, emphasis added.

Mutual Debates and Attempts at Understanding

Currently, it is a commonplace scholarly consensus that the term *allah* predates the time of Muhammad. It is also a consensus that—against the older scholarly view and still a regular popular opinion—the name did not originate in the context of moon worship in Arabia (even though the crescent became Islam's symbol and moon worship was known in that area).[41]

The term derives from Aramaic and Syriac words for God (*elah, alah*).[42] In that light, it is fully understandable that even among Christians in Arabic-speaking areas the term *Allah* is the designation for God. However, to say that both etymologically and theologically both Muslims and Christians refer to the same God when they speak of the Divine does not settle the issue of *what kind* of God that is.

Both Islam and Christianity claim to be based on divine revelation and seek to ground their understanding of the God believers worship, and to whom they devote their lives, on scripture. While those scriptures and the subsequent theological reflections and traditions share a lot in common, significant differences also complicate our clarifying the extent and meaning of the foundational consensus on the same referent of the term itself.[43]

This issue is not new to either tradition. As early as the eighth Christian century, John of Damascus, the most celebrated theologian in the Christian East, with firsthand knowledge of the Muslim faith, delved deeply into it in the last chapter of his *De haeresibus (On Heresies)*. Notwithstanding considering Muslims "idol worshippers," John seems to assume that both traditions worship the one and same God. Or consider the Catholic cardinal Nicholas of Cusa of the fifteenth century, who, following the ransacking of the holy city of Constantinople in 1453, in his *De pace fidei (On the Harmonious Peace of Religions)* sought a way to achieve a "harmony among religions" and "perpetual peace."[44] At the same time, he also exercised critical judgment on Islam's errors.

---

41. According to sura 3:67, there were monotheists (called *hanif*) in Arabia before the time of Muhammad.

42. See Timothy C. Tennent, *Theology in the Context of World Christianity: How the Global Church Is Influencing the Way We Think about and Discuss Theology* (Grand Rapids: Zondervan, 2007), 27–31; more widely, Imad N. Shehadeh, "Do Muslims and Christians Believe in the Same God?," *Bibliotheca Sacra* 161 (January–March 2004): 14–26.

43. See Lamin Sanneh, "Do Christians and Muslims Worship the Same God?," *Christian Century* 121, no. 9 (May 4, 2004): 35.

44. Nicholas of Cusa, *De pace fidei*, #68.

Even Martin Luther, with his well-known and deep suspicions toward Muslims (and Jews), assumed that "all who are outside this Christian people, whether heathen, Turks, Jews, or false Christians and hypocrites . . . believe in and worship only the one, true God."[45] While not often highlighted, it is a well-known scholarly fact that the identification of the Christian and Muslim God—even in the midst of highly polemic debates and mutual criticisms—was by and large the traditional Christian opinion;[46] in that sense, Luther followed tradition.

Prospects and Promise

What unites Muslim and Christian theologies is that both traditions speak of God in universal rather than "tribal" terms. Similarly to the Bible, the Qur'anic message "is a message for all people: all people should become Muslims, for God is the sovereign God of all people."[47] Part of the universalizing tendency is the important promise in sura 42:15: "God is our Lord and your Lord. Our deeds concern us and your deeds concern you. There is no argument between us and you. God will bring us together, and to Him is the [final] destination." This same sura also mentions that "had God willed, He would have made them one community; but He admits whomever He will into His mercy" (v. 8), and that "whatever you may differ in, the verdict therein belongs to God" (v. 10).

Hence, the important reason Muslim theology can unequivocally affirm the identity of the God of Islam and the God of Christianity has to do with the principle of continuity—in terms of fulfillment—between the divine revelations given first to the Jews, then to Christians, and finally, in the completed form, to Muslims (2:136; 6:83-89; 29:46).[48] While Christian tradition understands the principle of universality differently, materially it shares the same viewpoint: the God of the Bible, Yahweh, the Father of Jesus Christ, is the God of all nations and the whole of creation. Therefore, both faiths also are deeply missionary by nature.

An important asset to Christian theology for reflecting on the relation of Allah to the God of the Bible is its relation to Judaism. Hardly any Christians

45. Martin Luther, *The Large Catechism*, trans. F. Bente and W. H. T. Dau (St. Louis: Concordia, 1921), art. III, 76.

46. See Watt, *Islam and Christianity Today*, 45.

47. See Vroom, *No Other Gods*, 103-4.

48. For a current Muslim argument, see Umar F. Abd-Allah, "Do Christians and Muslims Worship the Same God?," *Christian Century* 121, no. 17 (August 24, 2004).

would deny that Yahweh and the Father of Jesus Christ are one and the same God. Yet the Jews no less adamantly oppose the Trinitarian confession of faith. This simply means that Christian tradition is able to confess belief in and worship one God even when significant differences exist in the understanding of the *nature* of that God. To confess one God does not require an identical understanding of the nature of God.

It is important to clarify the many Islamic misunderstandings about what the Christian Trinitarian confession means. What if it is true that "what the Qur'an denies about God as the Holy Trinity has been denied by every great teacher of the church in the past and ought to be denied by every orthodox Christian today"?[49] These include the typical misconceptions among the Muslims, including the inclusion of Mary in the divinity along with Father and Son, Arianist interpretations, and the blunt charge of tritheism. Having affirmed that Muslims and Christians believe in the same God, the Dutch Christian philosopher of religion Hendrik Vroom "would like to add that Christians, on the basis of the gospel, are better *able* to know God than Muslims are."[50] This is not an expression of a puffed-up spirit of superiority but rather a confident call to Muslims from a Christian perspective to consider rich values in the Christian Trinitarian conception of faith in one God. Muslim theologians undoubtedly would issue the same challenge to Christians.

Brahman and the Trinitarian God

Comparison in Perspective

A number of well-known challenges and unnuanced assumptions concerning Hindu and Christian views of the Divine complicate any serious comparative theological work: for example, the claims that

- whereas Christianity has a personal God, Hinduism has an impersonal god;
- whereas Christianity is monotheistic, Hinduism is polytheistic; and
- whereas in Christianity the Divine can take the form of humanity, in Hinduism the deity remains transcendently distant.

49. Volf, *Allah*, 14.
50. Vroom, *No Other Gods*, 113.

The following discussion seeks to investigate in detail these and related issues in order to compare and contrast these two traditions in terms of the relevant issues and topics. Whereas Christian-Jewish and Christian-Muslim dialogue must concentrate on the question of the Trinity versus monotheism, for the Christian-Hindu encounter, essential topics include whether their vastly differing concepts of the Divine share enough commonality even to facilitate the comparison.

Beyond the above-mentioned popular stereotypes, scholarly study must at all times be mindful of differences between the two traditions at deeper and more complex levels, like Christianity's solid doctrinal basis for faith (despite differences, say, in the formulation of the Trinitarian doctrine between the East and West) versus Hinduism's absence of such binding and commonly shared doctrinal basis. Indeed, while in the final analysis the majority of Hindus would conceive Brahman (often in the "person" of another god, whether Shiva or Vishnu or any of their associates) as the Ultimate Reality and thus affirm "monotheism," Hindus can also be more or less nontheistic (although hardly is there any atheistic movement after modern Western atheism) or agnostic about the existence of gods.[51] Furthermore, while by far the majority of Hindu adherents embrace a personal deity (most often in the form of Isvara, typically locally determined), theologically speaking it still seems to be the case that beyond the personal notion there is the "true" impersonal deity.

Add to these factors the deep differences in attitude about the role of history[52] (as explained above in the discussion of revelation), in terms of both its relation to the events and stories in scriptures concerning the "history of salvation" and the question of whether history is linear or cyclical. Deep differences in worldview and epistemology also often complicate the task of comparison.

A highly important theme in Hindu theology/philosophy regards how to negotiate the relationship between One and many, to use the classic expression: the One Ultimate "Brahman" and the cosmos in light of a generally monistic worldview (that is, there is ultimately only one "reality," as opposed to two or many). Complex and complicated philosophical debates have raged for ages among leading Vedanta theologians; those debates will be taken up in the chapter on creation. Here we will trace the evolvement of Hindu deities

51. See Francis X. Clooney, *Hindu God, Christian God: How Reason Helps Break Down the Boundaries between Religions* (Oxford: Oxford University Press, 2001), chap. 2.

52. Contra John Brockington, *Hinduism and Christianity* (New York: St. Martin's, 1992), 43–44.

and reflect on whether this religion is monotheist or polytheist. Thereafter will come a comparison between it and Christian Trinitarian faith.

Many Gods or One God?

The oldest Vedas, particularly Rig Veda, list a number of deities or *devas* (a more elusively envisioned "divine being" rather than god in the current sense of the word). Among them, Indra, the cosmic power, while a fairly late arrival in Vedic religion, plays the central role. Other important figures include Agni, the deity of fire, associated particularly with sacrifices; the lovely Savitri, "Mother Earth"; Aditi; and a host of others.[53]

A critical move toward the embrace of one major notion of the deity amidst the bewildering diversity of *devas* began in classical Hinduism, as represented by the last part of the Vedas, the Upanishads. The well-known answer in Brihadaranyaka Upanishad (3.9.1) to the question of how many gods there are altogether, drawn from a Vedic text, is 330,000, which then boils down to one, and this one god is Brahman. The many gods are "only the various powers of them." Ultimately, there is one Ultimate Divine, Brahman, represented by a number of individual deities.[54]

Here we come to the most important *theo*logical affirmation in theistic Hinduism: *atman* is Brahman.[55] Whereas Brahman is the ultimate notion of the divine, *atman* is the ultimate reality about us. While everything else in the world, including us, changes, *atman* does not. Though routinely translated as "soul," in no way is that individually driven Western concept a good way to communicate the meaning of the Sanskrit word.

Most typically, three deities are seen as the major manifestation of Brahman: Brahma (not to be confused with "Brahman"), the "creator" god; Vishnu, the "preserver" god; and Shiva, the "destroyer," or better, "consummator," god. The distant Brahman comes to be known and worshiped in any of these deities or their associates known as *isa* or *isvara*, the "Lord" or Bhagavan, the Exalted One. Typically the "Lord," be it Vishnu or Shiva—since the worship of Brahma by and large vanished almost completely a long time ago—becomes more or

---

53. Klaus Klostermaier, *A Survey of Hinduism*, 3rd ed. (Albany: State University of New York Press, 2010), chap. 7.

54. Arvind Sharma, *Classical Hindu Thought: An Introduction* (Oxford: Oxford University Press, 2000), 1.

55. Brihadaranyaka Upanishad 4.4.5 and 25; *SBE* 15:175, 181, respectively.

less an exclusive title in popular piety, although, theologically, either one and both of them manifest Brahman.

Hence, the proliferation of Hindu denominations, among which the most important are Shaivism (followers of Shiva) and Vaishnavism (followers of Vishnu), with an ever-increasing number of subsects. Either related to the main deities or separate from them, local and tribal deities, both male and female, and cults of worship dedicated to them fill India.

While it is of course true that the Hindu conception of the Brahman as the ultimate reality leans toward an impersonal notion unlike the personal God of Semitic faiths, it is also true that Hinduism is quite familiar with personal conceptions of deities. Not only does the personal deity come to the fore in the hugely popular and widespread folk piety based on the great epics of Mahabharata and Ramayana, as well as many Puranas, but even in the later stages of the Upanishads personal notions begin to emerge in various forms.

What is distinctive about Hindu deities is the prominent place of female deities; indeed, "Hinduism possesses a full-blown feminine theology."[56] Usually Shiva and Vishnu are accompanied by their wives, Parvati and Sri (Lakshmi). The prominent female deity is known as Sakti, "power," or Devi, the "Divine Mother." Sometimes Sakti is described as exercising the same powers as Vishnu and Shiva.

The Trinitarian God and the One Divine

The obvious starting point for considering any Trinitarian parallels in Hinduism is the above-mentioned "trinity" of classical deities, namely, Brahma, Vishnu, and Siva, named Trimurti. While never widely popular, a strand of Hindu piety developed cultic rites to honor the threeness. Recall that for almost all Hindus, different gods (these three or any others) are ultimately the expression of the One—an observation that in principle should be highly conducive to Christian confession of one God in three persons.

Before getting too excited about this alleged parallel, let us note that a main reason why the threefold conception never played an important role in either the popular or (particularly) scholarly Hindu world has to do with the virtual disappearance of the cult of Brahma—leaving only two major gods, Vishnu and Siva. Furthermore, even when the three Hindu deities are not conceived as three gods but rather as manifestations of one, Hindus still routinely

---

56. Sharma, *Classical Hindu Thought*, 68; see chap. 5 for a useful discussion.

consider one of them as supreme. Finally, in light of the fact that the deities are related with distinctive primary tasks (like Brahma with creation), it is more appropriate to regard the three as manifestations rather than "persons" of the one god.

Hence, it is understandable that efforts to find parallels have been lacking on the Hindu side, even if they have been quite pronounced at times for Christian theologians. Ram Mohun Roy, the founder of the strictly monotheistic neo-Hindu reform movement Brahma Samaj, states categorically with regard to the Christian Trinity: "After I have long relinquished every idea of a plurality of Gods, or of the persons of the Godhead, taught under different systems of modern Hindooism, I cannot conscientiously and consistently embrace one of a similar nature, though greatly refined by the religious reformations of modern times."[57]

For some, a more promising bridge may be found in the ancient concept of *saccidananda*, of three words meaning "being," "intelligence," and "bliss." Consider this statement by Brahmabandhab Upadhyaya, a famous nineteenth-century Hindu convert to Catholicism: "I adore the *Sat* (Being), *Cit* (Intelligence) and *Ananda* (Bliss), . . . the Father, Begetter, the Highest Lord, unbegotten, the rootless principle of the tree of existence . . . the increate, infinite Logos or Word, supremely great, the Image of the Father . . . [and] the one who proceeds from the union of *Sat* and *Cit*, the blessed Spirit (breath), intense bliss."[58]

Other Hindu converts and reformers have similarly shown more interest in this parallel than in the three deities discussed above. To put these and many other explorations in perspective, the Jesuit Hindu expert F. X. Clooney summarizes in a way worth repeating and affirming: "That the record is mixed should not surprise us. We know that the rich, deep Christian tradition of trinitarian theology, so nuanced and difficult, did not come together easily or suddenly in the earliest Church; rather, it took centuries to put together right insights into the three persons of God. . . . [Similarly] it was very hard indeed to explain in India the fine points of trinitarian thought, and as a result many did not see a great difference between Christian ideas of God and Hindu ideas."[59]

57. As cited in Francis X. Clooney, "Trinity and Hinduism," in *Cambridge Companion to the Trinity*, ed. Peter C. Phan (Cambridge: Cambridge University Press, 2011), 316 (I have been unable to secure the original source).

58. In Clooney, "Trinity and Hinduism," 317 (I have been unable to secure the original source).

59. Clooney, "Trinity and Hinduism," 320–21.

Any God(s) in Buddhism?

On the Conditions and Challenges of Mutual Dialogue

Except for the exchange between Nestorian Christians and Buddhists from the sixth to eighth centuries, unlike with Judaism and Islam, Christian and Buddhist traditions did not have much mutual engagement until the first occasional contacts in the nineteenth century.

By and large, Christian assessment of Buddhism was plagued by both ignorance and negative judgments leading to typical caricatures such as that Buddhism is atheistic (or idolatrous, as the adoration of images of the dead Gautama was mistakenly taken). Christians also routinely considered the Buddhist worldview nihilistic because of the doctrine of sunyata (emptiness) and life denying because of the principle of *dukkha* (suffering), and so forth.

Mutual dialogue faces significant challenges. To begin with, it is routinely asked whether Buddhism is a religion in the sense that other living faiths are. The reason is that Buddhism separated itself from the parent religion, Hinduism, because of its overly focused attention on deities and spirits that undermined one's own effort toward "salvation." Particularly the original Theravada Buddhism still seeks to be faithful to that vision, notwithstanding its acknowledgment of the existence of deities. Even in the current mainline movement, Mahayana, despite strong theistic orientations particularly in folk spirituality, deities and gods are not looked upon as saviors. On the other hand, all Buddhist denominations perceive some kind of "ultimate reality," even if that is not "god" in the traditional sense. As mentioned, Buddha is no savior.

The Buddhist Quest for the Ultimate Reality

Not only is Buddha not a savior, neither is he the "ultimate reality." Furthermore, in contrast to the parent religion Hinduism, Buddhism strictly rejects the idea of Brahman and *atman* as the ultimate answer. That said, the search for the ultimate reality appears easier with the mainstream Mahayana tradition. All scholars agree that its foundational idea of sunyata is the most likely proposal—but not the only one. Before looking at it, let us briefly consider other suggestions.

The Awakening of Faith, by the second century CE Indian dramatist and sage Asvaghosa, suggests one candidate for the ultimate reality, named simply "suchness" (and alternatively, "soul" or "mind," depending on the English translation). It "is the soul of all sentient beings," and it "constitutes all things in the world, phenomenal and supra-phenomenal."[60] While impersonal, suchness is active and dynamic, though changeless. Note that another key Buddhist concept foundational to Mahayana—Dharmakaya, the doctrine and wisdom taught by the Enlightened Buddha—is at times used as an alternative term for "suchness." These ways of speaking of the ultimate reality do not seem too far from a formal concept of deity in philosophical theology (but are a far cry from the personal).

Yet another classic pan-Buddhist candidate for the ultimate reality could be nirvana (*nibbana*),[61] the ultimate goal of all pursuit toward enlightenment. The famous and well-known "Udana Exclamation" (8.1), an ancient authoritative "small saying" among various Buddhist denominations, states it clearly: "There is that dimension where there is neither earth, nor water, nor fire, nor wind; neither dimension of the infinitude of space, nor dimension of the infinitude of consciousness, nor dimension of nothingness, nor dimension of neither perception nor non-perception; neither this world, nor the next world, nor sun, nor moon. And there, I say, there is neither coming, nor going, nor staying; neither passing away nor arising."[62] While this "definition"—of something indefinable!—strikes non-Buddhist sensibilities as negative, it is not, for it points to the final release, hence "salvation" in Judeo-Christian terms.

And now to the concept of sunyata. The leading academic interpreter of Mahayana Buddhism in the West, the Japanese Masao Abe, says, "The ultimate reality . . . is neither Being nor God, but Sunyata."[63] Notoriously difficult to translate and even harder to understand, "sunyata" literally means "(absolute) nothingness." However, it is not an "empty nothingness." It is only "empty" in terms of being "entirely unobjectifiable, unconceptualizable, and unattainable by reason or will."[64] According to the classic formulation of "the Heart Sutra," "Form is Emptiness, Emptiness is form. Emptiness does not differ from form, and form does not differ from Emptiness . . . in Emptyness [*sic*] there is no

---

60. Asvaghosa, *Awakening of Faith* II ["General Statement"], 53–54, in *Açvaghosha's Discourse on the Awakening of Faith in the Mahâyâna*, trans. Teitaro Suzuki (1900), available at http://sacred-texts.com/bud/taf/index.htm.

61. The former rendering is from Sanskrit and the latter from Pali (the language of the Theravada scriptures).

62. "Nibbana Sutta: Total Unbinding (1)" (Udana 8.1), available at "Tipitaka: The Pali Canon," ed. John T. Bullitt. The text can be found, e.g., at http://www.accesstoinsight.org/tipitaka/index.html.

63. Masao Abe, "Kenotic God and Dynamic Sunyata," in *DEHF*, 50.

64. Abe, "Kenotic God," 50.

form, no feeling, no recognition, no volitions, no consciousness; no eye, no ear, no nose, no tongue, no body, no mind . . . no ignorance and no extinction of ignorance . . . no aging and death and no extinction of aging and death; likewise there is no Suffering, Origin, Cessation or Path, no wisdom-knowledge, no attainment and non-attainment."[65] Furthermore, importantly, "Sunyata should not be conceived of somewhere *outside* one's self-existence, nor somewhere *inside* one's self-existence."[66] So, what, if anything, can be said of the potential convergences in relation to Christian tradition's doctrine of God?

God and the "Ultimate Reality" in a Comparative Perspective

Not all Christian interlocutors, after having engaged carefully the Mahayana concept of sunyata, believe that sunyata in any real sense could be taken as the Ultimate Reality. Reasons are many, such as that it seems not to be transcendent in the sense a theistic notion of god or Ultimate Reality is usually envisioned. Related to this, Christian intuitions consider that if there is a notion of the divine in Buddhism, it has to be equated with reality itself, that is, it leads to a sort of pantheism. That assumption seems to be confirmed by Buddhist experts themselves: "God *is* each and everything," and in this "completely kenotic God, personality and impersonality are paradoxically identical."[67] Noteworthy in this regard is the comment by a leading Christian comparative theologian, H. Küng, who concludes that while nirvana, emptiness, and Dharmakaya have "brought about a twilight of the gods or idols" as they have replaced the Hindu gods and Brahman as the ultimate explanation, "they have not put any other gods—not even the Buddha—in their place."[68]

After a careful dialogue with the Buddhist teachings about the ultimate reality, I myself came to this conclusion and recommendation:

> First, unlike any *monotheistic* tradition, Buddhism is happy with a plurality of answers to "one question" without suppressing the diversity; second, unlike any *theistic* tradition, Buddhism, even in its major Mahayana forms, makes every effort to resist the tendency to rely on gods (even if

65. Heart Sutra (no translator given, n.p., available at http://www.sacred-texts.com/bud/tib/hrt.htm).

66. Abe, "Kenotic God," 51.

67. Abe, "Kenotic God," 40, 41.

68. Hans Küng, "God's Self-Renunciation and Buddhist Self-Emptiness: A Christian Response to Masao Abe," in *DEHF*, 221.

their existence and role in the world thereby need not be denied after modern Western antitheistic ideology); and third, that therefore, Buddhism and Christianity represent deeply and radically different paths to liberation/salvation. Wouldn't that kind of tentative conclusion serve an authentic, hospitable dialogue better than a forced, I fear, one-sided (!) "*con*-sensus"?[69]

The last section of the chapter delves into the highly disputed question of whether religion and belief in god(s) necessarily leads to violence.

Religion, God(s), and Violence

On the Complexity of Linking Violence with Religion

The senior American scholar of public religion, Martin Marty, argues that "the collisions of faiths, or the collisions of peoples of faith, are among the most threatening conflicts around the world in the new millennium." This is because people of different faiths frequently divide themselves and others into competitive and suspicious groups of "belongers" and strangers.[70] Indeed, violence is part of religion's texture, each and every faith tradition's history[71]—hence, we see provocative book titles such as *Terror in the Mind of God.*[72]

That said, violence is also part of the record of atheistic and other secular ideologies; think only of the 70 million purported victims of communist regimes, among them a large number of believers of various faiths. This means that the alleged relationship between religion and violence has to be nuanced, particularly when we face unnuanced claims such as the new atheist Sam Harris's *End of Faith: Religion, Terror, and the Future of Reason.* It argues that since religions necessarily produce violence, the less religion, the better.[73]

---

69. Veli-Matti Kärkkäinen, *Trinity and Revelation*, vol. 2 of A Constructive Christian Theology for the Pluralistic World (Grand Rapids: Eerdmans, 2014), 415.

70. Martin E. Marty, *When Faiths Collide* (Malden, MA: Blackwell, 2005), 1–4, at 1.

71. Jack Nelson-Pallmeyer, *Is Religion Killing Us? Violence in the Bible and the Quran* (Harrisburg, PA: Trinity, 2003); Maurice Bloch, *Prey into Hunter: The Politics of Religious Experience* (Cambridge: Cambridge University Press, 1992).

72. Mark Juergensmeyer, *Terror in the Mind of God: The Global Rise of Religious Violence*, 3rd rev. ed. (Berkeley: University of California Press, 2003).

73. See chap. 7 in Ian S. Markham, *Against Atheism: Why Dawkins, Hitchens, and Harris Are Fundamentally Wrong* (Oxford: Wiley-Blackwell, 2010).

There is simply no basis for believing that with the demise of religion, violence would disappear. Rather, while "religion does some harm and some good, . . . most people, faced with the evidence, will probably agree that it does a great deal more good than harm."[74]

Violence and Abrahamic Traditions

Jewish Perspectives

The greatest challenge to all Abrahamic faiths with regard to violence is the concept of holy war. In Judaism,[75] holy war has important limits:

- War must be carried on as ordered by Yahweh and is meant for the glory of Yahweh.
- It is not by human force of arms but rather by the power of Yahweh that victory is won.
- Not only enemies but at times even the people of Yahweh are defeated by Yahweh, as in exile, and Yahweh at times uses enemies as an asset.

Very problematic is the concept of *herem*, total annihilation of enemies and their gods (the Amalekites being the prime example). Jewish tradition does not speak with one voice here: whereas current liberal Jews consider *herem* merely a spiritual/theological principle of total devotion to God, religious Zionists apply the principle to Palestinians and other Arabs. As in Christian hermeneutics, mainstream Jewish scholarship considers this a matter of development of revelation in Scripture.[76]

In marked contrast from the Old Testament, the Talmud by and large supports peace and active peacemaking, without advocating pacifism.[77] In contrast to political Zionism (Theodor Herzl), the *cultural* Zionism represented by Ahad Ha'am (d. 1927) denounces the use of violence against Arabs by Jews and advocates peaceful coexistence in the Holy Land; a similar ap-

74. Keith Ward, *Is Religion Dangerous?* (Grand Rapids: Eerdmans, 2006), 7.

75. For details, see Michael Dobkowski, "'A Time for War and Time for Peace': Teaching Religion and Violence in the Jewish Tradition," chap. 2 in *TRV*.

76. David Whitten Smith and Elizabeth Geraldine Burr, *Understanding World Religions: A Road Map for Justice and Peace* (Lanham, MD: Rowman & Littlefield, 2007), 75–76.

77. Haim Gordon and Leonard Grob, *Education for Peace: Testimonies from World Religions* (Maryknoll, NY: Orbis, 1987), chap. 3.

proach was taken by the philosopher Martin Buber.[78] The unique context for all contemporary Jewish reflections on war and violence is the haunt of the Shoah (Holocaust).[79]

Islamic Perspectives

For Islam the key violence-related challenges are not only holy war but also the way jihad is interpreted, whether as "the greater jihad," a personal struggle over spiritual obstacles and temptations, or as "lesser jihad," a call to a holy war.[80] Like the Old Testament, the Qur'an sets out fairly unambiguous rules for just war, including holy war:

- After seeking spiritual guidance from Allah, war should be resorted to only as the last means.
- Jihad should be led by an imam or at least a Muslim leader.
- Enemies should be given an opportunity to accept Islam first—or, if followers of another Abrahamic faith, merely be subject to Islamic political rule with a special tax and *zakat*, "almsgiving."[81]

On either lesser or greater jihad, Muslim tradition does not speak with one voice.[82] A number of contemporary reformists from various Muslim locations have spoken for the nonviolent way.[83] Similarly, some revisionist scholars and clergymen have advocated for a pluralistic, tolerant, and democratic Islamic theory of society.[84] The influential international group of Islamic scholars and clergy participating in the Muslim-Christian "A Common

---

78. See Marc H. Ellis, *Toward a Jewish Theology of Liberation: The Challenge of the 21st Century*, 3rd expanded ed. (Waco, TX: Baylor University Press, 2004).

79. See Richard L. Rubenstein and John K. Roth, *Approaches to Auschwitz: The Holocaust and Its Legacy* (Atlanta: John Knox, 1987).

80. For a highly nuanced discussion, see Amir Hussain, "Confronting Misoislamia: Teaching Religion and Violence in Courses on Islam," chap. 5 in *TRV*.

81. Smith and Burr, *Understanding World Religions*, 136–38. The well-known Qur'anic passages (2:90–93, 256) clearly state that no one should be forced to convert to Islam.

82. See C. W. Troll, H. Reifeld, and C. T. R. Hewer, eds., *We Have Justice in Common: Christian and Muslim Voices from Asia and Africa* (Berlin: Konrad-Adenauer-Stiftung, 2010).

83. Smith and Burr, *Understanding World Religions*, 141–42.

84. Abdulaziz Abdulhussein Sachedina, *The Islamic Roots of Democratic Pluralism* (New York: Oxford University Press, 2001); for an important theological study, see Winkler, *Contemporary Muslim and Christian Responses to Religious Plurality*.

Word" project strongly advocated the greater jihad as the only accepted form of interpretation, denounced terrorism and violence in the name of jihad, and urged interfaith activities.

Violence and Asiatic Traditions

Hindu Views

To an outsider, Hinduism offers a highly complicated case with regard to violence. The topic of *himsa* (harm) has been reflected on since the beginning of the Vedic religion. And currently, *ahimsa* ("noninjury," "nonviolence") is the most well-known trademark of Hindu reformism (although its roots go back to centuries before the common era).[85] Yet even the noted spokesperson for peace and nonviolence, Mohandas Gandhi, supported the caste system and thus, at least implicitly, sanctioned violence and oppression.[86]

What seems clear is that, in some real sense, war and violence are embedded in the Hindu system, as one of the four main castes of people is soldiers. It is the *dharma* of the Kshatriya to carry on that profession. The Bhagavad Gita, which includes the classic example of the duty of killing, even with regard to one's own kin, does not reconcile violence and its relation to war into a coherent vision.[87] Generally speaking, somewhat similarly to Christian tradition, *ahimsa* (nonviolence) does not apply to (just) war (neither to sacrificial cult). This argument in favor of violence is deeply problematic for Christian tradition. While it knows just war—as much as the details are debated—divinely authorized killing of one's kin never seems fitting under that rubric.

Buddhist Views

When it comes to Buddhism, not only is the popular picture of this tradition as a peaceful, inward, world-rejecting, and meditation-focused religion unnuanced,[88] but also its history, against common assumptions, knows the use of

---

85. Brian K. Pennington, "Striking the Delicate Balance: Teaching Violence and Hinduism," in *TRV*, 24–25.

86. See the introduction to Mohandas K. Gandhi, *The Bhagavad Gita according to Gandhi* (Blacksburg, VA: Wilder Publications, 2011), 6–12.

87. See Smith and Burr, *Understanding World Religions*, 12.

88. Brian Daizen Victoria, "Teaching Buddhism and Violence," in *TRC*, 74–76.

violence.[89] Furthermore, some of its key concepts, such as karma and rebirth, have been used to legitimate violence; the former in terms of justifying all kinds of diseases and ills as "judgment," and the latter as a way of helping ease an evil person's karmic effects by ending life.[90]

Consider the main historical figure, Asoka, the great ruler of India (third century BCE), who was converted to Buddhism and became its enthusiastic advocate as part of his military conquests.[91] He spread Buddhism with the sword, not unlike Christian crusaders, Islamic conquerors, and others during history.

In the contemporary world, Buddhist nationalisms and fundamentalisms are well known among scholars; they include the Sinhalese Buddhist nationalism in Sri Lanka at the turn of the twentieth century and the Khmer Rouge in Cambodia, whose ideology had "unequivocal roots in a version of reformist Buddhism."[92] In other words, against common assumptions, even the followers of the lotus flower have resorted to violence, including even His Holiness the Dalai Lama, who earlier in his career gave approval to the use of violence against the true enemies of the people.[93]

Christian Theology and Violence

The Old Testament, shared with Jewish people, not only issues the challenge of violence in general but especially violence linked with God. What do we do with these passages? And they are not totally missing even in the New Testament—just think of the Apocalypse. On this complex question, the following responses might be useful. First, in every society in the ancient world, violence was rampant and horrible. All living faiths' holy scriptures are ancient texts and share that feature; the Bible is no exception. Second, Christian the-

---

89. Charles F. Keyes, "Monks, Guns, and Peace," in *Belief and Bloodshed: Religion and Violence across Time and Tradition*, ed. James K. Wellman Jr. (Lanham, MD: Rowman & Littlefield, 2007), 145.

90. Victoria, "Teaching Buddhism and Violence," 77–87.

91. See the important source *The Edicts of Aśoka*, ed. and trans. N. A. Nikam and Richard McKeon (Chicago: University of Chicago Press, 1959).

92. Keyes, "Monks, Guns, and Peace," 156, with reference to Charles F. Keyes, "Communist Revolution and the Buddhist Past in Cambodia," in *Asian Vision of Authority: Religion and the Modern States of East and Southeast Asia*, ed. Charles F. Keyes, Laurel Kendall, and Helen Hardacre (Honolulu: University of Hawaii Press, 1994), 43–73.

93. Victoria, "Teaching Buddhism and Violence," 82–83.

ology of revelation builds on progressive revelation: God takes people at the level they are and patiently, over the ages, shapes them. To that progressive revelation also belong nuancing, balancing, and finally forbidding the right to violence. Third, the full revelation in Jesus Christ tells us that violence has been superseded and replaced with unconditional love and embrace. Fourth, in our kind of world, violence will not come to an end until the coming of the righteous rule of God.[94]

Finally, in the Christian vision, only God has the prerogative to exercise violence. God is all-loving, all-wise, all-patient, all-righteous. We humans are sinful and egoistic. In our hands, violence is always corrupted, evil, and destructive. In the sacrificial death of his Son, God has put violence to end.[95]

All ideologies based on the ontology of violence should be defeated. The representations of such ontologies in living faiths similarly should be subjected to criticism, as has already been noted in this discussion.

In sum: Christian theology of God and, derivatively, theology of creation are not based on violence, nor on a battle of the deities, as in many ancient myths; they are based on the divine pronouncement of the goodness of creation (Gen. 1:31), which refuses to ontologize violence, war, and conflict. Diversified unity, loving and accepting embrace of the other, and peace are ontologically founded in the triune God.

Acting on the basis of hospitality rather than violence, Christians should therefore be guided by the spirit of openness, inclusion, and welcoming the other. We can either "embrace," receive the other with outstretched arms that also, if need be, "struggle against deception, injustice and violence," or we can "exclude," go with these evil dispositions and acts, and be unwilling to make space for the other.[96] The will to embrace is based on and derives from the self-donation of the triune God that comes to its zenith on the cross. There are hopeful signs among Christian churches and in the ecumenical world of constructing hospitable, peaceful theologies and combating violence in all its forms.[97] While they are still limited, their importance should not be missed.

After this quite detailed discussion of God(s) in four living faith traditions in a sympathetic-critical dialogue with Christian theology, it is appro-

---

94. Ward, *Is Religion Dangerous?*; Markham, *Against Atheism*, chap. 5.

95. Miroslav Volf, *Exclusion and Embrace: A Theological Exploration of Identity, Otherness, and Reconciliation* (Nashville: Abingdon, 1996).

96. Volf, *Exclusion and Embrace*, 30.

97. See "Nurturing Peace, Overcoming Violence: In the Way of Christ for the Sake of the World," World Council of Churches, January 1, 2001; available at the WCC website.

priate to consider the doctrine of creation. This doctrine encompasses the two following chapters, the coming into existence and preservation of the cosmos with innumerable creatures (chap. 3) and humanity (chap. 4). Although, understandably, no unified doctrine of creation can be found among five faith traditions, they all forge a solid link between God/deities and what Christians call creation.

3 | Nature and Creation in Religions' Imagination

The Christian Doctrine of Creation

Alongside other Abrahamic faiths, Christian theology affirms the cosmos and humanity as the handiwork of God, the loving and sovereign Creator. Not only Creator, this same God is looked upon as the Provider and Consummator.

Theologically put: the Father, out of his abundant love, through the agency of the Son, in the power of the Spirit, brings about the cosmos and her creatures as well as cares for them. The Spirit of God is the principle of life and growth. Early in Christian tradition the original creative act came to be expressed with the help of the idea of *ex nihilo*, "out of nothing," a principle (though not necessarily the formula) shared with Judaism and Islam.

While traditional exegesis took Genesis 1–2 as a more or less literal description of both the origins and logistics of creation, having taken place in seven days a few thousand years ago, most contemporary theology affirms belief in creation in consonance with scientific evolutionary theory. According to theistic evolution, the Creator is "behind" the coming into existence and evolvement of the cosmos during the past approximately 13.7 billion years. Yet it shares the same central theological conviction: the world is neither self-originating nor self-supporting. Not surprisingly, it took almost a century for Christian theology to negotiate the religious and scientific explanations—and even nowadays fundamentalist movements oppose or at least struggle with those ideas.

A key challenge to contemporary theology of creation is how to best understand divine action, that is, God's continuing creative, sustaining, and "intervening" function in the world that God has made to follow natural laws.

This doctrine of providence, widely taught in the Scripture, cannot be understood in a way that would frustrate or negate the (relative) independence granted by the Creator God. Fortunately, negotiation between the law-like independent nature of the vast cosmos and God's caring and loving presence and action has been possible in recent decades.[1]

Another urgent challenge has to do with the preservation of nature and the environment against massive disastrous effects of human and other activity. In addition to scientific and mechanical initiatives and impulses, religious ones also play a role. Contemporary Christian theology of creation has found robust "green" resources to facilitate this work.

The Question of Origins in Comparative Perspective

In the preface to his discussion of the doctrine of creation, the late Christian theologian W. Pannenberg mentions that "the systematic presentation of Christian doctrine does not attempt a comparative evaluation of the Christian and other religious interpretations of the world and human life from the standpoint of the given understanding of the reality of God." Instead, he argues that this is the task of the philosophy of religion.[2] The current book obviously and decisively disagrees and rather argues that the comparative task is an urgent one in the contemporary world.

While engaging various faith traditions' myths, stories, and imaginations of the origins and fate of the cosmos, the comparative theologian should exercise similar caution and sensitivity as required of any theological comparison. The danger is simply this: a comparativist working from a particular perspective—and necessarily this is the position of everyone, even the allegedly "neutral" observer—should not uncritically assume that religions' accounts of origins are necessarily compatible with each other and so fit for comparison. Of particular concern is the well-known difference of orientation between the Abrahamic faiths' linear conception of history, from the beginning to the end, and Asiatic traditions' cyclical view, with infinite "beginnings" and "endings." That said, it seems that all living faiths do have an account of origins, and all of them have much to do with the divine reality.

---

1. For details of this complex issue, see chap. 7 in Veli-Matti Kärkkäinen, *Creation and Humanity*, vol. 3 of A Constructive Christian Theology for the Church in the Pluralistic World (Grand Rapids: Eerdmans, 2016).

2. Pannenberg, *ST* 2:xiv.

The discussion in this chapter falls in three uneven sections. First, each faith tradition's relation to scientific, particularly evolutionary, explanations will be investigated. Second, the main section will compare Christian teaching with visions of origins and workings of the cosmos in other faith traditions. Third, a short look at environmental resources among religions will be taken.

On Science-Religion Engagement in the Interfaith Context

The Significance of Science for Religions and Theology

The simple reason why contemporary comparative theology should be deeply interested in science is that science is a universal phenomenon and, as such, of great interest to all religions.[3] There is also the theological reason for dialogue: when "Christians confess God as the Creator of the world, it is inevitably the same world that is the object of scientific descriptions." As a result, theologians have the task of relating their statements to those of scientists.[4]

We will begin with relating sciences to Abrahamic faiths and thereafter to Asiatic faiths.

Science and Abrahamic Faiths

The Embrace of Science in Jewish Tradition

No other ethnicity can boast so many leading scientists throughout history and in the contemporary world as the Jewish people—from Galileo to Einstein. Of all Nobel Prizes in physics, Jews have gathered almost a third![5] And yet, Jews entered the scientific field relatively late, at the beginning of the twentieth century.

Until modernity, rabbis were sages who were looked upon also as intellectuals in science. In the contemporary world, that role has changed radically, even though there are still conservative rabbis who lean toward a literalist interpretation of Scripture and hence the American Christian Right type of

---

3. For details, consult the massive work of Patrick McNamara and Wesley Wildman, eds., *Science and the World's Religions*, 3 vols. (Santa Barbara, CA: Praeger, 2012).

4. Wolfhart Pannenberg, "Contributions from Systematic Theology," in *OHRS*, 359.

5. Noah J. Efron, *Judaism and Science: A Historical Introduction* (Westport, CT: Greenwood, 2007), 1–11; Gefforey Cantor and Marc Swetlitz, eds., *Jewish Tradition and the Challenge of Darwinism* (Chicago: University of Chicago Press, 2006).

creationism. This separation between the domains of religion and science, however, is a new development. For the defining medieval philosophers such as Moses Maimonides, nothing could have been stranger. Mainline Jewish theology nowadays sees no conflict with the theistic interpretation of evolutionism, including human evolution. Indeed, a significantly greater percentage of Jews in the United States accept evolution than do Christians.

The Old Testament, unlike the Qur'an, does not discuss cosmology as a separate topic; the little it offers is partially borrowed from the environment. Nor is there much attention to nature itself (unlike the Qur'an), although some of the sages, particularly Solomon, are depicted as masters of the knowledge of nature (1 Kings 3:10–15; 4:29–34). Rather than being mystical and speculative, for the most part the Old Testament's depiction of nature is that of an orderly cosmos brought about and controlled by Yahweh. This "disenchantment process" helped pave the way for the rise of scientific explorations.

Unlike the Muslims (and some Hindus), the Jews have never entertained the idea of a "Jewish science." Therefore, the sorts of science-religion clashes experienced among Christians (and much later in Muslim contexts) are by and large unknown (except for the more recent Orthodox rabbis' reservations mentioned above). As in mainline Christian tradition, evolutionary theory is currently embraced.

The Islamic Struggle with Modern Science

After the glorious rise of Islamic science, its "golden age" lasted until the eleventh century (CE) and featured such luminaries as Ibn Rushd (Averroes) and Ibn Sina (Avicenna), finally giving way to the "age of decline."[6] That said, however one judges the history of Islamic science, the current Western scientific and philosophical academia should remember its debt to the Islamic influence on the rise of the sciences.

Modern science came to Islamic lands only in the nineteenth century, and currently the Islamic world at large is in the process of catching up; leading Muslim scholars lament the status of scientific education at large in most Muslim lands. None of the main producers of modern science is a Muslim.

Unlike in the West, in Islamic contexts the link between religion and science is tight, so much so that, according to the Algerian astrophysicist Nidhal

6. Mohamad Abdalla, "Ibn Khaldūn on the Fate of Islamic Science after the 11th Century," in *ISHCP* 3:29–30.

Guessoum, even current textbooks are hardly much else than "a branch of Qur'anic exegesis."[7] The Iranian physics professor Mehdi Golshani's book *The Holy Quran and the Sciences of Nature* is a representative example. That said, unlike the Christian tradition (and more recently, Jewish tradition), religion-science dialogue is still a marginal phenomenon among Muslims.

As do many other religious traditions, Islamic scholars and scientists offer a fairly obvious typology of responses to modern science:

1. Rejection of science because of its alleged opposition to revelation.
2. An uncritical embrace of the technocratic practical results of Western science in pursuit of power- and competence-equality with (as they are perceived) more developed Western nations.
3. An effort to build a distinctively "Islamic science" based on the authority of the Holy Qur'an and Hadith.
4. An attempt to negotiate between the legitimacy and necessity of contemporary scientific principles and methods while at the same time critiquing the metaphysical, ethical, and religious implications of the scientific paradigm.[8]

The intuitive mind-set among Muslims follows the first category's opposition, particularly with regard to evolutionism.[9] So fierce is the opposition that it is not uncommon to find *fatwas* (more or less binding legal-religious rulings) on it.[10]

What is striking in Muslim countries is that not only a large majority of the general public but also university students and professors strongly and consistently oppose evolution, particularly human evolution. Even among American Muslims, fewer than half accept evolutionism.[11] The most important reason for opposition is the question of Adam.

7. Nidhal Guessoum, *Islam's Quantum Question: Reconciling Muslim Tradition and Modern Science* (London: I. B. Tauris, 2011), 180.

8. Adapted from Mehdi Golshani, "Does Science Offer Evidence of a Transcendent Reality and Purpose?," in *ISHCP* 2:96–97.

9. Mahmoud Ayoub, "Creation or Evolution? The Reception of Darwinism in Modern Arab Thought," in *SRPW*, chap. 11.

10. See Nidhal Guessoum, "Islamic Theological Views on Darwinian Evolution," in *Oxford Research Encyclopedia of Religion*, May 2016, https://dx.doi.org/10.1093/acrefore/9780199340378.013.36.

11. A 2008 Pew poll reports that only 45 percent of American Muslims embrace evolutionary theory.

Ironically, the advocates of the first category are rapidly losing ground in Islamic lands, not because Muslims by and large would endorse any part of the seeming atheistic ethos advanced by modern scientific culture but simply because of the uncritical embrace of the instrumental use of science in pursuit of technological, particularly military, competence (category 2). Because of the alleged neutrality and value-free nature of modern science, its practical fruits are being enjoyed unabashedly without much or any concern for the serious philosophical-ethical-religious challenges to core Islamic values. This has raised concerns in the minds of some leading Islamic theologians.[12]

Deeply critical of and disappointed with the antagonism of the secular scientific paradigm, some Muslim intellectuals have been envisioning the possibility and necessity of a distinctively Islamic science (category 3).[13] The main complaints against modern science and its "blind" use by Muslims include, among others:

- the lack of critical study of science produced in the West;
- the assumption of science's value-free, neutral nature; and
- the failure to acknowledge the disastrous effects of modern science on nature.

What would an Islamic science look like? According to Nasr, it would include "stop[ping] the worship-like attitude towards modern science and technology," returning to an in-depth study of authoritative Islamic sources, studying carefully pure sciences (including at the best institutions in the West) instead of focusing merely on applied fields, and rediscovering and reviving those fields of sciences in which Islam first achieved great competency, namely, medicine, agriculture, architecture, and astronomy.[14]

As an alternative to Islamic science, some leading scientists argue that there should not be in principle a contradiction between whatever science *qua* science discovers and Islamic faith (category 4). They strongly reject the whole idea of Islamic science and argue for the universal nature of the scientific pursuit and therefore its compatibility with Islam.[15]

12. Seyyed Hossein Nasr, "Islam and Science," in *OHRS*, 72.

13. Mehdi Golshani, "Islam and the Sciences of Nature: Some Fundamental Questions," in *ISHCP* 1:77–78.

14. Seyyed Hossein Nasr, *The Need for a Sacred Science*, Suny Series in Religious Studies (Albany: State University of New York Press, 1993).

15. Guessoum, *Islam's Quantum Question*, 129–35.

As in the Christian tradition, a vibrant Muslim creationist movement exercises wide influence among laypeople in various global locations.[16] Another similar kind of science-appealing development involves the search for "miraculous scientific facts in the Qur'an,"[17] a highly apologetic enterprise.

Modern Science and Asiatic Faith Traditions

On Evolutionary Theory at Large

Among the main Asiatic faith traditions, evolutionary theory has hardly caused any concern. Generally speaking, as will be discussed, Hindu traditions consider the origins and development of the whole reality in terms of evolvement and a common ancestry. Moreover, for Hindus, even the gods may assume animal features.[18]

Buddhism offers a number of reasons for its lack of concern. First, Gautama considered questions of origins to be secondary and marginal. Second, at least in some key Buddhist scriptural accounts, as discussed above, an evolutionary view (though not in its modern form) can be discerned. Third, the idea of no-self and impermanence leans toward evolvement and evolution.

Science in a Hindu Outlook

In contrast to the post-Enlightenment Western ideals of total objectivity and objectification of nature, traditionally Hindu vision has integrated scientific pursuit with religious and ritualistic domains. Religion and science are deeply intertwined. Consider this: "India is the one and only country in the world that simultaneously launches satellites to explore the space *and* teaches astrology as a Vedic science in its colleges and universities." In fact, since 2001, astrology has been taught as a scientific subject in Indian colleges and universities.[19]

Beginning in the mid-nineteenth century, a vast and wide intellectual renaissance started in India, resulting in its current great scientific pursuit;

---

16. For the Turkish creationist Harun Yahya, see https://harun-yahya.net/.

17. Chap. 5 in Guessoum, *Islam's Quantum Question*.

18. David L. Gosling, "Darwin and the Hindu Tradition: 'Does What Goes Around Come Around?'" *Zygon* 46, no. 2 (June 2011): 348.

19. Meera Nanda, "Vedic Science and Hindu Nationalism: Arguments against a Premature Synthesis of Religion and Science," in *SRPW*, 30.

that was also the time of introducing European educational systems (related to the British-led colonial project). Understandably, assessments of and attitudes toward modern science have varied. Bhikhu Parekh has famously classified Indian responses to Western (secularizing) influences under three categories:

- the "critical traditionalists," who believe Indian foundations can be redeemed even if some important aspects of the West are incorporated;
- the "modernists," who wish to adapt to the European lifestyle; and
- the "critical modernists," who envision a creative synthesis.[20]

Not unlike some Muslims, a group of Hindu scientists have attempted to develop a credible "Hindu science" (also called "Vedic science") paradigm.[21] Not surprisingly, this project has been subject to critique both by the scientific community and by some Hindu thinkers.

Buddhist Appraisals of Science

Modern Buddhism's relation to Western science does not differ radically from that of Hinduism. Its claims about science emerged in a polemical manner as Buddhists worked hard to convince Westerners, including Christians, that their understanding is not superstition but rather a rational, sound account of reality.[22]

The Buddhologist José Ignacio Cabezón suggests a typology not unlike those devised by Christian theologians. The first model, "Conflict/Ambivalence," is subscribed to by a small minority of Buddhists. Generally speaking, a negative attitude toward science among Buddhists in the contemporary world may have more to do with Western science's general hostility toward religion. By and large, however, rather than conflictual, Buddhism takes an attitude of "Compatibility/Identity." It can manifest itself either in terms of similarity between Buddhism and science or in the idea that "Buddhism is science" and therefore it and science

20. Bhikhu Parekh, *Colonialism, Tradition, and Reform: An Analysis of Gandhi's Political Discourse* (New Delhi: Sage Publications, 1989).

21. See Susmita Chatterjee, "Acharya Jagadish Chandra Bose: Looking beyond the Idiom," in *Science, Spirituality, and the Modernization of India*, ed. Makarand Paranjape, Anthem South Asian Studies (London: Anthem, 2008).

22. Donald S. Lopez, *Buddhism and Science: A Guide for the Perplexed* (Chicago: University of Chicago Press, 2008).

are more or less identical.[23] As in all other faith traditions, there is a growing body of contemporary (mostly popular) literature written by Buddhists around the world concerning the astonishing compatibility between, say, quantum mechanics and compassion, or emptiness and relativity theory.[24]

The final category is "Complementarity," which as a middle position seeks to negotiate both similarities (unlike the first option) and differences (unlike the second option). Whereas both Buddhism and science focus on "empirical" investigation of reality, Buddhism complements the reductionist materialism with the inclusion of the mental/spiritual/"inner." Whereas sciences rely only on rational, conceptual, and analytic methods, Buddhism also utilizes intuition, meditation, and "inner" resources.[25]

What about contemporary Christian theology's relation to science?

Science and Religion in Mutual Critical Dialogue: A Christian Position

The following typology helps us structure Christian approaches to science:[26]

- Theology in Continuity with Science
- Science in Continuity with Theology
- Theology and Science as Separate Realms
- Mutual Interaction of Theology and Science

For the first category, classical liberalism is a grand example. With its categorical separation between "nature" (the domain of facts) and "history" (the domain of human values), it made the former the realm of natural sciences and the latter that of "human sciences." Hence, no conflict arises. The critical point about this category is the timidity of its theology to engage natural sciences *critically*. Instead, there is accommodation.

The second category is rooted in the pre-Enlightenment worldview in which theology was seen as the queen of the sciences. As long as the Scripture

---

23. Henry S. Olcott, *The Buddhist Catechism*, 2nd ed. (London: Theosophical Publishing Society, 1903), 95–109, available at www.sacredtexts.com.

24. Lopez, *Buddhism and Science*, 2–4.

25. José Ignacio Cabezón, "Buddhism and Science: On the Nature of the Dialogue," in *Buddhism and Science: Breaking New Ground*, ed. B. Alan Wallace (New York: Columbia University Press, 2003), 41–56.

26. Anne M. Clifford, "Creation," in *Systematic Theology: Roman Catholic Perspectives*, ed. Francis Schüssler Fiorenza and John P. Galvin (Minneapolis: Fortress, 1991), 1:225–40.

principle (that is, the authority of the Bible) stayed intact, the authority of Scripture surpassed that of the sciences and philosophy. On the contemporary scene, the fundamentalist movement known as creationism, with its advocacy of an anti-evolutionary scientific paradigm as an alternative to mainline natural sciences, represents this category. It is based on literal interpretation of the biblical message, including matters of science, and a search for archaeological/ paleontological "evidence" in support of a young earth theory.[27] The obvious problem with this approach is that it lacks scientific credibility and hence even at its best remains a purely religious affair.

The third category is most notoriously represented by Karl Barth, who, in his massive discussion on creation in *Church Dogmatics*, simply refused to engage science.[28] More widely, the whole neo-orthodox movement separates theology and science with its fideistic (based on faith alone) elevation of divine revelation as the judge of all matters of knowledge; this position also accepts classical liberalism's categorical separation between nature and history. It simply rejects dialogue with sciences. The main liability, like that of category 2, is the failure of theology to have a public voice and also to make its own contribution to sciences.

The orientation recommended here is "Mutual Critical Interaction of Theology and Science."[29] The Roman Catholic Church, at Vatican II, stated that "earthly matters and the concerns of faith derive from the same God," and hence in principle cannot violate each other.[30] Among Protestant theologians, Pannenberg is a leading example of this view. He argues that while theology must be mindful of the differences in method between itself and natural sciences, it should also remember that theology should make every effort to critically integrate scientific results.[31] Many other leading Protestant theologians agree (J. Moltmann, T. F. Torrance, and others). Theology should not merely serve as science's religious interpreter; rather, it should also challenge and contribute to science's quest.

The following main section of the chapter will begin with a short statement on creation and cosmology in Abrahamic traditions because of the

---

27. Henry M. Morris, *Beginning of the World* (Denver: Accent Books, 1977).

28. Preface to *CD* III/1.

29. Adapted from Robert J. Russell's "Creative Mutual Interaction," in his *Cosmology: From Alpha to Omega; The Creative Mutual Interaction of Theology and Science* (Minneapolis: Fortress, 2008).

30. *Gaudium et Spes: Pastoral Constitution on the Church in the Modern World* (Vatican II), #36, available at www.vatican.va.

31. Pannenberg, *ST* 2:70–71.

foundational similarities of cosmologies among these "religions of the book." The bulk of the discussion then delves into the more detailed investigation of Buddhist and Hindu cosmologies and particularly views on origins because those are much less well known among theologians.

Origins of the Cosmos in Religions' Imagination

Creation Theologies in Abrahamic Traditions

Common Basis

All three Abrahamic traditions believe in God, the almighty Creator, who has brought about the cosmos and sustains and guides its life from the beginning to the end. The ultimate meaning of the confession of God as Creator is that the whole universe is ontologically dependent on God.[32] Everything derives from and is dependent on God.

The same Creator guides the creation with the help of the laws of creation he has put in place (Q 30:30). Thus, divine purposes are present in creation. While God and world can never be separated, neither can they be equated. God is infinite; the cosmos and creatures are finite.

Since Christian theology derived its creation theology from the Old Testament, there is no need in this context to delve into uniquely Jewish contributions; it suffices to highlight Islamic distinctives.

Islamic Theologies of Creation

Foundational to all Islamic traditions is Qur'anic teaching,[33] which "replaced the pagan Arabs' conception of nature with a new and vivid" theological interpretation.[34] Similarly to the Bible, the Qur'an describes God as the Creator in the absolute sense; that is, God brought into existence that which was not existent "before": "He is the First and the Last, and the Manifest and the Hid-

---

32. Seyyed Hossein Nasr, "The Question of Cosmogenesis: The Cosmos as a Subject of Scientific Study," in *ISHCP* 1:177.

33. Muzaffar Iqbal, *Islam and Science* (Aldershot, UK: Ashgate, 2002), chap. 2.

34. İbrahim Özdemir, "Towards an Understanding of Environmental Ethics from a Qu'ranic Perspective," in *I&E*, 6.

den and He has knowledge of all things. It is He Who created the heavens and the earth in six days, then presided upon the Throne" (Q 57:3-4), who never perishes (55:26–27).

In the Qur'anic interpretation, created order is "muslim." The term means "submission"; its root (*slm*) denotes "to be safe," "to be whole and integral." The idea behind the term is that one who submits to God avoids disintegration.[35] The Qur'an testifies: "to God prostrate whoever is in the heavens and whoever is in the earth, together with the sun and the moon, and the stars and the mountains, and the trees and the animals, as well as many of mankind" (22:18).[36]

No wonder Islam has a long tradition of natural theology not unlike Judaism and Christianity. All created realities are considered "signs" revealing the Creator (Q 30:22). Hence, the study of nature may draw us nearer to God (41:53). If all creatures are signs, then "it gives humans the impression that God is within us. If God reveals Himself" through all the created beings, "then it is not difficult to get the idea that wherever humans look we can easily feel the presence of God all around and within us."[37]

The foundational message signified by creation for Muslim theology is *tawhid*, the unity and oneness of God. Corresponding to—but also distinguishing itself from—the Christian *Trinitarian* theology of creation, the Qur'anic "principle of unicity of God (*tawhid*)" serves as the theological framework for both creation theology and the "unification of Sciences and Nature," argues Masudul Alam Choudhury.[38]

Codependent Origination: The Buddhist Vision of the Origins of the Cosmos

Although there is a connection between the Divine or the "Ultimate Reality" and the coming into existence of the world in Buddhist traditions, none of them considers the Divine as the "Creator" in any sense similar to the Abrahamic traditions, not even those Mahayana traditions that show much more pronounced interest in deities than does Theravada. In that sense, Buddhism is a "naturalist" philosophy closer to contemporary scientific materialism but

35. Fazlur Rahman, "Some Key Ethical Concepts of the Qur'an," *Journal of Religious Ethics* 11, no. 2 (1983): 183.

36. See further, Özdemir, "Towards an Understanding," 19.

37. Özdemir, "Towards an Understanding," 12.

38. Masudul Alam Choudhury, "The 'Tawhidi' Precept in the Sciences," in *ISHCP* 1:243.

with the crucial difference that, unlike scientific reductive materialism, even in Buddhism's nontheistic orientation it is the spiritual/mental that is primary. Nor is Buddhism atheistic, as is repeatedly explained above.

Keep also in mind that the Buddha discouraged speculations into abstract topics such as the origins.[39] That said, it is ironic that Buddhist cosmology is rich, variegated, and highly sophisticated.[40]

The main point about Buddhist cosmology is that there is no absolute "origin." As the Lotus Sutra, the "catechism" of the Mahayana tradition, categorically teaches, the cosmos was "not derived from an intelligent cause," nor has it any purpose.[41] Rather, the cosmos is everlasting and without beginning.[42]

All Buddhist schools agree that "[co]dependent origination" rather than creation is the key to the coming to existence and nature of the cosmos.[43] According to the leading Theravada teacher of Thailand, the Venerable P. A. Payutto, "dependent origination"[44] is the single most important principle that "describes the law of nature, which exists as the natural course of things." This principle applies not only to nature but also to human society, ethics, and other domains of life.[45] It is expressed classically like this:

---

39. *Majjhima Nikaya Sutta*, in *The Middle Length Discourses of the Buddha*, trans. Bhikkhu Ñānamoli and Bhikku Bodhi (Kandy, Sri Lanka: Buddhist Publication Society, 1995), #63; see Lily de Silva, "The Buddhist Attitude towards Nature," *Access to Insight*, June 5, 2010, http://www.accesstoinsight.org/lib/authors/desilva/attitude.html.

40. Two standard English-language primers are W. Randolph Kloetzli, *Buddhist Cosmology: Science and Theology in the Images of Motion and Light* (Delhi: Motilal Banarsidass Publishers, 1989), and Akira Sadakata, *Buddhist Cosmology: Philosophy and Origins*, trans. Gaynor Sekimori (Tokyo: Kōsei, 1997).

41. Lotus Sutra 5; quotation from 5.80 (*SBE* 21).

42. Lotus Sutra 13.19 (*SBE* 21).

43. Understandably, diverse Buddhist traditions entertain different kinds of speculations into origins (even though none of them knows a Creator, as mentioned). One of the more well-known speaks of eighty-two or eighty-nine constituent elements, *dhammas*, and the main point is that everything else is fleeting and conditioned, whereas the last one is nirvana, real and unconditioned. That is free from change and decay. See Buddhagosa, *Visuddhimagga, the Path of Purification: The Classic Manual of Buddhist Doctrine and Meditation*, trans. Bikkhu Nanamoli (Kandy, Sri Lanka: Buddhist Publication Society, 2011), 16.71; 522.

44. See Paticca-samuppada-vibhanga Sutta: Analysis of Dependent Co-arising (Samyutta Nikaya 12.2) for the famous analysis of Gautama concerning the idea of "dependent origination."

45. P. A. Payutto, *Dependent Origination: The Buddhist Law of Conditionality*, trans. Bruce Evans (Bangkok: Buddhadhamma Foundation, 1995), "Introduction" (n.p., so chapter numbers are given in references).

"When this is, that is."
"From the arising of this comes the arising of that."
"When this isn't, that isn't."
"From the cessation of this comes the cessation of that."[46]

In other words, according to the principle of effect, everything emerges in an interrelated manner through various sequences, finally consummating into ultimate liberation.[47] Everything is in a continuous process of change. The world passes through cycles of evolution and dissolution, *ad infinitum*, basically similarly to Hinduism. "Behind" this continuous process of the dependent origination is the process of the arising and cessation of *dukkha* (the first "Noble Truth").

Rather than using "suffering" (or "pain" or "stress") for *dukkha*, it is best to leave the term without English translation to avoid misunderstanding. It is intentionally an ambiguous word. With all their differences, all Buddhist schools consider *dukkha* the main challenge in life and, consequently, extinction of *dukkha* to be the main goal, the *summa* of everything in Buddhism and its scriptures,[48] a topic to be discussed in the context of "salvation" and eschatology.

Hindu Cosmologies of Origins

Endless "Beginnings" and "Ends"

While, similarly to Buddhism, Hinduism does not have any doctrine of *creation*, it is unusually rich in religious cosmologies and sacred cosmogonies. At the same time, Hinduism speaks of origins in diverse voices characteristic of its enormous plurality.

Notwithstanding the lack of the doctrine of "creation" strictly speaking, the Gita freely speaks of the Deity as the creator and sustainer of the world.[49] The Lord also resides in all things; he is likened to the taste of water and the light of sun and moon. He is also Om, the eternal "echo," the sound originating

---

46. Assutavā Sutta: Uninstructed (1) of Samyutta Nikaya 12.61.

47. Samyutta Nikaya 12.2; Payutto, *Dependent Origination*, chap. 1.

48. Saeng Chandngarm, *Arriyasatsee* [Four Noble Truths] (Bangkok: Sangsan Books, 2001), 9–14.

49. Bhagavad Gita 7.

from the mythic past (similarly Rig Veda 10.190). Not surprisingly, the Gita thus "affirms the interdependence of the spiritual and material nature."[50]

With all their differences, the various Hindu scriptural traditions affirm that God and nature are the same.[51] The description of "creation" in Brihadaranyaka Upanishad (1.4) is a case in point: Brahman first made himself split into two, bringing about male and female; out of female came cow and bull, out of them mare and ass, and so forth. Out of his body parts, further things were created.[52] No wonder the cosmos is sometimes compared to a cosmic being, a living organism.

What is more similar to the Semitic faiths is that "Hindu scriptures attest to the belief that the creation, maintenance, and annihilation of the cosmos is completely up to the Supreme Will."[53] The Gita puts it in a way that closely resembles the New Testament statement about Christ (Rev. 1:8): "I am the beginning and the middle and the end also of all beings."[54] What is different from the Abrahamic traditions is that all Hindu scriptural traditions also affirm rebirth and a cyclical worldview: hence, "creation" does not mean the absolute beginning, as in the Semitic traditions.[55]

On God-World Relationship

If the Divine and the cosmos are but one (that is, monism)—as expressed classically: "That Self [*atman*] is indeed Brahman"[56]—it raises the question of whether there is any difference between the two or any way to make a distinction. Here we come to the complicated and complex ancient debates

---

50. Jung Young Lee, *The Theology of Change: A Christian Concept of God in an Eastern Perspective* (Maryknoll, NY: Orbis, 1979), 105–6, 110 (105).

51. O. P. Dwivedi, "Classical India," in *A Companion to Environmental Philosophy*, ed. Dale Jamieson (Oxford: Blackwell, 2001), 45.

52. Brihadaranyaka Upanishad 1.4; *SBE* 15:85–91.

53. O. P. Dwivedi, "Dharmic Ecology," in *Hinduism and Ecology: The Intersection of Earth, Sky, and Water*, ed. Christopher Key Chapple and Mary Evelyn Tucker, Religions of the World and Ecology (Cambridge, MA: Harvard University Press, 2000), 6; see, e.g., Bhagavad Gita 10; *SBE* 8:87: "I am the origin of all, and that all moves on through me."

54. Bhagavad Gita 10.32.

55. That said, ironically, there are Hindu traditions that look at the emergence of the cosmos as a result of the Lord's love and benevolence toward the creatures and depict a theistic kind of picture! Just consider Svetasvatara Upanishad 6.16; *SBE* 15:265; see further, Keith Ward, *Religion and Creation* (Oxford: Clarendon, 1996), 82.

56. Brihadaranyaka Upanishad 4.4.5; *SBE* 15:176.

among Vedanta schools (the students of the Upanishads, the last part of the Vedas).[57] While all Vedanta theologians agree on the centrality of the monistic principle (technically called *advaita*, "not-two"), they have deep divisions concerning the nuances. For our purposes, the most noteworthy is the division between the strictly monistic schools, the nondualist *advaita* school represented most famously by Sankara of the eighth century, and the qualified nondualist (*visistadvaita*) school of Ramanuja of the eleventh century.[58]

For Sankara, Brahman is totally void of all limitations and is identical with *atman* (the "soul" or the "self"). Because of ignorance, the human soul is encumbered with body and mind and thus subject to *dukkha* (sorrow) and continuous samsara, endless cycles of birth and death, unless through knowledge one attains liberation when the identity between Brahman and *atman* is realized. Attaining this realization is the ultimate goal of the study of the Upanishads.

One of the fiercest critics of Sankara's strict nondualistic hermeneutics was Ramanuja. His qualified nondualist tradition refutes Sankara's absolute identity between Brahman and *atman* and allows for "inseparable" distinction (without compromising the unity), internal diversity, and complexity of the divine. Importantly, this qualified *advaita* became the mainstream of the spirituality of the common folk in India, themselves totally illiterate about these nuanced philosophical debates. Guided by the Gita and expressing itself in some form of *bhakti* devotion and spirituality with endless (often local) customs and colors (to which usually also belong local deities), this legacy of Ramanuja is typically linked with the deity Vishnu. According to this interpretation, everything is simultaneously one with and distinct from the Supreme Being, Lord.

On the "Appearance" Nature of Reality

Both Sankara's and Ramanuja's visions of (to use Christian parlance) the relationship between God and world have enormous implications, but those lie well beyond a primer such as this. Let us highlight here only one crucial issue, which comes to the fore most clearly in Sankara's absolute monism but is also the basic

---

57. For a succinct explanation, see Keith Ward, *Images of Eternity: Concepts of God in Five Religious Traditions* (London: Darton, Longman & Todd, 1987), chap. 2; more widely, John J. Thatamanil, *The Immanent Divine: God, Creation, and the Human Predicament; An East-West Conversation* (Minneapolis: Fortress, 2006).

58. These two views do not of course exhaust the Vedanta tradition, as there is also the influential thirteenth-century theology of Madhva, a qualified dualism, among others, but for our limited, comparative purposes, Sankara's and Ramanuja's theologies suffice.

intuition of much of Indian thought. It comes to fullest fruition in strict *advaita* and can be expressed in English as the "appearance" nature of reality.

To put it crudely: the cosmos we see and sense is not "real"; it is but "illusion" or "appearance," beyond which is the "real" world, nonmaterial or idealist (spiritual).[59] Why or how so? Simply put, if Brahman (the "Ultimate") and the cosmos are strictly one, only Brahman is real![60]

That said, we must hasten to add that notwithstanding its appearance nature, the empirical world of course exists. If not, we couldn't even be writing these lines! It just is not the ultimate.[61]

This idea of the appearance nature of the phenomenal world can be understood in a more negative or positive way (to use Western criteria). On the one hand, the world can be considered merely an illusion with no inherent value.[62] On the other hand, "the world can also be seen as the divine play, in which the One, though remaining complete in itself, manifests in diversity so as to realize its infinite potential in endless ways, and to enjoy that self-realization."[63]

Although some comparative notes have already been inserted in the discussion, it is useful to attempt a more "global" dialogue, paying special attention to the differences between two dramatically different orientations: the Abrahamic and the Asiatic. This comparison also includes a separate section on care for the environment.

Abrahamic and Asiatic Traditions in Comparison

The most radical difference between the Abrahamic and Asian faiths has to do with the affirmation of the doctrine of creation "from nothing" in the former

59. "In India as in Greece, the ultimate question must always be that of the relation between the supreme unchanging Reality and the world of coming-to-be and passing away, the eternal Self and what appears as non-Self." Sara Grant, RSCJ, *Towards an Alternative Theology: Confessions of a Non-dualist Christian*, with introduction by Bradley J. Malkovsky (Notre Dame: University of Notre Dame Press, 2002), 39–40.

60. Technically put: "The relation of Ruler and ruled does not exist" apart from the "phenomenal world." Sankara, Vedanta-Sutras 2.1.14; *SBE* 34:330.

61. Well-known illustrations of Sankara include mistaking a rope for a snake (Vedanta-Sutras 1.3.19; *SBE* 34:189) and elephants seen in dreams mistaken for real ones (1.2.12; *SBE* 34:123). See also, Julius J. Lipner, *Hindus: Their Religious Beliefs and Practices* (London: Routledge, 1994), 14.

62. See Keith Ward, *Religion and Human Nature* (Oxford: Clarendon, 1998), 13–14.

63. Ward, *Religion and Human Nature*, 15.

and the historical nature of the cosmos; it has both a beginning and an end. Buddhist and Hindu visions of endless "beginnings" and "ends" point in a completely different direction.

Another radical difference between Abrahamic and Asiatic faiths, particularly Hinduism, comes to the fore in the negotiation of God-world relationship. Whereas Hindu cosmology is based on a pantheistic equation between "God" and the world (monistic *advaita*), Abrahamic faiths require distinction although not separation. Even Ramanuja's qualified *advaita* is a far cry from Abrahamic faiths' need to establish the independence of God as the Almighty Creator and Provider. Indeed, the sophisticated nuances between *advaita* schools are just that, *nuances*, and from the Abrahamic perspective they all fail to make a proper distinction. Even in the most pan(en)theistically oriented versions of Christian theology, the world is not conceived to be a nondifferentiated extension of the Lord, as it is in Hinduism. There is an "unbridgeable gulf" between those theistic faiths that see the Creator as infinitely greater than the creatures and those that equate the two.[64]

Both Buddhism and Hinduism, albeit somewhat differently, deny the underlying Abrahamic belief in the value and purpose of creation, that is, "intentional creation."[65] For Buddhism, the endless origination of the cosmos is "natural" (that is, it belongs to the nature of reality) and the cosmos has no purpose per se. It just is. For Hinduism's appearance nature of reality, whether pessimistically or positively conceived, hardly any inherent value could be added. An offshoot from the purposefulness of creation in Judaism, Christianity, and Islam is its "sign" nature, to use Muslim vocabulary. In some real sense, creation speaks of and images the Creator. Not so in Asian views.

There is only a little truth to the mantra that whereas the Asiatic religions are cosmocentric, the Semitic faiths are anthropocentric; this claim is usually made without detailed engagement of scriptural and theological traditions.[66] In Hinduism's and Buddhism's cyclical worldview, respectively, worlds and universes succeed each other over an almost infinite time span. That would support the cosmocentric orientation. But the vision of "salvation" in terms of

---

64. R. C. Zaehner, *Mysticism, Sacred and Profane* (Oxford: Clarendon, 1957), 204.

65. Janet M. Soskice, "*Creatio Ex Nihilo*: Its Jewish and Christian Foundations," in *Creation and the God of Abraham*, ed. David B. Burrell et al. (Cambridge: Cambridge University Press, 2011), 29; with reference to David B. Burrell, "Freedom and Creation in the Abrahamic Traditions," *International Philosophical Quarterly* 40 (2000): 167.

66. A typical recent example is Steve Fuller ("Humanity as an Endangered Species in Science and Religion," in *SRPW*, 5), who names the orientations of Abrahamic and Asiatic faiths "anthropic" and "karmic," respectively.

each individual's enlightenment (variously described in Hindu and Buddhist traditions) certainly shifts the focus to anthropocentrism, or even individualism. Furthermore, the appearance nature of reality does not necessarily endorse cosmocentrism per se. While it is true that in Abrahamic faiths cosmogonies are written mainly from the perspective of humanity, this in no way means that their scriptural traditions lack a cosmic orientation. Indeed, it can also be argued that the Christian vision of eschatological salvation in terms of the renewal of the whole creation (to be detailed in the last chapter of this book) particularly supports a robust integrative approach to creation in which both humanity and the cosmos have their own places. Indeed, I suggest that a better term for Abrahamic traditions' relation to nature is "anthropocosmic."[67]

Substantial differences between Abrahamic and Asiatic traditions have also to do with the emphasis in Judaism, Islam, and Christianity on God as the source of moral order, and hence the importance of loving obedience and covenant, a topic briefly discussed above in the chapter on revelation and Scripture.

Yet another difference between a Western and an Asian outlook on life is that for Asians the world is more "spirited." The distinction between "material" and "spiritual" is far less categorical. What is spiritual is primary, while the material is secondary, a feature that runs contrary to much in the West.

On Ecological Resources and Challenges among Religions

The Role of Sacred Traditions in Relation to Nature

The pollution of creation is a well-documented, major crisis threatening not only the well-being but even the *being* itself of our planet, so much so that "if current trends continue, we will not."[68] This raises the question of the role of religions in helping overcome the impending eco-catastrophe. Happily, unlike in the past, most religions nowadays make claims to being "green."

---

67. The term comes from the Chinese Confucian scholar Tu Weiming; see, e.g., his "The Ecological Turn in New Confucian Humanism: Implications for China and the World," *Daedalus: Journal of the American Academy of Arts and Sciences* 130, no. 4 (2001): 243-64; William C. Chittick ("The Anthropocosmic Vision in Islamic Thought," in *God, Life, and the Cosmos: Christian and Islamic Perspectives,* ed. Ted Peters, Muzaffar Iqbal, and Syed Nomanul Haq [Surrey, UK: Ashgate, 2002], 125-52) applies the concept to Islam.

68. Daniel Maguire, *The Moral Core of Judaism and Christianity: Reclaiming the Revolution* (Philadelphia: Fortress, 1993), 13.

Although there is no denying religions' guilt for the environment's pollution—just think of some fundamentalist Christians' intentional neglect in hopes of an imminent eschatological consummation—the persistent criticism that asserts a necessary link between natural disaster and religion[69] is untenable. A related misconception is that whereas Abrahamic faiths are detrimental to the environment, Asiatic faiths by nature are "green." Is that so?

However we answer the questions above, critics routinely ignore the enormously devastating harm to nature done by atheists, from the former Soviet Union to China and beyond. Religions seem not to explain much here.

Asiatic Traditions

How "Green" Is the Buddhist View of Nature?

Supporters of Buddhism's green attitude routinely mention a number of features, from its alleged nonanthropocentrism, to its focus on this-worldly ethical pursuit rather than centering on transcendental salvation, to Buddha's compassion toward all beings as an example to follow, to its nondualistic approach to the world (in contrast to Judeo-Christian dualism).[70]

On the contrary, reports from Buddhist experts are far more cautionary and in many cases negative altogether.[71] Why the negative self-assessments? The most obvious reason has to do with the very "foundations" of Buddhism. Rather than the Christian vision of a new creation that encompasses the renewal of the whole of creation and all creatures, the Buddhist vision of seeking liberation from *dukkha* is deeply anthropocentric, individualistic, and oblivious of nonhuman beings.

Unlike in Abrahamic traditions in which nature has intrinsic value as the handiwork of a personal deity, in Buddhism and its cyclical view of time/

69. Lynn White Jr., "The Historical Roots of Our Ecological Crisis," *Science* 155, no. 3767 (March 10, 1967): 1203–7. For rebuttals, see Richard C. Foltz, "Islamic Environmentalism: A Matter of Interpretation," in *I&E*, 249–79; Norman Lamm, "Ecology in Jewish Law and Theology," in his *Faith and Doubt: Studies in Traditional Jewish Thought* (New York: Ktav, 1972).

70. Martine Batchelor and Kerry Brown, eds., *Buddhism and Ecology* (London: Cassell, 1992).

71. Ruben L. F. Habito, "Environment or Earth Sangha: Buddhist Perspectives on Our Global Ecological Well-Being," *Contemporary Buddhism* 8, no. 2 (2007): 131–47.

history, nature is doomed to a repeated cycle of emergence and destruction *ad infinitum*. This hardly leaves much energy or vision for the protection of this vanishing world.

All in all, these kinds of theological reasons that seem to obliterate or frustrate environmental pursuits and ethics among Buddhists are almost never mentioned in the popular promotional literature hailing "green" Buddhism.

Hinduism's Ecological Resources and Dilemmas

The significance of ecological attitudes among Hindus is immense in light of the huge environmental problems in India and surrounding areas.[72] There is no doubt that, as in Buddhism, the cyclical worldview of Hinduism potentially leans toward being oblivious to the conservation of the earth. Furthermore, Hinduism's appearance nature of reality or the cosmos as *lila* ("play," that is, an unintended "by-product") similarly may cause the faithful to consider this earth a secondary, temporary dwelling place, on the way to the "real world."

A number of other critical questions await response before the issue of Hinduism's relation to ecological concerns can be even tentatively defined: Can the strongly ascetic Hindu outlook (in pursuit of one's own deliverance) contribute to the communal and cosmic good?[73] What is the role of karma, the bondage to the world because of deeds in the past and present, with regard to environmental care? What about the deeply *theologically* based and (originally) divinely sanctioned hierarchic nature of society (the caste system) when it comes to ecological concern?

On the other side, there are some beautiful, inspiring scriptural resources extolling the beauty of nature. Just consider the long "Hymn to Goddess Earth" in Atharva Veda.[74] Many other such beautiful nature hymns can be found, particularly in Rig Veda (1.115; 7.99; 10.125; and so forth), somewhat similar to the nature psalms in the Hebrew Bible.

---

72. Dwivedi, "Dharmic Ecology."

73. Christopher Chapple, "Asceticism and the Environment: Jainism, Buddhism, and Yoga," *CrossCurrents* 57, no. 4 (2008): 514–25.

74. Atharva Veda, section X: Cosmogonic and Theosophic Hymns, 12.1, Hymns of the Atharva-Veda together with Extracts from the Ritual Books and the Commentaries; *SBE* 42, n.p.

Abrahamic Traditions

The Emergence of Ecological Awareness among the Jews

In the oldest Abrahamic faith, important resources can facilitate the flourishing of nature: the task of vice-regency given by God both in Hebrew-Christian and Islamic scriptures (see below, the theological anthropology discussion of chapter 4); the importance of history and time (because of a linear rather than a cyclical worldview); the covenant spirituality of the Hebrews that binds human beings to God, other humans, and nature; and so forth.

Similarly to others, the Jewish religion has only recently acknowledged the value of work for the environment.[75] Reasons for its recent appearance are many and understandable; one is that the survival of the small dispersed nation, particularly in the Holocaust world, including continuing threats from the surrounding nations, has not facilitated concern for the natural environment. Although secular Jewish eco-minded individuals excelled in green activities beginning from the 1960s,[76] the religiously driven pursuit started mainly among some Jews in the United States.[77]

Of course, nature has not been absent from Jewish life; just consider the many nature-related blessings and prayers in the liturgy, many of them based on Old Testament texts.[78] The annual feast of Sukkot, also known as the Feast of Tabernacles, during which people live in small huts for a week commemorating not only the forty years of survival in the desert but also nature and agriculture, is a great nature event. It is called nowadays the "Jewish Environment Holiday." Jewish scriptural tradition also testifies to the faithfulness of the Creator for the sustenance and well-being of nature (Gen. 8:22, among others).

Similarly to the Muslim tradition, Jews are cautious not to make nature an idol. Related to this concern is the debate among some leading eco-theologians whether to consider the earth sacred or not. According to Hava Tirosh-Samuelson, the following three tasks are routinely mentioned: "protection of vegetation . . . ; awareness of the distress of animals; and predicating

---

75. See Arthur Waskow, "Is the Earth a Jewish Issue?," *Tikkun* 7, no. 5 (1992): 35–37.

76. See Mark X. Jacobs, "Jewish Environmentalism: Past Accomplishments and Future Challenges," in *Judaism and Ecology: Created World and Revealed Word*, ed. Hava Tirosh-Samuelson (Cambridge, MA: Harvard University Press, 2002), 449–80.

77. For the Shomrei Adamah ("Keepers of the Earth") organization founded in 1988 by Rabbi Ellen Bernstein, see http://ellenbernstein.org/.

78. Neil Gillman, "Creation in the Bible and in the Liturgy," in Tirosh-Samuelson, *Judaism and Ecology*, 133–54.

social justice on the well-being of the earth itself." They all belong to and derive from the covenantal theology foundational to all Jewish tradition.[79]

Islamic Resources for Caring for the Environment

The US-based Muslim intellectual S. H. Nasr has harshly critiqued the technocratic use of nature in the modern West but has highlighted the spiritual and moral dimension of the crisis.[80] This is fully in keeping with mainline Islamic tradition, which attributes even the environmental crisis ultimately to "the loss of a relationship between humans, the natural realm, and Allah."[81]

Islamic creation theology's foundational idea of creation as a "sign" may have immense ecological impetus, as it links all creatures to the Divine. A related ancient Islamic resource is the concept of balance. Similarly to the heavens, which are sustained "by mathematical balance," human beings should be balanced, straight, and honest in relation to each other and natural resources.[82]

What are the role and place of creation (nature) vis-à-vis humanity? According to Muslim teachers, the resources of creation, unlike in modern science, are not meant for consumption by humanity but rather ultimately are meant for God's service. This is of course not to deny the great benefits of natural resources to men and women, but rather to put the matter in perspective.

Christian Contributions to Environment Care

Without unduly repeating the differences among Abrahamic (including Christian) and Asiatic traditions, let us end this discussion by briefly outlining some key Christian resources for the care of nature, bearing in mind that basically everything mentioned about Christianity's two sister faiths can also be embraced by the church.

---

79. Hava Tirosh-Samuelson, "Introduction: Judaism and the Natural World," in Tirosh-Samuelson, *Judaism and Ecology,* xxxviii.

80. Seyyed Hossein Nasr, *Man and Nature: The Spiritual Crisis in Modern Man,* rev. ed. (Chicago: Kazi Publishers, 1997 [1967]).

81. Saadia Khawar Khan Chishti, "*Fiṭra*: An Islamic Model for Humans and the Environment," in *I&E,* 69–71.

82. *Comments in The Holy Qur'an,* trans. Yusuf Ali, 5177–78, cited in Özdemir, "Towards an Understanding," 13.

Many contemporary theologians believe that Christian theology should be able to hold in a dynamic tension an attitude of reverent admiration for the beauty of creation in its endless diversity and creativity alongside a deepening concern for nature's vulnerability and suffering from the current global economic-industrial rape. This reverence does not have to make nature either divine or a "sacrament," notwithstanding the presence of sacramental elements in nature. The de-divinizing of nature affirms creation as *creation*, finite and vulnerable, as well as valuable because of its goodness.

What is very important for contemporary theology is to consider carefully the meaning of the mandate in Genesis 1:26–27 to act as God's faithful vice-regents. This does not justify abuse but rather is a call to responsible service on behalf of God's good creation. Regrettably, the command to "subdue the earth" has been too often taken in its literal sense in Christian tradition. Although the minor, alternative "green" tradition in Christianity includes mystics and saints to whom nature had intrinsic value and human dominion represented stewardship and care for creatures, in the main Christian tradition nature was conceived to have been made for humans and their benefit, and as a result, it was seen through a utilitarian lens.

The task of an ecological Christian theology is twofold: it has to clarify and help avoid ways of thinking and speaking of nature and creation that are detrimental to her survival and well-being, and it has to search for resources—theological insights, metaphors, approaches—that may help foster flourishing and continuing shalom of God's creation. Particularly helpful in this enterprise has been highlighting the Spirit's work for continuous healing of creation, a topic to be picked up below in the chapter on pneumatology. Similarly, a careful negotiation of the dynamic between the value of creation in this era and the eschatological hope for final redemption and consummation (attempted in the last chapter) has the potential of yielding fruitful results.[83]

As mentioned in the introduction to this chapter, the theme of creation in its wider sense includes both the coming into existence and nature of both the cosmos and human beings. The latter topic will be the focus of the following chapter.

---

83. The contemporary literature on "eco-theology" or "green theology" from a Christian perspective is wide and diverse. For starters, see C. Birch, W. Eaking, and J. B. McDaniel, eds., *Liberating Life: Contemporary Approaches to Ecological Theology* (Maryknoll, NY: Orbis, 1990); Ernst M. Conradie, *Hope for the Earth: Vistas for a New Century* (Eugene, OR: Wipf & Stock, 2005); Celia Deane-Drummond, *Eco-Theology* (London: Darton, Longman & Todd, 2008).

4 | Humanity and Human Nature in Religions' Teachings

Humanity and Human Nature in Christian Theology

The Image of God

Christian theology's most significant anthropological concept, *imago Dei*, claims to provide a foundational account of the human person and humanity in relation to the Creator, other creatures, and the cosmos as a whole. Notwithstanding the scarcity of direct references to the concept in the biblical canon—after three occurrences in the beginning (Gen. 1:26–27; 5:1; 9:6), the concept disappears until it is picked up in a couple of New Testament passages (1 Cor. 11:7; James 3:9)—from early on theological tradition made it an umbrella term. It is a comprehensive concept seeking to express Christian theological understanding of the nature, meaning, and destiny of humanity.

While there is no one fixed meaning given to the image of God in the biblical accounts (and therefore, the rise of diverse interpretations during the history of theology is understandable), it is taken for granted that it links humanity to Creator in a most unique way. Unlike other creatures with which human beings share their evolutionary and biological/physical basis, the Creator addresses men and women directly and in a personal manner. Human beings are made God's vice-regents; they are assigned special tasks such as naming other creatures, and most importantly, they are invited to a personal relationship. This special status also brings with it a unique responsibility (notwithstanding debates about the power and extent of free will): Christian theologians affirm that human beings have been given a say and responsibility in choosing to live with or flee from the Creator's presence.

The image of God also establishes human dignity and inviolability. No illness or defect, no suffering or torture, can take away the human dignity and value granted by the Creator. As taught in Genesis 1:26–27, humanity has been created as male and female, a reflection of the communion and relationality that Christian theology sees in the triune Creator.

Traditionally, Christian theology has emphasized the difference of humanity from the rest of creation rather than the continuity. With the embrace of evolutionary biology and etiology, current theology, while still holding to the uniqueness of humanity based on the theology of the image of God, duly acknowledges the continuity. The genetic evidence indicates that the oldest group of hominids goes back from 5 to 7 million years in history. While clearly different from the hominids, the modern human being (*Homo sapiens*)—which, according to current knowledge, emerged about 50,000–75,000 years ago—is the apex of that line.

Concerning the nature of human nature, alongside other religions and universal human intuition, Christian theology was traditionally dualistic, separating body and soul.[1] While dualism still reigns among the faithful and traditional theologies, nondualist holistic or monistic (particularly physicalist/materialist) views have emerged in the twentieth century, with no "canonical" position yet.

This chapter first introduces and compares religions' visions of humanity and the nature of human nature. Thereafter, in the second part, it delves into the question of what is wrong with humanity, known in Christian theology as the doctrine of sin and the Fall. Before anything else, without anticipating too much the ensuing detailed discussion, in the hopes of helping orient the reader, we provide a broad framework to distinguish and compare religions' conceptions of humanity and human nature.

Human Nature among Religions: A Big Picture

Despite deep differences in visions of human nature, virtually all religions agree that humanity is more than merely material; they affirm a spiritual (philosophically: idealist) view. This distinguishes religions from secular (scientific

---

1. History of theology knows versions of dualism alongside dichotomist body-soul and trichotomist body-soul-spirit distinctions; these main categories are but nuances of dualism.

and philosophical) naturalism, according to which all that there is, is nature; naturalism does not allow the nonmaterial (or nonphysical) dimensions any ultimate reality, even if mental, emotional, aesthetic, and other such properties are of course affirmed empirically.

At one end of the spectrum of religions is the view that only the spiritual dimension of humanity matters, not the bodily dimension or individuality in any sense (*advaita* Vedanta of Sankara). Thus, the whole point of the spiritual quest is to overcome the illusion of dualism. While the other major Vedanta school allows for some form of duality (the qualified nonduality of Ramanuja), the basic view of humanity is not much different. While radically different in many ways, the main schools of Buddhism, with their denial of the persistence of "self," all envision "salvation" in terms of transcending embodiment and thus also individuality.

Notwithstanding terminological differences and nuances (such as Islamic tradition's not using the term "image of God"), the three Abrahamic traditions agree materially on the idea of the human being having been made in some sense after the Creator. Furthermore, despite internal differences, all three Abrahamic faiths envision human nature as embodied soul or spirited body. They also make human existence finite and thus not immortal. Particularly in Jewish-Christian traditions, embodiment/materiality is an essential part of human nature, either because of a this-worldly eschatology (Judaism) or because of life in the resurrected body in the new creation (Christianity).

Humanity in Abrahamic Traditions

The Image of God among Abrahamic Traditions

In all Abrahamic faiths, the discussion of humanity is placed in relation to God and in the context of finite, moral life. Deeply embedded in the Jewish tradition is of course the belief shared with Christians that humanity has been created in the image of God. Jewish tradition, however, speaks with reservations about the *tselem*, "image of God," in order to avoid speaking of God too anthropomorphically.[2] The only main distinctive feature in the Christian account of the image of God has to do with the overall theological structure

2. See Jonathan Schofer, "The Image of God: A Study of an Ancient Sensibility," *Journal of the Society for Textual Reasoning* 4, no. 3 (May 2006).

stemming from the Trinitarian doctrine of God: Christian theology links the image of God particularly with the Son of God, who is the perfect and "original" image.

Although the Qur'an contains no direct statement about humanity being created in the image of God (as there is in the Hadith), the corresponding idea is there. The well-known passage of 30:30 comes close to it: "So set your purpose for religion, as a *hanif*[3]—a nature given by God, upon which He originated mankind. There is no changing God's creation." Here the term *fitrah* is used for "nature," which clearly has resemblance to the image in Christian-Jewish vocabulary. Somewhat similarly to the biblical testimonies, the human being is made of clay in the Qur'an (23:12–14). Not only that, but the one made of clay is also breathed into by the Spirit of God, and therefore even the angels prostrate themselves before him (15:26–30). In the Hadith, the idea of the image of God appears: "Allah, the Exalted and Glorious, created Adam in His own image."[4]

The technical term *fitrah*, used of human nature—"an inborn natural predisposition which cannot change, and which exists at birth in all human beings"[5]—has a number of interrelated meanings, including moral intuitions and religious instinct. According to the well-known Hadith statement, "Everyone is born according to his true nature and the command pertaining to the demise of the children of the infidels and of the children of the Muslims. There is none born but is created to his true nature (Islam). It is his parents who make him a Jew or a Christian or a Magian quite as beasts produce their young with their limbs perfect. Do you see anything deficient in them? . . . The nature made by Allah in which He has created men there is no altering of Allah's creation; that is the right religion."[6]

On the basis of this teaching, in Muslim tradition *fitrah* is universal, not limited to Muslims alone, and is an immutable feature of humanity. Very closely resembling the Christian idea of the innate knowledge of God, it "is the faculty, which He has created in mankind, of knowing Allah." As a result,

---

3. The exact meaning of the term is somewhat unclear (hence left without English translation here). A number of times it refers to "faith" (of Abraham) and also has the connotation of a nonpolytheistic faith. See Arthur Jeffery, *The Foreign Vocabulary of the Qur'an* (Leiden: Brill, 2007), 112.

4. Sahih Muslim, 40, #6809.

5. Yasien Mohamed, *Fitrah: The Islamic Concept of Human Nature* (London: Ta-Ha Publishers, 1996), 13.

6. Sahih Muslim, 33, #6423 (the last sentence is a citation from Q 30:30); similarly Sahih Bukhari, 60, #298.

belief in Allah (the confession of *tawhid*) is "natural" to human beings.[7] Therefore, Islam is at times called *din al-fitrah*, the religion of human nature, that is, religion that is in keeping with natural human instincts and a claim shared by Christian theologians regarding their own tradition.

All three Abrahamic traditions affirm the dignity of humanity in relation to God, the Creator. Just compare these two statements from Islamic and Christian writings, respectively: "When any one of you fights with his brother, he should avoid his face for Allah created Adam in His own image."[8] "Whoever sheds the blood of man, by man shall his blood be shed; for God made man in his own image" (Gen. 9:6).

A common theme for all three traditions is the idea of humanity as God's viceroy on earth. This idea is deeply embedded in Jewish tradition based on biblical teaching. In Islam, the idea of vice-regency is typically described in terms of caliph. According to Qur'an 2:30, when God announced to the angels, "Lo! I am about to place a viceroy [*khalifah*] in the earth," they demurred and wondered if God knew the risks involved because of the frailty of human nature! In response, the Lord taught them how to name the creatures, and that was a cause of marvel among the angelic beings. By extension, key figures such as Noah are appointed as caliphs as God's prophets and servants (10:71–73). A highly significant implication of the comprehensiveness of the vice-regency is the curious saying of 33:72: "Indeed We offered the Trust to the heavens and the earth and the mountains, but they refused to bear it and were apprehensive of it; but man undertook it." Importantly, the saying continues that the viceregent is "wrongdoer and ignorant" and that God is on the lookout for those who act wrongly (v. 73).[9]

The Embodied Ensouled Human Being: The Jewish Vision

As counterintuitive as it may sound at first, during the early periods of Old Testament history "the Jews were materialists," that is, they hardly had a developed eschatology, and therefore they regarded the blessings of God mainly in terms

---

7. Mohamed, *Fitrah*, 16. See also *Ibn Taymiyyah Expounds on Islam: Selected Writings of Shaykh al-Islam Taqi ad-Din Ibn Taymiyyah*, comp. and trans. Muhammad 'Abdul-Haqq Ansari (Fairfax, VA: Institute of Islamic and Arabic Sciences in America, 2007), 3–4.

8. Sahih Muslim, 32, #6325.

9. For details, see Kenneth Cragg, *The Privilege of Man: A Theme in Judaism, Islam, and Christianity* (London: Athlone Press, 1968), chap. 2.

of earthly goods.[10] A number of older Jewish traditions were influenced deeply by the Platonic tradition, as exemplified in Wisdom of Solomon, including the evil nature of the body (1:3) and the preexistence of the soul (provided it comes from God, 8:13). In Philo, the most famous Hellenistic Jew, the Platonic influence reached its zenith.

Later in tradition, the eleventh-century Spaniard Solomon Ibn Gabirol (a.k.a. Avicebron) creatively engaged the Hellenistic (and also to some extent Islamic) tradition and contributed significantly to issues of self, soul, and personal identity. His *Fountain of Life*[11] suggests a novel form of "materialism" in which, except for God, all substances, whether spiritual or physical, are composed of matter and form. The human soul (like that of the angels) is a kind of "spiritual matter." Avicebron's hylomorphism, thus, is a creative combination of Aristotelianism and Platonism; as in Plato, the soul acts something like the captain of the ship.[12]

The leading medieval Jewish philosopher Moses Maimonides set the tradition firmly in the Aristotelian camp and influenced greatly Christian scholarship. On the one hand, Maimonides builds on the Hebrew Scriptures' emphasis on the integral relationship between body and soul, and on the other hand, he continues the religious/philosophical tradition of allowing some kind of independence to the soul, particularly after death.[13] Postmedieval rabbinic theology in particular came to rediscover not only the anthropomorphic orientation of early tradition but also the importance of the human being's bodily nature for the image of God.

According to the twentieth-century Russian-born American rabbi Samuel S. Cohon, "The Jewish conception of human nature reaches its fullest expression in the belief that man is endowed with a divine soul." The immortal soul (immortality given by God) in the rabbinic teaching is "the life-principle and innermost self of man, [which] reveals and praises God, the abiding principle, the life and mind of the world."[14] Judaism thus operates dualistically, making a distinction between the material and immaterial

---

10. Raymond Martin and John Barresi, *The Rise and Fall of Soul and Self: An Intellectual History of Personal Identity* (New York: Columbia University Press, 2006), 42.

11. http://www.sacred-texts.com/jud/fons/index.htm.

12. Martin and Barresi, *Rise and Fall*, 85.

13. *Eight Chapters of Maimonides on Ethics (Shemonah Perakim)*, trans. and ed. Joseph I. Gorfinkle (New York: Columbia University Press, 1912), 37–46, http://archive.org/stream /eightchaptersofmoomaim#page/n9/mode/2up.

14. Samuel S. Cohon, *Jewish Theology: A Historical and Systematic Interpretation of Judaism and Its Foundations* (Assen, the Netherlands: van Gorcum, 1971), 346.

(spirit, soul) without in any way implying moral dualism of good and evil as in Platonism. This follows the normative rabbinic view of human nature regarding the human person as body and soul, the former linking with the earth, the latter with heaven. While closely related to the body, the soul is also independent and continues after death.[15] That said, Jewish dualism is thoroughly holistic and integral.

The Christian commentator may note several things about Jewish anthropology. First, the Old Testament anthropology, while employing a number of nonanalytic terms, majors in a holistic, embodied view of human nature with due acknowledgment of community and the link with earlier generations. Second, this is in keeping with not only the Old Testament but also the Jewish emphasis on "salvation" in this life, with much less stress on future eschatology than in Christian tradition. Third, like its Christian counterpart, Jewish anthropology was heavily shaped throughout history by influences from philosophical and religious traditions. In sum: it seems to me that a highly integrated hylomorphist account of humanity with the acknowledgment of the soul and belief in the resurrection of the body is an important current Jewish view.

The Human Being as Body and Soul: The Islamic Vision

Although the Islamic view of humanity is realistic, acknowledging many limitations and failures of human nature, the principle of *fitrah*, as discussed above, elevates the human person to a unique place among the creatures.[16] Notwithstanding some exegetical disputes, a number of sayings point to the divinely given status, for example, "Verily We created man in the best of forms" (Q 95:4; also 40:64). The status of human beings also appears in their inviolable dignity and invitation to serve as Allah's viceroy, discussed above. The Qur'anic creation accounts contain several references to humans having been presented before angels before they were created and having been assigned the lofty status of God's coregents (2:34). God's blessings and providence have been lavished upon humanity (7:10; 31:20; 17:70).

The reason the Qur'an (unlike Hadith) dares not to use the Jewish-Christian expression of the image of God is to safeguard the utter transcendence of Allah (42:11). That said, the Qur'an teaches that the Creator is "nearer

---

15. Cohon, *Jewish Theology*, 389–90.
16. Q 4:28; 10:12; 14:34; 16:4; 17:11; 33:72; 70:19; etc.

to him than his jugular vein" (50:16). After all, the human being made of clay is also breathed into by the Spirit of God (15:26–29).[17]

Islamic anthropology is deeply dualistic. The Qur'an and subsequent Islamic theology speak of the soul everywhere. In keeping with Abrahamic faiths, the normative Islamic tradition rejects the eternity and preexistence of the soul.

Aristotle became the guiding philosophical influence in Muslim anthropology. Avicenna (Ibn Sina) and Averroes, the leading scholars, were dualist; body and soul are separate substances, and personality is located in the soul and has its total independence from the body. Gleaning from Platonic sources, Avicenna viewed soul as "an immaterial substance, independent of the body," spiritual in its essential nature.[18] As for earlier influential medieval philosophers in his tradition, for Avicenna reason and intellect are the key aspects of the soul's capacities.[19]

The twelfth century—when a number of Islamic, Jewish, and Greek (Plato, Aristotle) works were translated and disseminated—was a fertile time for continuing interfaith debates about the soul-body problem.[20] Thomas Aquinas and Mulla Sadra, another Muslim authority, were united in criticizing the Neoplatonically based body-soul dualisms in which the body is a mere instrument in the employ of the soul. They put forth a hylomorphic account. Unlike Avicenna, Sadra worked toward a highly integrated body-soul connection.[21]

Generally speaking, current Muslim theology continues affirming traditional body-soul dualism, and only a few individual revisionist scholars have dared to tackle issues such as whether there is a soul in light of scientific knowledge.[22] As is evident from this brief discussion, basic Muslim theological

17. Mona Siddiqui, "Being Human in Islam," in *Humanity: Texts and Context; Christian and Muslim Perspectives*, ed. Michael Ipgrave and David Marshall (Washington, DC: Georgetown University Press, 2011), 16–17.

18. *Avicenna's Psychology* [*De Anima; The Treatise on the Soul*], trans. and ed. Fazlur Rahman (Oxford: Oxford University Press, 1952), 3.

19. Martin and Barresi, *Rise and Fall*, 82–84.

20. Reza Rezazadeh, "Thomas Aquinas and Mulla Sadrá on the Soul-Body Problem: A Comparative Investigation," *Journal of Shi'a Islamic Studies* 4, no. 4 (Autumn 2011): 415–28.

21. Daftari Abdulaziz, "Mulla Sadra and the Mind-Body Problem: A Critical Assessment of Sadra's Approach to the Dichotomy of Soul and Spirit" (PhD diss., Durham University, 2010), http://etheses.dur.ac.uk/506/.

22. For such an example, see Mahmoud Khatami, "On the Transcendental Element of Life: A Recapitulation of Human Spirituality in Islamic Philosophical Psychology," *Journal of Shi'a Islamic Studies* 2, no. 2 (2009): 121–40.

intuitions about humanity are very similar to those of the Christian tradition; the only major exception has to do with the doctrine of sin and the Fall, to be discussed below.

Humanity in Asiatic Traditions

The Many Hindu Visions of Humanity

Hinduism at large envisions *jiva*, "the living being" (sometimes also translated as "soul"), in terms of three bodies, namely, a physical ("gross"), a subtle, and a causal body. The causal body is a kind of "blueprint" that causes the human being to be what it is. The "subtle" body is the "mental" part of human nature with mind, intellect, activity of sense organs, vital energy, and so forth. As long as the human being falsely assumes separate individuality because of *avidya*, "ignorance," and has not yet grasped the insight of the identity of *atman* with Brahman, the subtle body represents the continuity in the process of transmigration (at death, the physical body is left behind and decays).[23]

Consider also the importance of the appearance nature of reality in Hindu cosmology and imagination, discussed in the previous chapter. Envisioning the visible world as merely an appearance of the "real" world of the spirit (ultimately everything is *atman*, that is, Brahman) is of course not to say that therefore the world does not exist; the world exists, but as appearance, and can easily mislead men and women to cling to what is *maya*, transitory and impermanent. Although one has to be careful in maintaining that the Semitic faiths are historical and Hinduism is not, it is also the case that history or embodiment certainly is not at the center of Indian vision.

In light of the appearance nature of reality, it is understandable that foundational to a Hindu understanding of humanity and human nature is the sharp distinction between the *real* self and the *empirical* self that lives in the phenomenal world. Whereas the latter is made of "stuff" such as earth, water, and light, and includes the "subtle body" of vitality (breath, mind, intelligence), it is not the "real" me, contrary to common intuitions. The real self is the *atman*, the eternal and formless, indeed the Brahman ("Spirit," "God," the Divine). This does not of course mean that "I" would not exist at all: even appearances, or dreams, or illusions exist in some sense. What the mainline

23. Arvind Sharma, *Classical Hindu Thought: An Introduction* (Oxford: Oxford University Press, 2000), chap. 10.

Hindu philosophy is saying is that I do not exist "ultimately" or "really." To realize this truth is the key to release.

Here we also come to internal divisions among the Vedanta theologies, already discussed in several contexts. Sankara's *advaita* school argues for an absolute, uncompromising nondualism, and hence, the identity of Brahman (god, divine, "spirit") with *atman* ("self" or "soul"). In contrast to this view, Ramanuja's *visistadvaita* allows for a qualified nondualism that refutes absolute identity between Brahman and *atman*, although it insists on their inseparability. Related to it, Vaishnava traditions, based on the teachings of the Bhagavad Gita, teach the eternity of each individual self.[24] This is taken to mean the existence of an infinite number of selves with no beginning and no end. This interpretation differs from that of *advaita*, according to which only the Absolute Self exists and all other "selves" are but appearances thereof.

The Vaishnavites also believe that the souls are created by God, the Absolute Soul, and are to serve the Lord (Krishna or similar).[25] In this sense, there is some commonality between how the souls are related to Krishna and the relation of individuals to Christ in Christian tradition. And somewhat similarly, Krishna is both unchanging and changing in nature and considers devotees dear to him.[26] While the devotion to Krishna seems to require a continued personal life and some form of embodiment, even the Vaishnava view rejects the idea that the self is to be identified with the material body.

Notwithstanding a wide variety of views among Hindus, it seems to me that Hindu anthropology is deeply dualistic. Consider this summative statement by the late Swami Adiswarananda: "According to Hinduism, man is essentially a soul that uses its body and mind as instruments to gain experience."[27] Part of this teaching is the separation between the apparent and real self as well as the eternity of the "soul." Clearly, these tenets are in deep conflict with all current notions of the natural sciences. Furthermore, the *advaita* view seems irreconcilable to Abrahamic theistic belief due to its ultimate conflating of the divine and the human (pantheism). Finally, Christian anthropology that resists body-soul dualism and lifts up the importance of embodiment and

24. Bhagavad Gita, chap. 2; *SBE* 8 (p. 44): "Never did I not exist, nor you . . . ; nor will any one of us ever hereafter cease to be."

25. Keith Ward, *Religion and Human Nature* (Oxford: Clarendon, 1998), 37-38.

26. The classic passage of devotion is in Gita 3.3.30: "Dedicating all works to Me in a spiritual frame of mind, free from desire, attachment, and mental grief, do your duty"; see also chaps. 12 and 18 (see Ward, *Religion and Human Nature*, 39, 43).

27. Swami Adiswarananda, "Hinduism," part 2 (Ramakrishna-Vivekananda Center of New York, 1996), http://www.ramakrishna.org/activities/message/message15.htm.

sociality definitely looks in the opposite direction from any attempt to divide human nature between the apparent and the real, and to consider the body only as the temporary "tool" of the eternal spirit.

Interdependence, No-Soul, and Dukkha: *The Buddhist Vision*

Three foundational and wide-reaching Buddhist principles govern talk about human nature: the principle of *dukkha*, interdependent origination, and the no-self teaching. The first two have been explained in the previous chapter on creation and will not be repeated here. Concerning the interdependent origination (or causal interdependence), it is essential to recall that it relates not only to the physical but also to other dimensions of reality, including the human.

Not only humans but everything else is impersonal or selfless (*anatta*, "no-self"). "What we call a 'being,' or an 'individual,' or 'I,' according to Buddhist philosophy, is only a combination of ever-changing physical and mental forces or energies."[28] There is no "self" or "soul" that is permanent. Calling the person a "self" is just an elusive, conventional way of referring to that fleeting combination of elements. To be liberated from the illusion of being permanent and hence clinging to something, one needs the "salvific" insight into the true nature of reality and being (release from samsara, the cycle of rebirths).

How would a Christian respond to the Buddhist teaching of no-soul? Keith Ward rightly notes that "from a theistic viewpoint, it will seem to be false that there is no enduring Self and that there is no permanent and noncontingent reality—for God is precisely such a reality." In that sense, "the whole Buddhist world-view and discipline leads away from theism."[29] Indeed, in the absence of self, it is impossible—at least for the Western mind—to imagine "who" is the one who clings to life due to desire, suffers from the effects of karma, and particularly comes to the enlightening realization (if it ever happens) that the samsaric cycle is now overcome. This reflects, it seems to me, a deep and wide difference of orientation between Semitic faiths and Theravada Buddhism, namely, the notion of individuality and the individual's relation to others. Furthermore, it seems impossible to think of ways to affirm the dignity of human personhood if there is nothing "permanent."

28. Walpola Rahula, *What the Buddha Taught*, rev. ed. (New York: Grove, 1974), 20.
29. Keith Ward, *Religion and Revelation: A Theology of Revelation in the World's Religions* (Oxford: Clarendon, 1994), 166.

It is often assumed that the Buddhist notion of humanity is pessimistic and gloomy. But it is not. It is rather realistic. As is well known, Gautama gave a long litany of things in life that are enjoyable and should be enjoyed, from economic security to enjoyment of wealth to happiness on account of living a good life.[30] Indeed, says Rahula, "a true Buddhist is the happiest of beings" because he or she has no fears or anxieties.[31]

What about the Buddhist notion of the nature of human nature in terms of body-soul/physical-spiritual distinctions? On the one hand, the Buddhist view of humanity is deeply holistic and resists dualisms. In keeping with the interrelatedness principles of Buddhist cosmology, all "five constituents" that one is made of interrelate and collaborate. On the other hand, ultimately the spiritual quest turns away from embodiment, and in that sense perennial dualism is present there. What about the soul? Although it is not difficult to establish the usage of the term "soul" in the Buddhist thesaurus, it is difficult to determine its meaning in relation to the typical terminology in Abrahamic faiths and Western philosophical traditions. For example: What is the meaning of "the soul of all sentient beings . . . that constitutes all things in the world"?[32] Hard to tell.

Having compared other religions' conceptions of humanity and human nature with Christian theological vision, we turn to the second part of the chapter, which focuses on the conceptions of sinfulness and corruption in humanity.

What Is Wrong with Us?
Sin and the Fall in Christian Theology

Alongside other Abrahamic traditions, Christian theology considers the human being currently in a state of deviation from original innocence. That said, Christian theology's explanations concerning the origin (and even perhaps the reason) differ drastically from those of even her Jewish counterpart, despite the same scriptural testimony. In Jewish theology Adam's "fall" (Gen. 3) plays no real role. Under the tutelage of former Jewish rabbi Saint Paul the apostle, Christian tradition speaks of the Fall as the origin of sinfulness. Even when, in modern theology, the narrative of Genesis 3 is generally considered a sa-

---

30. See, e.g., Anana Sutta: Debtless (Anguttara Nikaya 4.62).

31. Rahula, *What the Buddha Taught*, 27.

32. See, e.g., *Açvaghosha's Discourse on the Awakening of Faith in the Mahâyâna*, trans. Teitaro Suzuki (1900), II, 53–54, http://sacred-texts.com/bud/taf/index.htm.

cred myth rather than a historical story, the Fall is nevertheless a reality to be reckoned with. Islam shows even more distance from any theology of the Fall, despite the Qur'an's three references to a Genesis 3–type of narrative.

That said, Christian theology itself has no canonical account of sin and the Fall, despite the universal affirmation of the presence of sinfulness. In Western Christianity (Roman Catholicism, Protestantism, and Anglicanism), the Fall plays a significant role as the backdrop for sinfulness leading to divine judgment apart from God's grace. Many Western theologians also know the concept of "total depravity," a stark account of the influence of the Fall. Yet, that does not eradicate the image of God. Notwithstanding differences in nuances, most Western churches teach the transmission of sin from generation to generation. Although Roman Catholics consider fallen humanity lost apart from grace, in their understanding the capacity to choose between evil and good is not totally lost.

Among Eastern Orthodox churches, the idea of fall is depicted rather in terms of "children" (Adam and Eve) failing, in need of maturity and development. Eastern theology also insists on the freedom of will to choose between evil and good. Yet, even there it acknowledges sinfulness.

The acknowledgment of sinfulness leads all Christian churches to reject salvation by human means; only God is able to save.

The Human Condition in Religions' Visions

Sinfulness of Humanity in Abrahamic Traditions

Commonalities and Differences

As mentioned, among the Semitic faiths, there is no unified conception of human misery. Jewish and Muslim theologies insist on human freedom to choose and responsibility for one's choice. That said, all sister faiths place the discussion of sin in relation to God and derivatively in the human domain. All of them, though somewhat differently, consider the "origin" of sinfulness in the deviation of humanity from the Creator.

Not surprisingly, all three scriptural traditions therefore share the common narrative of the Fall and its consequences, even though their interpretations differ from one another quite dramatically. In many ways, Jewish and Muslim interpretations share more in common with each other than Christian interpretations do with the other two.

Good and Evil Inclinations in Jewish Tradition

Jewish theologians acknowledge that the Genesis 3 story contains "no doctrine of the fall of the race through Adam, of the moral corruption of human nature, or of the hereditary transmission of the sinful bias."[33] Adam plays no role in the rest of the Old Testament story. Jewish tradition also rejects his immortality before the Fall.

Instead of original sin, the Jewish (rabbinic) tradition speaks of two tendencies or urges in every human being, namely, *yetzer ha tov* and *yetzer ha ra'*, for good and evil, respectively. Even though the "inclination" to evil in itself is not evil, it is a matter of which of the two is the guiding force in life. Hence, the main term for repentance from evil is *teshuvav*, literally, "turning."[34] Every human being is engaged in a constant fight between the two urges.

This is not to undermine the seriousness of the sinful tendency. Just think of how radically the Yahwist account in Genesis speaks of the wide diffusion of moral evil (chap. 4; 6:5–12; 8:21; 9:20–27; 11:1–9). According to the biblical testimonies, human wickedness is great, and even the imaginations of the heart are evil (6:5; 8:21).

In other words, the evil urge is present at birth. But each person is responsible for sinful behavior; such responsibility is not inherited. Although the evil inclination plagues the human person, it neither robs the person of all moral integrity nor causes lostness, as in Christian tradition. It is of utmost importance for Judaism to affirm the freedom from depravity and innate evil of human nature despite the serious inclination toward evil. Second Baruch (54:15, 19; 19:3; 48:42–43; 59:2) teaches that even after Adam's sin, which brought about death, each new generation has to choose their own path.

That much can be said in general about traditional interpretation in Judaism. There are also differences of orientation. At the beginning of Christianity, at least three somewhat different conceptions of sin fought for recognition in rabbinic theology: first, corruption of humanity as hereditary; second, a vague connection between Adam's sin and subsequent generations' liability to punishment; and third, all sin as the fruit of the human person's own actions. Whereas the rabbinic tradition operated mainly, though not exclusively, with the third paradigm, Pauline and subsequent Christian tradition went with

---

33. Samuel S. Cohon, *Essays in Jewish Theology* (Cincinnati: Hebrew Union College Press, 1987), 220.

34. Louis Jacobs, *A Jewish Theology* (London: Darton, Longman & Todd, 1973), 243.

the first two (with the exception of Eastern Christianity, which also wanted to include key elements of the third).[35]

Both Jewish and Christian traditional ways of reading the Genesis narrative have undergone radical revisions as a result of the scientific advances concerning human evolution. At the same time, for the continuing dialogue to be meaningful, the differences between *theological* interpretations of the effects and the "source" of human sinfulness should be acknowledged.

Free Will and Human Disobedience in Islam

The Islamic tradition never envisioned Adam and Eve in terms of perfect paradise imagery after Christian tradition. Its account of humanity is realistic, as illustrated in Qur'an 95:4–6: "Verily We created man in the best of forms. Then, We reduced him to the lowest of the low, except those who believe and perform righteous deeds, for they shall have an unfailing reward." In a number of places the Qur'an speaks of weaknesses, frailties, and liabilities of humanity.[36] That said, according to mainline Muslim teaching, human nature is, generally speaking, good—or, at least, it is not sinful and corrupted, as in Christian teaching.

Although Islamic tradition, similarly to others, has had internal debates, particularly with regard to the presence or lack of evil inclinations, the normal Islamic theology assumes a more or less neutral view that takes the beginning of human life as a blank slate, thus emphasizing the role of free will—not unlike Christian Pelagianism. The mainline teaching in tradition and contemporary Islamic theology is by and large the "positive view"[37] of human nature.

That the Qur'an does not know the doctrine of original sin or the idea of moral depravity[38] does not mean that the concept of "fall" is not part of the Muslim tradition. The fall narrative can of course be found in the Qur'an—indeed, in three related narratives.[39] But its implications (like Judaism's) differ from those of Christian theology. In the (chronologically) earliest narrative

35. Cohon, *Essays in Jewish Theology*, 240–70.

36. Q 4:28; 10:12; 14:34; 16:4; 17:11; 33:72; 70:19; 96:6; 103:2.

37. See chap. 2 of Mohamed, *Fitrah*.

38. Muhammad Iqbal, *The Reconstruction of Religious Thought in Islam* (Lahore: Ashraf, 1960), 85.

39. For a detailed discussion, see Torsten Löfstedt, "The Creation and Fall of Adam: A Comparison of the Qur'anic and Biblical Accounts," *Swedish Missiological Themes* 93, no. 4 (2005): 453–77.

(20:115–27), after becoming forgetful of the covenant, all angels were invited by God to prostrate themselves before Adam, and they did, but Satan (named Iblis), who then promised to take Adam and Eve to the tree of immortality and knowledge, declined. They ate the fruit, became ashamed, and tried covering themselves with leaves. "And Adam disobeyed his Lord and so he erred" (v. 121). God called Adam again and advised him to leave the garden that had now become an "enemy" (obviously because Satan was said to be there, v. 117). God promised to guide the human or else blindness would follow for the one who previously was able to see. The punishment of blindness would be revealed on the day of resurrection, and even more severe forms of punishment might follow.

The later account in 2:30–38 repeats very closely the Genesis 3 story with only a few significant deviations. The third major passage, 7:10–25, speaks of the disobedient nature of Adam in starker terms and also mentions his leaving the garden in more certain terms (v. 27). Furthermore, all the accounts speak of enmity and distress as a result of the disobedience for which Adam himself (rather than Satan or Eve) is mainly responsible (albeit tempted and lured by Satan).

What is totally missing in Islamic theology of sin is the idea of transmission of "original sin" from one generation to another and its punitive effect on the progeny. Adam (along with Eve and Satan) himself is to be blamed for disobedience, not later generations. Importantly, the Qur'anic narrative does not link the Fall with lostness, as does Christian tradition.

The Human Condition in the Vision of Asiatic Faiths

Craving and *Dukkha*: The Buddhist Analysis

Gautama once used the simile of cloth to illustrate the difference between the pure mind and the defiled mind. The impure cloth absorbs all bad into its fabric, the end result of which is "an unhappy destination [in a future existence]," whereas a happy future awaits the pure minded. Particularly dangerous, so Buddha teaches, is the appeal of sensuality in its many forms.[40] With right knowledge and true effort, purification from all defilement can be attained. Even when the devotee looks upon the example of the Buddha, finds teaching in *dhamma*, and has the community of *sangha*, one is one's own savior.

---

40. Maha-dukkhakkhandha Sutta: The Great Mass of Stress of Majjhima Nikaya 13.

Following the *dukkha* principle, the persistent force of craving not only clings to life in general but is also accompanied with greed, hatred, and delusion. Although the craving and passion may be most intense, behind the human misery, *dukkha*, is the yearning to cling to what is merely fleeting, decaying, impermanent. That is the main problem for humans.

Whence this (evil) craving? As with all other topics, Buddha declined from speculating and rather focused on defeating it with the help of moral pursuit and right insight. (That there are in the Pali Canon mythical stories of the origins of craving does not change theologically the main orientation.)

From the Christian perspective, the only thing these two traditions have in common is the universal human condition as something requiring liberation, insight, or salvation. But both the diagnosis, as explained, and its remedy, as will be discussed in the chapter on salvation below, are radically different.

Ignorance and "Superimposition": The Hindu Diagnosis

The beginning point for the generic consideration of "sin"—human misery—in Hinduism at large is the notion of *dharma*, the positive standard against which all deviations must be compared. It is the "duty," the correct way of life, including all activities and spheres of life. Its opposite is *adharma*.

Somewhat similarly to Buddhism, Hindu traditions have developed detailed lists of vices to avoid, including delusion, greed, and anger, the roots of all vices.[41] Not unlike most religious traditions, Hinduism makes a distinction between great and lesser sins. The most grievous offense is the killing of Brahmin, which is unforgivable and occasion for the death penalty. Other examples of a great sin include drinking intoxicating beverages and stealing. In principle all great sins are unpardonable, with no possibility for atonement. For lesser sins, penance and atonement may be available. In keeping with the caste system, killing a person of a lower caste might be a less severe crime than slaughtering a cow![42]

Although there is some commonality with the Abrahamic faiths' conception of sin, the difference also runs deep. Whereas sin is ultimately transgression against God, *adharma* is basically a deviation from the "impersonal" law of the cosmos, reality.

41. Bhagavad Gita 16; *SBE* 8:114–17.
42. Klaus Klostermaier, *A Survey of Hinduism*, 3rd ed. (Albany: State University of New York Press, 2010), 141–46.

Adharma must be put in the wider context of Hindu philosophy of human "bondage" to *avidya*, "ignorance." Ignorance makes one cling to *maya*, "fiction," and thus be subject to effects of karma, leading to rebirths over and over again. Only with the removal of this "ignorance" can souls' essential nature as pure spirits be restored.[43]

Living faith traditions not only make claims about human misery and liberation from it, they also envision what would bring about release or salvation. That topic will be discussed in detail in chapter 8 below. Before getting there, following the logic of Christian theology with its focus on the Trinitarian God as the source, salvation, and consummation of human life, the next two chapters consider whether other faith traditions have any corresponding notion of Savior. Whereas the chapter that immediately follows focuses on Christology proper, to use classical Christian parlance, that is, the person and activity of Jesus Christ, chapter 6 zooms in on what is called "atonement" in traditional theological language and "reconciliation" here. That discussion leads to—again following Christian logic—the consideration of the third member of the Trinity, the Holy Spirit, and then salvation, wrought by the Son in his suffering, death, and resurrection, delivered by the same Spirit.

43. See further, Klostermaier, *Survey of Hinduism*, chap. 13.

5 | Jesus Christ and "Savior" Figures among Religions

Christian Christology in a Nutshell

The New Testament takes up the diverse and complex messianic expectations of the Jewish Torah and applies them to a historical person, Jesus of Nazareth, the Christian Messiah. Unlike in Jewish tradition, in the New Testament the Messiah is not only a divine figure but also deity, alongside the Father and Spirit. While the Synoptic Gospels present Jesus of Nazareth as a man sent by God to preach and call to repentance in submission to God's will, to heal and restore, as well as to liberate from oppressing powers, the (chronologically) first New Testament author, Paul, articulates a more theologically astute description of this God-man. John's Gospel also makes a significant contribution in speaking of the divine Word (*Logos*), an alleged reference to Christ's deity, as having become one of us (1:14).

The early creedal statements, in debate with what came to be determined heretical deviations from orthodoxy, sought to summarize and defend the incipient and narrative Christian theology of Christ in a more formal manner.[1] Notwithstanding centuries-long and still continuing debates about details, the following tenets of Christology are universally embraced by all churches: that Jesus Christ

---

1. The so-called Apostles' Creed from the third century, Nicene(-Constantinopolitan) Creed of 371, and Chalcedonian Creed (451) are considered binding by all Christians, notwithstanding a number of debates about details.

- is the second person of the Trinity, became truly human in the form of Jesus of Nazareth, and is confessed to be true man (human) and God (divine), of one "essence" with the Father and the Spirit (without the three being confused with each other or separated, though distinguished from each other);
- was conceived by the Holy Spirit and was born of the Virgin Mary;
- was sinless as totally obedient Son to the Father and by virtue of being divine;
- suffered as the innocent one, died on the cross, was buried, descended into "hell," and was raised to new life by his Father in the power of the Spirit, for our salvation; and
- subsequently ascended into heaven and now rules at the right hand of the Father and will return to establish God's kingdom, the righteous rule, and so help consummate the triune God's eternal purposes.

That the creeds do not speak of Jesus of Nazareth's earthly life and ministry with authoritative teaching, healings, exorcisms, and other miraculous acts is most likely because they were assumed and not contested among the opponents.

With the rise of modern biblical and dogmatic criticism most of these core beliefs came to be contested and even rejected, resulting in wide disagreements and debates in recent centuries, but this has not overruled the foundational importance of these classic christological doctrines. Still, it has to be mentioned that against this "high Christology" of the tradition, the modernist "low Christology" has little use for ancient beliefs in divinity, preexistence, and other god-like conceptions, and rather considers the meaning of Jesus Christ as a this-worldly ("immanentist") teacher, reformer, and visionary. This bifurcation with many sub-schools continues to characterize the contemporary theological scene and faith.

The comparative work in this chapter will begin with the closest tradition, the Jewish, to be followed by Islam. Thereafter, we will engage the two Asiatic faiths. As mentioned, the next chapter (6) continues christological themes but with a focus on the salvific effects of Jesus Christ's work ("atonement").

The Jewish Messiah—the Christian Messiah

Mutual Polemics and Misinterpretations

"When one asks the basic question of what separates Jews and Christians from each other, the unavoidable answer is: a Jew." This is the striking note from a Jewish New Testament scholar who is deeply engaged in dialogue with Christians, Pinchas Lapide. He continues: "For almost two millennia, a pious, devoted Jew has stood between us, a Jew who wanted to bring the kingdom of heaven in harmony, concord, and peace—certainly not hatred, schism, let alone bloodshed."[2] Yet another Jewish theologian, Susannah Heschel, reminds us that during the past two millennia, "Jews rejected the claim that Jesus fulfilled the messianic prophecies of the Hebrew Bible, as well as the dogmatic claims about him made by the church fathers—that he was born of a virgin, the son of God, part of a divine Trinity, and was resurrected after his death."[3]

It is one of the grand ironies of Christian history that for the first eighteen hundred years or more, Jewish theologians by and large ignored Christianity and particularly its claim that Jesus is the Messiah. We had to wait virtually until the twentieth century to have thoughtful Jewish responses to Christian messianism and Christology. Mutual polemics rather than seasoned dialogue had been the order of the day until then. The few writings by Jews on Jesus before that were mostly ignored by Christians. On the other side, Jewish interpretations of Jesus were (often intentionally) biased and skewed, going beyond authoritative original sources. It was not uncommon, for example, to attribute Jesus's miracles to sorcery rather than to God. A rare irenic exception to the polemics is the argument of the leading medieval Jewish theologian, Moses Maimonides, that not only Christianity but also Islam is part of the divine plan to prepare the world for the reception of the message of the biblical God; that said, he also considered Jesus of Nazareth a kind of heretic.[4]

The rabbinical writings—highly formative for most brands of Jewish tradition—present a definite and direct rebuttal of the claim to the divine Sonship of Jesus, "a blasphemy against the Jewish understanding of God." The Christian doctrines of the incarnation, atonement through the cross, and of course the Trinity, among others, "remained alien to normative Judaism and taboo to the rabbis."[5] That said, it is significant that even with the harshening of tone in later levels of the Talmud, the opposition was less targeted against

---

2. Pinchas Lapide, *The Resurrection of Jesus: A Jewish Perspective* (Minneapolis: Augsburg, 1983), 30.

3. Susannah Heschel, "Jewish Views of Jesus," in *JWF*, 149.

4. This paragraph is based on Heschel, "Jewish Views of Jesus," 149–51. For an informed discussion of several Jewish theologians of Christianity from three different time periods, see chap. 3 in Michael S. Kogan, *Opening the Covenant: A Jewish Theology of Christianity* (Oxford: Oxford University Press, 2008).

5. Pinchas Lapide, *Israelis, Jews, and Jesus*, trans. Peter Heinegg (Garden City, NY: Doubleday, 1979), 76–77.

the historical figure of Jesus of Nazareth and more against what was considered to be Pauline Christology and the subsequent patristic and creedal tradition. That became the focal point of opposition, at times even anger, among the formative Jewish writings.[6]

Somewhat similarly to early Muslim polemicists, medieval Jewish writers such as the legendary rabbi Saadia Gaon (d. 942), in his famous "Book of Beliefs and Opinions," paid close attention to different christological traditions among different churches and came to the conclusion that it was impossible to arrive at a single, uniform picture of Jesus.[7] The subtext of this observation is of course not to highlight only the inconsistency of Christian theology of the Messiah but also its self-contradictory nature.

Modern Attempts toward a Better Understanding

In the aftermath of the Enlightenment, and with the newly opening opportunities for Jews to participate in the wider European societies, interest in Jesus emerged, partly to help justify Judaism as a religion. Another famous Moses, namely, Mendelssohn, painted a picture of Jesus as a thoroughly Jewish religious figure, so much so that, "closely examined, everything is in complete agreement not only with Scripture, but also with the [Jewish] tradition."[8] Similarly influential nineteenth-century Jesus scholar Abraham Geiger[9] and the famous liberal rabbi of Stockholm, Sweden, Gottlieb Klein, at the turn of the twentieth century, stressed the thoroughly Jewish nature of Jesus and his self-understanding.[10] Encouraged by the quest of the historical Jesus and classical liberalism's subsequent interest in the "real" Jesus, divorced from the layers of dogmatic and creedal traditions, the Jewish quest for Jesus as a Jew was energized. Different from the "Jewish Jesus" paradigm, the first modern study on Jesus written in Hebrew, by Joseph Klausner, *Jesus of Nazareth: His Life, Times,*

6. Lapide, *Israelis, Jews, and Jesus*, 77.

7. See Lapide, *Israelis, Jews, and Jesus*, 86.

8. Moses Mendelssohn, *Jerusalem; or, On Religious Power and Judaism*, trans. Allan Arkush (Hanover, NH: University Press of New England), 134, cited in Heschel, "Jewish Views of Jesus," 151.

9. For Jewish scholars engaging Christian Christology, see Susannah Heschel, *Abraham Geiger and the Jewish Jesus* (Chicago: University of Chicago Press, 1998); Heschel, "Jewish Views of Jesus," 152.

10. Donald A. Hagner, *The Jewish Reclamation of Jesus: An Analysis and Critique of the Modern Jewish Study of Jesus* (Grand Rapids: Zondervan, 1984).

and Teaching, presented him as a Pharisee who "departed the boundaries of Jewish nationhood, implying that Jews who reject Zionism, end up like Jesus, as Christians."[11]

There were two agendas or at least effects of the modern Jewish reclamation of Jesus. First, there was the task of correcting the misrepresentation of earlier Jewish sources: "During late antiquity and the Middle Ages, Jews had commonly caricatured Jesus as a sorcerer who had attempted to beguile the Jewish people and lead them astray. The modern Jewish scholarly reassessment stripped away such earlier misconceptions, restored respectability to Jesus' image, and then reclaimed him as a Jew who merited a rightful place in Jewish literature alongside those of ancient Jewish sages."[12]

Second, although the emphasis on Jesus's Jewishness was in keeping with the Christian quest, the Jewish search for the Jewish Jesus also wanted to develop "a counterhistory of the prevailing Christian theological version of Christianity's origins and influence."[13]

Among the Christian students of Jesus Christ, recent decades have brought about an unprecedented interest in the Jewishness of Jesus, beginning with the first generation of the "New Perspective (on Paul)" in the 1970s. Conversely, it is remarkable that some contemporary Jewish scholars are now arguing that what happened with the rise of Christianity was not "the parting of ways" and that Judaism was not the "mother" religion out of which the younger religion emerged. Rather, both religions emerged simultaneously within the matrix of the Mediterranean world.[14]

Whether Christology Is Inherently Anti-Semitic

Anti-Semitism has a sad and long track record in Christian tradition. It goes all the way from the church fathers, to the Reformers, to twentieth-century theologians, and includes even the highest-ranking church leaders such as numerous popes. Alone, the destruction of Jerusalem by the gentiles in 70 CE should have led Christians to reach out to their suffering Jewish brothers and sisters in sympathy and love—yet it did not!

11. As paraphrased by Heschel, "Jewish Views of Jesus," 156.

12. Michael J. Cook, "Jewish Perspectives on Jesus," in *The Blackwell Companion to Jesus*, ed. Delbert Burkett (Oxford: Wiley-Blackwell, 2011), 224.

13. Heschel, "Jewish Views of Jesus," 152.

14. Adam H. Becker and Annette Yoshiko Reed, eds., *The Ways That Never Parted: Jews and Christians in Late Antiquity and the Early Middle Ages* (Tübingen: Mohr Siebeck, 2003).

More than the acknowledgment of this sad history of violence against the Jews, there is a suspicion among many current Christian theologians that something in Christian faith makes it inherently anti-Semitic. Particularly Christology has been named as the source of that attitude. These thinkers consider the New Testament and the way Christian theology has interpreted it as inherently anti-Semitic. The most vocal among those critics is the feminist Rosemary Radford Ruether, who argues in her *Faith and Fratricide: The Theological Roots of Anti-Semitism* that anti-Judaism is the result of what she calls the "left hand" of Christian Christology.[15] Ruether wonders if it is possible to confess Jesus as Messiah without at the same time saying that "the Jews be damned."[16] She opines that because anti-Judaism is intimately intertwined with the christological hermeneutic of the early church, the only way to purge it is to radically reconceive Christology along two lines. First, faith in Jesus as the Christ must be understood as proleptic and anticipatory rather than final and fulfilled. Second, Christology must be understood paradigmatically rather than exclusivistically: "The cross and the resurrection are contextual to a particular historical community."[17] Hence, in this outlook, Jesus's paradigmatic role should be abandoned in order to avoid a supersessionist Christology.

Ruether's presuppositions and charges against the New Testament are sweeping and unnuanced, and they ignore different types of christological trajectories and traditions and their complex and complicated development in the canon. The Jewish scholar Thomas A. Idinopulos and the Christian Roy Bowen Ward carefully investigated Ruether's claims and concluded that "the appearance of anti-Judaic thought in certain documents in the New Testament does not lead to the conclusion that anti-Judaism is necessarily the left hand of christology." They looked carefully at the parable of the vineyard in Mark 12, which Ruether considers a showcase for inherent anti-Jewishness and the beginning of anti-Semitism in the New Testament, and they came to contest Ruether's interpretation.[18]

A critical investigation of the seemingly most anti-Jewish passage in the Pauline corpus, 1 Thessalonians 2:14–16 ("the Jews, who killed both the Lord

---

15. Rosemary Radford Ruether, *Faith and Fratricide: The Theological Roots of Anti-Semitism* (New York: Seabury, 1974); chap. 2 focuses on the anti-Jewish materials in the New Testament.

16. Ruether, *Faith and Fratricide*, 246.

17. Ruether, *To Change the World: Christology and Cultural Criticism* (New York: Crossroad, 1981), 43.

18. Thomas A. Idinopulos and Roy Bowen Ward, "Is Christology Inherently Anti-Semitic? A Critical Review of Rosemary Ruether's *Faith and Fratricide*," *Journal of the American Academy of Religions* 45, no. 2 (1977): 196.

Jesus and the prophets"), another key passage for Ruether, similarly does not support her reasoning. First of all, the interpretation of that passage is full of problems and unanswered questions of which Ruether seems to be ignorant. One of her omissions is that in the Thessalonian correspondence Paul is talking to a gentile audience rather than to Jews; in Romans, Paul clarifies in no uncertain terms his understanding of the continuing special status granted to the chosen people. Idinopulos and Ward conclude:

> It is difficult to understand how Ruether can conclude that "Judaism for Paul is not only *not* an ongoing covenant of salvation where men continue to be related in true worship of God: it never was such a community of faith and grace." It is only Gentiles, not Jews, that Paul characterized as those who "knew not God." Paul himself boasts of his Jewishness and can even say that "as to righteousness under the law [he was] blameless" (Phil 3:6). He never says that Judaism was a false worship of God; rather, he claims that a new righteousness has been revealed (Rom 1:17; 3:21; 10:3) which causes him to move into a new phase in the history of salvation. Nor does his acceptance of the gospel lead him to deny the holiness of the law (Rom 7:12) nor the election of the Jews (Rom 11:28). It is difficult to see how Paul is any more anti-Judaic than other Jewish sectarians such as those at Qumran, who like Paul, believed that God was doing a new thing in the history of salvation. Unlike the Qumran sectarians who expected the destruction of "Mainstream" Jews (whom the sectarians considered apostate), Paul hoped for/expected the salvation of all Israel (Rom 11:26).[19]

There is also an important difference between the time prior to and the time following the destruction of Jerusalem in 70 CE, which, according to common theological wisdom, has to do with the worsening relations between the Christian church and the Jews. Whereas in the earlier part of the New Testament ("earlier" in time of writing), such as most of the Pauline correspondence, there is very little in terms of attributing the death of Jesus to Jews, in the Christian writings after the disaster, motivated by Christians' desire to distance themselves from the Jews and so show evidence of alliance with Rome, the tone gets harsher. The apocryphal Gospel of Peter relates the crucifixion in a way that basically removes the Romans from the scene and

---

19. Idinopulos and Ward, "Is Christology Inherently Anti-Semitic?," 198–99; citation in the text from Ruether, *Faith and Fratricide*, 104.

leaves the responsibility for it to the Jews.[20] Even if the nuances of this common interpretation may be debated, it cannot be ignored, as Ruether does.

Yet another historical observation has to be considered before charging the birth of anti-Semitism to the New Testament; it is that anti-Jewish attitudes precede Christianity. The Jewish thinker Salo Baron speaks for many when he states the commonplace fact that "almost every note in the cacophony of medieval and modern anti-Semitism was sounded by the chorus of ancient writers."[21] This is of course not to absolve Christians of the guilt of anti-Semitism—far from that. But it is to put the question under consideration in perspective.

In criticizing the unnuanced attribution of anti-Jewish attitudes to the New Testament, I do not deny the "hardening of attitudes"[22] toward the Jews in Matthew or the quite negative presentation of the Jews in the Gospel of John (however the dating of these documents goes). This criticism of Jewish people, usually their religious leaders, however, must be put in proper perspective. The Matthean critique of the Jewish people, especially in chapter 23, is not necessarily any different from or untypical of the harsh criticism of one Jewish group by another Jewish group at the time.[23] Even when the whole people is addressed, usually the target of the criticism is the religious or political leadership that is deviating from the will of God.

The late New Testament scholar Raymond Brown reminds us that at first "there was nothing anti-Jewish in depicting the role of the Jewish authorities in his death: for Jesus and his disciples on one side and the Jerusalem Sanhedrin authorities on the other were all Jews." Only later was the passion narrative "'heard' in an anti-Jewish way." The change into the predominantly gentile composition of the church of course was a main factor here.[24] Brown also remarks that a careful comparison of the gospel narratives of crucifixion oscil-

---

20. So, e.g., Birger Pearson, "I Thessalonians 2:13–16: A Deutero-Pauline Interpolation," *Harvard Theological Review* 64 (1971): 79–94.

21. Salo W. Baron, *A Social and Religious History of the Jews* (New York: Columbia University Press, 1951), 1:194, cited in Idinopulos and Ward, "Is Christology Inherently Anti-Semitic?," 200. For a careful discussion of anti-Semitism before Christianity and its continuation apart from Christianity, see Edward H. Flannery, *The Anguish of the Jews: Twenty-Three Centuries of Antisemitism*, rev. ed. (New York: Paulist, 1985 [1971]).

22. Ruether, *Faith and Fratricide*, 75.

23. Raymond E. Brown, *An Introduction to the New Testament* (New York: Doubleday, 1997), 222; for a detailed discussion, see Luke T. Johnson, "The New Testament's Anti-Jewish Slander and the Conventions of Ancient Polemic," *Journal of Biblical Literature* 108 (1989): 419–41.

24. Brown, *Introduction to the New Testament*, 166–67.

lates between making the Romans (gentiles) responsible for and executors of the crucifixion and blaming the Jewish authorities.[25] Hence, it is an unfounded charge by Ruether that John's Gospel makes the blame of the Jews "very close to what will become the charge of 'deicide'"[26]—that the Jews are "murderers" of God's Son—even though that accusation became a commonplace throughout history in the mouths of Christians.

As mentioned, the question of the Messiah is central to these two faiths. Let us take a closer look at it.

Why Has the Messiah Not Yet Come in Jewish Expectation?

The Christian theologian J. Moltmann aptly sets the stage for contemporary consideration of the role and meaning of Messiah between these two religions: "The gospels understand his [Jesus Christ's] whole coming and ministry in the contexts of Israel's messianic hope. Yet it is the very same messianic hope which apparently makes it impossible for 'all Israel' to see Jesus as being already the messiah."[27] Hence, every Christian theology of Christ should seek to consider and respond, if possible, to the Jewish no to the New Testament Messiah. Martin Buber formulated the Jewish objection in 1933 in dialogue with the New Testament scholar Karl-Ludwig Schmidt:

> We know more deeply, more truly, that world history has not been turned upside down to its very foundations—that the world is not yet redeemed. We *sense* its unredeemedness. The church can, or indeed must, understand this sense of ours as the awareness that *we* are not redeemed. But we know that that is not it. The redemption of the world is for us indivisibly one with the perfecting of creation, with the establishment of the unity which nothing more prevents, the unity which is no longer controverted, and which is realized in all the protean variety of the world. Redemption is one with the kingdom of God in its fulfillment. An anticipation of any single part of the *completed* redemption of the world . . . is something we cannot grasp, although even for us in our mortal hours redeeming and redemp-

25. Brown, *Introduction to the New Testament*, 39; see also Raymond E. Brown, *The Death of the Messiah: From Gethsemane to the Grave* (New York: Doubleday, 1994), 1:388, 396, 831–39.

26. Ruether, *Faith and Fratricide*, 114.

27. Jürgen Moltmann, *The Way of Jesus Christ: Christology in Messianic Dimensions*, trans. Margaret Kohl (Minneapolis: Fortress, 1993 [1989]), 28.

tion are heralded. . . . We are aware of no centre in history—only its goal, the goal of the way taken by the God who does not linger on his way.[28]

Many other Jewish thinkers have expressed the same sentiment. In the words of Schalom Ben-Chorin, the Jewish mind is "profoundly aware of the unredeemed character of the world," which means that the "whole of redemption" has not yet taken place since the Messiah has not yet arrived.[29] Behind the Jewish no to the Christian claim for the arrival of the Messiah is hence a different concept of redemption. Rightly or wrongly, Jewish theology considers the Christian version of redemption "happening in the spiritual sphere, and in what is invisible,"[30] whereas for Jewish hopes, it is the transformation happening in the most visible and concrete ways, including the removal of all evil.

Without downplaying and certainly not dismissing this profound difference in understanding of what the coming of Messiah and the ensuing redemption mean, Moltmann poses the question to the Jewish counterpart that needs to be asked here. This is the "gentile" question to the Jews: "*Even before the world has been redeemed so as to become the direct and universal rule of God, can God already have a chosen people, chosen moreover for the purpose of this redemption?*" Furthermore: "Does Israel's election not destroy Israel's solidarity with the unredeemed humanity, even if the election is meant in a representative sense?" All this boils down, says Moltmann, to the simple and profound query: "can one already be *a Jew* in this Godless world?"[31]

Another important counterquestion—or, more irenically, invitation to mutual dialogue—has to do with the one-sided, if not reductionistic, interpretation by Jewish theology of the Christian hope for redemption. As will be discussed in the next chapter on the many dimensions and metaphors of atonement, Christian theology is not bound to limit redemption only to the inner personal and invisible notion. Christian eschatological hope, focused on the crucified and risen Messiah who now rules with the Father and Spirit, includes the total transforma-

28. Martin Buber, *Der Jude und Sein Judentum: Gesammelte Aufsätze und Reden* (Cologne: n.p., 1963), 562, cited in Moltmann, *Way of Jesus Christ*, 28–29. See also Martin Buber, "The Two Foci of the Jewish Soul," in *Israel and the World: Essays in a Time of Crisis* (New York: Schocken Books, 1963), 28–40. For an informed discussion of Buber's views in this respect by a contemporary Jewish theologian, see Kogan, *Opening the Covenant*, 90–95.

29. Schalom Ben-Chorin, *Die Antwort des Jona, zum Gestaltwandel Israels* (Hamburg: n.p., 1956), 99, cited in Moltmann, *Way of Jesus Christ*, 30.

30. Gershom Scholem, "Zum Verständnis der messianischen Idee," *Judaica* 1 (Frankfurt: n.p., 1963), 7, cited in Moltmann, *Way of Jesus Christ*, 30.

31. Moltmann, *Way of Jesus Christ*, 30.

tion of the world, a foretaste of which has already come in this messianic age.[32] Yes, a great difference between the expectation and full realization still continues: whereas Jewish theology discerns the coming of Messiah as the fulfillment of all hopes for redemption, Christian tradition—slowly and painfully, as New Testament eschatology shows—came to understand the coming of Messiah in two stages. The consummation of redemption is yet to come. That difference must be acknowledged and honored, but it doesn't have to block continuing dialogue.

With the Christian idea of incarnation in mind, a comparative theologian may wonder if the idea of God taking human form is absolutely unknown to Jewish faith. While most Jews think it is, some current theologians are willing to look for parallels, such as "God walking in the garden" (Gen. 3:8), or the Lord appearing to Abraham in the form of the angel and sharing a meal (Gen. 18), or Jacob's wrestling match with a man of whom he says, "I have seen God face to face" (Gen. 32:24, 30), or Israelite leaders under Moses claiming that they "saw the God of Israel" on the mountain (Exod. 24:9–11). The Jewish scholar Michael S. Kogan draws a conclusion from these kinds of texts: "For Jewish believers, then, the thought may come to mind that, if God can take human form in a series of accounts put forward in one's own sacred texts, one would be unjustified in dismissing out of hand the possibility that the same God might act in a similar fashion in accounts put forward in another text revered as sacred by a closely related tradition."[33] This is of course not to push the similarities too far; the differences are obvious, particularly in light of Christian creedal traditions that speak of the permanent "personal" (hypostatic) union of the human and divine in one particular person, Jesus of Nazareth. But it nevertheless points to the possibility of early Christians making such claims while still not leaving behind the confession of faith in the unity of the God of Israel.

The Holocaust and the Suffering Messiah

Over the resurgence of interest in Jesus among Jewish scholars and the heightened Christian interest in the Jewishness of Jesus looms large the shadow of the horrors and crimes of the Holocaust.[34] It is a continuing task for Christian

---

32. See further, Moltmann, *Way of Jesus Christ*, 30–32.

33. Kogan, *Opening the Covenant*, 115. For a highly promising and constructive essay on Jewish views of incarnation, see Elliot R. Wolfson, "Judaism and Incarnation: The Imaginal Body of God," in *Christianity in Jewish Terms*, ed. Tikva Frymer-Kensky et al. (Boulder, CO: Westview, 2000), 239–53.

34. Consult C. Klein, *Anti-Judaism in Christian Theology*, trans. Edward Quinn (Phila-

theology to more fully understand how it was ever possible for such a horrendous ethos to develop in "Christian" soil. Christian theology in general and Christology in particular must resist any notion of imperialism, whether in terms of political hegemony and crimes against the Jewish people as under the Nazi regime, or in terms of "realized eschatology" claiming the eschatological glory and rule already now. The Messiah confessed in Christian theology is the crucified one "who heals through his wounds and is victorious through his sufferings . . . the Lamb of God, not yet the Lion of Judah."[35]

This kind of "theology of the cross" makes it possible for Christian theology to tolerate and appreciate the Jewish "no" rather than assuming, as has happened in Christian history, that God has abandoned the people of Israel because of their reluctance to acknowledge the Messiah.

> The Christian "yes" to Jesus' messiahship, which is based on believed and experienced reconciliation, will therefore accept the Jewish "no," which is based on the experienced and suffered unredeemedness of the world; and the "yes" will in so far adopt the "no" as to talk about the total and universal redemption of the world only in the dimensions of a future hope, and a present contradiction of this unredeemed world. The Christian "yes" to Jesus Christ is therefore not in itself finished and complete. It is open for the messianic future of Jesus. . . . This means that it cannot be an excluding and excommunicating "yes," not even when it is uttered with the certainty of faith.[36]

A systematic account of the redemption in Christ and its rejection by the people of the Messiah needs to be worked out in the context of the doctrine of atonement. Similarly, in the context of ecclesiology, the relation of the Christian church to Israel and the question of the continuing legitimacy of a rightly configured mission to Israel have to be investigated in detail.

On the Conditions and Promise of Mutual Dialogue

A dialogue about Messiah and other corollary christological issues between Christians and Jews is meaningful only if there is mutual trust to allow both

---

delphia: Fortress, 1978); Thomas A. Idinopulos, "Christianity and the Holocaust," *CrossCurrents* 28, no. 3 (Fall 1978): 257–67.

35. Moltmann, *Way of Jesus Christ*, 32.

36. Moltmann, *Way of Jesus Christ*, 32–33.

parties to represent their positions faithfully.[37] The challenge to the Jewish faith is to stop "constructing Jewish conceptions of Jesus . . . and try to confront Christian claims about him as we [Jews] actually hear them from Christians." That said, it is also important for Christian theologians to acknowledge that the "Jews . . . cannot and should not see Jesus through the eyes of Christian faith, but . . . try to understand that faith in the light of" their own.[38] This does not mean that the Jews do not have the right to comment on Christian doctrines and views of Jesus; yes, they do. That is an opportunity also for Christians to learn more about their own faith. Nor does this mean that Christians should refrain from presenting Jesus as the Messiah to all men and women, gentiles as well as Jews. Similarly, Jewish counterparts should be granted the same right to defend their "no" to Christian interpretation.

Only such an encounter may also open up new ways of looking for thematic and material parallels in the midst of foundational differences. A patient, common search of both real differences and potential common themes does not necessarily promise "results" but is a process to which all believers, regardless of religion, are called. This is wonderfully represented in the following statement from the Jewish theologian Michael S. Kogan:

> But Jews do not ask Christians in the dialogue to give up core doctrines. How would Jews respond if Christians who have problems with Zionism demanded that Jews give up the theological claim that God has given us the land of Israel? . . . The divine bestowal of the Holy Land is a core doctrine of Israelite faith that cannot be given up for the sake of the dialogue or to suit anyone's preferences. . . . Similarly, the incarnation and resurrection are essential experiences of Christian faith. In Christ the transcendent God comes down to earth as, in the gift of land to God's people, the Holy One acts in the world and its history. These doctrines are parallel concretizations of the divine activity crucial to the respective faiths.[39]

---

37. Hence, compromising basic christological beliefs for the sake of dialogue is not recommended, as happens in Clark Williamson, *A Guest in the House of Israel: Post-Holocaust Church Theology* (Louisville: Westminster John Knox, 1993).

38. Kogan, *Opening the Covenant*, 112.

39. Kogan, *Opening the Covenant*, 102.

Jesus in Light of Islamic Interpretations

The Challenges and Prospects of Dialogue about Jesus

The main challenge to Islamic-Christian engagement around Jesus Christ is not the lack of interest on the Muslim side but rather the somewhat ironic fact that for a faithful Muslim, Jesus of Nazareth plays an important role. Indeed, one cannot be a true Muslim and ignore Jesus! Counterintuitively, "Islam is the only religion other than Christianity that *requires* its adherents to commit to a position on the identity of Jesus"![40] So much so that "[in] the Islamic tradition, Jesus ('Isa) was a Muslim,"[41] which accounts for titles such as *The Muslim Jesus*.[42]

There are roughly one hundred references or allusions to Jesus (and his mother) in the Qur'an alone, and the commentary literature is rich with allusions and references to him.[43] Alongside 'Isa (Jesus), a number of significant nomenclatures are applied to Jesus in the Qur'an, including the Prophet (e.g., 4:163), Messiah (4:171), and—astonishingly—even God's "Word" and "Spirit" from God (4:171). Unbeknownst to many, Jesus's figure as an eschatological prophet and his awaited return play a crucial role in Islamic theology (to be studied in the last chapter). Of course, the Qur'an contains nothing like the New Testament Gospel narratives. Instead, there are a number of references to key events in Jesus's life, from conception to earthly ministry to death/resurrection to his eschatological future (the last theme is dealt with in much more detail in Hadith tradition).

Yet, interpretations about Jesus's meaning differ drastically and are typically a source of deep discord. This complex state of affairs is well captured in Vatican II's *Nostra Aetate*: "Though they [Muslims] do not acknowledge Jesus as God, they revere Him as a prophet. They also honor Mary, His virgin Mother; at times they even call on her with devotion."[44] While Jesus matters a lot to both

---

40. Gregory A. Barker and Stephen E. Gregg, "Muslim Perceptions of Jesus: Key Issues," in *JBC*, 83.

41. Reem A. Meshal and M. Reza Pirbhai, "Islamic Perspectives on Jesus," in Burkett, *The Blackwell Companion to Jesus*, 232.

42. Tarif Khalidi, *The Muslim Jesus: Sayings and Stories in Islamic Literature* (Cambridge, MA: Harvard University Press, 2000).

43. For details, see Kenneth Cragg, *Jesus and the Muslim: An Exploration* (London: Allen & Unwin, 1985; Oxford: Oneworld, 1999), chap. 2; Oddbjørn Leirvik, *Images of Jesus Christ in Islam*, 2nd ed. (New York: Continuum, 2010), 20–24.

44. *Nostra Aetate: Declaration on the Relation of the Church to Non-Christian Religions*

traditions, christologically focused mutual exchange and dialogue have not so far been very important. The meaning of Jesus is a sensitive issue, linked with apologetics and polemics rather than mutual learning. Even the fact that both the Islamic canonical tradition and the rich and variegated later commentary tradition speak so much of Jesus Christ has not necessarily facilitated dialogue, as the two traditions' interpretations differ so widely. Not surprisingly, many observers seriously doubt if any "practical results" can come from this dialogue.[45]

The ambiguity about Jesus has characterized Muslim-Christian exchange from the beginning—with problems on both sides. On the Christian polemical side, from the beginning of the encounter a handful of arguments have persisted, often used in an uncritical and unnuanced manner against any Muslim interpretation of Jesus. These arguments claimed that

- what the Qur'an says of Jesus is hopelessly distorted;
- there are clear mistakes in the Qur'anic presentation of Jesus;
- Muhammad received much of his information from heretical or otherwise suspect sources; and
- some elements of the Qur'anic presentations of Christ are more "Christian" than Muslims suppose, including pointers to Jesus's divinity and the affirmation of his death on the cross.[46]

For a long time, a typical Muslim engagement added to the references in the Qur'an and Hadith ideas based on Christian legends and gospel materials, including gospels not ratified by Christians, especially the Gospel of Barnabas, whose influence even today is immense in anti-Christian polemics.[47] This development culminated in the mystical Sufi spirituality and continues. Some contemporary Muslim theologians have also utilized historical-critical tools of New Testament studies to discredit key christological beliefs.[48]

Although a serious dialogue has to acknowledge and carefully weigh these kinds of challenges, the matrix of both traditions provides reasons for continuing and deepening Muslim-Christian dialogue. In this exchange more

(Vatican II, October 28, 1965), #3, http://www.vatican.va/archive/hist_councils/ii_vatican
_council/documents/vat-ii_decl_19651028_nostra-aetate_en.html.

45. Smail Balić, "The Image of Jesus in Contemporary Islamic Theology," in *We Believe in One God*, ed. A. M. Schimmel and Abdoldjavad Falaturi (London: Burns & Oates, 1979), 7.

46. These are conveniently listed and discussed in detail in Neil Robinson, *Christ in Islam and Christianity* (New York: State University of New York Press, 1991), chap. 2.

47. For a useful discussion, see Leirvik, *Images of Jesus Christ*, 132–44.

48. See further, Leirvik, *Images of Jesus Christ*, 2.

is at stake than just the need to make pedagogical contact for the sake of better relations:

- Christology is the heart of Christian theology and must be taken seriously as a central point of reference in the self-understanding of the church. The church has great need to continually rethink the question of Christology in an Islamic context—as part of the more general task of a contextualized theology.
- Christology is in fact dealt with as an issue from the Muslim side—both in Muslim polemics, medieval and modern, and in more dialogical contributions from Muslims.
- Christology is not an isolated subject but touches upon fundamental issues in anthropology and theology as well as in ethics. This is true both for Christians and, in a different sense, for Muslims.[49]

Jesus and Muhammad—Christ and the Word of God

As mentioned earlier, in many ways it is neither fair nor useful to compare Jesus Christ to Muhammad. First of all, even though Christ is of course named a "prophet"[50] in the Qur'an, it is Muhammad who is the "seal of the prophets" and thus occupies a unique role. That said, unlike Christian faith, which is determined by belief in Christ, Islam is not based on Muhammad but rather on the Qur'an and Allah. Neither Christ nor Muhammad in Islamic interpretation is divine; only God is.[51] The closest parallel to Christ in Islamic faith could be found between Christ's role as the living Word of God and the divine revelation of the Qur'an.[52]

Notwithstanding the incompatibility between the two prophets, in the Hadith collections a number of sayings seek to clarify the relation be-

49. Leirvik, *Images of Jesus Christ*, 222.

50. It may be significant that in the Sunni Hadith collection Bukhari, which almost gained canonical status, most of the references to Jesus occur in "The Prophets."

51. In some strands of Islam, particularly in the esoteric Sufism, the veneration of Muhammad goes way beyond the established tradition, making him not only an embodiment of "Perfect Man" but also a carrier of divine light and expression of divine attributes. Leirvik, *Images of Jesus Christ*, 47.

52. Hence the heading "The 'Christ of Islam' Is the Koran," in Josef Imbach, *Three Faces of Jesus: How Jews, Christians, and Muslims See Him*, trans. Jane Wilde (Springfield, IL: Templegate Publishers, 1992), 87.

tween Muhammad and Jesus. Among them is the important, oft-quoted, and highly respectful statement by Muhammad of Jesus: "Prophets are brothers in faith, having different mothers. Their religion is, however, one and there is no Apostle between us (between me and Jesus Christ)."[53] As is well known, Muhammad's own relation to Christianity and Christian tradition in general, especially in the early phases of his career, was fairly positive and constructive.[54]

Because neither the person nor the work of Christ is in any way as central to Islam as it is to Christianity, the Qur'an sets the portrayal of Jesus in a different context.[55] Jesus is put in the line of a number of Old Testament prophets beginning with Moses and Abraham. Furthermore, Mary's role is much more prominent in the Qur'anic presentation. Both of the two main suras that contain the most references to Jesus, 3 and 19, are named after Mary.[56]

Even the fact that Jesus is a miracle worker in the Qur'an, unlike Muhammad, does not imply that therefore he should be lifted up higher than the Prophet of Islam; the miracles wrought by Jesus are similar to those performed by Moses and other such forerunners of Muhammad.[57] In other words, the most the miracles can do is confirm Jesus's prophetic status; they cannot confirm his divinity.[58] Even the fact that Jesus is described as sinless in Hadith and legendary tradition, whereas it is not quite certain whether Muhammad is—although in the Shi'ite tradition all imams are!—does not make Jesus superior.

The Pakistani-born bishop of the Church of England Michael Nazir-Ali makes the pointed remark that many of the traditional and contemporary Islamic Christologies seem to find a lot in common with Christian interpretations of Jesus that work with a "low Christology," basically reducing Jesus's significance to his role as a human person.[59]

---

53. Sahih Muslim, *Kitāb al-Fadā'il*, book 30, chap. 37, quoted in Leirvik, *Images of Jesus Christ*, 38. For sayings clarifying the relation between Muhammad and Jesus, see Leirvik, 37–38.

54. See Robinson, *Christ in Islam*, chap. 4.

55. That said, there are a number of parallels between the two "founders" of religions as carefully delineated in Robinson, *Christ in Islam*, chap. 5. For a standard, masterful study, see Geoffrey Parrinder, *Jesus in the Qur'an* (London: Sheldon; Oxford: Oneworld, 1995).

56. "The House of Imrān" (Mary's father's house; sura 3) and "Maryam" (sura 19).

57. David Thomas, "The Miracles of Jesus in Early Islamic Polemic," *Journal of Semitic Studies* 39, no. 2 (1994): 221–43.

58. See Thomas, "Miracles of Jesus," 240.

59. Michael Nazir-Ali, *Frontiers in Muslim-Christian Encounter* (Oxford: Regnum, 1987), 25.

What about the Messiah?

Islam is not a messianic religion in the way the two older Abrahamic traditions are. Yet the designation "Messiah" is known in their scripture. Indeed, the only title that is uniquely reserved for Jesus in the Muslim tradition is Messiah (4:171). It is difficult, however, to determine the distinctively Islamic interpretation of that term. Christian theology has been aware of and interested in Muslim interpretations of this important passage; John of Damascus of the eighth century, in the last chapter of *De haeresibus (On the Heresies)*, discusses this passage.[60]

In Christian tradition, of course, Messiah, the Anointed One, is integrally connected with the Spirit of God. Interestingly enough, an important passage in the Qur'an that names Jesus the Messiah also makes the same connection: "The Messiah, Jesus son of Mary, was only a messenger of Allah, and His word which He conveyed unto Mary, and a spirit from Him" (4:171). Notwithstanding continuing ambiguity about the Islamic interpretation, it seems clear that there is a direct linking in the Qur'an with the life-giving power of creation (as in connection with Adam in 15:29): "Christ himself is seen as a creation of the life-giving spirit, but at the same time as a privileged vehicle of the spirit, aided by the Holy Spirit in his mighty signs" (2:253).[61]

Although it would be tempting to read these and similar descriptions that have clear Christian parallels through the lens of Christian theology, the warning by the late Finnish New Testament scholar Heikki Räisänen merits hearing: "The Qur'an must be explained by the Qur'an and not by anything else." Hence, in the Qur'anic interpretation, "Jesus became an example and a precursor of Muhammad, a guarantor of Muhammad's message who had experienced similar things."[62]

Ultimately, the loftiest status granted to Jesus in the Qur'an is that of the "highest" predecessor of Muhammad—something like the Baptist to Jesus himself.[63] That said, Räisänen cautiously finds parallels between some New Testament and Qur'anic portraits of Jesus. The Lukan Christology with a focus

---

60. The last chapter of *De haeresibus* (100/101) is unusually long. See further, John E. Merrill, "John of Damascus on Islam," *Muslim World* 41 (1951): 88–89, www.answering-islam.org/Books/MW/john_d.htm.

61. Leirvik, *Images of Jesus Christ*, 24.

62. Heikki Räisänen, "The Portrait of Jesus in the Qur'an: Reflections of a Biblical Scholar," *Muslim World* 70 (1980): 124.

63. See Leirvik, *Images of Jesus Christ*, 29–30; Robinson, *Christ in Islam*, 40.

on Jesus's subordination to God as exemplified in his voluntary submission under God's plan (Acts 2:22–23) and his servanthood (Acts 3:13; 4:27) provides such parallels.[64] This Qur'anic perspective has to be kept in mind as we next touch the most controversial christological issues between Muslims and Christians: claims of his deity and incarnation.

The Divinity of Jesus between Muslims and Christians

A contemporary Muslim scholar sets the question of the divine Sonship and deity of Jesus in a proper perspective: "Jesus the 'Christ,' the 'eternal logos,' the 'Word made flesh,' the 'Only Begotten Son of God' and second person of the trinity has been the barrier separating the two communities [Muslims and Christians]."[65] This judgment is consonant with Muslim tradition going back to its beginning, and it must be remembered at all times on the Christian side. To the credit of the Christian tradition, several early theologians (after the rise of Islam), such as John of Damascus (d. 749), showed an extensive understanding of Islam and its main beliefs.[66]

When investigating this issue, it is hard to establish exactly how much early Muslim thinkers knew of the details of established orthodox tradition when they began to engage Christian claims about Jesus and the Trinity. Even some Muslim scholars admit that these early Muslims' assessments were hardly informed by a clear knowledge of Christian creeds and teachings.[67] A complicating factor here is that Christian tradition did not of course always speak with one voice—even after Chalcedon (451). By the time of the rise of Islam, especially the Eastern Christian tradition was deeply divided into different groups and orientations, some affirming, others resisting or revising, key Chalcedonian formulae.

---

64. Räisänen, "Portrait of Jesus," 127.

65. Mahmoud Ayoub, "Jesus the Son of God: A Study of the Terms *Ibn* and *Walad* in the Qur'ān and *Tafsīr* Tradition," in *Christian-Muslim Encounters*, ed. Y. Y. Haddad and W. Z. Haddad (Gainesville: University of Florida Press, 1995), 65.

66. Two of the writings by John of Damascus contain an account of Islam: "The Heresy of the Ishmaelites," in his *De haeresibus (On Heresies)*, and *Disputatio Saraceni et Christiani (Dialogue with a Saracen)*. English translations of these texts (as reprints) can be found in N. A. Newman, ed., *The Early Christian-Muslim Dialogue: A Collection of Documents from the First Three Islamic Centuries (632–900 A.D.); Translations with Commentary* (Hatfield, PA: Interdisciplinary Biblical Research Institute, 1993), 133–68.

67. See, e.g., Ayoub, "Jesus the Son of God," 66.

The Qur'an contains only a handful of direct references to the Christian claim of Jesus as the Son of God and his divinity—and bluntly denies it (4:171; 9:30; 19:35). Similarly denied is the idea of Allah having a son (2:116; 4:171; 17:111; 39:4; 72:3). In the first place, Allah, the all-sufficient One, has no need for anything (10:68). The Qur'an also denies the idea of sonship because it is seen as linked with Allah having a consort (6:101).

For the Christian reader it is essential to bear in mind that the Qur'anic affirmation of the virgin birth of Jesus does not imply any divinity, nor even the linking of Jesus with God's Spirit or God's Word. According to Qur'an 21:91, God "breathed into Mary and caused her to become pregnant with Jesus"; and according to 4:17, Jesus is called "a spirit from Him." Even when it is well known that the Qur'anic hermeneutic (*tafsir*) knows a number of debates about the details of these verses, the deity of Jesus is absolutely ruled out.

That said, it is clear that the linking of Jesus with God's Spirit and Word is meant to speak of Jesus's high status as a religious figure. Yet, at the same time, in the very same passage in the Qur'an (4:171) in which the reference to the Spirit and Word occurs, there is also one of the strongest denials of the Trinity and the divine Sonship of Jesus: "So believe in Allah and His messengers, and say not 'Three'—Cease! (it is) better for you!—Allah is only One God. Far is it removed from His Transcendent Majesty that He should have a son. His is all that is in the heavens and all that is in the earth. And Allah is sufficient as Defender." This is clearly a polemic against any allusion to the deity of Jesus and thus to the Trinity.

Incarnation between Muslims and Christians

To their credit, early Muslim polemicists and commentators were fairly well aware of the many different interpretations and nuances among various Christian interpretations of the incarnation. Indeed, these early Muslim thinkers often considered the nuances in Christian interpretations (among the "schools" of Melkites, Nestorians, and Jacobites) more carefully than usually happens in contemporary debates.

The Muslim rebuttals of the Christian doctrine of the incarnation of Jesus Christ, as presented in the anti-Christian Muslim literature during the first centuries of Islam's existence, can be classified under two broad sets of arguments.[68] First, incarnation is allegedly inconsistent with both Muslim and

68. Reda Samuel, "The Incarnation in Arabic Christian Theology from the Beginnings

Christian Scripture. Muslim scholars quoted Qur'anic passages that refute Jesus's divinity (e.g., 5:72, 73) while employing Qur'anic passages that speak of the mere humanity of Jesus (e.g., 5:75). As for the Bible, Muslim scholars devoted considerable attention to the sayings that speak of Jesus's humanity, such as his being the son of David and Abraham (Matt. 1:1) and that he ate, drank, slept, traveled, rode a donkey, suffered, and died; similarly, his need to pray, his temptations, and so forth. On the other hand, Muslim commentators also downplayed the importance of Christian interpretation of a few passages in which they saw direct claims to Jesus's divinity. Second, these early Muslim commentators argued that the Christian doctrine of incarnation is inconsistent with Muslim and Christian teachings at large. On top of this argumentation was the central Muslim idea of *tawhid*, the oneness of God, which by default rejects not only all notions of incarnation but also the corollary Christian doctrine of the Trinity. *Tawhid* was seen as taught not only by the Qur'an but also by the Bible, especially the Old Testament (Deut. 6:4).

A related concern among Muslim commentators is the incompatibility of incarnation with God's transcendence, affirmed firmly in both faiths. To Muslim sensibilities, the idea of God becoming flesh violates the principles of God's glory and greatness. Furthermore, Jesus's physical conception and birth as part of the doctrine of incarnation were seen as incompatible with both Christian and Muslim teachings. A logical problem here is the exact moment the two natures were united, whether in conception or birth or afterward. A final Muslim concern about the incarnation is that it involves itself in *shirk*, the greatest sin of all, associating with God what should not be associated with him.

Although the impasse remains, deepening mutual dialogue is not useless. It is particularly important for the sake of mutual learning. As mentioned regarding the Trinity, a number of Islamic beliefs about Christ (and the Christian God) are gleaned from heretical sources.

Toward a Faithful and Integral Dialogue

A tempting way to try to ease the tension between two vastly different portraits of Jesus in these two religions would be to "water down" the New Testament account of Jesus—for the sake of the dialogue. The classic work in

---

to the Mid-Eleventh Centuries" (PhD tutorial, Fuller Theological Seminary, School of Intercultural Studies, Spring 2010).

Christian-Muslim relations by Kenneth Cragg, *The Call of the Minaret*, warns against that orientation. It recommends that for the sake of a genuine dialogue, Christians should present Jesus to Muslims in the fullness of his personality as it is revealed in the Gospels.[69] This means that Christians are required to present Jesus to Muslims in the fullness of both his humanity and his divinity. "To concentrate only on elements in Jesus that Muslims can at once accept is to fail Jesus himself," Cragg asserts.[70] Thus, to be content with only Jesus the prophet-teacher would not do justice to the Muslims' need.[71] On the other hand, "a simple reassertion of the Christian doctrine of Christ will not suffice" either, without a conscious effort to face honestly the difficulties Muslims face in trying to understand the Christian interpretation.[72]

For fruitful dialogue to occur, both parties face challenges. Here the recommendation from the Roman Catholic Hans Küng is worth following. He reminds us of the need to acknowledge the difference between Christian and Islamic interpretations. Furthermore, Küng advises Christians not to read Christian meanings into the Qur'an but rather to interpret it from its own point of view: "For the Qur'an, Jesus is a prophet, a great prophet, like Abraham, Noah, and Moses—but nothing more. And just as in the New Testament John the Baptist is Jesus' precursor, so in the Qur'an Jesus is the precursor—and highly encouraging example—for Muhammad."[73]

Commensurately, Küng advises Muslims to evaluate Jesus on the basis of the historical sources of the Gospels: "If we on the Christian side make an effort to reevaluate Muhammad on the basis of Islamic sources, especially the Qur'an, we also hope that for their part the Muslims will eventually be prepared to move toward *a reevaluation of Jesus of Nazareth on the basis of historical sources* (namely the Gospels) as many Jews have already been doing."[74]

The implication that the Qur'an gives a faulty picture of Jesus, however, is a deeply troubling challenge to devout Muslims. It goes way beyond the unwillingness to reconsider one's own interpretative framework. A leading Muslim thinker, the American-based Seyyed Hossein Nasr, in dialogue with

69. Kenneth Cragg, *The Call of the Minaret*, rev. ed. (Maryknoll, NY: Orbis, 1985 [1956]), 258–60.

70. Cragg, *Call of the Minaret*, 258.

71. Cragg, *Call of the Minaret*, 259.

72. Cragg, *Call of the Minaret*, 258.

73. Hans Küng, "A Christian Response [to Islamic perspective]," in *Christianity and World Religions: Path of Dialogue with Islam, Hinduism, and Buddhism*, ed. Hans Küng et al. (New York: Doubleday, 1986), 110.

74. Küng, "A Christian Response," 111.

Küng, made this point in a most forthright way: "To suggest that the Qur'ān had the wrong Christology makes absolutely impossible any dialogue with Islam. . . . It must always be remembered that for Muslims the Qur'ān, the whole Qur'ān, and not only parts of it, is the Word of God."[75] Against Küng's historical interpretation of Muhammad's prophecy, Nasr says: "One should be very clear on this point and on the role of the Prophet in the process of the revelation of the Sacred Text. It is because of this Islamic belief in the nature of the Qur'ān as the direct Word of God that any consideration of the Prophet of Islam as having learnt this view of sacred history and Christology from Jewish and Christian sources is the greatest blasphemy in the eyes of Muslims."[76]

From Abrahamic traditions, we now move to consider potential parallels between Christian Christology and Buddhism and Hinduism. Here, again, we need to proceed cautiously in order not to assume too much compatibility if the evidence does not warrant it.

Jesus and Buddha: Christian-Buddhist Engagement on Jesus

The Slow Buddhist Engagement of Jesus

Unlike the relationship with Islam, the interaction between Jesus traditions and Buddhist traditions had not been wide and deep until the twentieth century. Particularly in the Theravada tradition, given the fact that Buddha taught no fewer than forty-five years, establishing a solid and coherent tradition to follow, the teaching ministry of Jesus—comprising only three years at most and not yielding any kind of systematic and organized body of tradition—does not easily gain much respect.

That said, in terms of life history there are obvious similarities between Sakyamuni (Gautama) Buddha and Jesus of Nazareth, even if the historical details of Gautama's life are very scarce, including the lack of precise dating of his birth.[77] Both founders of religions had miraculous elements attached to their birth, including cosmic signs and phenomena, as well as ominous threats;

---

75. Seyyed Hossein Nasr, "Response to Hans Küng's Paper on Christian-Muslim Dialogue," *Muslim World* 77 (1987): 100.

76. Nasr, "Response," 99.

77. Gajin Nagao, "The Life of the Buddha: An Interpretation," *Eastern Buddhist*, n.s., 20, no. 2 (1987): 1–31.

both faced temptations, one in the forest, the other in the desert; both became itinerant preachers and teachers who also were considered miracle workers; both were men of prayer and meditation; and so forth.[78]

Potentially the Mahayana tradition's stress on the transcendent and "salvific" presence of Buddha might find bridges with Christian faith more easily. The major difference, however, has to do with its vision of multiple Boddhisattvas (the Enlightened Ones) vis-à-vis Christian faith's focus on one single savior. Furthermore, "That Jesus prayed to a deity that is self-caused, self-existent, and independent of the created world conflicts with both the notion of co-independent origination as well as the non-dualistic goal of a self merged with all consciousness."[79]

Silence, rather than aggressive polemics, has been the defining characteristic of Buddhist reaction to Jesus. With all their appreciation of Jesus's ethical life, ministry, and teaching, occasionally criticisms such as the illicit status of Mary and the coming of Jesus at such a late moment of history are presented.

Jesus and Boddhisattva

If one were to look for a defining problem for the Buddhist assessment of Jesus as interpreted in Christian theology, without doubt it would have to do with the claim to deity. To be more precise, in the words of the leading Tibetan Buddhist scholar and practitioner José Ignacio Cabezón: "The problem lies not in the claim that Jesus is the incarnation or manifestation of a deity. What I find objectionable is (a) the Christian characterization of the deity whose incarnation Jesus is said to be, and (b) the claim that Jesus is unique in being an incarnation."[80] That the idea of incarnation in itself is not a problem for Buddhists is based on the belief prevalent among all Mahayana Buddhists that the universe is populated by enlightened beings who, having attained the buddhahood, have the capacity to incarnate for the welfare of others.

Further complications for Buddhist acknowledgment of Jesus as divine come from Christian Trinitarian teaching. If Christ is divine, that means one

---

78. Leo D. Lefebure, *The Buddha and the Christ: Explorations in Buddhist and Christian Dialogue* (Maryknoll, NY: Orbis, 1993), chap. 2.

79. Gregory A. Barker, "Buddhist Perceptions of Jesus: Key Issues," in *JBC*, 220.

80. José Ignacio Cabezón, "Buddhist Views of Jesus," in *JWF*, 21.

has to acknowledge the God of the Bible. To begin with, Buddhists are not willing to approve the notion of a creator God, one who has no beginning in time, and other corollary Christian theistic notions.[81]

To consider Jesus as incarnate on the basis of his extraordinary teaching, miracles, and ethical life is not to say that therefore he "possessed the quality of maximal greatness (enlightenment), that is, that he was a Buddha."[82] In many respects, Jesus might be better compared with Boddhisattva, a Buddha-in-the-making, as it were, who for the sake of others is willing to suffer and postpone one's own enlightenment (as happens in Mahayana traditions).[83]

In the Pure Land tradition, similarly, Jesus can be respected as a Boddhisattva, a compassionate being who helps others, a manifestation of Amitabha.[84] Even then there is no ultimacy to the role of Jesus after the Christian tradition.[85] Between the Theravada tradition and the Christian interpretation of Jesus are even wider differences, as Theravada does not emphasize the idea of enlightened manifestations of the divine incarnating for the benefit of others. What matters in the oldest Buddhist tradition is the following of *dhamma*, the way of training (*vinaya*), and *sangha*, the community in which assistance may be received from others but which has no salvific effect.[86]

Reasons behind Differing Visions of the "Savior" and "Salvation"

Behind the Buddhist refusal to grant a salvific role to Jesus lie a number of doctrinal presuppositions. In Buddhist thought, every sentient person is responsible for his or her destiny. *Dukkha* (suffering), the ultimate problem that demands "salvation," is caused by each and every person, and consequently one cannot refer to a source of deliverance apart from one's own efforts. The idea that salvation of men and women would be dependent on any historical event such as the crucifixion is totally unknown to Buddhism.

---

81. See Cabezón, "Buddhist Views of Jesus," 22–23.

82. Cabezón, "Buddhist Views of Jesus," 21–22 (22).

83. See Rita M. Gross, "Meditating on Jesus," in *Buddhists Talk about Jesus, Christians Talk about the Buddha*, ed. Rita M. Gross and Terry C. Muck (New York: Continuum, 2000), 45–47.

84. Amitabha is the original Sanskrit name for the central Buddha in Pure Land; it means, literally, "Infinite Light." In Japanese, the title is Amida. See further, Alfred Bloom, "Jesus in the Pure Land," in *JWF*, 31.

85. See further, Bloom, "Jesus in the Pure Land," 31–32.

86. Sister Ajahn Candasiri, "Jesus: A Theravadan Perspective," in *JWF*, 25.

Furthermore, Buddhism includes no temporal end to the continuing path of salvation, not even physical death. Mere belief or doctrine cannot save the human person; only effort toward enlightenment can lead to the end goal.[87]

Behind the differences between Buddhist and Christian notions of the "Savior"—including that of the Pure Land tradition, which comes closest to Christianity—are their approaches to questions of faith and history. Whereas the claims of Christian Christology are historically founded—just think of the creedal statement "suffered under Pontius Pilate"—that is not the case with Buddhism (or with Hinduism). Particularly for Mahayana (including Pure Land) traditions, the stories and happenings "are mythical beyond any history with which we are familiar."[88] Furthermore, as mentioned, all Buddhist traditions grant the existence of multiple Buddhas, whereas Christian tradition of course denies many Christs.

The Buddhist Rita M. Gross makes the insightful observation that Christian tradition tends to "locate truth in the messenger, whereas Buddhism tends to focus on the message." This is linked with the fact that Christian tradition has a tendency "to personify the ultimate while Buddhists tend toward nonpersonal metaphors about ultimate reality."[89]

Any Buddhist Parallel to Incarnation?

Are there any similar motifs or parallels between the two religions and the founding figures? Anyone who knows Buddhism in its everyday manifestation—even in the Theravada form—knows how highly Buddha is venerated. The story of Brahman Dona in the Pali Canon presents an illustrative example. Having found Buddha's footprints, Dona, in his amazement and awe, went to ask Buddha of their origin. Buddha explained that they belong neither to a *deva* (celestial being) nor to a spirit nor to a human being since all those forms of existence still are stuck within the bounds of samsara leading to rebirths. Instead, Buddha has transcended all that—and that's what makes him *Buddha!*[90]

The state of buddhahood is also the key to the Buddhist notion of incarnation. Buddha identifies himself with *dhamma* (the doctrine, teaching): "He

---

87. Cabezón, "Buddhist Views of Jesus," 23–24.

88. Bloom, "Jesus in the Pure Land," 35–36 (36).

89. Gross, "Meditating on Jesus," 44.

90. Dona Sutta: With Dona of Anguttara Nikaya 4.36.

who sees Dhamma . . . sees me; he who sees me sees Dhamma."[91] Undoubtedly, this resembles the Johannine Jesus's words about the unity between him and the Father (John 10:30). Indeed, Buddhist tradition speaks of the kind of "visible Dhamma" in terms of the life of the person who has freed himself or herself totally from hatred, delusion, and greed.

The final form of the (Mahayana) Buddhist doctrine of incarnation is the idea of trikaya, three bodies: first, "Transformation Body," the earthly Buddha, a transient and illusionary form of existence; second, "Enjoyment Body," the form of existence for the sake of others; and third, "Dhamma Body," the ultimate form of existence that indeed is no longer a "form" of existence but formless. In other words, the last "body" transcends the form and laws of existence. It is inconceivable and ineffable.[92] Although there are some interesting similar motifs in Buddhist and Christian doctrines of incarnation, including the ascent-descent/descent-ascent dynamic, "salvific orientation," and the dialectic between the "historical" and "suprahistorical" forms of existence, even a cursory look reveals profound differences, many of which have already been alluded to above.

What about Parallels to Jesus's Self-Emptying?

The most promising connecting point between (Mahayana) Buddhism and Christology can be found in the correlation of the main concepts of sunyata and the self-emptying of Christ. As discussed, notoriously difficult to translate and even more complicated to understand, sunyata literally means "(absolute) nothingness." However, it is not "empty nothingness," since it is what in Western terms should be called the ultimate, absolute reality.[93]

In comparative comments on Philippians 2:5-8, the Buddhist Masao Abe notes, first, the "abnegation of Christ as the Son of God," and second, that this self-emptying "indicates the self-sacrificial love of Christ for humankind," as a manifestation of the "unfathomable depth of God's love." This Japanese Buddhist opines that the abnegation was full and thoroughgoing. By that he means that a radical transformation took place as "the Son of God

91. Vakkali Sutta: Vakkali of Samyutta Nikaya 22.87.

92. Perry Schmidt-Leukel, "Buddha and Christ as Mediators of the Transcendent: A Christian Perspective," in *Buddhism and Christianity in Dialogue*, ed. Perry Schmidt-Leukel, Gerald Weisfeld Lectures 2004 (London: SCM, 2005), 157-59.

93. Masao Abe, "Kenotic God and Dynamic Sunyata," in *DEHF*, 50; Heinrich Ott, "The Convergence: Sunyata as a Dynamic Event," in *DEHF*, 127-35.

abandoned his divine substance and took on human substance," all the way to the cross. Indeed, he concludes that "Christ as the Son of God is *essentially* and *fundamentally* self-emptying or self-negating." This (and some other related moves, particularly a revision of the doctrine of preexistence) allows him to provide a seemingly self-contradictory account of incarnation, based on the logic of sunyata: "The Son of God is not the Son of God (for he is essentially and fundamentally self-emptying); precisely because he *is not* the Son of God he *is* truly the Son of God (for he originally and always works as Christ, the Messiah, in his salvational function of self-emptying)."[94] For Christian intuitions—and Western logic—this is a difficult idea to swallow or to grasp.

The Christian commentator Wolfhart Pannenberg wonders what really is the meaning of Abe's talk about the seemingly contradictory (at least to Western logic) notion of emptiness not only emptying everything else but also itself. In Christian theology this did not mean that Jesus Christ ceased to be the Son of God.[95] For this foundational reason and related others (concerning the above-mentioned reference to Christ's preexistence, the details of which we will not take up here), Pannenberg's summative comment on Abe's constructive interpretation makes a valuable point: "The notion of kenosis is of limited value in Buddhist-Christian dialogue, though I recognize its merit in providing inspiration for the initial phase of that dialogue. . . . In contrast with Buddhist emptiness the Christian idea of kenosis presupposes an agent, the Son, in relation to another agent, the Father, whose action is not kenotic." Furthermore, as Pannenberg also rightly points out, the most foundational question involves whether there is a "god" (personal or nonpersonal) distinct, if not separate, from the finite human world.[96] For Christian theology this is axiomatic; for Buddhist theology it is not, or at best it is an open question.

This is not to say that the comparison between sunyata and a christological understanding of *kenosis* is useless; it is just to follow our methodological rule of highlighting not only convergences and promising areas of common understanding but also differences and differing orientations. The same rule will be followed in our last comparative exercise in this chapter, one regarding Hindu thought.

94. Abe, "Kenotic God," 32–33.
95. Wolfhart Pannenberg, "God's Love and the Kenosis of the Son: A Response to Masao Abe," in *DEHF*, 247–48.
96. See Pannenberg, "God's Love," 245–46 particularly.

Christ and Avatars: Hindu-Christian Engagement on Jesus

The Hindu Appreciation of Jesus's Ethics and Teaching

Although it is probable that as early as the first (or at least second) century there was a Christian presence in India, no evidence of Hindu perceptions of Jesus survives; we have to wait until the seventeenth century. The earliest modern Hindu interpretation of Jesus was offered in the early nineteenth century by Raja Ram Mohun Roy, who focused on Jesus's ethical meaning and denied divine incarnation.[97]

Beginning from the end of the nineteenth century, a new wave of interpretations of Christ emerged that were deeply rooted in the religious (Hindu) soil of Asia, the so-called Indian Renaissance or neo-Hindu reform. Consider these book titles: Raimundo Panikkar's *Unknown Christ of Hinduism* and M. M. Thomas's *Acknowledged Christ of the Indian Renaissance*. The contemporary Indian theologian Stanley J. Samartha's *The Hindu Response to the Unbound Christ* reminds us that while many Indians attached themselves to the person of Jesus Christ—who reflects the features of Hindu avatars (incarnations of Hindu gods such as the famous Krishna or Vishnu)—they also detached that person from the institutional church.

Several Hindu writers were excited by the social teachings of Christ but did not make a personal commitment to him, for example, Swami Vivekananda of the Ramakrishna order, who elevated Jesus among the highly revered figures of Buddha and Krishna, generally believed to be the incarnation of Vishnu. Well known is Mahatma Gandhi's admiration of Jesus as an ethical teacher, reflecting the same principles that guided his own pacifist fight for the liberation of the Indian people, namely, *satyagraha* (the search for truth) and *ahimsa* (nonviolence).[98]

Finally, there are Hindus who have become Christians but insist they have remained Hindus, one of the best known of whom is Brahmabandhab Upadhyaya. His spirituality is based on a deep personal experience of the person of Jesus the Son of God, who becomes at once his guru and his friend. Whether Jesus was divine or not is not the point.[99]

---

97. R. Neufeldt, "Hindu Views of Christ," in *Hindu-Christian Dialogue: Perspectives and Encounters*, ed. Harold Coward (Maryknoll, NY: Orbis, 1990), 162–75.

98. Mohandas K. Gandhi, *The Message of Jesus Christ* (Bombay: Bharatiya Vidya Bhavan, 1963 [1940]).

99. See Jacob Kavunkal, "The Mystery of God in and through Hinduism," in *Christian Theology in Asia*, ed. Sebastian C. H. Kim (Cambridge: Cambridge University Press, 2008), 28–30.

By and large, Hindu perceptions of Jesus are positive. This is similar to Buddhist views and different from a number of Jewish and Islamic views. With sweeping generalizations, the Hindu perceptions, including the twentieth-century ones, can be described in this way: "(1) Jesus is a rational teacher of universal values; (2) Jesus is an incarnation of God among other incarnations; and (3) Jesus is a spiritual teacher. These positions are not, of course, mutually exclusive."[100]

What makes the mutual dialogue between Hindus and Christians both promising and challenging is that there are few, if any, doctrinal boundaries that are exclusively Hindu or that require followers to subscribe to. Add to that a bewildering variety of beliefs, rites, rituals, "favorite" local gods and goddesses—and you get a feel of a "religion" very different from that of most other living faiths.

The Divinity of Jesus in Hindu Estimation

Among the Hindu commentators are those who consider Jesus of Nazareth a mere human teacher, albeit a highly respected and honored one. These interpreters of Christ also reject the belief of Jesus as the incarnation of God. Others, such as Keshub Chunder Sen, replace the doctrine of the Trinity with the biunity of Father and Spirit, which falls short of regarding Jesus as the divine incarnation, his "Divine Humanity."[101]

Many contemporary Hindu interpreters of Jesus, perhaps a majority of them, are willing to grant divine status to Jesus Christ, something parallel to Krishna, the avatar of Vishnu. That said, important qualifications and clarifications are in order. It is a commonplace in Hindu thought to believe that some dimension of the human being is divine. The possible realization of the divine lies within the reach of any human being; however, in most cases that does not happen. Jesus is one among those in whom the realization of the divine occurred.[102] Hence, Jesus's importance lies in his role as the symbol of the potential of the realization of the divine in the human person. In that outlook, even the cross may be appropriated as the form of an ultimate self-sacrifice.[103]

---

100. Gavin D. Flood, "Jesus in Hinduism: Closing Reflection," in *JBC*, 202.

101. Editors' explanation as an introduction to Chunder Sen's lectures, Keshub Chunder Sen, *Jesus: The Ideal Son; Keshub Chunder Sen's Lectures in India*, 2nd ed. (Calcutta: Brahmo Tract Society, 1886), 25–27, reproduced in *JBC*, 165–66 (165).

102. Chakravarthi Ram-Prasad, "Hindu Views of Jesus," in *JWF*, 85.

103. Ram-Prasad, "Hindu Views of Jesus," 85.

Some strands of Hinduism, such as the Hare Krishna movement, consider Jesus as Guru. It focuses on love and devotion rather than on doctrine, particularly toward Krishna, the avatar of Vishnu. The ultimate goal of this pursuit is active love and desire for God. Avatars, divine embodiments empowered with divine *shakti* (power), help revive the devotion to God. Jesus is one of those divinely empowered incarnations.

If possible, even higher status is granted to Jesus in *The Gospel of Sri Ramakrishna*, written by the nineteenth-century great Bengalese guru Ramakrishna Paramahansa. He even claimed to have a number of mystical encounters with Jesus.[104] His most famous disciple, Swami Vivekananda—best known for his influential speech at the first World's Parliament of Religions in Chicago (1893) and as the founder of Vedanta Societies—wrote the highly honoring preface to the (unfinished) Bengali translation of Thomas à Kempis's *Imitation of Christ*.[105]

Similarly to Buddhist faith, we inquire next into whether there are parallels in Hindu religion to the Christian idea of incarnation.

Incarnation and Avatars

With all the differences and diversity among Hindu traditions, it is safe to say that in classical Hinduism, the one Brahman in its "manifested" form is known as the Hindu Trimurti, namely, Brahma (the "Creator God"), Vishnu (the "Preserver God"), and Shiva (the "Destroyer God" [or "Completer God"?]). As it is the task of Vishnu to make sure the universe and its order will not be destroyed in an undue manner, through various forms of avatars, Vishnu intervenes in the affairs of the world. This "descent," as the word literally means, can be expressed in terms of the word "incarnation," as the often-cited passage in Bhagavad Gita (4.7–8) renders it:

7. Whenever, O descendant of Bharata, there is decline of Dharma, and rise of Adharma, then I body Myself forth
8. For the protection of the good, for the destruction of the wicked, and for the establishment of Dharma, I come into being in every age.[106]

---

104. Sri Ramakrishna, *The Gospel of Sri Ramakrishna: Translated into English with an Introduction by Swami Nikhilananda* (New York: Ramakrishna-Vivekananda Center, 1984 [1942]), 34, reproduced in *JBC*, 173.

105. *The Complete Works of Vivekananda* (Calcutta: Advaita Ashrama, 12th impr., 1999), 8:159–60; reproduced in *JBC*, 177–79.

106. Trans. Swami Swarupananda, http://www.sacred-texts.com/hin/.

The purpose, hence, of the "coming down" of God is the establishment of *dhamma*, the right order, "righteousness" (as it is rendered in some English translations). It has little to do with the Christian notion of atonement. It has everything to do with what we might call enlightenment (true knowledge, right insight) in our terminology. Sandy Bharat puts it thus: "The purpose . . . is to help people return to the Source [Brahman, 'ultimate reality'] by remembering their true Selves and so be free from *avidya* (ignorance) and its conditioning. It is *avidya* that keeps one in the spell of *maya* (delusion) and separated from God. Most Hindus believe that, to help people return to the Source, Truth is revealed through descents of divine beings."[107] Or: "Avatars come then to bring a new or renewed revelation of Truth, expressed through the example of their lives. This enables people to know that they can change and become like the avatars."[108] Chapter 4 in Bhagavad Gita, in which the above-quoted important statement about the divine descent is found, can be titled "The Way of Renunciation of Action in Knowledge," which is a (divine) solution to the human effort in "The Way of Knowledge" (literally: Transcendental Knowledge) of chapter 2 and "The Way of Action" (literally: Path of Karma Yoga) in chapter 3. The divine descent is both the aid, as it were, and the way of renunciation of the yogic path on the way to a fuller realization.

Hindu mythology includes numerous accounts of incarnations. Among those, an established doctrine widely shared by various Hindu strands is *dasavatara*, ten incarnations of Vishnu beginning from a fish and tortoise and continuing all the way to Rama and Krishna, the two most cherished avatars of all, and finally to the Buddha. The last one-to-be-waited-for is Kalki at the end of this degenerate era.[109] An illustrative example of the multiplicity of incarnations is the possibility of multiple avatars of the one and same figure of Krishna. Based on Vedic teaching and embraced by even contemporary Hindu piety, six such incarnations are often discerned: Purusa Avatars, Lila Avatars, Guna Avatars, Manvantara Avatars, Yuga Avatars, and Satyavesa Avatars.

Furthermore, unlike Christian tradition, it is customary for Hindu thought to conceive of avatars in degrees, from a partial to a fuller to a fullest measure of incarnation. Srila Prabhupada, the founder of the International As-

107. Sandy Bharat, "Hindu Perspectives on Jesus," in *The Blackwell Companion to Jesus*, ed. Delbert Burkett (Oxford: Wiley-Blackwell, 2011), 250–51.

108. Bharat, "Hindu Perspectives," 255; so also Swami Yuketswar, *The Holy Science* (Los Angeles: Self-Realization Fellowship, 1972), 32.

109. A reliable, nontechnical exposition is offered by Arvind Sharma, *Classical Hindu Thought: An Introduction* (Oxford: Oxford University Press, 2000), 6–7, 82–86.

sociation for Krishna Consciousness,[110] says it is also therefore understandable that, in contrast to the traditional Christian view of incarnation of the divine in one particular person at a certain point in history in a particular place, Hindu religion not only speaks of multiple "descents" of the divine but also speaks of them in universal terms.[111]

Similarly to the logic of Christian pluralisms in which Christ as a universal principle of divine presence is separated from the historical figure of Jesus, Hindus customarily make a distinction between Jesus and Christ. The title Christ appeals to them, as it speaks of universal application. The founder of the Self-Realization Fellowship and one of the ablest communicators to the West of Hindu religion, Paramahansa Yogananda (d. 1953), says this well: "There is a difference of meaning between *Jesus* and *Christ*. Jesus is the name of a little human body in which the vast Christ Consciousness was born. Although the Christ Consciousness manifested in the body of Jesus, it cannot be limited to one human form. It would be a metaphysical error to say that the omnipresent Christ Consciousness is circumscribed by the body of any one human being."[112] In this framework, "Christ" does not mean a particular individual but rather "the state of realization of Truth." Hence, each and every one of us can become Christ.[113]

From the Christian point of view (unless one subscribes to the typical pluralistic idea of a rough parity of all religions), this divorces Christology from all historical contours and makes the history of Jesus devoid of any meaning that the New Testament and the creeds assign to it. It of course also frustrates Christianity's claim to the uniqueness of Christ's work, including incarnation.

Over against the Christian view of "God-as-human" (the Word made flesh), the Hindu formula is "God-in-human." In this outlook, "the divine and human are ultimately identical, or the divine is the spark of potential in the human, or something else. . . . In all of them, everyone is potentially divine,

---

110. A. C. Bhaktivedanta Swami Prabhupāda, *Bhagavad-Gita As It Is*, abridged version (Los Angeles: Bhaktivedanta Book Trust, 1976), 69, cited in Bharat, "Hindu Perspectives on Jesus," 251.

111. See Swami Krishnananda, *The Philosophy of the Bhagavadgita* (Rishikesh, India: Divine Life Society Sivananda Ashram, n.d.), 99, https://www.swami-krishnananda.org /gita_oo.html.

112. Paramahansa Yogananda, *Man's Eternal Quest* (Los Angeles: Self-Realization Fellowship, 1975), 297.

113. Swami Abhedananda, *Vedanta Philosophy* (Kolkata: Ramakrishna Vedanta Math, 1959), 40.

and Jesus is an outstanding . . . embodiment of the human who has realized his divinity." Consequently, Hindu interpretation of Jesus knows no idea of atonement or reconciliation similar to that of Christian tradition.[114]

Because of these foundational differences, patient mutual dialogue between Hindu and Christian traditions is both necessary and useful. Even if it may not be able to resolve differences in the understanding of the deity of the "Savior(s)," incarnation, and the intervention of God, it may lead to a mutual trust and respect, as well as learning from the Other.

114. Ram-Prasad, "Hindu Views of Jesus," 88.

6 | "Atonement" and Reconciliation among Religions

Christian Theology of Atonement

The traditional Christian term used to refer to what Jesus Christ—sent by his Father for the salvation of humankind, in the power of the Spirit—has done to bring about reconciliation between God and humans, as well as among men and women, is "atonement." Not without reason, traditional "atonement theories," as they have been called, focused on the suffering, death, and resurrection of the Son of God, without which no Christian account of salvation can be had. Particularly in the Christian East, beginning from the very first centuries, incarnation, the "assumption" of human life and its cleansing and sanctification by the Son of God, was also stressed, as well as the resurrection and ascension of Christ.

Importantly, none of the ancient creeds rules on which specific theory of atonement the church should endorse. As already implied, the Eastern churches highlight the importance of incarnation and resurrection/ascension, whereas Western Christianity (both Protestant and Roman Catholic) has focused on suffering and the cross. For the former, the biggest problem of humanity has to do with mortality, or to put it positively, the possibility of gaining life eternal in communion with God. For the latter, the greatest atonement effect has been in defeating the effects of sin and the Fall, namely, guilt and judgment that result in condemnation apart from atonement. Notwithstanding the different emphases (which can be seen as complementary rather than alternative), all churches assign atonement and reconciliation to the triune God. This is the heart of the Christian theology of atonement, and it also distinguishes it from most other religious accounts. In Christian theology, the human being can never work out salvation for oneself—nor can another person; only God is able to.

In recent times, without in any way leaving behind the great tradition, Jesus Christ's life, ministry, and proclamation have also been highlighted as the basis of salvation, but only when linked to his whole history. Similarly, recently, topics such as the alleged link of the Christian story of the suffering and dying Messiah with violence and oppression have been reconsidered.

In today's pluralistic world, a vital challenge to all Christian theologies of atonement comes in relation to other living faiths' visions of "atonement" and reconciliation. The quotation marks around the term "atonement" remind us that it is questionable whether other faith traditions even have, or need to have, anything like the Christian substitutionary and "atoning" process. Be that as it may, it is reasonable to have a tentative expectation that living faith traditions (as long as they are theistic in any real sense of the word) envision ways of "reconciliation" both in relation to the deity and among human beings, and if, as in the Theravada tradition, "reconciliation" may not be theistically directed, some real material similarity still allows comparison. Our investigation begins with the Abrahamic traditions and then moves to the Asiatic traditions—again, paying special attention to particularities and nuances rather than lumping together incompatible accounts.

The Messiah of Israel and the Savior of the Nations: A Jewish-Christian Engagement

The Rejection of the Messiah by His Own People and the Salvation of the Gentiles

Most counterintuitively and ironically, it was only after the rejection of the Messiah by his own people that Jesus's suffering, death on the cross, and resurrection made him the "Savior of the nations."[1] Indeed, had not the messianic people of Israel rejected their Messiah, "Christianity may have remained an intra-Jewish affair."[2] In other words, the Messiah of Israel, the covenant people,

---

1. Pannenberg, *ST* 2:312; so also Jürgen Moltmann, *The Way of Jesus Christ: Christology in Messianic Dimensions*, trans. Margaret Kohl (Minneapolis: Fortress, 1993 [1989]), 34.

2. Carl E. Braaten, "Introduction: The Resurrection in Jewish-Christian Dialogue," in *The Resurrection of Jesus: A Jewish Perspective*, by Pinchas Lapide (Minneapolis: Augsburg, 1983), 18.

died for the people outside the covenant, the gentiles. Of course, this is not to deny the validity of Jesus's death for the people of Israel; Christians have to bear in mind that the Messiah of Israel, even when rejected, died first for the salvation of his own people.[3] The *Christian* theological statement about the Messiah's work for the gentiles highlights the universal efficacy of the salvific work of Israel's Messiah. Perhaps it is also justified to say from the Christian point of view that Christians could also now serve as the go-between for Israel and her Messiah and so anticipate the consummation of the divine plan that "all Israel will be saved" (Rom. 11:26).[4] Be that as it may, according to the New Testament, "salvation is from the Jews" (John 4:22).

It is significant that the influential Jewish philosopher of religion Franz Rosenzweig, in his mature work *The Star of Redemption*, came to affirm the role of the Christian church in the preaching of the gospel to the gentiles. The contemporary Jewish ecumenist Pinchas Lapide, among others, has continued this reasoning.[5] These testimonies by Jews at least make reasonable, if they do not totally justify, the Christian claim for the universal salvific effects of the death of Israel's Messiah.

That said, Christians should at all times bear in mind that the cross as a cultural-religious symbol is highly offensive to Judaism[6]—and not only generally speaking but also due to its cruel and violent abuse by Christians down through history. As discussed in the previous chapter, while Christian Christology does not have to be anti-Jewish, its narration has to be highly sensitive to Jewish intuitions after two millennia of wounded relations, and often under the shadow of the cross of the conquerors and oppressors. Not only that, but rather than reaching out to the Jewish people in seeing the passion story of the Messiah as a way of identification in solidarity with the suffering of the messianic people, the Christian church has interpreted the passion stories of the Gospels in terms of hostility toward Israel.[7]

---

3. John G. Kelly, "The Cross, the Church, and the Jewish People," in *Atonement Today*, ed. John Goldingay (London: SPCK, 1995), 166–67.

4. Braaten, "Introduction," 19.

5. Pinchas Lapide and Jürgen Moltmann, *Jewish Monotheism and Christian Trinitarian Doctrine: A Dialogue by Pinchas Lapide and Jürgen Moltmann*, trans. Leonard Swidler (Philadelphia: Fortress, 1981), 71.

6. Edward H. Flannery, *The Anguish of the Jews: Twenty-Three Centuries of Antisemitism*, rev. ed. (New York: Paulist, 1985 [1971]); Daniel Cohn-Sherbok, *The Crucified Jew* (London: HarperCollins, 1992).

7. See Elisabeth Schüssler Fiorenza and David Tracy, eds., *The Holocaust as Interruption*, Concilium 175 (Edinburgh: T&T Clark, 1984).

The Atonement in Jewish Estimation

An important task here is the comparison between Jewish and Christian theologies of atonement, a topic that, surprisingly, has not loomed large in the agenda of mutual talks. Each side has much to learn from the other. The idea of vicarious atonement after the Christian interpretation, with a view for the salvation of the world rather than for the benefit of the nation, as in the Maccabean martyrs' case, "seems strange and foreign to Jews who believe that the problem of sin had already been dealt with in the Torah."[8] This is because, first of all, Jewish theology does not hold to the Christian tradition's view of the Fall, which necessitates divine initiative as with the death on the cross.[9] Second, the transcendent goal of salvation in the afterlife is not as central either in the Old Testament or in later forms of Judaism as it is in Christian tradition, even though the idea of divine reward and punishment after death is not to be ignored in rabbinic and most other Jewish traditions. Following the Torah and its commandments, as the chosen people, and thus testifying to God's unity and holiness, is the way of "salvation" in Judaism.[10] That said, Jewish scholar Michael S. Kogan rightly acknowledges that it was on the basis of Hebrew Scriptures such as Isaiah 53:4–6 that Christian theology came to interpret the vicarious suffering of their Messiah.[11]

There is no denying that particularly the early Christian views and early rabbinic views evolved in close connection with the Old Testament atonement traditions. The concept of sacrifice is one of the important connecting links between the two religions. In both religions, sacrifice is an atoning act, notwithstanding differences registered above, and it calls for human response.[12] The Old Testament prophetic literature, which both traditions embrace, time after time targets worshipers who merely perform the cultic acts without repentance, mercy, and works of justice.

So, how would Jewish tradition interpret such key New Testament statements as "Behold, the Lamb of God, who takes away the sin of the world!"

---

8. Michael S. Kogan, *Opening the Covenant: A Jewish Theology of Christianity* (Oxford: Oxford University Press, 2008), 116.

9. See further, Steven Kepnes, "'Turn Us to You and We Shall Return': Original Sin, Atonement, and Redemption in Jewish Terms," in *Christianity in Jewish Terms*, ed. Tikva Frymer-Kensky et al. (Boulder, CO: Westview, 2000), 293–319.

10. Kogan, *Opening the Covenant*, 11–13.

11. Kogan, *Opening the Covenant*, 116.

12. John C. Lyden, "Atonement in Judaism and Christianity: Towards a Rapprochement," *Journal of Ecumenical Studies* 29, no. 1 (Winter 1992): 47–48, 50.

(John 1:29)? According to Jewish scholar Steven Kepnes, Jews may gain insight into its meaning through the lens of the biblical notions of purity and impurity, sacrificial offices and systems, including the rituals of the sanctuary, as well as the temple. Reference to the Lamb who takes away sin, of course, is based on the slaughtering of lambs for the expiation of sins. Christ's self-sacrifice also connects with Jewish liturgical days such as Yom Kippur.[13]

Differences, however, are noteworthy. Even though Jesus may be called metaphorically the high priest, in Jewish faith the high priest conducts the sacrificial act, whereas in Christian faith Jesus is the sacrifice, the sacrificial Lamb. This is not to say that Jewish faith doesn't know substitutionary suffering for others; of course it does, both in terms of the "Suffering Servant" of Second Isaiah and in terms of righteous martyrs, as during the Maccabean era. Still, the onetime finished self-sacrifice of Jesus after the Christian interpretation is markedly different from the continuing sacrificial cult administered by the priesthood in Judaism. Not only the finality of the sacrifice of Jesus but also its universality marks its divergence from the understanding of the Jewish tradition.

Further differences come to the fore when we bear in mind that Jesus's sacrifice, even in the context of the work of the triune God, is contingent on the relation to his person, a claim without parallel in Judaism and a stumbling block to its monotheism. The role of the Messiah in Judaism is to serve as the agent of reconciliation but not as the one who reconciles—only Yahweh can do that. Finally, a foundational difference has to do with the offer and object of the sacrifice. Whereas in Judaism people offer the sacrifice to Yahweh, in Christian theology it is God who reconciles the world to himself (2 Cor. 5:18–19).[14]

This brief comparison clearly shows that while there are profound common points between the two Abrahamic faiths, as both of them speak of sacrifice and atonement, the commonality should not be taken as implying a common understanding. In the matrix of the wider theological outlook, including differing theological anthropologies, much more work awaits the comparativists.

The Christian Theology of the Cross in Light of the Islamic Interpretation

As much as Jesus of Nazareth's significant role in both religions helps draw Christians and Muslims together around a common dialogue table, his death on the

13. Kepnes, "Turn Us to You," 297–301.
14. Lyden, "Atonement in Judaism," 50–53.

cross is a true scandal and cause of division. One of the reasons the suffering Messiah does not appeal to Muslims is that "paragons of success and vindication" such as Abraham, Noah, Moses, and David are much more congenial with the vision of God's manifest victory on earth. Simply put, "Islam refuses to accept this tragic image of Passion. Not simply because it has no place for the dogma of the Redemption, but because the Passion would imply in its eyes that God had failed."[15]

When it comes to the event of crucifixion itself, Muslim tradition does not speak with one voice. That said, without oversimplification, it is justified to claim that for most Muslims, if death on the cross even happened in the first place, it was not Jesus who died but rather a substitute in his stead (Simon of Cyrene or, as often presented in folk religion, Judas Iscariot).[16] So, what is believed to have happened to Jesus himself? According to tradition, "Allah took him up to Himself,"[17] up to heaven, from whence he will return at the eschaton (more in chap. 10).[18] This is based on the main Qur'anic passage (and, indeed, the only explicit reference to the crucifixion of Jesus), 4:157-58:

> (157) And because of their saying: We slew the Messiah, Jesus son of Mary, Allah's messenger—they slew him not nor crucified him, but it appeared so unto them [or "but a semblance was made to them"]; and lo! those who disagree concerning it are in doubt thereof; they have no knowledge thereof save pursuit of a conjecture; they slew him not for certain.
>
> (158) Nay, God raised him up to Him. [But Allah took him up unto Himself.] God is ever Mighty, Wise.[19]

Christian apologetic has advanced two different positions as a response to the standard Muslim denial of Jesus's death on the cross.[20] The first one is that

15. M. A. Merad, "Christ according to the Qur'an," *Encounter* (Rome) 69 (1980): 14, 15, quoted in Oddbjørn Leirvik, *Images of Jesus Christ in Islam*, 2nd ed. (New York: Continuum, 2010), 4.

16. See Leirvik, *Images of Jesus Christ*, 67–69.

17. See Clinton Bennett, *Understanding Christian-Muslim Relations: Past and Present* (London: Continuum, 2008), 51–52.

18. Understandably, attacks against the Christian teaching of the crucifixion have played a significant role in Muslim anti-Christian polemics and continue to do so, as illustrated in the widely influential pamphlet by the Indian–South African Ahmed Deedat, *Crucifixion or Cruci-fiction?* (Durban: Islamic Propagation Centre International, 1984).

19. Translation in square brackets from Neil Robinson, *Christ in Islam and Christianity* (New York: State University of New York Press, 1991), 106.

20. This paragraph is based on Robinson, *Christ in Islam*, 108–9.

the Qur'an is inconsistent: on the one hand affirming the death of Jesus (19:33; 3:55), and on the other hand denying it (4:157). The second apologetic argument has advanced the thesis that, indeed, the Qur'an is not denying the crucifixion because the contested passage of 4:157–58 can be interpreted otherwise and because it is hard to deny the apparent affirmation of Jesus's death in other passages.

Be that as it may, even Muslim exegetes have widely debated the exact meaning of the passage "Allah took him up unto Himself" (v. 158). Similarly, the reference to "a semblance was made to them" in 4:157 (following Robinson) is difficult. Muslim theology agrees with Robinson's conclusion almost unanimously: "Despite differences of opinion about the details the commentators were agreed that 4:157 denies that Jesus was crucified. The most widespread view was that it implies that the Jews erroneously crucified Jesus' 'semblance' and not Jesus himself."[21]

These debates aside, what is clear and without dispute is that in standard Muslim understanding "'God was *not* in Christ reconciling the world to himself': he was with Jesus withdrawing him to heaven."[22] Sin is not atoned for through a substitutionary death in Islam, so Jesus's death on our behalf does not even make sense in the framework. Hence, Muslim and Christian accounts of reconciliation are even further from each other than Jewish from Christian.

Reconciliation and "Savior" in Buddhist Perspectives

A foundational difference between the Buddhist and Christian visions is that "Savior has no place in the Buddhist worldview. An individual must control and be responsible for his or her own destiny."[23] One is one's own refuge, and no one else—not even Buddha—can save one from the law of *kamma*.[24] Buddhists simply "balk at the idea that any deity is capable of granting salvation to others simply through an act of will."[25]

21. Robinson, *Christ in Islam*, 140, at the end of the chapter-long detailed study of this expression in the Qur'an and commentary literature.

22. Kenneth Cragg, *Jesus and the Muslim: An Exploration* (London: Allen & Unwin, 1985; Oxford: Oneworld, 1999), 167–68.

23. Satanun Boonyakiat, "A Christian Theology of Suffering in the Context of Theravada Buddhism in Thailand" (PhD diss., School of Theology, Fuller Theological Seminary, 2009), 114.

24. John R. Davis, *Poles Apart: Contextualizing the Gospel in Asia* (Bangalore: Theological Book Trust, 1998), 98–104.

25. José Ignacio Cabezón, "Buddhist Views of Jesus," in *JWF*, 23.

The death on the cross of the Savior for the sins and salvation of others is an idea totally unknown in all traditions of Buddhism. That said, the generic idea of redemptive or "vicarious" suffering on behalf of others is not unknown in Buddhism; think, for example, of the commonly known story in Thai (Theravada) Buddhism of the sixteenth-century Queen Srisuriyothai's self-sacrifice to save her people who were threatened by the king of Burma.[26] Apart from this kind of noble human self-sacrifice, resorting to any kind of vicarious act done by another person, even a divinity, would mean shrinking from one's own responsibility to deal with one's *kamma*. In Mahayana Buddhism, the Boddhisattva—unlike the *arahant* of Theravada who has stepped into nirvana—is willing to postpone his own entrance into *nibbana* to help others reach the goal. Even that, however, is the function not of a "savior" but rather of a "good neighbor."

What about Pure Land Buddhism? Is the path outlined by this Buddhist tradition compatible with the Christian view of salvation? No, it is not, although there are remarkable common themes, unlike in any other major form of Buddhism. The main savior figure is Boddhisattva Dharmakara, who, through the rigorous and pure practice of forty-eight vows, reached enlightenment and became Amitabha Buddha. He opened the path of salvation in primordial times by establishing the Western Pure Land and made it possible for all sentient beings reborn in that land to reach enlightenment, "salvation."[27] "The Buddha embodied his virtue in his Name for all beings, enabling them to enter the Pure Land at death. Through their faith in, and meritorious recitation of the Name, they are saved by its power."[28] With all his great reservations about human religiosity, Barth felt deep sympathies for the Pure Land tradition, the existence of which was "a providential disposition" parallel to Reformed Christianity based on the logic of grace. He considered carefully the form of Pure Land developed by Shinran with an appeal to faith.[29]

---

26. Summary of the story on the web page regarding the memorial to Srisuriyothai, under "Ayutthaya," on BangkokSite, accessed March 14, 2019, http://www.bangkoksite.com /AyutthayaPage/ChediSriSuriyothai.htm.

27. Boddhisattva is a Buddha-in-the-making seeking enlightenment. Indeed, there is more than one Pure Land in those traditions. Wherever there is an enlightened Buddha, there is Pure Land. The Western Pure Land created by Boddhisattva Dharmakara is the main Pure Land and combines teachings and features of others.

28. Alfred Bloom, "Jesus in the Pure Land," in *JWF*, 33.

29. Barth, *CD* I/2, 340–42 (342).

Reconciliation and the Cross in Hindu Assessment

Similarly to Buddhism, Hinduism does not know reconciliation through a vicarious death by another person; even the main theistic traditions do not. Raja Ram Mohun Roy, who had a high regard for Jesus as an ethical teacher, expresses the Hindu opposition to the Christian idea of atonement in his correspondence with an anonymous Christian priest. Against the Christian minister's reasoning that Jesus can be called a "Saviour of men" only if "he died in their stead to atone for their sins" rather than just helping them live an ethical life, Roy contends that the title "Saviour" is "applied frequently in the divine writings to those persons who had been endued with the power of saving people." In support, Roy refers to Old Testament Scriptures such as Obadiah 21, Nehemiah 9:27, and 2 Kings 13:5, which use the term translated in many renderings as "savior." Furthermore, Roy notes that Jesus himself at times refers to his salvific work on the basis of "the inculcation of the word of God," as in John 15:3, 5:24, and 6:63. For Roy, the conclusion follows that, on the one hand, there is no way to attribute any "atoning" power to Jesus's influence and that, on the other hand, it wouldn't diminish Jesus's significance for him to be revered as a "Divine Teacher."[30] Apart from exegetical inaccuracies, Roy accurately expresses the radical difference between the two faiths regarding the topic of "salvation."

In other words, the biblical idea of Jesus as the Lamb of God (John 1:29) sacrificed for the sins of the world is foreign to all Hindu strands. That said, as mentioned earlier, the idea of self-sacrifice for the sake of others and their well-being is very much part of Hindu thought. The sacrificial lamb imagery can only make sense if it is understood in its "cosmological"—we could probably also say metaphorical—sense and linked with the basic Vedic principle of *rita* (right order). This multifaceted term denotes cosmic order as well as moral order, and also the right order of sacrifices. Sacrifices offered to gods were the basic means of securing order in ancient Hinduism. Indeed, "sacrifice" is called in Rig Veda the "center of the universe."[31] The New Testament and early Christian atonement theories include perspectives related to these kinds of cosmic ramifications of the cross. However, in Christian tradition they are integrally related to the bib-

---

30. *The English Works of Raja Ram Mohun Roy*, vol. 3, *The Precepts of Jesus—a Guide to Peace and Happiness; Extracted from the Books of the New Testament Ascribed to the Four Evangelists with Translations into Sungscit and Bengalee* (Calcutta: Baptist Mission Press, 1820), part I, 172–75, reproduced in *JBC*, 162–64.

31. Rig Veda 1.164.35.

lical narrative of the triune God breaking the power of evil and resistance to divine purposes in Christ, reconciling everything in heaven and earth with God.

One aspect of salvation in Christian theology has to do with forgiveness. That is not a totally foreign idea to Hinduism, even though it is not a central one. Bhagavad Gita (18.66) says, "Relinquishing all Dharmas take refuge in Me alone; I will liberate thee from all sins; grieve not."[32] To properly understand this statement, one has to stick with the Hindu view of what "sin" is, namely, "that which keeps the mind attached to sense perception and objects of the senses. Such attachment produces restlessness, which clouds perception of the soul."[33]

That said, the idea of grace properly understood is not unknown in Hinduism, particularly in Vaishnavism (Vishnu god–based theistic religion) and as taught particularly in Bhagavad Gita. That topic will be carefully studied in chapter 8, on salvation.

Whereas in Christian tradition the emphasis is "on the God who is offering salvation," in Hinduism (Siva god–based) and other traditions, it is "on the effort of the individual seeking salvation."[34] Put otherwise, "In the Christian doctrine of Grace, therefore, we confront an act of God," whereas in the Hindu view, liberation is a matter of human initiative and accomplishment.[35] Ultimately, the Christian view of salvation is linked with the salvific work of the triune God in the context of the cross.[36]

Christian Trinitarian logic suggests that, after discussing the Father's role as the Creator and the Son's role as the Redeemer, it is time to turn to the Holy Spirit, the energy of life and vitality who is also linked with the reception of salvation and sanctification by men and women. Somewhat similarly to Christology, pneumatology (the doctrine of the Holy Spirit) consists of two mutually intertwined main themes, namely, (1) pneumatology "proper," which deals with the nature and personhood of the Spirit, including the Spirit's work in general, and (2) soteriology, the doctrine of salvation, with the focus on salvific gifts communicated by the Spirit to the believers on the basis of Christ's atoning work. Since other spirits and powers are believed to be in the cosmos and among religions, pneumatology typically discusses them also.

32. Swarupananda translation.
33. Cited in Sandy Bharat, "Hindu Perspectives on Jesus," in *The Blackwell Companion to Jesus*, ed. Delbert Burkett (Oxford: Wiley-Blackwell, 2011), 256.
34. Sabapathy Kulandran, *Grace in Christianity and Hinduism* (Cambridge: James Clarke, 2000 [1964]), 245.
35. Kulandran, *Grace in Christianity*, 242.
36. Chap. 2 in John Brockington, *Hinduism and Christianity* (New York: St. Martin's, 1992).

7 | Holy Spirit and the S/spirit(s) of Religions

Holy Spirit and Spiritual Powers in Christian Theology and among Religions

The Spirit and Spirits in Christian Theology

As mentioned above, it is useful to define the domain of pneumatology, the doctrine of the Holy Spirit, in two interrelated areas. The first one might be called pneumatology "proper." It deals with the nature and personhood of the Spirit, including the Spirit's work in the cosmos, creation, and the world. Since there are believed to be other spirits and powers, good and evil, in the cosmos and among religions, pneumatology typically also discusses them under the elusive title "angels, demons, and other spiritual powers." This is a fertile area of comparison in relation to Islamic, Jewish, Buddhist, and Hindu traditions (although Theravada's nontheism stretches its limits). The second main domain, typically named soteriology, the doctrine of salvation, deals with salvific gifts communicated by the Spirit to the believers on the basis of Christ's atoning work. They range from divine election and calling, to repentance and forgiveness, to justification and sanctification, to union and glorification. This so-called order of salvation will be the topic of chapter 8. Although to other faith traditions most of these Christian nomenclatures are foreign, there is enough material similarity in the general vision of "salvation" to facilitate cautious comparisons.

In Christian theology, the third member of the Trinity, the Holy Spirit, is fully divine along with the other two Trinitarian members, a conviction established in early centuries, thus completing the doctrine of the Trinity. Not surprisingly, this classic view came under much pressure and challenge in the aftermath of the Enlightenment. Modern theologians sought to diminish, at times even virtually reject, a distinction between the divine and human spirit(s), resulting in this-worldly ("immanentist") accounts of the Spirit. As is true of Christology and some other Christian doctrines, this kind of bifurcation still continues and characterizes the diversity of theologies and beliefs.

Similarly to the Father and Son, the Holy Spirit functions in many areas in Christian faith, from serving as the principle of life to facilitate the life of all living beings and creation, to inspiring the Scriptures and enlivening its reading in the Christian community, to helping distinguish between God-sent spirits and their opponents. That said, the Holy Spirit is looked upon particularly as the agent who brings to men and women the salvific gifts acquired by the Son in his incarnation, suffering, death, and resurrection. Throughout history, and more recently in the rapidly growing Pentecostal/charismatic movement, the Spirit's charisms have also belonged to the gifts, including healing and prophecy.

Under and subservient to the Holy Spirit (and more widely, the triune God), Christian tradition, based on the Old Testament teaching, knows spiritual powers and energies, named angels and demons. Teaching on these spiritual powers is less fully developed than the doctrine of the Holy Spirit (proper), and they are typically conceived of as created beings who possess some real power (and often also will). As to the origin of demons and evil powers, mythical stories allegedly hinted at in the biblical canon are often mentioned, though no canonical opinion exists.

The Theological Significance of the Spirit(s) among Religions

As the Indian theologian Joseph Pathrapankal states, the Spirit is "the foundational reality which makes possible for the humans to exercise their religious sense and elevate their self to the realm of the divine."[1] No wonder, then, that part of the cosmic orientation of all traditional and most contemporary cultures in the Global South has to do with the deep and wide sense of spirits and spiritualities in religions.

Hence, the importance of the theme of the discernment of the Spirit and spirits in the religiously plural world. But, as another Indian theologian,

---

1. Joseph Pathrapankal, "Editorial," *Journal of Dharma* 33, no. 3 (1998): 299.

Stanley J. Samartha, observes, in recent years the question of the discernment of the spirits has "somewhat aggressively thrust itself on the theological consciousness of the church"[2] without the needed readiness. Not surprisingly, theological textbooks lack discussions of the topic.[3] A necessary asset to any exercise of the discernment of the spirit(s) has to do with the basic knowledge of other traditions, attempted here.

This comparative discussion proceeds in three unequal parts. Part 1 will engage pneumatology proper in four living faith traditions, beginning with the two cousin Abrahamic religions and then going to Asiatic religions. The short second part will take up the issue of spiritual powers and energies in all these traditions, in the same order of discussion. Finally, part 3 introduces the theme of the discernment of the spirit(s) from a Christian point of view.

Ruach ("Spirit") in Jewish Traditions

Rabbinic and Mystical Interpretations

Because Christians share with Jews the major part of the sacred Scriptures, no separate study of the Old Testament pneumatologies is attempted here.

In the vast rabbinic literature, the interest in the *Shekinah*, the divine immanence of Yahweh, overshadows discussion of the *ruach*.[4] An obvious reason for focusing less on the "Holy Spirit" in postbiblical Jewish theology seems to be apologetic, that is, the avoidance of making too close a connection with the New Testament and emerging Christian theology of the Spirit. Be that as it may, we must also consider the well-known (but widely debated) fact that according to the rabbinic sources, God's Spirit has left Israel. That, however, never meant that interest in the Spirit was therefore lost. Based on the scriptural teachings, the rabbinic literature considers *Ruah ha-Kodesh*, "holy spirit" or "spirit of holiness," to be the divinely given power of prophecy and leadership.[5]

---

2. Stanley J. Samartha, *Between Two Cultures: Ecumenical Ministry in a Pluralist World* (Geneva: WCC Publications, 1996), 187.

3. Stanley J. Samartha, *Courage for Dialogue: Ecumenical Issues in Inter-Religious Relationships* (Geneva: WCC Publications, 1981; Maryknoll, NY: Orbis, 1982), 76.

4. Joshua Abelson, *The Immanence of God in Rabbinical Literature* (London: Macmillan, 1912).

5. Julie Hilton Danan, "The Divine Voice in Scripture: *Ruah ha-Kodesh* in Rabbinic Literature" (PhD diss., University of Texas at Austin, 2009), http://repositories.lib.utexas.edu /bitstream/handle/2152/17297/dananj31973.pdf?sequence=2.

Pneumatology in Judaism has undergone significant revisions and transformations, including diverse medieval movements. The Zoharic literature, compiled in the late thirteenth century, represents a culmination of the mystical kabbalistic traditions and a response to Christian teachings of the Holy Spirit. It focuses on mystical spiritual experience and the union with God. As in rabbinic literature, the Holy Spirit is identified with the *Shekinah*. It accompanies the people of God and represents the powerful divine immanence in the world, including guidance of the people of God.[6]

Something curious about the pneumatology of *Zohar* is not the existence of evil spirits or "nonholy spirit" but that it "posits secondary 'holy spirits,' that derive from the *Shekinah* and other emanation-related holy spirits."[7] Even angels can be called holy spirits.

Contemporary Jewish Pneumatologies

From a Christian perspective, it is interesting to note the influence of Greek-Hellenistic and later modernist philosophies on the conception of the Spirit in Judaism as well. The chapter entitled "The Holy Spirit" in Hermann Cohen's (d. 1918) *Religion of Reason: Out of the Sources of Judaism* builds on the Enlightenment. It follows strictly an ethical-moral (Kantian) lead beginning with the question: "What is human morality?"[8] The only "religious" meaning of the Holy Spirit relates to holiness. The presentation of the theme of the Spirit in Samuel S. Cohon's *Jewish Theology: A Historical and Systematic Interpretation of Judaism and Its Foundations* (1971) follows the same kind of immanentist and humanity-focused line.

A markedly different approach is the 2011 pneumatology titled *Breath of Life*, by the contemporary American rabbi Rachel Timoner, which bears much resemblance to current Christian pneumatologies. Unlike her predecessors, Timoner links *ruach* with "life-giving breath, a simple wind, and the spirit that animates creation."[9] She also forges a link with redemption in a most ho-

---

6. Elliot B. Gertel, "Holy Spirit in the Zohar," *CCAR Journal: A Reform Jewish Quarterly* 56, no. 4 (2009): 80–102.

7. Gertel, "Holy Spirit," 88.

8. Hermann Cohen, *Religion of Reason: Out of the Sources of Judaism*, translation and introduction by Simon Kaplan, 2nd rev. ed. (New York: Frederick Ungar, 1972 [1919]), 100.

9. Rachel Timoner, *Breath of Life: God as Spirit in Judaism* (Brewster, MA: Paraclete, 2011), xviii.

listic manner, a move missing in her tradition. In keeping with an important trend in contemporary Christian pneumatology, Rabbi Timoner also discusses topics such as "embodied spirit"[10] and deep interconnection and relationality between the physical and mental/spiritual, personal and communal, human and the rest of creation, and so forth.

This kind of bifurcation of the accounts of the Spirit corresponds quite neatly with the diversity in Christian tradition and thus makes mutual dialogue highly useful and informational.

The Spirit of Yahweh and the Holy Spirit

Between the Jewish and Christian theologies, talk about the Spirit has to do with how to conceive of the Spirit of the one God in relation to the divine persons (Father, Son, Spirit), as discussed above in chapter 2 on the Trinity. Even when that discussion is not likely to lead to unanimity, the conversation partners speak of one and the same God, the Spirit.

Despite deep differences, Christians and Jews should appreciate the great cross-fertilization between the two traditions when it comes to pneumatology. Christian pneumatology owes everything to the Jewish scriptural traditions of the Spirit of God.[11] The dramatic reorientations in contemporary Christian pneumatologies that have dramatically widened the sphere and ministry of the Holy Spirit are but a rediscovery of the Old Testament teaching on *ruach Yahweh*.

The other Abrahamic faith's conception of the Spirit bears significantly less similarity to Christian pneumatology.

Ruh ("Spirit") in the Qur'an and Islamic Spiritualities

The Spirit in the Qur'an

The Muslim teaching about the Spirit is deeply indebted to older Abrahamic traditions. The basic term *ruh* is, of course, a Hebrew cognate with shared meanings of breath, wind, and air. The twenty Qur'anic references to *ruh* can

---

10. Timoner, *Breath of Life*, 17–19.
11. Michel René Barnes, "The Beginning and End of Early Christian Pneumatology," *Augustinian Studies* 39, no. 2 (2008): 169–86.

be divided into four "sense-groups."[12] The first relates to the sayings about the angels and the Spirit (97:4). Here the Spirit is (semi)personified.

The second sense-group is about the sharing of Allah's spirit with humans. Here the Qur'an makes a definite shift from a (semi)personal agent to an impersonal breath, as in Genesis 2:7. Interestingly, this breathing relates only to Adam (Q 15:29; 32:8; 38:72) and Jesus, including the passages in which Mary's virginal conception is mentioned (4:171; 19:17; 21:91; 66:12). What is the meaning of the Qur'anic saying that Jesus is a spirit from Allah? Neither divinity, nor Trinity, as the same sura hastens to add: "So believe in God and His messengers, and do not say, 'Three'" (4:171).

The third sense-group of *ruh* sayings in the Qur'an is the least understood: "Say: 'The Spirit is of the command [*amr*] of my Lord'" (17:85; also 16:2; 40:15; 42:52). The exact meaning of *amr* is disputed: Is it "command" or "affair" or something else?

The final sense-group relates to the important theme of "Holy Spirit," the "Spirit of Holiness." These occurrences emerge at the end of the Prophet's ministry, as he also becomes better informed on Christian faith and the role of Jesus. Three times it is linked with Jesus in terms of Allah "strengthening" or "confirming" him (2:87, 253; 5:110); some other faithful ones are also strengthened with a spirit from Allah (58:22).

Mystical and Charismatic Experiences of the Spirit in Sufism

Grassroots-level enthusiasm of the spiritual experience, similar to that found in other faiths, is manifest in Islamic mystical Sufism and related movements. The rapid and steady growth of Sufism and related spiritualist movements is explained at least partly by full embrace of the spiritual experience and manifestations.[13] No wonder that throughout the years "power encounter" and miraculous acts have been enthusiastically acknowledged and claimed to lie behind many conversions.[14] Particularly important is Sufism's virtual identification of the Spirit of Holiness/Holy Spirit with God himself.

12. Thomas J. O'Shaughnessy, *The Development of the Meaning of Spirit in the Koran* (Rome: Pont. Institutum Orientalium Studiorum, 1953).

13. Duncan B. Macdonald, "The Development of the Idea of Spirit in Islam: II," *Moslem World* 22, no. 2 (1932): 166.

14. Sobhi Malek, "Islam Encountering Spiritual Power," in *Called and Empowered: Global Mission in Pentecostal Perspective*, ed. Murray W. Dempster, Byron D. Klaus, and Douglas Petersen (Peabody, MA: Hendrickson, 1991), 180–97.

While doctrinally suspect, Sufi mysticism focuses on love and spiritual unity as well as on spiritual experiences. It is said of Husayn ibn Mansur Al-Hallajah, a famous ninth-century Sufi mystic, that he "was so full of the Holy Spirit that he could no longer distinguish himself from God," an abomination to the establishment, leading to his crucifixion in 922.[15]

Discerning Differences and Searching for Commonalities

Many common points include the close relationship of *ruh* to Jesus, including the virginal conception, its relationship to the Word of God, the ministry of strengthening the faithful, and so forth. At the same time, one must be careful not to interpret common theological terms such as "spirit" and "word" without taking into consideration the underlying deep theological differences.

An interesting interfaith debate has to do with how to translate and interpret the identity of the Johannine metaphor of the Holy Spirit, Paraclete. A long and wide tradition, particularly in folk Islam, identifies the Paraclete with Muhammad. The dispute goes back to the interpretation of Qur'an 61:6: "And when Jesus son of Mary said, 'O Children of Israel, I am indeed God's messenger to you, confirming what is before me of the Torah and bringing good tidings of a messenger who will come after me, whose name is Ahmad.' Yet when he brought them, they said, 'This is manifest sorcery!'"

The *parakletos* ("Counselor") of John 16:7 is equated with "Ahmad" of Qur'an 61:6 (in many English renderings, the "Praised One"). In Islamic tradition, a version of Muhammad's name is Ahmad.[16] There are, however, a number of problems with this identification, the most obvious one being that there is absolutely no textual evidence for it in Greek manuscripts of the New Testament. Furthermore, it is doubtful that Muhammad himself would have endorsed this interpretation.

One related theme may find commonality between Islamic and Christian spiritualities: "remembering." The main task of the Johannine Paraclete is to "bring to your remembrance all that I [Jesus] have said to you" (John 14:26). The theme of remembering is crucial to Islamic tradition; indeed, the Qur'an itself is named *Al-Dhikr*, the "Reminder." Hence, the central exhortation and

---

15. James Kritzeck, "Holy Spirit in Islam," in *Perspectives on Charismatic Renewal*, ed. Edward D. O'Connor (Notre Dame: University of Notre Dame Press, 1975), 110.

16. William Montgomery Watt, "His Name Is Ahmad," *Muslim World* 43, no. 2 (1953): 110–17.

promise: "So remember Me, I will remember you; and be thankful to Me, and be not ungrateful towards Me" (Q 2:152).[17]

Atman and the Holy Spirit: Pneumatology in Hindu-Christian Perspective

Atman *Is Brahman*

Hindu traditions are united in the common belief in the Spirit[ual] as the ultimate reality.[18] What is much more challenging is defining more precisely how to best express in Hindu terms what Christian faith speaks of when stating "God is spirit" (John 4:24). Reasons are many, including the fluidity and open-endedness of demarcation lines in Hinduism between any "personal" god/deity and spiritual powers and energies, including those in nature. Note also that Hindu philosophy uses a number of words that could be translated (something like) "spirit": *atman*, *antaryamin*, and *shakti*, to name the most obvious ones.

Nevertheless, any inquiry into the "pneumatology" of Hinduism must begin with the most foundational statement in Vedic Upanishadic texts: "that Self [*Atman*] is indeed Brahman,"[19] a topic already dealt with in various chapters above. As the ultimate reality, Brahman is beyond all qualities, definitions, limits; to use the Western philosophical terminology, it is absolutely infinite.

Still the question persists: How exactly is this related to pneumatology within the Hindu framework? Are there any parallels with Abrahamic faiths?

In Search of Parallels between Hindu and Christian Concepts of the Divine Spirit(s)

In light of the deep spirituality of Hindu cultures and religions, it comes as no surprise that Indian Christian theologians have shown remarkable interest in the Holy Spirit through the lens of Indian spiritualities.[20] Two

---

17. Kenneth Cragg, *Jesus and the Muslim: An Exploration* (London: Allen & Unwin, 1985; Oxford: Oneworld, 1999), 260–62, 269, 272–74.

18. M. M. Thomas, "The Holy Spirit and the Spirituality for Political Struggles," *Ecumenical Review* 42, nos. 3–4 (1990): 216.

19. Brihadaranyaka Upanishad 2.5.2; *SBE* 15:113.

20. See Robin H. S. Boyd, *An Introduction to Indian Christian Theology* (Madras: Christian Literature Society, 1969), 241–43.

kinds of tactics have been tried in this search for potential correlations between the two "pneumatologies." One focuses on the concept of "spirit" per se; the other one places the Spirit in the Trinitarian context and looks for any links.[21]

As a representative of the first category, we may look at the alleged connecting point between the concept of *shakti* and God's Spirit. *Shakti* is extraordinary power and energy, not limited to the workings of humans but also related to some deities, particularly Durga and Kali, the prominent female deities. Even more important regarding parallels with the Holy Spirit is the belief in *shakti* as the energy of creation; at times it is called the "Universal Creator."[22] For the Indian Christian theologian R. Panikkar, this was a key: "From the Hindu perspective, the Spirit can be described as the 'Divine *Sakti* penetrating everything and manifesting God, disclosing him in his immanence and being present in all his manifestations.'"[23] That said, from the Christian perspective, the parallel stays at a highly generic level.

More work has been done with the second category, spirit in relation to Trinity. Having investigated Trinitarian parallels at large in chapter 2, we highlight here the Spirit's role. In reference to the ancient concept of *saccidananda* ("being," "wisdom," "bliss"), discussed in that chapter, some Indian theologians have seen parallels between *Ananda* ("bliss") and the Holy Spirit, the bringer of joy and blessedness.[24] While this Hindu interpretation cannot be reconciled with the normative Christian view for obvious reasons, such as its lack of "personhood," as a *Hindu* interpretation it deserves attention. But, as said before, the general cash value of the attempts to find a parallel between the Christian Trinity and Hindu Trimurti is meager, at least in light of investigation done so far. Still, continuing these dialogical exercises is necessary and useful.

21. P. V. Joseph, *Indian Interpretation of the Holy Spirit* (Delhi: ISPCK, 2007); Kirsteen Kim, "The Holy Spirit in Mission in India: Indian Contribution to Contemporary Mission Pneumatology" (presentation at Overseas Christian Missionary Society, April 6, 2004), http://www.ocms.ac.uk/docs/TUESDAY%20LECTURES_Kirsteen.pdf.

22. B. J. Christie Kumar, "An Indian Appreciation of the Doctrine of the Holy Spirit: A Search into the Religious Heritage of the Indian Christian," *Indian Journal of Theology* 30 (1981): 29.

23. Raimundo Panikkar, *The Unknown Christ of Hinduism: Towards an Ecumenical Christophany*, rev. ed. (Maryknoll, NY: Orbis, 1981, 1991), 57.

24. Peter May, "The Trinity and Saccidananda," *Indian Journal of Theology* 7, no. 3 (1958): 92.

Pneumatology in Buddhist-Christian Perspective

The Quest for the Ultimate Reality

If possible, the search for correlates between the Christian Holy Spirit and conceptions of the S/spirit(s) in Buddhist traditions is an even more complicated task, beginning with (Theravada's) intentional flight away from deities. That said, Buddhist "theology" and cosmology are still foundationally idealist, that is, based on the primacy of the spirit[ual] rather than natural (materialist). Having discussed the issue of an ultimate reality (chap. 2), it suffices to mention that the only viable candidate for comparison would be sunyata (emptiness).

Indicative of the scarcity of comparative precedents and lack of specification in rare cases where sunyata and *pneuma* have been set in parallel is the leading Christian comparative pneumatologist Amos Yong's stance. He obviously assumes at the general level some commonality between the two but fails to specify it in any exact manner. Indeed, Yong rightly mentions at the outset that "in the Buddhist case *shunyata* functions in a non-theistic context," and therefore he finds it useful to relate it to pneumatological anthropology and the discussion of creation at large rather than to the Holy Spirit strictly speaking.[25]

Another potential comparative parallel could be found between Christian Spirit and the "three bodies" (trikaya) doctrine of the Mahayana, discussed in chapter 5, on Christology, particularly its middle category, the "blissful body" (*sambhogakaya*). But even that stays at such a general level that at the moment we need merely register the effort.[26] That said, the parallels also are severely limited by the Christian confession of the Spirit as God.

The remaining two sections of this chapter, much shorter than the first one, will first compare spiritual powers and energies among faith traditions and then introduce the task of the discernment of the spirit(s). In the immediately following section, we will first introduce briefly the topic in four traditions and then attempt a short comparative dialogue.

---

25. Amos Yong, *Pneumatology and the Christian-Buddhist Dialogue: Does the Spirit Blow through the Middle Way?* (Leiden: Brill Academic, 2012), 59; a similar tactic is followed in his *The Cosmic Breath: Spirit and Nature in the Christianity-Buddhism-Science Trialogue* (Leiden: Brill, 2012).

26. J. C. Cleary, "Trikaya and Trinity: The Mediation of the Absolute," *Buddhist-Christian Studies* 6 (1986): 65.

Spirits and Powers among Living Faith Traditions

Angels and Demons in Abrahamic Traditions

Jewish Angelology

Although belief in angels, demons, and spiritual beings among secular Jews (a majority of whom reside in the United States) is mixed, over half of them no longer affirm the traditional belief.[27] Among religious Jews, that belief is still high, and spiritual powers have a definite place in the scriptural tradition.[28]

As is well known, the Old Testament term *malak* (messenger) can be used of both divine and human agents; the context determines the meaning. A special category is the "angel of Yahweh" (Gen. 19; Exod. 14:19; among others), at times identifiable with God himself. Somewhat like Christian tradition, in which medieval theology brought about the most sophisticated angelology, in the mystical Jewish kabbalah the most creative reflection on spiritual beings emerged.

The appearance of demons, evil spiritual beings, in the Old Testament is infrequent, particularly in the postexilic period—although throughout the canon there are less pronounced and more elusive themes of cosmic conflict and chaos (Job 3:8; 38:8–11; Pss. 29:3–4; 89:9–10; Isa. 51:9–11).[29] Differently from Asiatic and other pagan traditions, the role of both good and evil angels is always subordinated to Yahweh, thus avoiding dualism. Even the role of Satan, which gradually evolves over history, is that of a subordinate—in some cases, even Yahweh's servant (as in Job). This clear and uncompromising distinction between God and other spiritual beings carried over to Christian tradition beginning from the church fathers.

Muslim Angelology

Of the three Abrahamic faiths, it is in Islam that angels and spiritual beings play the most significant role, whether in scriptural tradition or in folk piety.[30]

---

27. Pew Research Center, *U.S. Religious Landscape Survey*, June 1, 2008, http://www.pewforum.org/2008/06/01/u-s-religious-landscape-survey-religious-beliefs-and-practices/.

28. Among the main Jewish movements in New Testament times, only the Sadducees refused to believe in spirits (Mark 12:18; Acts 23:8).

29. Gregory A. Boyd, *God at War: The Bible & Spiritual Conflict* (Downers Grove, IL: InterVarsity Press, 1997), 73–113.

30. Peter G. Riddell, "How Allah Communicates: Islamic Angels, Devils and the

181

Belief in angels is one of Islam's key tenets, and their denial is regarded as a rejection of the Word of God. Their importance is also highlighted in that, unlike Jewish-Christian tradition, there is a well-known scriptural teaching about angels' creation prior to that of humans and about Allah's consultation with them before creating humans (Q 38:71–72). Somewhat similarly to the Old Testament, the Qur'an provides various kinds of artistic portraits of angels (such as their having hands and two, three, or four wings; 35:1; 6:93) and speaks of their ministering in various kinds of tasks of service and messaging, including intercession (53:25). A further similarity is an allusion to the hierarchy of angels, Gabriel being the most prominent, and Michael second. The most important angelic task is that of Gabriel as the messenger from whom Muhammad received the divine revelation. No wonder that highly sophisticated angelologies were constructed by leading Islamic philosophers and theologians.

A special class of heavenly beings, the jinn—hugely important in folk Islam—are mentioned often in the Qur'an. They are made of fire (as opposed to humans, who are made of clay). They are endowed with freedom of the will, and there is ambiguity about whether they are evil or good; mostly they are taken as evil. Jinns are believed to interact in various ways with humanity. In folk religion, they are frequently invoked for magical and miraculous purposes. Spiritual healers often address the jinn as part of their rituals.[31]

Spiritual Beings and Powers in Asiatic Faiths

Powers and Energies in Hinduism

The role and nature of angelic beings and powers in Asiatic faith traditions are more complex than in monotheistic traditions. In Hinduism, the contours and definitions are quite elusive. It is often particularly difficult to make a clear distinction between deities and nondivine spiritual beings.[32] In contrast to

---

2004 Tsunami," chap. 8 in *A&D*; Bill A. Musk, "Angels and Demons in Folk Islam," chap. 10 in *A&D*.

31. Gordon D. Newby, "Angels" and "Jinn," in *The Oxford Encyclopedia of the Modern Islamic World*, ed. John L. Esposito (Oxford: Oxford University Press, 1995), *Oxford Islamic Studies Online*, http://www.oxfordislamicstudies.com/Public/book_oemiw.html.

32. Chris Gnanakan, "The Manthiravadi: A South Indian Wounded Warrior-Healer," in *A&D*, 141.

Abrahamic traditions, even the main deities (such as Vishnu) get entangled in numerous ways in the lives and workings of what Western terminology would name less-than-divine beings. Furthermore, not all demons are evil, as in Abrahamic traditions.[33]

The belief in reincarnation blurs any absolute distinction between human and "superhuman" (angelic, demonic) beings. To make the issue more complicated, even *devas* (the godlike or divine beings) are subject to reincarnation; but also, it is not impossible for humans in some cases to be reincarnated as *devas*. Given the complex, multimillennial history of religious and cultural beliefs, it is no wonder that there is a rich diversity of beliefs and traditions and rituals related to either invoking good spirits or trying to cast away evil spirits.

Powers and Energies in Buddhism

Buddhist traditions also have wide and rich demonological traditions with many local colors.[34] Somewhat similar to the temptations of Jesus on the eve of his public ministry, in early Buddhist tradition Mara, the arch-devil, along with his three daughters, Rati (Desire), Raga (Pleasure), and Tanha (Restlessness), sought to dissuade Gautama from achieving enlightenment.[35]

Although the Theravada tradition soon (against its initial intentions, one may argue) began to develop quite sophisticated visions of spiritual beings, that development was even more massive in the various Mahayana traditions and their extremely rich folk piety. Mahayana was also deeply influenced by local cultures, particularly in China, Japan, Tibet, and beyond.

Summative Comparative Remarks from a Christian Perspective

This brief discussion of "other spirits" in four living faiths reveals a remarkable consistency concerning the place of spiritual beings across different tradi-

---

33. Walter Stephens, "Demons: An Overview," in *ER* 4:2275; Michael Witzel, "Vedas and Upanisads," in *The Blackwell Companion to Hinduism*, ed. Gavin Flood (Oxford: Blackwell, 2003), 71–73.

34. See Yong, *Pneumatology*, chap. 9.

35. Ananda W. P. Guruge, "The Buddha's Encounters with Mara the Tempter: Their Representation in Literature and Art," *Access to Insight* 23 (July 2013): particularly section 2, http://www.accesstoinsight.org/lib/authors/guruge/wheel419.html.

tions—monotheistic, polytheistic, and "non"-theistic (Theravada). Similarly, belief in spiritual beings seems not to be limited to any cultural or geographical location or to any specific racial group.

It is also clear that the basic structure and orientation of the religion, whether strictly monotheistic or not, determine the place of the powers vis-à-vis the Ultimate Reality. In Abrahamic faiths, they are strictly put under the lordship of God. Furthermore, it seems that a division into evil and good forces is a basic human religious intuition even when the boundary line may be variously (or at times ambiguously) drawn.

It seems warranted to assume that all major faith traditions include a belief in the influence of spirits on the affairs of humans and the world. It is curious that what is now considered the normative opinion in post-Enlightenment academia in the West—that spirits are but an archaic, outdated, and mistaken imaginary fantasy—is historically a new and novel view.

At the same time, it also seems uncontested that it is typical for religious people to believe that we humans, under the power and authority of deities, may exercise influence on spiritual beings and powers. This is manifested in the universal reliance among religious adherents on the rituals and techniques of exorcism, not only in Judeo-Christian tradition but also in Islam,[36] Buddhism,[37] and Hinduism.[38] Bear in mind that no scholar contests that the narrative of the New Testament presents a portrait of Jesus as an itinerant healer and exorcist.[39]

Christian Guidelines for the Discernment of the Spirit(s) among Religions

Beginning from of old, Christian tradition has sought to construct biblically and theologically responsible guidelines for the discernment of the Spirit/spirits among religions.[40] That said, the discernment of spirits in the biblical

---

36. "Simple Guide on Islamic Exorcism," https://islamicexorcism.wordpress.com/ (4/20/17).

37. Yong, *Pneumatology*, 208–17.

38. Morris E. Opler, "Spirit Possession in a Rural Area of Northern India," in *Reader in Comparative Religion: An Anthropological Approach*, ed. William A. Lessa and Evon Z. Vogt (Evanston, IL: Row, Peterson & Co., 1958), 553–66.

39. Graham H. Twelftree, *Jesus the Exorcist: A Contribution to the Study of the Historical Jesus* (Tübingen: Mohr-Siebeck, 1993).

40. Veli-Matti Kärkkäinen, "'How to Speak of the Spirit among Religions': Trinitarian

canon is set in a different context from the multifaith world of ours, as it usually connects discernment to encounters with false prophets. Interestingly, the postbiblical church in its turn linked discernment with issues of spirituality and morality.[41] The New Testament's contribution is that the "discernment of spirits" is named as one of the gifts of the Holy Spirit (1 Cor. 12:10).[42]

Indeed, discernment of the spirit(s) among religions is a topic the Bible addresses only very marginally. Hence, it is understandable that the church and theological tradition have had to exercise chastened constructive imagination in this task. An emerging ecumenical consensus is forming according to which the main question is not about "*whether* or not the Spirit is at work among people of other faiths" but rather about "how to *discern* the presence and work of the Spirit."[43]

That said, there are "no simple phenomenological criteria by which we can test the presence of the Holy Spirit."[44] Ultimately, it is a theological and spiritual process of judgment and assessment. Christology is the most important criterion: "Every spirit which does not confess Jesus is not of God" (1 John 4:3). As the late missionary bishop to South India Lesslie Newbigin used to say, "the Holy Spirit does not lead past, or beyond, or away from Jesus."[45] The appeal to ethical and liberative praxis, along with Christ, is also important.[46]

Christians have to keep in mind at all times that our task is discernment, not controlling the Spirit of God. "To ask whether or how the Holy

'Rules' for a Pneumatological Theology of Religions," *International Bulletin of Missionary Research* 30, no. 3 (July 2006): 121-27; Yong, *Pneumatology*, 8-21.

41. Joseph T. Lienhard, "On 'Discernment of Spirits' in the Early Church," *Theological Studies* 4 (1980): 505-29; Amos Yong, "Discernment; Discerning the Spirits," in *Global Dictionary of Theology*, ed. Veli-Matti Kärkkäinen and William Dyrness (Downers Grove, IL: InterVarsity Press, 2008), 232-35.

42. Eduard Schweizer, "On Distinguishing between Spirits," *Ecumenical Review* 41 (July 1989): 406-15; F. Martin, "Discernment of Spirits, Gift of," in *The New International Dictionary of Pentecostal and Charismatic Movements*, ed. Stanley M. Burgess and Eduard M. van der Maas, rev. and expanded ed. (Grand Rapids: Zondervan, 2002), 582-84.

43. Stanley J. Samartha, "The Holy Spirit and People of Other Faiths," *Ecumenical Review* 42, nos. 3-4 (July 1990): 259.

44. Paul G. Hiebert, "Discerning the Work of God," in *Charismatic Experiences in History*, ed. Cecil M. Robeck (Peabody, MA: Hendrickson, 1985), 151.

45. Lesslie Newbigin, *The Light Has Come: An Exposition of the Fourth Gospel* (Edinburgh: Handsel, 1982), 216-17.

46. Amos Yong, "The Holy Spirit and the World Religions: On the Christian Discernment of Spirit(s) 'after' Buddhism," *Buddhist-Christian Studies* 24 (2004): 199.

Spirit is at work in the world is to remind the church that the Spirit is not under our control and that it may even challenge us to repent and reform."[47] A work in progress, discernment is not only provisional but also communal and deeply ecumenical in nature; ultimately, it calls for engagement beyond faith traditions.

47. Jeremy M. Bergen, "The Holy Spirit in the World," *Vision: A Journal for Church and Theology* 13, no. 1 (Spring 2012): 84.

8 | Visions of "Salvation" and Liberation among Religions

Christian Theology of Salvation

The "Order of Salvation"

Whereas chapter 5, integrally linked with Christology, approached the question of *how* salvation was made possible and brought about in Christian vision, namely, through Christ's incarnation, suffering, death, and resurrection, the current chapter continues that conversation by looking at the ways men and women *receive* and appropriate the salvific gifts. In the Trinitarian logic, this latter domain is most integrally connected with the work of the Spirit. Christian tradition came to speak of this distinction in terms of Christ's *objective* and the Spirit's *subjective* works toward our salvation: "The *ordo salutis* [order of salvation] describes the process by which the work of salvation, wrought in Christ, is subjectively realized in the hearts and lives of sinners. It aims at describing in their logical order, and also in their interrelations, the various movements of the Holy Spirit in the application of the work of redemption."[1] Even if in contemporary theology this distinction is handled with greatest care (if used at all), pedagogically it may still be useful to help understanding.

The biblical text speaks of diverse dimensions and aspects of the salvific gift using many metaphors, concepts, and pictures. Thus, Christian understandings of salvation are manifold. The biggest difference regarding soteriology (the doctrine of salvation) appears between the Christian East and West.

1. Louis Berkhof, *Systematic Theology* (Grand Rapids: Eerdmans, 1996), 415–16.

In the East, the main concept of salvation is deification or divinization (from the Greek word *theōsis*). Based on biblical passages such as 2 Peter 1:4, which speaks of participation in the divine nature, early patristic theology and Orthodox theology at large envisioned salvation in terms of true participation of human beings with God, in Christ, through the Spirit. This divinization, which begins here on earth and will be finalized in the eschaton, is full and real. That said, this does not lead to pantheism (that is, confusion between the divine, the uncreated, and the human, the created nature) because the human participates in the divine "energies," as they are called, but not in God's mysterious, hidden divine "essence."

The Christian West (Protestant, Anglican, and Roman Catholic) uses different biblically driven images and concepts. Although it took until almost the time of the Protestant Reformation for a systematic "order of salvation"— that is, a listing of particular "steps" or "aspects" of soteriology—to appear, basic concepts began to be used quite early on, including election/calling, justification, sanctification, and glorification. Biblical passages that appealed to the more analytic effort in the West included Romans 8:29–30. This passage lists calling, foreknowledge, predestination, conformation to Christ's image, justification, and glorification.

Notwithstanding analytic-conceptual differences among Christian churches, the details of which do not concern us in comparative exercises, currently the typical order of salvation looks something like this: divine foreknowledge and election; calling of sinners to salvation; conversion, repentance, and faith in Christ; justification (which can be understood primarily in terms of declaring the sinner just or also making the sinner righteous, thus blurring the distinction between justification and sanctification); sanctification; union with God (which can be placed in different locations in the order and which resonates with some key ideas of Orthodox *theōsis*); and glorification in the eschaton.

Contemporary theology and church life have felt a need to widen and make more comprehensive the vision of Christian salvation. Going back to biblical testimonies regarding Jesus of Nazareth as an itinerant healer and exorcist, as well as the continuation of healing and exorcism in the early church and later throughout history, the topics of healing, restoration, and freedom from oppressive powers have been embraced. Most recently Pentecostal/charismatic Christianity has made these key concerns, as well as charismatic empowerment, another biblical and ancient Christian emphasis. Hence, the comparison below will also note the theme of healing, both physical and mental.

The Topic of "Salvation" in Interfaith Context

Any soteriological comparison has to begin with this all-important question: How justified is it to apply the Christian notion of salvation to other religions, particularly Asiatic religions? Even among Abrahamic faiths, the question of salvation is utterly complex.[2] A counterargument is—in keeping with the current project—that as long as careful discernment of differences among religions is kept in mind, it is legitimate to consider the ultimate goals of religions using a concept particular to one religion, in this case to Christianity.

To do justice to each of the four dialogue partners, it is important to begin the comparison with a careful outlining of the "big" vision of salvation—or "liberation" or "release," which seem more apt terms among Asiatic faiths. This language helps ensure that we do not force a Christian template of "order of salvation," which seems to point in a dramatically different direction, upon the religious Other.

Only after we outline this comprehensive vision of each faith tradition will we attempt a careful and cautious comparison with Christian tradition. That comparison, however, for the most part cannot and should not be done following the (Western) Christian tradition's highly analytic order of salvation but should rather rely on larger and more elusive concepts used in each tradition. It simply is the case that nothing like the technical *ordo salutis* is found in any of the four counterparts, not even among the Abrahamic faiths.

So, the plan for this chapter consists of two interrelated sections. In the first, each of the four traditions' soteriological, liberative visions will be presented with some Christian engagement at a more general level. The second main section will comparatively investigate a number of case studies (related to, but not artificially "squeezed" into, the *ordo salutis*), including election, repentance, forgiveness, and healing.

Salvation as Redemption and Submission in Abrahamic Faiths

The Common Basis

As discussed in chapter 4, somewhat counterintuitively the Semitic faiths do not share a unified conception of human misery. The traditional Christian

2. See Kenneth Cragg, "God and Salvation (an Islamic Study)," *Studia Missionalia* 29 (1980): 156.

doctrine of original sin (however that is formulated) is not shared by Jewish and Islamic traditions. They understand sin in terms of "incurring the 'punishments' or disadvantages of ignorance of God, lack of self-control, and short-sighted restriction of moral concern."[3] These two Abrahamic traditions insist on human freedom to choose and responsibility for one's choice.

Notwithstanding these important differences from Christian theology, it is also important to underline the significant common basis. All three Abrahamic faiths place humanity before God and in that light assess what is wrong with us. Though somewhat differently, they all consider the "origin" of sinfulness in the deviation of humanity from the Creator. In other words, because sin is ultimately deviation from God, it takes God to fix the problem, notwithstanding graced human response and collaboration. Hence, not surprisingly, all three scriptural traditions share the common narrative of the Fall and its consequences, even when their interpretations differ from each other quite dramatically.

Jewish and Muslim interpretations share more in common with each other than Christian views do with them.

Redemption in Jewish Theology

As discussed, instead of original sin, the Jewish (rabbinic) tradition speaks of two tendencies: good and evil. What matters is which of the two inclinations is the guiding force in life. Hence, the main term for repentance from evil is *teshuvav*, literally "turning" (to God).[4] This is not to undermine the seriousness of the sinful tendency, which is "not an isolated act, but a state of consciousness, so that one sin leads to others." Indeed, it is the goal of the Yahwist account to highlight the wide diffusion of moral evil (Gen. 4; 6:5–12; 8:21; 9:20–27; 11:1–9).[5] Yet this is no "original sin."[6]

Rather than "salvation," Jewish theology speaks typically of "redemption"; a key idea of the term has to do with deliverance.[7] Consider how often

---

3. Keith Ward, *Religion and Human Nature* (Oxford: Clarendon, 1998), 175.

4. Steven Kepnes, "'Turn Us to You and We Shall Return': Original Sin, Atonement, and Redemption in Jewish Terms," in *Christianity in Jewish Terms*, ed. Tikva Frymer-Kensky et al. (Boulder, CO: Westview, 2000), 293–319.

5. Samuel S. Cohon, *Essays in Jewish Theology* (Cincinnati: Hebrew Union College Press, 1987), 225.

6. 2 Baruch (54:15, 19; 19:3; 48:42–43; 59:2) teaches that even after Adam's sin, which brought about death, each new generation has to choose their own path.

7. Harold Coward, *Sin and Salvation in the World Religions: A Short Introduction* (Ox-

the term "redeemer" (and "to redeem") appears in the most common Jewish daily prayer, the Amidah.[8] While not limited to national deliverance, the idea is present in most Jewish traditions even beyond Zionism. Similar to creation, which is the work of the past, present, and future, redemption covers all tenses.[9]

What about faith and belief? According to Israel Abrahams, in the Jewish "Bible there are no articles of faith or dogmas in the Christian or Islamic sense of the terms." Rather than invitation to believe (in an intellectual sense), the biblical call is for faithfulness, which can be used of both God and the human person. The reason for the absence of catechism (in the Christian sense) is the emphasis on conduct and ethics. That is not to deny the presence of theological reflection and doctrines in later Judaism. Those came, however, largely because of apologetic need and external pressure. The Shema (Deut. 6:4) is of course the basis and foundation of Jewish faith. Yet monotheism is more than a belief; it is the central thrust of Jewish (and Islamic) faith tradition.[10]

As discussed regarding Christology, while both traditions are messianic, their conceptions are widely different. Jews are still awaiting the Messiah; for Christians he has arrived. But even then, the role of the Messiah in Judaism is to serve as the *agent* of reconciliation rather than the one who reconciles; only Yahweh can do that.[11]

As also discussed, although the sacrificial system is part of the Jewish tradition, the Christian idea of vicarious atonement, on which the salvation of the world is based, is not part of Jewish theology because "the problem of sin had already been dealt with in the Torah."[12] Particularly in Talmudic traditions, "the sages know nothing of a miraculous redemption of the soul by external means. There is no failing in man, whether collectively or as an individual, which requires special divine intervention and which cannot be

---

ford: Oneworld, 2003), 5. The term appears about 130 times in the Old Testament; see Donald Daniel Leslie et al., "Redemption," in *EJ* 17:151–55.

8. English translation can be found at "Translation of the Weekly Amidah," Chabad .org, accessed March 15, 2019, http://www.chabad.org/library/article_cdo/aid/867674/jewish /Translation.htm.

9. Jacob Neusner, *The Way of Torah: Introduction to Judaism* (Encino, CA: Dickenson, 1970), 14.

10. Israel Abrahams, Jacob Haberman, and Charles Manekin, "Belief," in *EJ* 3:290–91.

11. John C. Lyden, "Atonement in Judaism and Christianity: Towards a Rapprochement," *Journal of Ecumenical Studies* 29, no. 1 (Winter 1992): 50–54.

12. Michael S. Kogan, *Opening the Covenant: A Jewish Theology of Christianity* (Oxford: Oxford University Press, 2008), 116.

remedied, with the guidance of the Torah, by man himself."[13] (Only in mystical kabbalah are the "inner" aspects of redemption prominent.)[14] Following the Torah and its commandments, as the chosen people, and thus testifying to God's unity and holiness, is the way of "salvation" in Judaism.[15]

Importantly, "the prophets emphasized that what the Torah required from people was not just religious observance but also moral behavior—indeed that both morality and religion form a unity in the teaching of the Pentateuch as they do in the nature of God."[16] The "new obedience" required of the people of God is not based on sacrifice but on the covenant. Covenant will give true knowledge of God, as God's will "would be engraved in the very heart of the people. . . . Thus shall the knowledge of God become the common possession of all Israel and through Israel all the nations of the world."[17]

What about contemporary Jewish theology? Notwithstanding great diversity, this much can be said: "In modern Jewish thought redemption has been viewed as referring to the eventual triumph of good over evil, to the striving of individuals to self-fulfillment, to the achievement of social reforms, and also in terms of the reestablishment of a sovereign Jewish state."[18] Importantly, even some leading Orthodox thinkers such as Joseph B. Soloveichik, for whom redemption is linked with faith and *mitzvot* (commandments), include in the concept "the idea that the human capability of renewal and self-transformation manifests itself especially in times of human distress"; the human person's control over himself or herself is a sign of redemption.[19]

What about the youngest Abrahamic tradition and its salvific vision?

Submission and Overcoming Ignorance in Islam

Islam's understanding of the human condition is closer to that of Judaism than to that of Christianity. Even more vehemently than the Jews, Muslims deny all notions of original sin and basically affirm the goodness of human nature (chap. 4). Needless to say, the Christian notion of the lostness of humanity does

---

13. Leslie et al., "Redemption," 152.

14. See Leslie et al., "Redemption," 153.

15. Kogan, *Opening the Covenant*, 11–13.

16. Coward, *Sin and Salvation*, 7.

17. Isidore Epste, *Judaism* (New York: Penguin Books, 1987), 61, cited in Coward, *Sin and Salvation*, 8.

18. Leslie at al., "Redemption," 154–55 (154).

19. Leslie et al., "Redemption," 155.

not resonate at all. The parallel to the idea of "lostness" is the ignorance of the right way and unwillingness to submit to Allah, acts that are conscious choices.

For these reasons, Muslims do not envision redemption in the way Christian tradition does, namely, as a divine gift,[20] and there is absolutely no doctrine of atonement. Nor does sacrifice play any salvific role at all. Muslim theology has a hard time intuiting why the justice and fairness of God would ever require a sacrifice and shedding of blood. Allah is of course sovereignly free to forgive (or not to forgive) apart from any such requirements. And on the basis of Qur'anic teaching, it may be legitimate to infer that no one else can "pay" for the sins of others, not even Allah.[21] There is no need to add that in Islam there is hardly anything like what Christianity names "redemption" or "regeneration."[22]

This is not to deny the presence of grace and mercy in Islam. Even a cursory look at the Qur'an shows the prevalence of the idea of Allah as merciful.[23] Consider this important sura: "Were it not for Allah's grace upon you and His mercy, not one of you would have ever been pure, but Allah purifies whom He pleases" (24:21). That mercy, however, does not translate in Islam into an idea of "justification by faith." Everything is about submitting to the will of Allah, particularly by observing the Five Pillars. Access to paradise will be granted as a "reward for what they used to do" (56:24). "Allah has prepared . . . forgiveness and a mighty reward" for those who "submit" and "obey"; obedience includes almsgiving and fasting (33:35).[24]

Where the mercy of Allah comes to the fore is in the completion beyond the balancing act of good and bad as evidenced in this statement (6:160): "Whoever brings a good deed, he shall have ten like it, and whoever brings an evil deed, he shall be recompensed only with the like of it, and they shall not be dealt with unjustly."[25] While one's efforts and good deeds certainly are required to gain access to paradise, God's mercy is also necessary as a surplus.

---

20. See Kare Zebiri, *Muslims and Christians Face to Face* (Oxford: Oneworld, 1997), 216–17.

21. Q 6:164; see also 2:233.

22. James Robson, "Aspects of the Qur'anic Doctrine of Salvation," in *Man and His Salvation: Studies in Memory of S. G. F. Brandon*, ed. Eric J. Sharpe and John R. Hinnells (Manchester: Manchester University Press, 1973), 217.

23. See further, Cragg, "God and Salvation," 155–66.

24. For many more such references, see Munawar A. Anees, "Salvation and Suicide: What Does Islamic Theology Say?," *Dialog* 45, no. 3 (Fall 2006): 275–76.

25. Similarly, e.g., 64:17. See also Paul Martindale, "A Muslim-Christian Dialogue on Salvation: The Role of Works," *Evangelical Missions Quarterly* 46, no. 1 (2010): 69–71.

It is in this respect that the numerous references to the merciful nature of Allah—indeed, in the first line of each sura of the Qur'an[26]—have to be interpreted. According to the Islamic tradition (Hadith), this principle applied even to the Prophet himself.[27]

To summarize, "salvation" in Islam means simply submission to Allah. But the fact that salvation ultimately depends on whether or not one wishes to submit does not mean that believing is thus marginalized.[28] One cannot submit if one persists in ignorance of the revealed will of God.[29] Belief goes hand in hand with repentance (Q 3:16–17; 19:60) and "the works of righteousness," that is, good deeds (4:57).[30]

While submission to Allah is a personal matter, in Islam it is also integrally linked with the *ummah* (community) and confession of faith.[31] In its widest sense, the "total submission of human will to the will of God" is expressed in three forms:

1. through *islam*, which determines the institutionalized way of worshiping God;
2. through *iman*, which is faith in God, his angels, his prophets, his books—all the revealed books of God—and the last day, that is, the day of resurrection; and
3. through *ahsan*, which refers to good actions, or righteous living, and which the Prophet interpreted as worshiping God "as though you see him, for if you do not see him he nonetheless sees you." So to be a true *muslim* (that is, to be in "submission") to God, whether you are a Christian, a Jew, a Hindu, a Buddhist, or whatever, is always to live in the presence of God.[32]

26. The only exception is sura 9.

27. Anees, "Salvation and Suicide," 276.

28. The six mandatory tenets are the unity of God, divine predestination, angels, Qur'an, prophets, and last day. For details, see Sayyid Muhammad, *A Compendium of Muslim Theology and Jurisprudence*, trans. Saifuddin Annif-Doray (Sri Lanka: A. S. Nordeen, 1963), 3–15.

29. See Coward, *Sin and Salvation*, 63.

30. Q 4:57; similarly 4:122.

31. For details, see Jacob S. Dharmaraj, "Sin and Salvation: Christianity and Islam," *Bangalore Theological Forum* 30 (1998): 54; J. D. Greear, "Theosis and Muslim Evangelism: How the Recovery of a Patristic Understanding of Salvation Can Aid Evangelical Missionaries in the Evangelization of Islamic Peoples" (PhD diss., Southeastern Baptist Theological Seminary, 2003), 139–41.

32. Mahmoud Ayoub, "Trinity Day Lectures," *Trinity Seminary Review* 32 (Winter–Spring 2011): 8.

Although the technical term "salvation" (*najat*) occurs only once in the Qur'an (40:41), the verbal from which it derives is fairly common, particularly denoting deliverance from dangers of various kinds.[33] Another common word is *furqan*, which appears frequently in the Qur'an (2:53, 185; 3:4; 8:29, 42; 21:48; 25:1). Its basic meaning (beyond salvation) is "distinction" or "criterion" (between right and wrong).[34] Yet another important soteriological term is *falah* (success). The main point is not only that success may happen both in this life and in the life to come but also that ultimately the human person is faced either with a positive outcome, success, or a negative one, failure.[35]

While deliverance from sin does not have to be excluded from the Islamic vision of salvation, it is fair to say that deliverance from eternal punishment, often depicted as "fire"[36] of hell, seems to be at the forefront.[37] Indeed, "'salvation' in the *Quran* is not the bestowal of a new creation, nor an act of power and victory over sin and death; rather, it is primarily an escape from judgment and entry into paradise."[38]

What about "assurance of salvation"? Although Qur'anic promises to those who believe and do good deeds seem assuring, there are also warnings throughout not to fall away.[39] Although one may lose salvation, every believer can also trust Allah's "guidance" (an almost technical term in the Qur'an referring to the divine help for believers, as in 4:51; 6:157; 17:84; 28:49; 67:22; and so forth).[40] Ultimately, Allah is absolutely sovereign in his dealings with humanity, and therefore the Christian (Calvinistic) idea of the "perseverance of the saints" is foreign to Islam.

Like other faith traditions' mystical movements—and unlike the "textbook" official teaching—Sufism focuses on personal devotion and repentance. Sufi mysticism has an amazingly wide appeal among the ordinary faithful,

33. Robson, "Aspects of the Qur'anic Doctrine of Salvation," 205. See further, Gordon Nickel, "Islam and Salvation: Some On-Site Observations," *Direction* 23, no. 1 (Spring 1994): 4–5; Arya Roest Crollius, "Salvation in the Qur'an," *Studia Missionalia* 29 (1980): 125–39.

34. "Furqan, al-," in *The Oxford Dictionary of Islam*, ed. John L. Esposito, *Oxford Islamic Studies Online*, accessed March 22, 2019, http://www.oxfordislamicstudies.com/article/opr /t125/e684.

35. Frederick Mathewson Denny, "Salvation in the Qur'an," in *In Quest of an Islamic Humanism*, ed. A. H. Green (Cairo: American University in Cairo Press, 1984), 206.

36. See, e.g., Q 2:24, 39, 80–81, 119, 126, 167, 174–75, 201, 217, 221, 257, 266, 275.

37. Robson, "Aspects of the Qur'anic Doctrine of Salvation," 205–6.

38. Greear, "Theosis and Muslim Evangelism," 130; similarly, Roland Miller, "The Muslim Doctrine of Salvation," *Bulletin of Christian Institutes of Islamic Studies* 3, nos. 1–4 (1980): 145.

39. Q 6:82; see also 4:13.

40. For details, see Robson, "Aspects of the Qur'anic Doctrine of Salvation," 215–26.

probably influencing deeply more than half of all Muslims. In their spirituality the idea of union with God—theologically a most scandalous idea in light of normal Muslim teaching—comes to the forefront: "The Sufi doctrine of a direct and personal experience with God passed by the claim of the orthodox theologians that they were the guardians of the truth, in exclusive possession of the science of theology and law. *But they could not stem the tide of Sufism, for it seemed to fill a great need in the soul of many Muslims.* Finally the great Muslim theologian, Al Ghazzali, managed to combine orthodoxy and Sufism into one system of thought, in which he retained all the tenets of orthodoxy and at the same time made Sufi thought respectable."[41] No wonder some interesting parallels have been discerned between the Christian doctrine of *theōsis* and the Sufi pursuit of union with God.[42]

We have outlined briefly the ways of redemption and submission in two Abrahamic faiths, and before engaging similarly Asiatic traditions, a brief Christian engagement is in order.

A Summative Christian Engagement of Sister Traditions

As discussed in the beginning of this section, in many ways Judaism and Islam are closer to each other in terms of human diagnosis and its solution than they are to Christianity. In relation to both, the dividing issue is christological. With all the diversity of Christian views regarding the human condition and its solution, they all are christologically directed. Hence, a deep gulf separates Jewish and Muslim views from the view of Christ as the gate, source, and goal of salvation.

Also, even though Jewish and Christian religions are messianic, their messianism is so different that it does not build a bridge with regard to salvation but rather the opposite. For the mother faith, the Messiah is yet to appear, and when that happens, the Messiah is not the savior; Torah (and ultimately Yahweh, the giver of the law) is.

Islam's denial of the sinfulness of humanity—not empirically, as in denying that there is something wrong with us, but theologically, meaning that men

---

41. Miller, "Muslim Doctrine of Salvation," 188, cited in Greear, "Theosis and Muslim Evangelism," 162. A highly useful and accessible presentation of all things Sufi by Dr. Alan Godlas of the University of Georgia titled "Sufism—Sufis—Sufi Orders" is at http://islam.uga.edu/Sufism.html, accessed March 15, 2019.

42. Seyyed Hossein Nasr, "The Prayer of the Heart in Hesychasm and Sufism," *Greek Orthodox Theological Review* 31 (1986): 195–203.

and women will not be denied salvation due to some kind of innate sin—is the foundational obstacle for the Christian side. Regarding Jesus Christ, somewhat similarly to the figure of Messiah between Jewish and Christian teachings, he is as much a divider as the common denominator. The blunt and categorical denial of Jesus's atoning death (regardless of historical nuances) blocks the way of salvation by faith through grace to the Muslim, according to the basic Christian vision.

This fairly rigid summative categorization and comparison is not meant to stall dialogue; had it been done in the beginning of the discussion—or apart from a careful comparative investigation into authoritative teachings of each tradition—that might have been the implication. This stark picture of the differences among these three sister faiths is rather meant to demonstrate the need for careful, painstaking, and patient comparative dialogue. Resources for this work are immense between Judaism, Islam, and Christianity: partially shared scriptural tradition, monotheism, and a number of shared doctrines, including creation, eschatology, and others.

The Human Condition in Hindu Vision(s): Diagnosis and Solution

The Diagnosis: Ignorance

Any attempt at a generic description of Hindu views of liberation is virtually impossible because Hinduisms have virtually no binding doctrinal or creedal basis but have an unbelievable diversity of views, local beliefs and rites, and so forth. Also, there is no concept of sin, let alone the Fall. That said, there is a deep intuition that something is wrong with us, as discussed in chapter 4.

The standard for what is right and true among all Hindu movements is *dharma*, the "duty," the correct way of life, including all activities and spheres of life. "Sin,"[43] as its opposite, is *adharma*.[44] The ultimate beginning point for the investigation of human misery in Hinduism—as in Buddhism—however, is not the analysis of wrong deeds, behavior, or attitudes. *Adharma* belongs to

---

43. Similarly to Buddhism, Hinduism has worked out lists of sins to avoid; Bhagavad Gita 16.2; see also Klaus Klostermaier, *A Survey of Hinduism*, 3rd ed. (Albany: State University of New York Press, 2010), 141–46.

44. See Benjamin Khan, *The Concept of Dharma in Valmiki Ramayana*, 2nd ed. (New Delhi: Munshiram Mannoharlal Publishers, 1983), 34.

the wider context in Hindu philosophy of human "bondage" to *avidya*, "ignorance." Ignorance makes one cling to *maya*, "fiction," and thus subject to effects of karma, leading to rebirths over and over again. Only with the removal of this "ignorance" can the soul's essential nature as pure spirit be restored.[45] This is the general principle that applies to most Hindu traditions. As also discussed, what is distinctive in the *advaita* version involves the concept of "superimposition" (that is, assigning the attributes of the self to the object, and vice versa), as a result of which humans envision themselves as finite, vulnerable, and decaying, thus not identical with the changeless, eternal Brahman (and, even worse, they attribute finite characteristics to the Absolute).[46]

The Christian reader, however, must be reminded that there is absolutely no sudden "fall" either in the life of humanity at large or in each human person's life; rather, it is a matter of ignorance, the lack of releasing insight into the true nature of reality. Furthermore, unlike in theistic forms of Hinduism, in *advaita* there is "no God to be afraid of."[47] Here is a profound difference between the diagnoses of nontheistic Hinduisms (as well as Theravada Buddhism) and those of Abrahamic traditions.

Any Grace for Hindus?

What, then, about grace in Hindu doctrine? Something similar to "grace" can be found in theistic Hinduism and, indeed, is a steady part of the *bhakti* tradition, particularly in the Bhagavad Gita.[48] Consider this oft-quoted verse (18.58): "When your mind becomes fixed on Me, you shall overcome all difficulties by My grace."[49] Regarding the pursuit of salvation, theistic forms of Hinduism such as Vaishnavism (whose most famous philosopher was Ramanuja, who

---

45. See further, Klostermaier, *Survey of Hinduism*, chap. 13.

46. Useful here is John J. Thatamanil, *The Immanent Divine: God, Creation, and the Human Predicament; An East-West Conversation* (Minneapolis: Fortress, 2006), chap. 2 (although I do not agree with all of his interpretations of Sankara; see chap. 15 in Veli-Matti Kärkkäinen, *Creation and Humanity*, vol. 3 of A Constructive Christian Theology for the Church in the Pluralistic World [Grand Rapids: Eerdmans, 2016]).

47. Vivekananda, "Is Vedanta the Future Religion?," in *The Complete Works of Vivekananda*, vol. 8 (under "Lectures and Discourses") (n.p.), http://www.ramakrishna vivekananda.info/vivekananda/complete_works.htm.

48. See further, Sebastian Painadath, "The Integrated Spirituality of the Bhagavad Gita—an Insight for Christians: A Contribution to the Hindu-Christian Dialogue," *Journal of Ecumenical Studies* 39, no. 3–4 (2002): 305–24.

49. Similarly 18.62 (trans. Swarupananda).

held to qualified *advaita*) emphasize *bhakti*, devotion to a personal god (which may often be locally determined). Sri Sarvepalli Radhakrishnan reminds us that notwithstanding many differences in doctrine, all Vaishnava schools "agreed in rejecting the conception of māyā, in regarding God as personal, and the soul as possessed of inalienable individuality, finding its true being not in an absorption in the Supreme but in fellowship with him."[50]

Importantly to our comparative purposes, differently from *advaita*, Bhagavad Gita clearly assumes a relationship to a personal God. According to Paulos M. Gregorios, the Gita teaches that the personal God is above the impersonal Brahman, whereas in the Upanishads and in the Vedanta system, especially in Sankara, the personal God is only a permissible form in which to conceive an ultimate reality that in fact is purely without any attributes at all.[51] Gregorios supports his thesis with the well-known passage from the Gita: "Setting aside all noble deeds, just surrender completely to the will of God (with firm faith and loving contemplation). I shall liberate you from all sins (or bonds of karma). Do not grieve."[52] In Sankara, however, the human person's own initiative and commitment to the pursuit of liberative knowledge are the key. For Sankara's advaitic vision, "the nature of liberation is a state of oneness with Brahman."[53]

In sum, although the concept of grace and divine benevolence is not completely foreign to Hindu traditions, the clear emphasis is on human striving and quest.[54] The key is the enlightenment insight into the true nature of reality. Indeed, the quest for final liberation might be the most distinctive feature of all Hindu paths of salvation. Rather than "salvation," the common term *moksa*, "liberation" (also called *mukti*), is used in Hinduism. It is safe to say that, by and large, Hindu movements "aim at the practical end of salvation. The systems mean by release (moksa) the recovery by the soul of its natural integrity, from which sin and error drive it." Because ignorance is the main problem, an insight or "realization" is needed for release.[55] The ultimate goal of all sacred

---

50. Sir Sarvepalli Radhakrishnan, *Indian Philosophy* (New York: Macmillan; London: Allen & Unwin, 1958 [1927]), 2:661–62; for the importance of *bhakti* to Ramanuja, see also 703–5.

51. Paulos Mar Gregorios, *Religion and Dialogue* (Kottayam, India: ISPCK, 2000), 68.

52. Bhagavad Gita 18.66. One can also refer to passages such as 11.44 and 18.56.

53. Radhakrishnan, *Indian Philosophy*, 2:639.

54. For a highly important study, see Bradley J. Malkovsky, *The Role of Divine Grace in the Soteriology of Śaṃkarācārya* (Leiden: Brill, 2001).

55. Radhakrishnan, *Indian Philosophy*, 2:27. See K. Sivaraman, "The Meaning of Moksha in Contemporary Hindu Thought and Life," in *Living Faiths and Ultimate Goals: Salvation and World Religions*, ed. S. J. Samartha (Maryknoll, NY: Orbis, 1974), 2–11.

scriptures—whose divine authority, particularly that of the Vedas, is strongly affirmed—is to help gain this liberative insight. In Hinduism, release can be experienced either in this life or in a life to come. In an emancipated person after death, all desire has come to an end.[56] The still-living liberated person (called *jivan-mukti*) can be called a "saint," using wider religious language.[57]

Three Paths to "Release"

The Path of Devotion

By now it is evident that there are differing diagnoses of the human condition among various Hindu movements. Hence, the tradition provides various types of paths with distinctive emphases. While not exhaustive in any way, a typical textbook presentation knows three *margas*: one focused on devotion (*bhakti*), one on knowledge (*jnana*), and one on effort (or work [karma]).[58] For the common folks following theistic Vaishnavism in its wide denominational and geographic diversity (as well as other less-known theistic interpretations), the devotional *bhakti-marga* is the way of salvation. The teaching of the Gita is the guide here: "But, to those who worship Me as the personal God, renouncing all actions to Me; setting Me as their supreme goal, and meditating on Me with single minded devotion; I swiftly become their savior, from the world that is the ocean of death and transmigration, whose thoughts are set on Me, O Arjuna. Therefore, focus your mind on Me alone and let your intellect dwell upon Me through meditation and contemplation. Thereafter you shall certainly come to Me" (12.6–8). In the Bhagavad Gita, devotion is often focused on Krishna, the most important *avatara* of Vishnu.[59]

Although based on the Gita, the way of devotion and love of God is not unknown in Vedic scriptures either. Recall that the very first hymn of Rig Veda, the oldest scripture, speaks of the devotion to and intimacy with the Lord. While in general the notion of *bhakti* is hardly mentioned, some of the

---

56. Surendranath Dasgupta, *A History of Indian Philosophy* (Cambridge: Cambridge University Press, 1922), 2:245. On *moksa* during one's lifetime, see Sankara, *Brahma Sutra* 4.1.15, 19.

57. Sanjukta Gupta, "Jivanmukti," in *ER* 7:4925–26.

58. Klostermaier, *Survey of Hinduism*, chap. 8 (karma), chap. 11 (*jnana*), and chap. 14 (*bhakti*). The rest of part 2 of the book includes details on each of those.

59. See Kristin Johnston Largen, *Baby Krishna, Infant Christ: A Comparative Theology of Salvation* (Maryknoll, NY: Orbis, 2011).

Upanishads clearly teach it (Katha Upanishad, Mundaka Upanishad, and Vetasvatara Upanishad particularly). "It is an affective participation of the soul in the divine nature, a most intense devotion to God, by which one tries to unite oneself with the supreme."[60] Although the strict *advaita* of Sankara prefers other paths (although his own writings are not devoid of devotional materials either!), in the qualified *advaita* of Ramanuja, Vishnu devotion, *bhakti*, is an important part.[61] It is rightly said that Ramanuja helped to save (folk) Hinduism from "philosophers-only religion" and to connect it with the rich and variegated Vishnu and Shiva theistic spiritualities.[62]

On the contemporary scene, *bhakti* devotion is widely known in the West through the work of Swami Bhaktivedanta (d. 1977) and his International Society for Krishna Consciousness.[63] According to him, Krishna created all humans from his own nature, and his "grace is there waiting, but it is the duty of the devotee to remove the obstacles to Krishna's grace so that Krishna consciousness will result. One must surrender and engage in devotional service," helped by detailed practical exercises.[64]

The Path of Knowledge

If *bhakti* is for common folks, on the other end of the spectrum, among the most philosophically minded thinkers, particularly within the strict *advaita* of Sankara, *jnana-marga* is the way to pursue release from superimposition and ignorance. Indeed, "One can never think of Advaita without leaving a note on the concept of knowledge. It is a system built upon the foundation of knowledge, both of God and of the self as sources of enlightenment. The path of knowledge is the best Advaitic approach to the realization of God. The end and goal of all morality is jñāna or realization."[65] This kind of liberative knowl-

---

60. Santhosh Thomas Karingadayil, *From Darkness to Light: The Concept of Salvation in the Perspectives of Thomas Aquinas and Sankara* (Frankfurt am Main: Lang, 2011), 158–59; for a great discussion, see A. K. Majumdar, *Bhakti Renaissance* (Bombay: Bharatiya Vidya Bhavan, 1965).

61. Vasudha Narayanan, "Karma, Bhaktiyoga and Grace in the Srivaisnava Tradition: Ramaniya and Karattabvan," in *Of Human Bondage and Divine Grace: A Global Testimony*, ed. John Ross Carter (La Salle, IL: Open Court, 1992), 57–94.

62. See Coward, *Sin and Salvation*, 111.

63. For teachings and activities, see the society's website: http://iskcon.org/.

64. Coward, *Sin and Salvation*, 114–15.

65. Karingadayil, *From Darkness to Light*, 164.

edge that discerns the absolute unity is based on the scriptures (Upanishads) but can be had only when that indirect insight becomes direct and immediate, as in enlightenment.[66] Modern advaitic Hinduism as represented by teachers such as Swami Vivekananda (d. 1902) stresses even more the importance of the "personal experience" of enlightenment insight, in contrast to mere knowledge of it on the basis of scripture.[67]

It is clear that whereas *bhakti-marga* as a universal way of salvation (according to the Gita) is available to all, *jnana-marga* is only for some few.[68] The attainment of liberation is a long process: while sin and evil (in the Abrahamic traditions' sense) are not the main obstacle, those who pursue liberation also seek to overcome selfish, evil, and negative attitudes and acts.[69] Nevertheless, the Upanishads are optimistic about final perfection at the end of the spiritual path that leads to enlightenment.[70] Particularly important in its pursuit is continuous meditation (on which advaitic Vedanta has much to say and teach).[71] The knowledge path culminates in renunciation, which at its core means the "denial of anything real outside of or additional to the infinite reality of God"; ultimately, renunciation means to "bid good-bye" not only to the body but also to one's own ego. Only Brahman remains.[72]

The Path of Works

The third path, *karma-marga*, holds a most fundamental position in Indian religious thought and is not necessarily an alternative to the other two. It is closely related to the notion of transmigration. "Karma marga is considered as the best way suited for people who are particularly drawn by social service, alleviation of human suffering and organizational activity, and whose constant compulsion for work is directed towards the divine."[73] Karma is also connected with liberation because liberation consists in the complete freedom from karma and from

---

66. Karingadayil, *From Darkness to Light*, 164–65; see Mundaka Upanishad 3.2.3; also 3.1.9; 3.2.1.

67. See Coward, *Sin and Salvation*, 107–8.

68. See Karingadayil, *From Darkness to Light*, 164–65.

69. On purification as a result of liberative pursuit, see Maitri Upanishad 4.4; Brihadaranyaka Upanishad 5.14.8.

70. See further, Coward, *Sin and Salvation*, 99–100.

71. See Karingadayil, *From Darkness to Light*, 171–84.

72. Karingadayil, *From Darkness to Light*, 184–88.

73. Karingadayil, *From Darkness to Light*, 154.

all its consequences.[74] The Upanishads speak of the greatness of *karma-marga*, which emphasizes that a person, by his or her very nature, is divine and can attain liberation by the person's own moral forces and good deeds.[75]

The complementary nature of the *trimarga* is indicated by the importance the Gita places on it. The most famous passage in this regard is the teaching of Lord Krishna to Arjuna on proper duty. The key is the right motivation: the duty has to be done without any consideration of the gain to oneself.[76] In the twentieth century, the most well-known advocate of this path has been Mahatma Gandhi. Incidentally, he called the Gita his "spiritual dictionary."[77]

Even Sankara, with his total focus on knowledge, never rejected the importance of the works path; he just took it as subservient to a higher way.[78] Having now discussed some important Hindu movements' diagnoses of and proposed solutions to the human condition, we finish the chapter by highlighting Buddhist analyses and visions.

Dukkha and Enlightenment: Buddhist Visions of Liberation

The Diagnosis: Dukkha *and* Kamma

As discussed in detail above (particularly in chap. 4), the foundational term for Buddhist diagnosis of the human condition, *dukkha*, is best left untranslated, as renderings such as "suffering" (or "pain" or "stress") have implications foreign to this tradition (for example, that it would be negative or life-escaping per se). *Dukkha* persists as long as there is craving, based on ignorance of the true nature of reality, that is, its impermanence. One is under the law of *kamma*, leading to transmigration ("rebirth") as long as the enlightening insight is not achieved.[79] That said, no "fall" after Christianity is affirmed, any more than in Hinduism.

---

74. See Bhagavad Gita 4.16 for the well-known questions of what is karma and a-karma.

75. Karingadayil, *From Darkness to Light*, 155.

76. Bhagavad Gita 2.47–48. For Ramanuja's comments on this passage, see the *Gitabhasya of Ramanuja*, 55.

77. See Coward, *Sin and Salvation*, 117. For Gandhi's comments on the Gita passage (2.47), see Mohandas K. Gandhi, *The Bhagavad Gita according to Gandhi* (Blacksburg, VA: Wilder Publications, 2011), 14.

78. Karingadayil, *From Darkness to Light*, 155–56.

79. See Malcolm David Eckel, with John J. Thatamanil, "Beginningless Ignorance: A Buddhist View of the Human Condition," in *The Human Condition: A Volume in the Comparative Ideas Project*, ed. Robert Cummings Neville (Albany: State University of New York Press, 2001), 49–72.

Inquiring into the way of "salvation" in Buddhism is appropriate in light of Gautama's own focus on liberation rather than on abstract, meaningless speculations. That said, the Christian reader is reminded that in no Buddhist movement is Gautama a deity after Christian tradition, and therefore a "Savior" has no place in the Buddhist worldview. An individual must control and be responsible for his or her own destiny."[80] The person is one's own refuge, and no one else, not even Buddha, can save one from the law of *kamma*.[81] In other words, Buddhism, particularly in its original "orthodox" (Theravada) version, is "an atheistic and humanistic system that locates human beings at the center of their existence and believes that humankind can overcome the problem of human suffering by their own endeavors. It also implies the denial of . . . [a] Savior who delivers humankind from suffering."[82]

Although many movements of Mahayana acknowledge the concept of grace and (divine) assistance in search of liberation, ultimately liberation is dependent on one's own effort. Buddha taught his disciples: "Monks, be islands unto yourselves, be your own refuge, having no other; let the Dhamma be an island and a refuge to you, having no other."[83] Gautama's role is that of a mentor or guide, similar to that of *dhamma*.[84] Hence, not "faith" but confidence in the Teacher's instructions is needed.[85]

The Solution: "Enlightenment"

"Enlightenment"—or insight—is the favored soteriological term among all Buddhist schools. Following the teachings of Buddha as expressed in the Noble Eightfold Path[86] and emulating his experience move one toward the goal of "direct, embodied knowledge of the unconditioned, Nirvana."[87] This sim-

---

80. Satanun Boonyakiat, "A Christian Theology of Suffering in the Context of Theravada Buddhism in Thailand" (PhD diss., School of Theology, Fuller Theological Seminary, 2009), 114.

81. Dhammapada 12.4; *SBE* 10 (in some other versions, 12.160); similarly 20.4 (*SBE* 20:276).

82. Boonyakiat, "Christian Theology of Suffering," 115.

83. Attadiipaa Sutta: An Island to Oneself, of Samyutta Nikaya 22.43.

84. For the close relationship between Gautama and *dhamma*, see Samyutta Nikaya 22.87.

85. See Walpola Rahula, *What the Buddha Taught*, rev. ed. (New York: Grove, 1974), 8.

86. For "the Middle Way" or the Noble Eightfold Path, see Rahula, *What the Buddha Taught*, chap. 5.

87. John J. Makransky, "Buddhist Analogues of Sin and Grace: A Dialogue with Au-

ply means defeating the power of *dukkha*. Buddha's foundational distinction between "conditioned" and "unconditioned" existence means a distinction between the *dukkha* existence, under the power of craving, leading to samsaric rebirth over and over again, and the release from under the power of *kamma*.[88]

What I have so far explained about the human condition and human effort to pursue the liberative insight is shared by all Buddhist traditions. As in Hinduism, there are denominational differences. The basic distinction for our purposes is between Theravada and the Mahayana families. These later movements have adopted a more theistically oriented cosmology and have highlighted the importance of notions of grace and mercy. Mahayana has also developed a growing tradition of spiritual exercises in pursuit of liberative insight.[89] In Mahayana, the Boddhisattva—different from the Theravada *arahant*—is willing to postpone his or her own entrance into *nibbana* to help others reach the goal. Even that, however, is not the function of a "savior" but rather the function of a "good neighbor," even when the Boddhisattva may grant his own merit to help the other.[90]

The Distinctive Nature of the Pure Land Vision

The most distinctive vision of liberation can be found in the Mahayana Pure Land tradition developed by Shinran (1173–1263), which, as is well known, entertains some ideas materially close to Christian soteriology.[91] It can be illustrated with the ancient Indian distinction between two kinds of determinative metaphors of salvation. The "monkey path," depicted by a baby monkey clinging tightly to the back of the mother on a dangerous walk, signifies self-power, whereas the "cat path," illustrated by the kitten being held by the mother at the nape of its neck, speaks of Other-power. The Pure Land (known also as Shin

---

gustine" (presentation at 2001 Thagaste Symposium, Merrimack College, 2001), 5, http://www .johnmakransky.org/article_12.html.

88. Makransky, "Buddhist Analogues," 7–8.

89. See Kristin Johnston Largen, *What Christians Can Learn from Buddhism: Rethinking Salvation* (Minneapolis: Fortress, 2009), 108–29.

90. For differences between Mahayana and Theravada in this respect, see John R. Davis, *Poles Apart: Contextualizing the Gospel in Asia* (Bangalore: Theological Book Trust, 1998), 98–104.

91. Paul S. Chung, *Martin Luther and Buddhism: Aesthetics of Suffering*, 2nd ed. (Portland, OR: Pickwick, 2008), 381–93; more widely, Alfred Bloom, *Shinran's Gospel of Pure Grace*, Association for Asian Studies Monographs 20 (Tucson: University of Arizona Press, 1965).

Buddhism), which is predominantly a Japanese and Chinese phenomenon, represents the latter.

The main savior figure is Boddhisattva Dharmakara, who, through the rigorous and pure practice of forty-eight vows, reached enlightenment and became Amitabha Buddha, also known as Avalokitesvara. He opened the path of salvation in primordial times by establishing the Western Pure Land and made it possible for all sentient beings reborn in that land to reach enlightenment. "The Buddha embodied his virtue in his Name for all beings, enabling them to enter the Pure Land at death. Through their faith in, and meritorious recitation of the Name, they are saved by its power."[92]

Reflecting the mainline Mahayana teaching, Boddhisattva Dharmakara's enlightenment in the Pure Land was contingent on the inclusion of others.[93] The Christian reader, however, has to be reminded that behind this salvific outreach of Amitabha there is absolutely no idea of sacrificial suffering and death for the atonement of sins.[94] Different from other forms of Buddhism, Pure Land speaks of faith as "a gift infused in the heart-mind of a person in fulfillment of the Buddha's Vow. The source of the name and Faith is in Amitabha Buddha." As a result, "gratitude for a salvation received characterizes the religious life of a devotee."[95]

As we did with the Abrahamic faiths, we conclude this section with a brief Christian engagement, before continuing with more detailed comparisons regarding specific topics.

A Summative Christian Engagement of Two Asiatic Traditions

Asiatic Traditions in the Wider Context of Abrahamic Faiths

For the sake of Christian engagement, it is useful to place the two Asiatic traditions in the wider concept of Abrahamic ones. Even with internal differences, the three Semitic faiths share worldview and religious insights that differ quite starkly from Asiatic ones. Here we highlight only those pertinent to soteriology.

---

92. Alfred Bloom, "Jesus in the Pure Land," in *JWF*, 33; see also 32.
93. For the eighteenth vow, see Hisao Inagaki, *The Three Pure Land Sutras* (Kyoto: Nagata Bunshodo, 1994), 243.
94. See Bloom, "Jesus in the Pure Land," 34.
95. Bloom, "Jesus in the Pure Land," 34.

The Christian philosopher-theologian Stephen T. Davis offers an interesting comparison between "karma" and "grace," archetypes of a sort of two religious orientations. He does this by abstracting from religions such as Hinduism and Buddhism on the one hand and Christianity and Judaism on the other hand. While different in many ways, these two systems of salvation—Asiatic and Abrahamic—share some foundational similarities, including the view that the deepest human need is spiritual, that moral right and wrong are in some sense "objective" realities, and that justice is a transcendent reality beyond this world.[96]

The differences, however, are great and many, argues Davis. The karmic religions reject the idea of a personal God and rather assume an impersonal absolute "reality." The karmic view is based on a strict cause-and-effect formula. It envisions "salvation"[97] as a release from the karmic cycle as one progresses on the path of "enlightenment." Basically, karma attributes the human predicament to lack of awareness or insight. In contrast, Davis continues, grace religions assume a personal God in whose image human beings have been created and to whom they are responsible. The initiative of salvation comes from God, apart from one's own merits. Only God is able to resolve the main human dilemma: sin stemming from the Fall.[98]

Whether or not professional scholars of religion would endorse all the details of Davis's somewhat general description of Asian religions (for example, concerning personal deity, as also discussed above), I think it makes a useful orientational observation in terms of differences between Abrahamic and Asiatic traditions. That said, there are also more complex common threads. Consider the Buddhist Alfred Bloom's striking book discussing Pure Land tradition, titled *Shinran's Gospel of Pure Grace*, and Hinduologist Bradley J. Malkovsky's book *The Role of Divine Grace in the Soteriology of Śaṃkarācārya*. On the Abrahamic side, think of the centrality of ethical pursuit and "works" in the soteriology of both Judaism and Islam. These observations help us strike a dynamic balance for comparison.

---

96. Stephen T. Davis, "Karma or Grace," in *The Redemption: An Interdisciplinary Symposium on Christ as Redeemer*, ed. Stephen T. Davis, Daniel Kendall, SJ, and Gerald O'Collins, SJ (Oxford: Oxford University Press, 2004), 237–38.

97. Of course, the notion of "salvation" itself is a grace-based concept, owing to Christianity, Judaism, and perhaps Islam.

98. Even though my exposition is based on S. T. Davis, "Karma or Grace," 238–42, I have also expanded it.

Christian and Asiatic Visions in Comparison

Asiatic faiths' diagnosis of what is wrong with humanity is drastically different from that of all Judeo-Christian traditions, notwithstanding the importance of the wisdom motif in the Bible, in both the Old and New Testaments. Ignorance of the will of God, as revealed in the Scripture, is a result of something more foundational, particularly in Christian theology's concept of the Fall and sinfulness. Even for Islam, in which ignorance plays a bigger role as the explanation for "sin," as discussed, it is integrally related to the need to submit to God as a way of remedy, a requirement foreign to Asiatic faiths (though less so to *bhakti* devotionalism). Because sin in Abrahamic traditions at large is Godward, so also are salvation and its reception.

When it comes to Christian soteriology in particular, its uncompromised link with the work of Jesus Christ is the foundational divider in relation to Asiatic (as well as other Abrahamic) faiths. Theravada Buddhism, relying solely on human resources, seems to be most distant from and foreign to the Christian dependence on Christ's work to be received by faith through grace. Similarly *advaita* Hinduism's reluctance to embrace a personal deity and a salvific, graceful offer of salvation distances it significantly from Christian teaching.

Mahayana Buddhism's openness to divine assistance with regard to the enlightening insight and Ramanuja's personal deity–driven Vaishnavist, particularly *bhakti*-oriented devotional religion, resonate much more closely with Christian intuitions. They differ significantly, however, in their rejection of any idea of a vicarious work of atonement. Deities are there to help and grant grace but without any need or possibility to atone.

What about the Pure Land's grace- and "faith"-based approach? Of course, as routinely mentioned, it comes closest to a Christian vision. That said, similarly to all Asiatic (and even two Abrahamic) traditions, there is no death-dying-rising scheme of the Savior for the sake of the salvation of men and women, even though in Pure Land vision the deity is the savior.

The schematic, summative comparison can be significantly deepened and better draw out details and nuances when case studies in some specific topics of soteriology are taken up in the second main section of this chapter. Here we follow the Christian "order" of salvation logic while mindful of the need not to impose it on others. Rather, our aim is to find topics that might resonate with the self-understanding of each tradition (even if Christian vocabulary is being employed).

Comparative Case Studies in Aspects of Salvation among Religions

Determinism, Fatalism, and Freedom of Will among Religions

A Brief Statement on Christian Understanding

With all other living faiths, Christianity affirms that human beings have been endowed with some form of real power to choose between right and wrong, as ultimately revealed in the sacred Scripture. At the same time, this general statement comes with two caveats. First, all Christian churches acknowledge that the Fall, however that is understood precisely, has real effects on the power of the human will. Second, all Christian churches consider God's election as a significant influence on human choices, without which no man or woman is able to turn to God. In other words, even the desire to place one's faith in God is initiated by the same God.

That said, Christian tradition does not speak with one voice about the power of human will and divine determinism. Eastern Orthodox tradition, with its thin understanding of the negative effects of the Fall, highlights the power of human responsibility and human will to the point that the human person may choose to follow God or not. Some forms of Western Christianity, in contrast, particularly Augustinian-Calvinist traditions, with their "total depravity" view of the Fall, seem to assign election mainly (at times, exclusively) to divine determinism. Hence, the concept of "double predestination," that is, God has chosen some to salvation and others to damnation. Among the Protestants, the Arminian camp and its affiliates make every effort to find a balance between divine election (determinism) and limited but real human capacity to choose. In the Roman Catholic tradition, the Fall's weakening of the exercise of the human will to choose rightly is acknowledged but not to the point of making the human being capable by himself or herself to fully respond to divine initiative. All Christian traditions reject Pelagianism, which assumes that the human person is capable of freely choosing whether to place his or her faith in God or not.

Placed in the wider world of religions, we can say, on the one hand, "the essential presupposition of most major religions is that humans are born with freedom of choice";[99] on the other hand, most of the religions at the same time embrace the idea of divine election or divine determinism of some sort. With this in mind, let us look at the details and attempt a comparative discussion.

---

99. Ileana Marcoulesco, "Free Will and Determinism," in *ER* 5:3200.

Election and Free Will in Abrahamic Traditions

The most peculiar and formative doctrine of election can be found in Judaism. The idea of a "chosen people" defines her identity. It is based on the covenant between Yahweh and his people, going back to Abraham. Deuteronomy 7:6 summarizes election succinctly: "For you are a people holy to the LORD your God; the LORD your God has chosen you to be a people for his own possession, out of all the peoples that are on the face of the earth" (see also 14:2).[100]

Election is solely based on Yahweh's love and purposes. It happens despite the unworthiness of the elected one. The selection of some is for the sake of the people and her mission to other nations rather than for their own benefit.

As with everything else in Jewish tradition, catastrophic events helped consolidate and reshape theological views. With regard to election, the exile was the first such formative event, and the destruction of the temple and ensuing Diaspora in 70 CE was another. The rabbinic emphasis on Yahweh's election also had to do with the strong resistance to Christian theology's implication that Israel was no longer the chosen people.

What about freedom of the will? Differently from Christian and Islamic versions of robust predeterminism, Jewish tradition does not interpret divine action in a way that would frustrate the exercise of human free will and, consequently, responsibility. According to Moses Maimonides's oft-cited statement, "man does what is in his power to do, by his nature, his choice, and his will; and his action is not due to any faculty created for the purpose." Not only that but also, "all species of irrational animals likewise move by their own free will."[101]

In Islam, election does not play the same crucial role as in Judaism. Islamic theology emphasizes the election of several key persons such as Noah, Abraham, and prophets. The greatest stress understandably is placed on the election of the Prophet, Muhammad, and the community established by him (*ummah*). Somewhat similarly to Judaism, the Qur'an teaches that while other nations might have known God, only Muslims know Allah intimately and are rightly related to God (37:40; 38:40).[102]

A dominant principle of the Qur'anic teaching has to do with human responsibility, the shorthand for which is obedience (submission) to Allah.

---

100. Ellen M. Umansky, "Election," in *ER* 4:2744.
101. Maimonides, *The Guide for the Perplexed*, trans. M. Friedländer (1903), 3.17, 285, http://www.sacred-texts.com/jud/gfp/index.htm#contents.
102. Umansky, "Election," 2748.

Indeed, there are hundreds of such Qur'anic texts.[103] That said, other important Qur'anic passages seem to deny any notion of human freedom of choice. Consider 35:8: "Indeed God leads astray whomever He will and guides whomever He will" (also 8:17–18). Hence, similarly to Christian theology, fierce, continuing debates in Islamic philosophy and theology have been fought.

Already at the end of the first Islamic century, a vigorous protest arose to challenge and refute the prevailing deterministic, often fatalistic, emphasis on divine determinism. One of the most ironic—if not also confusing—terms in Muslim tradition is "Qadarites." From the term "to determine," *qadar*, it was applied astonishingly to both those who subscribed to divine determinism and those who excluded human free choice from under divine determination![104] The term, however, eventually came to be applied to the latter group. Generally speaking, the Qadarites wished to affirm human free will, which in turn justified God's punishment for intentional wrongdoings. In other words, freedom of will entails responsibility. Later the influential Mu'tazilite movement adopted materially the Qadarite view in contrast to the fierce opposition by the dominant Asharite tradition, ratified by the majority Sunni movement. The most famous philosopher, al-Ghazali, an Asharite, helped found "occasionalism," a theory of causation according to which God is the sole acting agent and created beings are not acting agents. This, however, does not rule out all human freedom.

Modern Muslim commentators argue that, notwithstanding diversity, the Qur'an endorses the concept of human freedom in choosing one's belief and human responsibility for human actions. God has foreknowledge of human actions, but this divine knowledge does not compel humans to commit sin.[105]

Determinism, Fatalism, and Free Will in Asiatic Traditions

The following statement helps put in perspective Abrahamic and Asiatic traditions in this regard: "The main traditions of Hinduism and Buddhism do not posit a personal deity with an omnipotent will, and thus the polarity of free will and predestination in relation to the salvation of souls has not been so

---

103. M. A. Rauf, "The Qur'ān and the Free Will [I]," *Muslim World* 60, no. 3 (1970): 206.

104. William Montgomery Watt, *Islamic Philosophy and Theology: An Extended Survey* (Edinburgh: Edinburgh University Press, 1962), chap. 5.

105. William Montgomery Watt and Asma Afsaruddin, "Free Will and Predestination: Islamic Concepts," in *ER* 5:3213.

prominent as in Judaism, Christianity, and Islam. The doctrine of *karma* can constitute a kind of determinism whereby an individual's lot in life is determined by his behavior in past lives, but the doctrine can also imply that a soul is in charge of its future destiny; its modern proponents therefore sometimes consider the doctrine to imply freedom more than fatalism."[106]

From the perspective of the Abrahamic faiths, it is not readily evident how to negotiate freedom and determinism in relation to karma, an ironclad principle. The freedom principle comes to the fore particularly in the ancient concept of *svaraj* (self-ruling), which Mahatma Gandhi took as the basis for his social activism.[107] The Hindu expert Klostermaier affirms, "*Karma* does not cancel free will and genuinely free decision, nor do free will and one's own decisions neutralize *karma*."[108] Be that as it may, a whole spectrum of interpretations is found in diverse Hindu traditions.[109]

To all Buddhists, talk about divine election is even more marginal than to a Hindu. This is not to deny the possibility of an idea of divine favor or election among some theistically driven Mahayana movements; it is rather a summary statement about Buddhist doctrine at large.[110] Scriptures add to the complexity. Because of causal relations and the interdependence of the world, as well as the denial of the existence of "soul," there seems to be very little room for personal choice, even responsibility. On the other hand, because there is no god to depend on, the human person is left totally on his or her own in the pursuit of "salvation."[111] Following the Buddhist "middle way," a fitting conclusion goes something like this: "The Buddha rejected the philosophical extremes of both determinism and indeterminism and discouraged his followers from embracing any view that might undermine their inspiration to devote themselves to an ethical life in the pursuit of liberation."[112]

106. Dewey D. Wallace, "Free Will and Predestination: Christian Concepts," in *ER* 5:3204.

107. Mohandas K. Gandhi, *Hind Swaraj and Indian Home Rule*, online version available at https://www.mkgandhi.org/ebks/hind_swaraj.pdf.

108. Klostermaier, *Survey of Hinduism*, 176.

109. For the complexity of the issue in theistic, particularly *bhakti*, spiritualities, see Ankur Barua, "The Dialectic of Divine 'Grace' and 'Justice' in St. Augustine and Sri-Vaisnavism," *Religions of South Asia* 4, no. 1 (2010): 46.

110. Nicholas F. Gier and Paul Kjellberg, "Buddhism and the Freedom of the Will: Pali and Mahayanist Responses," in *Freedom and Determinism*, ed. Joseph Keim Campbell, Michael O'Rourke, and David Shier (Cambridge, MA: MIT Press, 2004).

111. Asaf Federman, "What Kind of Free Will Did the Buddha Teach?," *Philosophy East & West* 60, no. 1 (2010): 1–19.

112. B. Alan Wallace, "A Buddhist View of Free Will: Beyond Determinism and Indeterminism," *Journal of Consciousness Studies* 18 (2011): 217–33.

Christian Engagement

The discussion above of Jewish and Islamic views has revealed that for all Abrahamic traditions the topic of election is deeply God-driven. This sets them apart from Asiatic faiths. Notwithstanding great differences among Semitic faiths, and even debates and disputes within them (particularly Christian and Islamic faiths), the Godward orientation is crucial. More so than any other faith, Judaism highlights the importance of the election of the people. Indeed, Judaism's foundational belief is Yahweh's choosing of one people out of all other peoples of the earth to make her God's own people. While the election of the peoplehood is not foreign to Christian tradition, it is not as crucial, although the concept of the church as the chosen and elected people has been duly acknowledged.

Indeed, in Christian tradition, the doctrine of election has been focused on the question of who might be saved and who not. That discussion is not dominant in Judaism. Of the three Abrahamic faiths, the theme of election, either individually or communally, plays a smaller role in Islam. There, the human response to Allah's call to submit is the key. The downplaying of election makes sense given the lack of a doctrine of human sinfulness and the robust emphasis on the power of the human will even when debates about divine determinism have raged over centuries.

In Asiatic faiths, even in the deistic Mahayana and *bhakti* Hinduism, it seems to the Christian observer, election is not a needed or familiar concept. The solution to the human dilemma, ignorance (widely understood, encompassing both faith traditions), lies in the hands of the human person and in his or her effort. No one, not even a deity, can make a choice for the human person. Needless to say, in this kind of environment, any concept of communal (peoplehood) election hardly finds any fruitful soil.

Having now looked at the divine initiative in salvation, we naturally move to the human response under the classic rubric of conversion, repentance, and forgiveness of sins. Whether the given faith tradition assigns any meaning to divine election (or even if, as in some Christian ones, election is solely God's business), they all speak of the importance of human response with regard to the human problem. Would the three Christian concepts mentioned above find any resonance in other faiths?

Conversion, Repentance, and Forgiveness among Religions

A Brief Statement on Christian Understanding

The very first public announcement of Jesus in Mark's Gospel has to do with repentance (1:15). Like the main term denoting conversion in the Old Testament, *shuv*, the New Testament *epistrephō* means "to turn (around)." The religious usage of these terms entails turning away from evil and disobedience to serving God in gratitude and obedience.

The traditional Christian *ordo salutis* includes, under conversion, "repentance" as the way to turn away from sin, with accompanying regret and remorse as conditions for turning to Christ in faith.[113] This template holds, notwithstanding the above-mentioned differences among various Christian traditions about the role of human will and divine determinism in election (and subsequent divine calling for repentance). Depending on one's theological tradition, conversion is either followed or preceded by regeneration/new birth.

Conversion is followed by divine forgiveness. Abrahamic traditions commonly agree that only God has the standing to forgive. In Christian theology, forgiveness is based on reconciliation (atonement) brought about by the triune God in Christ. The risen Christ authorized and mandated his church to pass on forgiveness to the world: "If you forgive the sins of any, they are forgiven; if you retain the sins of any, they are retained" (John 20:23).

While Christian tradition does not speak with one voice on whether divine forgiveness is without prerequisite (conversion and repentance), all agree that forgiveness is God's work. At the same time, derivatively from divine forgiveness, Christian tradition, alongside Jewish and Islamic traditions, emphasizes forgiveness among human beings. Men and women, forgiven by God, ought to forgive others.

"Conversion," a common term among all religions,[114] has a loaded history, as it has been linked with proselytism, colonialization, and similar suspicious activities. In the ensuing brief comparative discussion on topics of conversion, repentance, and forgiveness, Christian engagement is embedded in each section. Hence, a separate summative subsection is not needed.

---

113. Hugh T. Kerr and John M. Mulder, eds., *Conversions: The Christian Experience* (Grand Rapids: Eerdmans, 1983; republished as *Famous Conversions: The Christian Experience*, 1994).

114. Bryant M. Darroll and Christopher Lamb, eds., *Religious Conversion: Contemporary Practices and Controversies* (New York: Cassell, 1999).

Repentance, Forgiveness, and Conversion in Jewish Tradition

In Jewish tradition, the basic scriptural word for repentance is *sub*, which develops into the rabbinic term *teshuvah*, "to return." In Torah it "is constantly and closely connected with eschatological ideas of the Judgment and of the Messianic Age."[115] The Christian message of repentance and forgiveness in John the Baptist's and Jesus's ministries of course builds on these same themes.

Although the idea of forgiving was known by the Israelites since the beginning of their existence, the topic became all the more important as the elected people, as people of God, continued sinning. Particularly in the aftermath of the exile, the importance of repentance became an urgent theme.[116] The availability of God's forgiveness was taken as the confirmation of election and covenant. Even more widely, "the conception could involve the prophetic notion of restoration as well as the conversion of pagans."[117] Although God is the ultimate source of forgiveness, obedience to Torah based on the covenant is emphasized.

What about the role of sacrifices? According to a defining Mishnah text (Yoma 8:8–9), sin offering atones for all unintentional sins, but intentional sins require repentance and returning to God—even though full atonement may come only at death or through the Day of Atonement (provided that the sinner refrains from further intentional sins).[118] Jacob Neusner concludes that although the "sinner should be, and is punished . . . sin is not indelible. If the sinner repents of the sin, atones, and attains reconciliation with God, the sin is wiped off the record, the sinner forgiven, the sinner's successors blameless." Forgiveness entails repentance because without it the rule of justice is violated as repentance "defines the key to the moral life."[119]

Like revivalist movements, mystically oriented Jewish movements such as Hasidism have focused much on repentance and forgiveness as a way to ensure the genuine nature of spiritual life. The kabbalistic tradition's emphasis on repentance as the way of rectification (*tikkun*) belongs to the same category.[120]

115. C. G. Montefiore, "Rabbinic Conceptions of Repentance," *Jewish Quarterly Review* 16, no. 2 (January 1904): 211.

116. Louis Jacobs, *A Jewish Theology* (London: Darton, Longman & Todd, 1973), chap. 17.

117. David E. Aune, "Repentance," in *ER* 11:7755.

118. Jacob Neusner, "Repentance in Judaism," in *RCP*, 64.

119. Neusner, "Repentance in Judaism," 60, 61–62, respectively.

120. Simon Shokek, *Kabbalah and the Art of Being: The Smithsonian Lectures* (London: Routledge, 2001), 135–40.

Similar to other Abrahamic faiths, Jewish tradition highlights the importance of forgiveness in relation to the neighbor as well. Divine forgiveness cannot be had if an intentional violation against the neighbor has been committed and there is not yet reconciliation.

Islamic Interpretations

Similar to the Old Testament, the earliest Qur'anic passages were not calling people to convert to a new religion. Rather, the Meccans were called to "worship the Lord of this House [Ka'ba]" (Q 106:3).[121] Only later, with the rising opposition from the worshipers of local deities, was a decisive break announced and the confession became "There is no god except God" (37:35).[122]

Because the Qur'an teaches that "there is no compulsion in religion" (2:256), conversion should be a matter of one's choice.[123] This is not to deny—similar to Christian history—occasions of forced conversions, but those have to be considered anomalies rather than the norm.[124] What, however, is strictly forbidden is conversion from Islam to another religion, an apostasy potentially resulting in punishment by death.

Conversion to Islam entails confession of two simple but necessary tenets: that Allah is the only God and that Muhammad is the Prophet of God (usually recited in Arabic and followed by "the greater ablution" of the whole body). Part of the conversion process is a continuous mind-set of penitence and contrition, although there are no mandatory formal rites or rituals. The internal process of remorse and repentance is accompanied with ritual prayers and *zakat*, "almsgiving" (Q 9:5, 11); submission (*islam*) to God is part of the act of conversion (39:54).

Recall that Muhammad declared, "I am the Prophet of repentance."[125] In the Qur'an, and particularly in the later Hadith tradition, repentance plays an important role. Among several terms denoting repentance and remorse, the

---

121. The Ka'ba is the center of the holy place in Mecca.

122. J. Dudley Woodberry, "Conversion in Islam," in *HRC*, 24.

123. Yohanan Friedmann, *Tolerance and Coercion in Islam: Interfaith Relations in the Muslim Tradition* (New York: Cambridge University Press, 2003, 2006).

124. William M. Brinner and Devin J. Stewart, "Conversion," in Esposito, *The Oxford Encyclopedia of the Islamic World*, http://www.oxfordislamicstudies.com/article/opr/t236/e0165.

125. Quoted in Atif Khalil, "Early Sufi Approaches to *Tawba*: From the Qur'ān to Abū Ṭālib al-Makkī" (PhD diss., University of Toronto, 2009), 2.

key scriptural term, akin to Hebrew, is *tawbah* (Q 3:90; 4:17; 40:3; 42:25), meaning not only "to return" but also to do so frequently.[126] The Qur'an speaks of the process of returning in terms of "people entering God's religion in throngs" and asking for forgiveness (110:2, 3). While forgiveness is based on God's grace, clearly human initiative is needed: "Indeed God does not alter the state of a people unless they have altered the state of their souls" (13:11).

Continuous repentance is particularly important in Sufi mysticism, which is deeply concerned about repentance and conversion in its desire for deepening spiritual life.[127] The normative medieval theologian al-Ghazali, who also gleans from Sufi mysticism, names repentance as the starting point for followers of the spiritual path, and therefore "it must be put first in the Quarter of Salvation."[128]

What about its conditions? It requires a true change of heart. A prideful and arrogant attitude blocks forgiveness. That said, materially similar to Judeo-Christian tradition, "God's mercy takes precedence over God's wrath."[129] Yet—again like other Abrahamic traditions—Islamic theology also must maintain God's justice.

As in the other Abrahamic traditions, forgiveness in Islam encompasses both divine and human forgiveness. In keeping with Judeo-Christian teaching, before praying to God one must be reconciled with one's neighbor. It calls for a change of heart toward the violator without excluding the need to expose and judge the wrong act.[130]

Conversion, Repentance, and Forgiveness in Hinduism

Rather than conversion, what counts in Hinduism is a religious experience, spiritual "realization," and conduct.[131] Rather than "deliverance from sin,"

---

126. Mahmoud Ayoub, "Repentance in the Islamic Tradition," in *RCP*, 96–98; Frederick Mathewson Denny, "The Qur'anic Vocabulary of Repentance: Orientations and Attitudes," *Journal of the American Academy of Religion* 47, no. 4 (1979): 649–64.

127. Khalil, "Early Sufi Approaches," iii.

128. *Al-Ghazzali on Repentance*, trans. M. S. Stern (New Delhi: Sterling Publishers, 1990), 30, pub.flowpaper.com/docs/http://www.en.islamic-sources.com/download/E-Books /Intellectual/philosophy/Al-Ghazali-on-Repentance.pdf.

129. Bahar Davary, "Forgiveness in Islam: Is It an Ultimate Reality?," *Ultimate Reality and Meaning: Interdisciplinary Studies in the Philosophy of Understanding* 27, no. 2 (2004): 135.

130. Davary, "Forgiveness in Islam," 128–29.

131. Sir Sarvepalli Radhakrishnan, *The Hindu View of Life* (London: Allen & Unwin, 1961 [1927]), 13.

conversion is "progressive enlightenment in which the ignorance and desire that keep us trapped in our human dilemma are expelled."[132] With this view, Hinduism rejects the Abrahamic traditions' call for conversion. In India, the continuing heated discussions around conversion also have everything to do with proselytism and the question of the legitimacy of evangelization. Beginning from the time of independence, Christians and Hindus, including government representatives, have carried on lively and at times heated conversations about conversion.[133]

Why do Hindus convert to Christianity? At the sociological level, different kinds of explanations have been offered. A popular reason has to do with the socioeconomic change provided by Christianity, particularly for those from lower levels of the societal hierarchy.[134] A related factor has to do with enhanced feelings of dignity and self-respect, as well as belonging. In other words, the argument is that "Christian conversion, unlike Sanskritization, was able to facilitate structural change and that conversion movements represent caste mobility or the realization of a communal identity."[135] Whereas this paradigm obviously highlights discontinuity with the past, a competing type of explanation seeks to discern more continuity. In that template, conversion in India has much more to do with "people's assimilation of new ideas and values in the course of their own progress towards modernity."[136] It is not of course possible to arbitrate that complicated debate in this discussion; let it suffice to mention the complexity of the issue(s) of conversion in contexts such as India and the need for theologians to look at conversion through interdisciplinary lenses.

Notwithstanding the hesitancy against conversion, Hinduism knows not only the reconversion of lapsed faithful but also active missionary efforts to convert "pagans." This was certainly the case in the third to fifth centuries during the establishment of Hindu rajas in South India to replace Buddhism.

132. Paul G. Hiebert, "Conversion in Hinduism and Buddhism," in *HRC*, 10.

133. A detailed history and theological/missiological assessment can be found in Sebastian C. H. Kim, *In Search of Identity: Debates on Religious Conversion in India* (Oxford: Oxford University Press, 2003).

134. Geoffrey A. Oddie, "India: Missionaries, Conversion, and Change," in *The Church Mission Society and World Christianity, 1799-1999*, ed. Kevin Ward and Brian Stanley (Grand Rapids: Eerdmans, 2000), 228-53.

135. Kim, *In Search of Identity*, 2, with reference to S. M. Michael, *Anthropology of Conversion in India* (Mumbai: Institute of Indian Culture, 1998).

136. Kim, *In Search of Identity*, 3, with reference particularly to the important work by Susan Bayly, *Saints, Goddesses, and Kings: Muslims and Christians in South Indian Society, 1700-1900* (Cambridge: Cambridge University Press, 1990).

More recently, Hare Krishna and a number of less well-known revival movements in the West have sought new converts.

What about repentance? Notwithstanding a radically different theological context from that of Abrahamic faiths, in both classical Vedic religion and theistic (particularly *bhakti*) traditions repentance is present. The seriousness of sin is certainly present, although, unlike the classical Christian interpretation, there is no "original sin" but rather a form of contamination and defilement. Related to the key Vedic concept of *rita*, the cosmic and moral order, sin in Hinduism ultimately has to do with violation of this cosmic order, the guarantee of peace, harmony, and blessings. This accrues "debt," which should be paid in order to regain balance.[137]

Somewhat like Christian tradition, some Vedic traditions made a distinction between unintentional and intentional sins. Whereas the former can be cleansed with the help of reciting proper Vedic passages, the latter can only be rectified by restitution. The most serious offenses can be "burned off" only in the process of numerous reincarnations, including temporary time spent in various hells. In Hinduism, the reconciliation of the most serious offenses may also entail various kinds of vows, a practice echoing the rationale of merits to be earned in the process of penance (rite of reconciliation) in Roman Catholic tradition.

Although atonement by the deity is not an unknown idea in Vedic religion, the emphasis by and large is still on "self-atonement." The situation is different with *bhakti* spirituality: grace and divine forgiveness stand in the forefront, as taught in the Bhagavad Gita (18.66): "Setting aside all noble deeds, just surrender completely to the will of God (with firm faith and loving contemplation). I shall liberate you from all sins (or bonds of Karma). Do not grieve." Various opportunities and ways for forgiveness are offered in these traditions, from pilgrimage to a sacred site, to bathing in the sacred river Ganges, to being tutored by the Guru (who is believed to bear sins as well), and so forth. Particularly important is the recitation of Sanskrit hymns and divine names.[138]

Similar to Abrahamic traditions, there are Hindu teachings about the need to extend forgiveness also to fellow humans. Rig Veda (5.85.7) contains the plea to Varuna: "if we have sinned against the man who loves us, have ever wronged a brother, friend, or comrade, The neighbour ever with us, or a stranger, O Varuṇa, remove from us the trespass."

---

137. Jeanine Miller, *The Vision of Cosmic Order in the Vedas* (London: Routledge & Kegan Paul, 1985), 142.

138. Guy L. Beck, "Fire in the Ātman: Repentance in Hinduism," in *RCP*, 85.

Buddhist Perspectives

As in Hinduism, Buddhist traditions display an ambiguity concerning conversion.[139] On the one hand, it looks as though beginning from Gautama's enlightenment experience, a radical break with the past is the norm; on the other hand, it can also be argued that (apart from some exceptions such as conversion by force)[140] the people who joined the movement hardly underwent any radical crisis experience. One way to reconcile this apparent tension is to argue that only when the religious seeker made the firm decision to break off from the "world" and become a Theravadin (an ascetic) was the break a crisis. That said, a significant number of disciples who joined Gautama already belonged to religious movements.[141]

As a general rule, with perhaps the exception of Pure Land, forgiveness is not linked with divine pardon for ensuring entrance to eternal blessedness. Gods play little (or virtually no) role in conversion, repentance, and forgiveness. Furthermore, "the early Buddhist doctrine of kamma allows for mitigation, though not eradication, of the consequences of actions under some circumstances";[142] the kind of expiation of sins present in Hindu traditions discussed above is not present, however. In the forefront in the Buddhist tradition are "practices of self-examination, feelings of remorse, the renunciation of unwholesome patterns of life, and the possibility of radical moral change."[143]

The major difference exists between Theravada and Mahayana: whereas in the former the renunciation of the world ideally means devotion to full-time religious life with a view to personal salvation, including joining the community (*sangha*), the latter accepts the simple fact that for most of the masses this radical call is too much. Hence, Mahayana, with its theistic orientation, offers the way of "salvation" somewhat similarly to forms of theistic Hinduism, that

139. Asanga Tilakaratne, "The Buddhist View on Religious Conversion," *Dialogue* (Colombo, Sri Lanka) 32–33 (2005–2006): 58–82.

140. Charles F. Keyes, "Monks, Guns, and Peace," in *Belief and Bloodshed: Religion and Violence across Time and Tradition*, ed. James K. Wellman Jr. (Lanham, MD: Rowman & Littlefield, 2007), 145–63.

141. Torkel Brekke, "Conversion in Buddhism?," in *Religious Conversion in India*, ed. Rowena Robinson and Sathianathan Clarke (New York: Oxford University Press, 2007), 181–91.

142. Jayarava Michael Attwood, "Did King Ajātasattu Confess to the Buddha, and Did the Buddha Forgive Him?," *Journal of Buddhist Ethics*, n.d., 279, http://blogs.dickinson.edu /buddhistethics/files/2010/05/attwood-article.pdf.

143. Malcolm David Eckel, "A Buddhist Approach to Repentance," in *Repentance: A Comparative Perspective*, ed. Amitai Etzioni and David E. Carney (Lanham, MD: Rowman & Littlefield, 1997), 122.

is, with devotion to the Ultimate Reality ("divinized" Buddha figure), and encourages delaying one's own stepping into nirvana for the sake of helping others. In keeping with other faith traditions, all Buddhist traditions highlight the importance of forgiving other persons.[144]

Justification, Deification, and Holiness among Religions

A Brief Christian Statement

While the term "justification" does not appear frequently in the Bible—in comparison to terms such as "justice" and "righteousness," with regard to both God and the demand for people to imitate it—in the Western Christian order of salvation, justification (or righteousness) by faith became a dominant theme particularly by the time of the Protestant Reformation. As alluded to in the beginning of this chapter, justification by faith can be understood in two distinct ways, and this has been historically taken as a leading reason for the split between Protestants (and Anglicans) and Roman Catholics.

The Roman Catholic tradition has continued the early Christian understanding, going back to Augustine (fourth-fifth centuries) and Thomas Aquinas (thirteenth century), in which justification meant primarily making the sinner just. This means that as a result of justification the justified person begins to do good deeds, or else one might wonder if justification had happened in the first place. The Protestant Reformation's insistence on keeping distinct this effective sense (making just) and forensic sense (declaring the sinner justified even if the person might not yet be just) led to a fairly categorical separation between what came to be called justification and sanctification. It also led to undermining the importance of good deeds out of the fear of "works righteousness." It took until the end of the second millennium for Protestants and Catholics to come to a shared understanding of the need for both making and declaring just and of the importance of good works as the fruit of salvation. Even with remaining differences of emphasis, all Christians believe that one can be justified only by faith, through the grace of God in Christ, in the power of the Holy Spirit.

The Protestant (and Anglican) family includes an important "holiness" tradition: Wesleyans, Methodists, and others who, while holding on to the

144. Kinrei Bassis, "Forgiveness," Berkeley Buddhist Priory, accessed February 25, 2019, https://berkeleybuddhistpriory.org/?page_id=832.

distinction between justification and sanctification, still wanted to save Protestantism from complacency. Thus, they significantly approach the Roman Catholic teaching.

Whereas the Christian East has never employed the terminology of "justification by faith," its chosen concept, deification or divinization (*theōsis*), basically says the same as the combined understanding mentioned above. Divinization, however, also means more, namely, that the saved person begins to become like God, even divinized, sharing in God's nature (although not his essence, to avoid pantheism, as explained above).

Would these two cardinal Christian soteriological concepts find any currency among world religions? The general response is this: they do not easily yield to interfaith comparisons. Hence, the following section is quite short! (The brevity of that section reminds us that one result of comparative work can be the acknowledgment of a lack of common basis, to the point that comparison is hardly meaningful!)

Justification, Sanctification, and Deification among Religions

While a distinctively Christian vision of salvation and liberation is absent, some formal parallels can be found in particular religious traditions with regard to justification, sanctification, and deification. The most obvious one is the importance of "faith" (trust) and "grace" in Pure Land Buddhism or forms of piety in (deeply) theistic *bhakti* traditions of Hinduism, as discussed above. Those parallels, however, have to be handled with great care when set in the wider context of each religious tradition. Indicative of that, in a project called "Explorations in Lutheran Perspectives on People of Other Faiths,"[145] the term "justification by faith" (unless used to describe generally Lutheran soteriology) is virtually absent in all comparative exercises.

Although the Jewish scriptural tradition knows the idea of justification by faith, its meaning differs vastly from Christian teaching because Christian theology claims that even the salvation of Abraham (Gen. 15:6) ultimately depends on the work of Jesus Christ, the Messiah. Israel's faith categorically rejects all those claims. Instead, the Jewish vision of redemption and deliver-

145. Paul Martinson, "Explorations in Lutheran Perspectives on People of Other Faiths: Toward a Christian Theology of Religions," in *Theological Perspectives on Other Faiths: Toward a Christian Theology of Religions*, ed. Hance A. O. Mwakabana, LWF Documentation 41 (Geneva: Lutheran World Federation, 1997).

ance focuses on the following of Torah. Unlike the Christian vision, its eschatological dimension is marginal, with its focus on this-worldly renewal with the coming of the yet-awaited Messiah of Israel. No need to mention that to Jewish intuitions, the idea of salvation by faith being contingent on the sacrificial death of the innocent Messiah borders on blasphemy.

Salvation in Islam is about submission to Allah and has little to do with the Christian idea of justification by faith; the only role of "faith" in Islam has to do with the knowledge of the Qur'anic (and later, the Prophet's traditional) teachings and confidence in the truth of Islam. Furthermore, a significant difference between Christian and Islamic traditions is that whereas in the former, forgiveness "costs" God (and hence, requires a sacrifice or satisfaction or similar), in Islam God just forgives, without any sacrifice.[146] While "salvation" in Islam is ultimately dependent on Allah, the idea of an "undeserved" gracious gift is foreign to that sister tradition.

The differences between the Christian doctrine of justification by faith and Asiatic traditions are too deep and wide to facilitate a meaningful comparison. A potential bridge might be found in some aspects of the doctrine of deification. Work on this connection, however, is about to be started at the time of this writing, and no report can yet be provided. Although holiness and sanctity are common themes among religions, the commonality with the Christian theology of sanctification based on the work of salvation by God is foreign to Asiatic faiths.

The last case study in interreligious soteriology looks at the theme of healing and restoration.

Healing and Sickness among Religions

A Brief Christian Statement

Healings feature prominently in the Bible.[147] The New Testament Gospels narrate numerous healings and miraculous cures, and the Synoptic Gospels add to the picture acts of deliverance and exorcisms.[148] Jesus used various "methods," from touch, to laying on of hands, to healing from a distance, to curious things

---

146. For this I am indebted to the British Islamicist David Marshall of Duke University.

147. Michael L. Brown, *Israel's Divine Healer* (Grand Rapids: Zondervan, 1995).

148. Steven L. Davies, *Jesus the Healer: Possession, Trance, and the Origins of Christianity* (New York: Continuum, 1995).

such as use of saliva (Mark 7:33; 8:23; John 9:6). No doubt, there are similarities to shamanic healing techniques, widely known in ancient cultures.

The healing ministry of Jesus makes a robust statement about the all-inclusive nature of the Christian vision of God's salvation; it includes the physical and emotional as well as the spiritual. Christian theology affirms the close link between the atonement and healing based on Old Testament testimonies (Isa. 53:4–5) and their creative use in the New Testament (Matt. 8:17; 1 Pet. 2:24). The healings and restorations anticipate the final salvation in the eschaton when all sickness and sorrow are over.

As mentioned above, only recently have healing, exorcism, and other forms of restoration been attached to the order of salvation. Despite their formal absence, they are well known and well documented throughout Christian history. Similarly, health and sickness feature prominently in religions.[149] All scriptural traditions deal with the problem of sickness and the possibility of restoration.

Abrahamic Traditions

All three Abrahamic traditions speak of healing and well-being as a promise of God. Well known are the Old Testament promises of Yahweh as healer. Indeed, in the Israelite faith both calamity and healing come from one and the same Lord (Deut. 32:39). So deeply is healing instilled in Jewish scriptural tradition that a petition from Jeremiah (Jer. 17:14) is recited in daily Jewish liturgy: "Heal us, O Lord, and we shall be healed."[150]

According to the Qur'anic promise in 41:44, the divine word is "guidance and a healing" for believers but brings about deafness to the disobedient. God is the healer (26:80). The Hadith tradition continues and deepens this idea. According to the Prophet, "There is no disease that Allah has created, except that He also has created its treatment."[151] Not surprisingly, all Islamic traditions also invite the faithful to pray for healing; it is particularly important in the mystical Sufi tradition. Folk healing tradition runs long and wide in Islam.[152]

---

149. David Kinsley, *Health, Healing, and Religion: A Cross-Cultural Perspective* (Upper Saddle River, NJ: Prentice Hall, 1996).

150. David L. Freeman and Judith Z. Abrams, eds., *Illness and Health in the Jewish Tradition: Writings from the Bible to Today* (Philadelphia: Jewish Publication Society, 1999).

151. Sahih Bukhari 7.71, #582; Fazlur Rahman, *Health and Medicine in the Islamic Tradition* (New York: Kazi Publications, 1998).

152. See, e.g., "Islamic Folk Healing," Islamic Healing Systems, accessed March 18, 2019, http://islamichealingsystems.wordpress.com/islamic-folk-healing/.

Asiatic Traditions

If there is a common denominator among widely divergent Asiatic faith traditions concerning insights into wellness, it has to do with harmony and balance.[153] The human being's health is part of a larger cosmic network. Although all faith traditions locate sickness and health in a matrix of influences and factors, from religious to secular, in Hinduism the network of causes and effects is unusually wide. It includes not only karma, the spiritual "cause-effect" chain, and other foundational theological themes such as "ignorance," as well as complicated rules and rites regarding ritual pollution and purity, but also caste and class, gender, and other such issues related to the sociocultural hierarchy. The medical and religious are deeply intertwined.[154] Some diseases are conceived to be the result of the anger of a god. Commensurately with other faith traditions, Hinduism also provides for deliverance from possession and demonic influence.[155]

The question of the place of suffering and sickness in all diverse Buddhist traditions is of course linked with the concept of *dukkha*. Another foundational concept, namely, the interrelatedness of all the cosmos, comes into play here: "Suffering is not unique to those who struggle with chronic disability or illness. The point is that even those who are physically healthy and materially wealthy nonetheless experience a chaotic, continually festering dissatisfaction."[156]

If the original Theravada tradition has focused much more energy on "healing" in terms of spiritual healing, the theistically oriented Mahayana traditions imagine healing as both spiritual and physical. Not unlike other theistic traditions, Mahayana can link healing directly to Buddha.[157] Indeed, one of the most interesting developments in this regard is the emergence of the "Medicine Buddha," a hugely important object of worship and prayer in

153. Ivette Vargas-O'Bryan, "Keeping It All in Balance: Teaching Asian Religions through Illness and Healing," in *Teaching Religion and Healing*, ed. Linda L. Barnes and Inés Talamantez (New York: Oxford University Press, 2006), chap. 4.

154. Prakash N. Desai, *Health and Medicine in the Hindu Tradition: Continuity and Cohesion* (New York: Crossroad, 1989).

155. B. S. Bharathi, "Spirit Possession and Healing Practices in a South Indian Fishing Community," *Man in India* 73, no. 4 (1968): 343–52.

156. Darla Schumm and Michael Stoltzfus, "Chronic Illness and Disability: Narratives of Suffering and Healing in Buddhism and Christianity," in *Disability and Religious Diversity*, ed. Darla Schumm and Michael Stoltzfus (New York: Palgrave, 2011), 164.

157. Raoul Birnbaum, *The Healing Buddha* (Boulder, CO: Shambhala, 1989), 3–26.

devotional movements throughout East Asia.[158] An authoritative, widely used manual is *The Sutra of Medicine Buddha*.

A Christian Engagement

While Abrahamic traditions make a general connection between the Fall and sickness, in terms of living in a world yet to be fully redeemed, the Scriptures, generally speaking, discourage trying to find the ultimate source of sickness— unless, as in the Old Testament, it is just left to the hand of God. Asiatic faiths provide fairly complex scenarios related to the order of the world and its processes regarding the origin and causes of sickness.

Although in all Asiatic theistic traditions deities may play a role in healing and restoration, in all Abrahamic traditions God is the healer (in Christian Trinitarian grammar, the healing work is typically assigned to Jesus). Theistic Buddhism comes closer in this regard by considering the Buddha the healer. Abrahamic traditions make a link between faith and human desire for and willingness to seek divine help from God. In Asiatic traditions, faith's role is ambiguous (as in theistic Hinduism) or lacking (as in Theravada).

In Christian faith, healing and restoration also have a future orientation, a sign of the awaited eschatological fullness of health and integrity. While a future orientation is not lacking in other Abrahamic traditions, they do not make it a theme, as does the Christian tradition.

---

158. Deepak Chopra, *Journey into Healing: Awakening the Wisdom within You* (London: Ebury, 2010).

9 | The Church and Religious Communities

Ecclesiology, the Christian Doctrine of the Church

Ecclesiology, the doctrine of the church, encompasses a wide array of interrelated topics, including the nature of the Christian community, her sacraments and liturgical life, her ministry and mission, as well as the quest for unity. Regardless of debates concerning the "founding" of the church (including Peter's role therein), Christian theology affirms an integral link between the ministry, death, and resurrection of Christ and the community he left behind to continue the mission of the kingdom of God, the righteous rule of his Father, to be consummated in the eschaton. Rooted in the peoplehood of Israel in the Old Testament, reflected in the band of the twelve closest disciples, the New Testament church came into existence as a result of the pouring out of the Spirit at the day of Pentecost. Catapulted into worldwide mission of proclamation, healing ministry, and service, this community has grown to be the largest in the history of religions, now encompassing about one-third of the world's population in all its diversity and plurality.

From of old, the Christian community has been described with a number of biblical metaphors: as the people of God (linking with Israel as the first people), as the body of Christ (Christ being the head), and as the temple of the Spirit. Following the example of the first Christian church, the church of the book of Acts, the Christian community has studied and listened to the Scripture; prayed and worshiped; practiced sacraments, particularly water baptism and Eucharist (the two universal rites present in all communities); and cultivated communion (fellowship). Tightly linked with this "inner" life of the community, the church has also been involved in diverse ministries, including preaching, healing, exorcism, as well as service to the poor and other disadvantaged persons. This mission includes both local and global dimensions, as Christianity, alongside Islam and early Buddhism in particular, is a deeply missional faith, unlike Judaism and Hinduism.

While all Christian communities make a distinction (though not a separation) between the clergy and the laity, what vary are leadership patterns and practices as well as theologies of ordination (that is, setting apart for a professional, usually theologically trained, ministerial leadership). Historically the oldest one is probably the three-tiered bishop, priest, and deacon/deaconess model. Alongside this pattern practiced in older churches (Orthodox, Roman Catholic) and the Anglican Church, there are two-tiered models, consisting of pastor and deacons, or something similar.

The worship and liturgical life of the church has never been uniform; yet, common elements can be found in weekly or other regular gatherings: reading the Scripture, homily, prayers, singing, and sacraments. While the majority of churches expect the leader of the worship and liturgical gathering to be an ordained minister, particularly when it comes to administering the Eucharist, a growing number of churches may or may not have that rule.

Beginning from the early centuries, the one church of Christ has undergone divisions and splits. The most well-known dividing moments have been the 1054 CE split between what are now the Eastern (Orthodox) Church and the Western Church (Roman Catholic, Anglican, Protestant, free churches, and independent communities). At the time of the sixteenth-century Reformation, the Western Church further divided into two main families, Roman Catholics on one side and Anglicans and all Protestants on the other side. In the Protestant family of churches, yet another significant split took place as what are now called free churches (Baptists, Quakers, many Methodists and Holiness movements, and countless others) and mainline (or magisterial) Protestants (Lutherans, Reformed, and some others) emerged.

While less like a split and more like a new development, the birth of the Pentecostal movement and its offshoot, the charismatic movements (Pentecostal-type communities both within and outside other churches), dramatically helped spread and diversify the church. Currently Roman Catholics (about 50 percent) and Pentecostals/charismatics (about 25 percent) make up the largest segments of the church, followed by the Eastern Church and then all the rest. Furthermore, over 70 percent of all Christians can be found in the Global South (Africa, Asia, and Latin America), making the formerly dominant Euro-American Caucasian population a minority—even if theological education, publishing activities, and a number of leadership organizations still reside in the old heartlands.

Among a number of great challenges and opportunities facing the global Christian church are the challenge of ecumenism, the search for unity, as well as the opportunities presented by religious plurality and forms of religious pluralism (that is, an ideological take on the fact of the diversity of religions).

Visions of Community among Religions: An Orientational Note

Although it would make little sense to speak of "ecclesiology," the doctrine of the church, in pan-religious terms, "it is part of the belief-structure of most religions that there should be a particular society which protects and sustains their basic values and beliefs, within which one may pursue the ideal human goal, as defined within the society"[1] and religion itself.[2] That said, the importance and role of the community vary greatly from religion to religion; similarly, the community's relation to the Divine differs among traditions. In terms of orientation, it is useful to highlight three broad theologically/ecclesiologically significant differences.[3]

First, whereas the Abrahamic (Jewish, Muslim, and Christian) traditions are integrally and deeply communal in orientation, neither of the Asiatic faiths engaged here is; commensurately, the Asiatic faiths' visions of "salvation" focus neither on the whole of humanity nor on the reconciliation of the cosmos as in the Abrahamic faiths, particularly the Jewish-Christian traditions. In Buddhism, the communion involves basically the religious "professionals," monks, and only indirectly laypeople, through their contact with the monks. Hinduism is basically individualistic, and its communal structures are highly diverse—and to the outsider, endlessly complex and elusive.

Second, whereas for Abrahamic traditions the religious community is deeply rooted in a "personal" God and divine election (notwithstanding differences in election theologies), in Asiatic faiths that is not the case. In Buddhism,

1. Keith Ward, *Religion and Community* (Oxford: Oxford University Press, 1999), 1.

2. Here it is not possible to delve into the continuing, complex scholarly debates about the concept of "religion" itself (and cognate terms such as "world religions"), which is a modern Western invention. An up-to-date, highly useful discussion for theologians is Harold A. Netland, *Christianity and Religious Diversity: Clarifying Christian Commitments in a Globalizing Age* (Grand Rapids: Baker Academic, 2015), chap. 1 (with rich, diverse literature), which also clarifies the meaning of "worldview" and "culture" in relation to religion.

3. See the somewhat similar kind of reflection in Ward, *Religion and Community*, 1–4.

particularly in its original Theravada form, the community is about ethico-religious pursuit, and in Hinduism, even in theistic forms (which constitute the majority of popular religiosity throughout India), the communities' relation to the Divine (however diversely understood) is complex and ambiguous.

Third, with little exaggeration it can be said that whereas the Asiatic faiths major in the renunciation of society in pursuit of final release, particularly the Christian faith (with many variations, of course) seeks to both renounce "the world" and penetrate it for the sake of its flourishing in this age and salvation (of many) in the eschaton. With Judaism and Islam, that issue is a bit more complex, although still essentially different from that of Asiatic faiths.

Now, with each of the four religious traditions, three descriptions are attempted: first, the nature of the religious community; second, her liturgical and ritual life; and, third, her relation to other religious communities. Following that "neutral" presentation, an intentionally dialogical engagement from a Christian perspective will be attempted with each of the dialogue partners.

Synagogue—the Jewish Community

The Emergence of the Jewish People and Community

Like her Abrahamic sister faiths, Judaism is communally oriented and community centered. Unlike them, it is the only religion that originally was purely tribal and still continues to be ethnic. While beliefs, particularly uncompromising monotheism (Deut. 6:4), came to be part of Jewishness from early times, the basis of the Jewish identity "is not a creed but a history: a strong sense of a common origin, a shared past and a shared destiny."[4] Indeed, one's Jewishness is not cast away by a lack of faith or even pronounced atheism—an unthinkable situation for a Muslim or Christian. One either is a Jew, by birth (of a Jewish mother), or one is not.

So far the term "Jewish" has been used in the established contemporary sense. However, totally differently from sister Abrahamic faiths (and Buddhism), the emergence or birth of the religion of Judaism is unique in that it happened in two distinct phases and over a millennium-long time span. The "Israelite" community has its defining origin in Moses's legacy, as recounted in the Tanak (i.e., the Christian Old Testament). "Judaism" emerged beginning

---

4. Nicholas De Lange, *An Introduction to Judaism* (Cambridge: Cambridge University Press, 2000), 26.

from the renewals led by Ezra following the Babylonian exile in the sixth century BCE. Its defining identity was shaped by the rabbinic tradition's Talmud. The emergence of the synagogue as the religious community in that phase is an important event. In the following, however, the terms "Israel" and "Judaism" are used interchangeably.

As discussed, Israel's distinctive identity is based on Yahweh's election of her as a "chosen people," based on covenant and its call for total devotion to Yahweh. Basically, separatism follows from this status and at the same time a claim on a specific territory, the Holy Land. Due to separatism, intermarriage has not been encouraged (as common as that has been in various eras), nor are conversions sought, although proselytism is possible under certain conditions.[5] Separatism and ethnic orientation, however, are only one part of the Jewish identity. A strong trend in the Old Testament is a missionary calling to help other nations of the world to know the name of Yahweh and to be a vehicle of divine blessings (Gen. 12:1–3). Although Israel's missional vocation is not similar to that of Islam and Christianity in terms of making concentrated efforts to reach nonbelievers, it still is embedded in Israel's identity in terms of expecting a universal end-time pilgrimage to Jerusalem to worship God (Isa. 2:1–4; Mic. 4:1–4).

A further defining feature of Jewish identity and her community is the continuing diaspora status beginning from the fall of Jerusalem in the sixth century BCE and continuing all the way to the founding of Israel in 1948. The large majority of Jews still live in diaspora outside the Holy Land, with a majority in the United States.

Liturgy and Religious Cycle

The origin of the Jewish religious community, the synagogue,[6] stems from the sixth century BCE crisis of losing the land and the temple, the beginning of (what became) rabbinic Judaism. The first synagogues were like ordinary houses, but the desire for the perception of holiness later led to fairly elaborate sacred building structures. Ten men are usually needed to establish a synagogue. Traditionally women have been separated from men into a different space in the synagogue; in modern and contemporary times, that varies.[7]

---

5. David Shatz, "A Jewish Perspective," in *OHRD*, 369–71.

6. The Greek-derived word "synagogue" means "gathering together," that is, community, and thus resembles *ekklēsia*.

7. Joseph Gurmann and Steven Fine, "Synagogue," in *ER* 13:8920–26.

Led by an elected council or official, synagogues are autonomous, without any authoritative superstructure. Unlike most Christian churches but similar to Islam, no professional clergy are needed to lead prayers and worship in the synagogue. That said, in practice the rabbi, the religious leader and teacher since the founding of (rabbinic) Judaism, presides over the liturgy—but a rabbi's status should not be confused with the role of a priest.[8] As in other religions, rabbis used to be only men; nowadays, in diaspora Judaism, many Reform movements endorse a gender-inclusive view.

Jewish (rabbinic) liturgy is founded around the Shema (Deut. 6:4-9) and the related Eighteen Benedictions (or prayers, the Amidah).[9] Another ancient habit is the encouragement to recite one hundred prayers per day, covering all aspects of life and faith. The reading of Torah is an essential part of worship. Contemporary diaspora, particularly in the United States, has produced a wide variety of liturgical patterns and orientations.

Not unlike other religions, there is a religiously ordered pattern for both the Jewish person's life cycle[10] and the life of the community following the sacred calendar.[11] What is unique is the centrality of weekly Sabbath around which the weekly religious ritual is totally centered, beginning with the common Friday evening pre-Sabbath service.

Perceptions of the Religious Other

The main thrust—and dynamic—in the Jewish relation to others is this: as much as Yahweh's covenant with Israel calls for unreserved commitment, it also implies that the same God could also covenant with other nations. In other words, there is both particularity (separatism) and universalism (missionary calling). Just consider Deuteronomy 32:8-9. No wonder Israel's relation to other religions has fluctuated over the centuries between exclusivism and inclusivism. Diversity of approaches has only intensified in contemporary times.[12]

Important theological reasons lie behind the wide-openness projected toward the religious other, particularly the "Talmudic position that embracing Judaism is not necessary for a Gentile's entering the world to come" for the

8. De Lange, *Introduction to Judaism*, 121-22.
9. Ruth Langer, "Worship and Devotional Life: Jewish Worship," in *ER* 14:9805-9.
10. De Lange, *Introduction to Judaism*, 110-12 and 147-50, respectively.
11. De Lange, *Introduction to Judaism*, 141-47.
12. Alan Brill, *Judaism and Other Religions: Models of Understanding* (New York: Palgrave Macmillan, 2010).

simple reason that "God wants to give all people just rewards."[13] This is not to deny the presence of exclusivism, particularly toward Christians, but rather to appreciate the fact that despite horrible and inhumane treatment of Jews throughout the centuries and particularly in the twentieth, there is this robust inclusivist impulse.

The Church and the Synagogue

Jews and Christians as the People of God

As discussed in the section on Christology above, what makes the encounter between Jews and Christians ironic and unique is that only after the Jewish people had rejected Jesus, the Messiah, did he become the "Savior of the nations."[14] Along with these and related theological reasons, what has damaged the relations between the two Abrahamic communities is the "supersessionist ideolog[y] of Christian identity," which rejects the idea that Israel continues to be the people of God,[15] and its corollary, Christian anti-Semitism.

It is against this sad and regrettable background—including also Jewish omission, until modern times, of a thoughtful engagement of Christianity and the proliferation of caricatures and prejudices—that promising signs of a fruitful mutual dialogue are on the horizon.[16] A key here is the right theological understanding of the meaning of the peoplehood. In Christian understanding, the concept of the "people of God" includes both Jews and Christians. Consequently, the idea of the church as the "new" people replacing Israel as the "old" people is to be rejected.

As orientation to this complex discussion, it may be useful to outline briefly (but hopefully not in an oversimplified manner) the main options among Christian theologians with regard to this issue:[17]

---

13. Shatz, "A Jewish Perspective," 367.

14. Pannenberg, *ST* 2:312.

15. John G. Kelly, "The Cross, the Church, and the Jewish People," in *Atonement Today*, ed. John Goldingay (London: SPCK, 1995), 168.

16. Edward Kessler and Neil Wenborn, eds., *A Dictionary of Jewish-Christian Relations* (Cambridge: Cambridge University Press, 2005); Edward Kessler, *An Introduction to Jewish-Christian Relations* (Cambridge: Cambridge University Press, 2010).

17. Following, with minor modifications, Donald G. Bloesch, *The Last Things: Resurrection, Judgment, Glory* (Downers Grove, IL: InterVarsity Press, 2004), 43–46 and chap. 10; this discussion is indebted to this source.

- In the *supersessionist* (or traditional) view, the church as the "new people" replaces Israel and takes her place in the divine economy.
- *Dispensationalists* make a categorical distinction between God's dealings with the church and with Israel, and they expect a literal fulfillment of Old Testament prophecies, including the rebuilding of the temple and its cult in the eschaton before the final consummation.[18] Because this view is novel and therefore marginal in Christian theology, it will not be further engaged.
- The *revisionists* expect ultimate redemption for both Israel and the church, and while for the latter it is through Christ, for the former it is not; indeed, the nonacceptance of Jesus as the Messiah for Israel is made a matter of obedience to God in this scheme.
- In *reunionism*, God's covenant with Israel will never be annulled but rather fulfilled through Christ, who is Israel's and all peoples' Messiah. Ultimately, both peoples of God, that of the Old Testament and that of the New Testament, will be reunited and saved.

Generally speaking, contemporary Christian tradition embraces either the revisionist or reunionist view and rejects the first two. In support of the reunionist vision—and thus rejecting supersessionism—it seems clear in the biblical testimonies, first, that God's covenant with Israel is irrevocable (Amos 9:14–15; Rom. 11:1, 29). Although for Paul the church embodied the true Israel (Rom. 2:29; 9:6; Phil. 3:3), this did not mean God put Israel aside (Gal. 3:17) after the supersessionist scheme. Second, in the divine plan of salvation, Israel plays a unique role as the "light" to the nations (Isa. 42:6; 49:6; Acts 13:47). That commission is not made void by Israel's disobedience. Third, in Jesus Christ, Israel's Messiah and the Savior of the whole world, the line of enmity between the chosen people and gentiles has been eradicated forever (Eph. 2:12–22), hence making possible the coming eschatological reunion.

Taking for granted the inviolability of God's covenant, in Romans 9–11 Paul holds that Israel is the "trunk" of God's tree and that the church, as the newcomer, can be compared to branches. In God's plan the branches could be united with the trunk (9:25)! This is a diametrically opposite angle from later Christian theology in which the starting point usually is the idea of the church as *the* people and the question focuses on whether Israel can also be God's people! At the same time, Paul is of course deeply troubled with Israel's unwillingness to embrace Christ as the Messiah, although he finds some consolation

18. Robert G. Clouse, "Fundamentalist Eschatology," in *OHE*, 263–77.

in the Old Testament remnant theology. He is confident that Israel's current "hardening" is but temporary and, ironically, is being used by God to further God's plans for the salvation of the whole world (11:11). As a result, God's purposes will be fulfilled: "a hardening has come upon part of Israel, until the full number of the Gentiles come in, and so all Israel will be saved" (11:25–26). There is thus a united eschatological goal for both Israel and the church, and they are set in mutual, yet distinct, roles in relation to each other. All this means that the church should take a careful and self-critical look at herself as the people of God.[19]

While holding to the continuation of God's covenant with Israel, the Christian church and theology also should exercise critical judgment in not identifying that status with the current secular state of Israel. Israel's political sins and wrongdoings, similarly to those of her Arabic neighbors, should be subjected to the same kinds of ethical and theological judgments as are other nations' deeds.

The Unique Nature of the Christian Mission to the Jews

Unlike Judaism, Christianity—similarly to Islam—is an active missionary faith. Again, contemporary Christian theology does not speak with one voice, as revisionists typically reject or at least marginalize any attempt at evangelizing the Jews. Reunionists, on the other side, affirm mission to Israel but hasten to remind us of its unique nature. What might be the reasons for the reunionist position? The main argument in favor of mission is biblical: neither Paul nor the rest of the New Testament was advocating a "special path" for Israel in terms of the Jews not needing Jesus the Messiah. The one people of God will all be saved in and through Christ. Not only did Paul preach to both gentiles and Jews (Acts 9:15), but he also considered bringing the gospel of Christ to Israel to take priority over other works of mission (Rom. 1:16).

At the same time, as mentioned, the unique and special nature of Jewish evangelization and mission has to be noted. The gospel of Christ, even when rejected by Jews, is not calling the people of God into something "new" in the way gentiles are being called. After all, Jesus Christ is Israel's Messiah before he is the Savior of the world. Mission to the Jews should also include a contrite and repentant spirit and acknowledgment of guilt for the sins in which Christians have participated throughout history. At the same time, Christians

19. Pannenberg, *ST* 3:476–77 (476).

should acknowledge their indebtedness to Israel for the message of salvation and the Messiah.

These two broad theological principles help us better appreciate this continuing dynamic tension facing Christian theology, put well by a Jewish theologian: how "to be faithful to the New Testament command to witness for Christ to all peoples and to convert all nations, while, at the same time, affirming the ongoing validity of the covenant between God and Israel via Abraham and Moses."[20] At the center of this tension lies the obvious but important fact that "historically Christianity has been theologically exclusive and humanistically universal, while Judaism has been theologically universal and humanistically exclusive." Christian theological exclusivism, however, does not entail a view to disqualifying others from salvation but—as the sympathetic Jewish observer further rightly notes—is funded by the conviction that Christ's salvific work is meant for the benefit of all.[21]

Ummah—the Islamic Community

The Birth and Meaning of the Ummah

As mentioned, Islam as a religion shares with Judaism and Christianity a deep communal orientation anchored in one God.[22] The term for the community, ummah, appears in the Qur'an over sixty times with diverse meanings.[23] The incipient universal vision of early Islam is evident in Qur'an 10:19: "Mankind was but one community; then they differed," obviously implying an original "single ummah with a single religion."[24]

There is a marked development in the relation of the ummah to the other during the Prophet's lifetime, beginning with inclusion of Muslims, Jews, and Christians, based on belief in one God, toward a narrower view limited basically to the followers of the Prophet. A definite limiting took place after

---

20. Michael S. Kogan, *Opening the Covenant: A Jewish Theology of Christianity* (Oxford: Oxford University Press, 2008), xii.

21. Kogan, *Opening the Covenant*, xii–xiii.

22. Ward, *Religion and Community*, 33.

23. Abdullah Saeed, "The Nature and Purpose of the Community (Ummah) in the Qur'ān," in *The Community of Believers: Christian and Muslim Perspectives*, ed. Lucinda Mosher and David Marshall (Washington, DC: Georgetown University Press, 2015); Frederick Mathewson Denny, "The Meaning of Ummah in the Qur'ān," *History of Religions* 15, no. 1 (1975): 34–70.

24. Brannon Wheeler, "Ummah," in *ER* 14:9446.

his death, with also a shift toward the presence of more sociopolitical and juridical aspects.

The idea of the superiority of this community was established with appeal to passages such as Qur'an 3:110: "You are the best community brought forth to men, enjoining decency, and forbidding indecency, and believing in God." At times, however, a more hospitable interpretation could also include other God-fearing communities as exemplary.

The Divisions of the *Ummah*: The Emergence of the Sunnis and Shi'ites

The major division, between the Sunnis and Shi'ites, arose over the issue of the Prophet's successor after his death (632 CE). The father of the Prophet's beloved wife Aisha, Abu Bakr, was made the first leader (*amir*, "commander") by the majority, but that did not settle the matter, as the minority of the community preferred as leader Ali, the husband of Muhammad's daughter Fatima. Both theological and political issues were involved. Whereas for the majority, the leadership choice after the passing of the Prophet belonged to the *ummah* at large, for the rest it was God's choice falling on Ali—with the ambiguous claim that he had both divine endorsement and the Prophet's.

The majority wanted to stay in the line of Mecca's dominant tribe, the Prophet's own tribe, Quraysh, whereas a minority received support from Medina. Full separation of the *ummah*, however, did not come about until after the brief leadership of Umar I and the longer office of the caliph Uthman, whose assassination in 656 brought Ali to power for half a decade, during which virtual civil war was fought. At the end, the community's separation was final, between the majority Sunnis (currently over 80 percent) and a minority of Shi'ites following Ali's legacy. Both sides further continued splitting internally, leading to the kind of complex denominationalism characteristic of most religions.

All Shi'ites share the belief in the divinely ordered status of Ali as the successor to the Prophet (Q 2:124; 21:72–73).[25] By far the largest and most important Shi'ite denomination, "the Twelvers," has developed a highly sophisticated genetic line of succession from Ali through his two sons (Hasan and Husayn) all the way to the twelfth one. The most distinctive claim therein has to do with the last imam (after Hasan ibn Ali al-Askari of the ninth century), titled Muhammad b. Hasan, who allegedly went into "occultation" (that

---

25. Najam Haider, *Shī'ī Islam* (Cambridge: Cambridge University Press, 2014).

is, concealment) and whose return they await. All imams in this interpretation possess inerrancy in order to be able to prevent the community from being led astray. That said, there are a number of fiercely debated issues among the three main Shi'ite traditions (the Twelvers, the Ishmaelites, and the Zaydis, the first two sharing much more in common concerning the imamate) about the line of succession and related issues.

What is amazing and confusing to the outsider about the global Muslim community is that, despite how extremely much they share in tradition and doctrine, their mutual relationships are so antagonistic and condemnatory. Both parties share the same Qur'an, the same prophethood, and the Five Pillars, including prayers, fasting, and other rituals (albeit somewhat differently nuanced and practiced).[26] Yet, it seems like any kind of global ecumenical reconciliation is not on the horizon,[27] although the Qur'an mandates work for unity: "And hold fast to God's bond, together, and do not scatter. . . . Let there be one community" (3:103–4; see also 103:5).

Spiritual Life and Worship

Obedience and submission to Allah, including willing service and honoring *tahwid*, the absolute unity/oneness of God, shape all aspects of Muslim life, including what we call devotion and liturgy.[28] This piety consists of "five pillars"—confession, ritual prayer, fasting, pilgrimage, and alms—routinely preceded by the important rites of purification, both physical and spiritual.[29]

Ritual prayer is the most visible form of piety. Muslims ought to pray five times a day at designated times, regardless of their location. Prayer is preceded by ablution and employs a prescribed form and content, mostly recital of Qur'anic verses. Prayer is also the main activity in the mosque;[30] nowadays the

26. Shmuel Bar, "Sunnis and Shiites: Between Rapprochement and Conflict," in *Current Trends in Islamist Ideology*, ed. Hillel Fradkin et al. (Washington, DC: Center on Islam, Democracy, and the Future of the Muslim World, Hudson Institute, 2005), 2:87–96.

27. Feras Hamza, "Unity and Disunity in the Life of the Muslim Community," in Mosher and Marshall, *The Community of Believers*, 74.

28. Vernon James Schubel, "Worship and Devotional Life: Muslim Worship," in *ER* 14:9815–20.

29. Frederick Mathewson Denny, *An Introduction to Islam*, 2nd ed. (New York: Macmillan, 1994), chap. 7.

30. Rusmir Mahmutcehagic, *The Mosque: The Heart of Submission* (New York: Fordham University Press, 2007).

Friday afternoon gathering there includes a sermon. Holy scripture is highly honored and venerated. Since there is no clergy and no theologically trained priesthood, any male in principle is qualified to lead; he is usually chosen from among those most deeply knowledgeable in the tradition.

Although the Prophet Muhammad was but a human being, particularly in folk Islam and forms of Sufism his status gets elevated to a (semi)divine object of veneration. Sufi mysticism also knows a number of saints similarly highly elevated, particularly Ali (even among the Sunnis).

As in other religions, the annual life cycle follows the religious calendar, starting from the honoring of the date when Muhammad migrated from Mecca to Medina. Friday is not considered a holy day, although it is the day of congregation. Instead, a number of other holy days commemorate significant days in the life of the Prophet and early *ummah*.[31] Globalization has caused much diversity in rituals and rites but not in doctrine and prayers.

Mission to Nonbelievers and Perception of the Religious Other

Similarly to Christianity, Islam's outlook is universal. Echoing biblical theology, the Qur'an teaches that "'to God belongs the kingdom (*mulk*) of the heavens and earth' (e.g., 2:107)."[32] The Qur'an instructs us that "had God willed, He would have made them one community" (42:8; see also 42:10). The key verse is well known: "God is our Lord and your Lord. Our deeds concern us and your deeds concern you. There is no argument between us and you. God will bring us together, and to Him is the [final] destination" (42:15).

In this light, it is understandable that the earliest Qur'anic passages were not calling people to convert to a new religion; rather, the Meccans were called to "worship the Lord of this House [Ka'ba]" (106:3).[33] Only later, with the rising opposition from the worshipers of local deities, was a decisive break announced, and the confession became "There is no god except God" (37:35). We know that in Medina the Prophet with his companions lived among the Jews, and we may safely infer that he obviously assumed that the new faith

31. George W. Braswell Jr., *Islam: Its Prophet, Peoples, Politics, and Power* (Nashville: Broadman & Holman, 1996), 77–80.

32. J. Dudley Woodberry, "The Kingdom of God in Islam and the Gospel," in *Anabaptists Meeting Muslims: A Calling for Presence in the Way of Christ*, ed. James R. Krabill, David W. Shenk, and Linford Stutzman (Scottdale, PA: Herald, 2005), 49.

33. The Ka'ba is the holiest place in Islam; it is in Mecca.

was in keeping with theirs, as well as with Christian faith (2:40–41). Recall also that at that time the term *muslim* could be applied to non-Muslims such as Solomon (27:15–44) and disciples of Jesus (3:52). Only when the Jews rejected the Prophet was the direction of prayer changed from Jerusalem to Mecca (2:142).

In keeping with this history is the special status assigned to Abrahamic sister faiths. Between what Muslims call "the Abode of Peace and the Abode of War," a third region was acknowledged, "the Abode of the People of the Book," that is, Jews and Christians.[34] These two traditions enjoy a unique relation to Islam (2:135–36; 5:12, 69), implying that in some real sense the diversity of religions is not only tolerated by Allah but even planned and endorsed, at least when it comes to those who are the "people of the book" (48:29; 5:48; 3:114).

This inclusive tendency notwithstanding, Islam retains a unique place in God's eyes. The inclusion is similar to Roman Catholic inclusivism: while other nations might have known God, only Muslims know Allah intimately and are rightly related to God. That is most probably the meaning of the Qur'anic statements that Muslims, in distinction from others, are "God's sincere servants" (37:40) and "are of the elect, the excellent" (38:47). Therefore, ultimately even Jewish and Christian traditions suffer from corruption and misunderstanding of the final revelation.

At her core, Islam is an active missionary community, based on the Qur'anic mandate to reach out to nonbelievers (16:125–26). This is often expressed with the Arabic term *da'wah*, literally "call, invocation, or summoning."[35] Combining a universalizing tendency and fervent missionary mandate, Islam's goal of outreach is comprehensive, including ideally social, economic, cultural, and religious spheres. Ideally it would result in the establishment of Shari'a law and the gathering of all peoples under one *ummah*.[36]

Although the Qur'an prohibits evangelism by force (2:256), similarly to Christianity, alliance with earthly powers, militarism, and economic interests were all employed to spread Islam with force and brutality.[37] In other words, not only Christianity but also Islam bears the long legacy of colonialism.

---

34. William Montgomery Watt, *Muslim-Christian Encounters: Perceptions and Misperceptions* (London: Routledge, 1991), 26–27.

35. William D. Miller, "Da'wah," in *ER* 4:2225–26.

36. Badru D. Kateregga and David W. Shenk, *Islam and Christianity: A Muslim and a Christian in Dialogue* (Ibadan, Nigeria: Daystar, 1985), 79–81.

37. Miller, "Da'wah," 4:2225.

Church and Ummah

Muslim-Christian Relations in a Theological Perspective: A Brief Assessment

Not only does Judaism stand in a unique position in relation to Christianity, so does Islam, albeit differently. That said, it is too rarely appreciated how different the Christianity first encountered by the Prophet and the early Muslim *ummah* was from what the contemporary global Christian church is now. In the seventh century, notwithstanding internal differences, there was one undivided church (at least formally). Importantly, the segments of the church that early Islam engaged were either marginal or heretical in the eyes of mainstream Christianity, namely, the advocates of Nestorianism[38] and Monophysitism (of various sorts).[39] Most ironically, many of the objections of Muslims against the orthodox Christian doctrines of the Trinity and Christology either stem from or are strongly flavored by these Christian divergences.[40]

On the one hand, the Christian-Muslim encounters throughout history have been characterized by misperceptions, misrepresentations, and even hostility. On the other hand, more often than not there has been more tolerance than would be expected from, say, cultures of the Middle Ages.[41] There was also a shift in Christian perception: whereas for Christian apologists beginning from the seventh century, such as John of Damascus, Islam was represented more as a heresy, from the late medieval period onward it was taken as a false religion, apostasy. In the contemporary situation, a number of promising signs indicate that concentrated efforts are under way to continue constructive mutual engagement, heal memories, and improve understanding of the two faiths.[42]

Recall the wise words from the Roman Catholic Vatican II (1962–1965) document *Nostra Aetate*: "The Church regards with esteem also the Moslems.

---

38. Nestorians were charged for separating Christ's divine and human nature in a way that compromised their integral union.

39. Monophysitism (literally "one-nature") was charged with lumping together Christ's divine and human nature in a way that compromised the distinction between the two (making the divine the only "nature").

40. Watt, *Muslim-Christian Encounters*, chap. 1.

41. Clinton Bennett, *Understanding Christian-Muslim Relations: Past and Present* (London: Continuum, 2008); Watt, *Muslim-Christian Encounters*.

42. For the "A Common Word" project, see http://www.acommonword.com/; for "The Building Bridges Seminar," see https://berkleycenter.georgetown.edu/projects/the-building -bridges-seminar.

They adore the one God, living and subsisting in Himself; merciful and all-powerful, the Creator of heaven and earth, who has spoken to men; they take pains to submit wholeheartedly to even His inscrutable decrees, just as Abraham, with whom the faith of Islam takes pleasure in linking itself, submitted to God. Though they do not acknowledge Jesus as God, they revere Him as a prophet. They also honor Mary, His virgin Mother; at times they even call on her with devotion."[43] The church and the *ummah*'s common basis in monotheism, scriptural heritage, doctrine of creation, theological anthropology, eschatology, and the person of Jesus, detailed above—these alone mandate continuous, sustained dialogue. Commonalities and differences also come to the surface in the missional orientation of both traditions.

Mission, Colonialism, and Political Power: Shared Concerns

Similarly to Judaism, Islam sees "the appropriate way to human fulfillment in obedience to a divinely revealed law," named in that tradition the Shari'a, which differs from Judaism in that it is "given to be followed by all humanity, and not just by one special community."[44] How does Christian mission relate to that claim? Instead of a divinely given law to govern all of life as in a theocracy, Christian mission aims at providing a holistic way of life based on love of God and neighbor, leaving open issues of government (most inclusively understood).

From a Christian perspective, it is highly ironic that the Islamic pursuit of global Shari'a has from the beginning been closely allied with a specific ethnicity and language (Arabic) and, in modern and contemporary times, often allied with nationalism, particularly in the regions of the world colonized by European powers.[45] How would a universal reach to all humanity be reconciled with that? "If Islam is indeed meant to be a global community, then it is self-defeating for Islam to oppose 'the West,' when Westerners should be Muslims, too, and when many are."[46]

As mentioned above, both Islam and Christianity carry the legacy of colonialism as part of their mission history. Unbeknownst to many is the fact

43. *Nostra Aetate: Declaration on the Relation of the Church to Non-Christian Religions* (Vatican II, October 28, 1965), #3, http://www.vatican.va/archive/hist_councils/ii_vatican_council/documents/vat-ii_decl_19651028_nostra-aetate_en.html.

44. Ward, *Religion and Community*, 31.

45. See Bernard Lewis, *Islam and the West* (Oxford: Oxford University Press, 1993).

46. Ward, *Religion and Community*, 32–33 (33).

that "while from the first there were considerable numbers of Christians under Muslim rule, yet until the appearance of European colonialism there were virtually no Muslims under Christian rule except for limited periods."[47] Everywhere Christians lived under Muslim rule, the Shari'a law totally forbade Christian sharing of the gospel with Muslims. Indeed, according to Shari'a law, the penalty for apostasy—the Islamic perception of converting to Christianity—is death.[48]

After this engagement of Abrahamic sister faiths, the rest of the chapter delves into Asiatic traditions, beginning, again, with a description.

Hindu Spiritual Life and Community

In Search of Hindu Identity and Religious Community

Both Judaism and Hinduism emerged over a long period of time. Neither one has a human founder. They are also similar in that while one can be a Jew only by birth (through a Jewish mother), the assumption is that being born in India makes one Hindu. Doctrine does not determine belonging in either tradition, although holy scriptures are honored in both.

Differently from Abrahamic faiths, community does not play an essential role in Hinduism, as the religion's main goal is the spiritual release of the individual rather than either reform of the society or communal (let alone cosmic) eschatological renewal. This does not mean in any way to undermine the deeply and widely communal orientation of Indian culture and, as part of that, the celebration of religious rites in communal settings in family, village, or temple. Rather, it means that the basic *theological* orientation of Hinduism lacks an internal and ultimate communal goal. In keeping with this, there is no single term to describe the communal side of Hindu spirituality. Perhaps closest in intention comes the term *sampradaya*, which, however, is not universally nor even very widely used.[49]

The plurality of Hinduism allows a plethora of local deities to be worshiped. That said, the existing diversity does not translate into personal choice of the deity, as might be misunderstood in the manner of the hyperindivid-

---

47. Watt, *Muslim-Christian Encounters*, 74.

48. See Watt, *Muslim-Christian Encounters*, 70.

49. Gavin D. Flood, *An Introduction to Hinduism* (Cambridge: Cambridge University Press, 1996), 134.

ualism of the Global North. Rather, one follows the religion and rites of the family and wider community.

Hindu "Sacraments" and Ways of Spirituality

Without any claim for material similarity between Christian sacraments and Hindu life-cycle-related *samskaras*, through which one becomes a full member of the community and society, the Christian interpreter may duly identify them as "Hindu sacraments." Similarly to rites of passage in most all religions, they cover all life from birth to death, as prescribed in the sacred literature.[50]

Highly important is one called "the second birth," which occurs at eight to twelve years of age. The exact time of this rite of initiation is determined by an astrologer, and it helps the person make the shift from childhood to the first of the four ashrams, which is studenthood, including religious education.

A central role is also played by the last sacrament, that of death, universally practiced by all Hindus, even secular ones. The funeral, in which the body is burned, includes elaborate rites and rituals. Following the funeral, ancestor rites typically continue over the years to "establish the deceased harmoniously within their appropriate worlds and prevent them from becoming hungry and haunting their living descendants."[51]

As explained in the section on soteriology, Hinduism knows three paths to liberation, namely, devotion, knowledge, and work. The most typical at the grassroots level is the first path, and for the large majority, this *bhakti* devotion comes in the form of theistic Vaishnavism. Based on the Bhagavad Gita, this loving, intimate devotion is often focused on Krishna.

In India's worship life, "space and time are permeated with the presence of the supreme."[52] Among the conveyors of the divine, the most profound is *murti*, or image, which can also be called "embodiment," the highest form of manifestation of the divine. In temples, the devout Hindus are surrounded and embraced by this divine presence. In that presence, masses of devotees may experience *darsana*, the special kind of spiritual "seeing" or insight.[53] Indeed, this "auspicious seeing" is mutual as, on the one hand, the deity makes her-

---

50. Klaus Klostermaier, *A Survey of Hinduism*, 3rd ed. (Albany: State University of New York Press, 2010), chap. 10.

51. Paul B. Courtright, "Worship and Devotional Life: Hindu Devotional Life," in *ER* 14:9821.

52. Klostermaier, *Survey of Hinduism*, 263.

53. Klostermaier, *Survey of Hinduism*, 263–68.

self or himself to be seen and, on the other, the god is "seen" by the devotee. Regular *pujas*, acts of worship to the deities, open to all Hindus, take place from day to day to celebrate the divine presence.[54] Closely related to the centrality of divine presence is a special kind of prayer rite, originating in Vedic religion,[55] the mantra "Om," which functions as the representation not only of God (Brahman) but in some sense also of the whole reality. It is typical for the head of the household to utter this word first thing in the morning after purification rituals.

Similarly to other religious traditions, along with rites of passage, a rich and diverse annual festival menu is an essential part of Hindu devotion and worship life. Although the basic structure of festivals may be simple, to outsiders these festivals look extremely complex. They may last several days and exhibit unusually rich local and denominational diversity.

As do other faiths, Hinduism has a "professional" religious class, the Brahmins, related to the ancient class system of India, formerly a caste society.[56] Whereas ordinary devotees have Puranas, the rich narrative and epic literature, as their holy scripture, only the Brahmins are experts in Vedic literature. Another related structure of Indian society and culture has to do with the four ashrams. Ideally one reaches at the end of life the final stage of the "renouncer," after studenthood, family life, and the period of forest hermit. Only a tiny minority of Hindus belong to the Brahmin class or reach the stage of renouncer. Along with these two classes, there is an innumerable group of gurus of various sorts, many highly respected, others less so. Around the guru, a *sampradaya* is formed, a main concept regarding community for the masses of Hindus.

The Perception of Religious Diversity Both within and in Relation to the Other

Hinduism embraces diversity in a way no other major living tradition does. This diversity, however, differs from the modernist Western pluralism in many respects. First of all, Hindus, even in their tolerance of other rites and deities,

54. For details, see Theodore M. Ludwig, *The Sacred Paths: Understanding the Religions of the World*, 4th ed. (Upper Saddle River, NJ: Pearson, 2006), 109–10; Courtright, "Worship and Devotional Life," 9823.

55. The classic passage is Rig Veda 3.62.10.

56. The four classes are Brahmins, Kshatriyas, Vaishyas, and Shudras. Arvind Sharma, *Classical Hindu Thought: An Introduction* (Oxford: Oxford University Press, 2000), chap. 19.

typically take their own beliefs as true. Second, Hindu tolerance has much to do with the idea that since God is bigger than any other concept of ours, various ways of approaching God are complementary in that, beyond and transcending any particular path, there is the infinite Divine, Brahman.[57]

What about mission and desire to convert others? It is clear that Hinduism is not a missional religion like Buddhism, Christianity, and Islam. Considering itself the "original" religion, it tends to assimilate others under its own purview, not necessarily inviting them to change.

Understandably, Hinduism faces grave difficulties when encountering Christian and Islamic types of claims for the finality of revelation and uniqueness of God.[58] In keeping with the assimilationist principle, Hindus resist and oppose any efforts at evangelization by other traditions. In that light, it appears inhospitable that some Hindu movements, such as Arya Samaj, opposed the conversion of Hindus to Islam and Christianity while at the same time strongly advocating reconversion of recent converts to Christianity back to Hinduism.[59]

The Church and Hindus

Differences of Orientation

Because of the difference of orientations between Hindu and Christian traditions, namely, the former's individualistic pursuit of release and the latter's deeply communal faith, dialogue focused on ecclesiology yields fewer results and areas of shared concerns than between the church and the synagogue or the *ummah*.

In the discussion on Hindu spiritual life and devotion above, it became evident that in many ways it is oriented differently than Judeo-Christian tradition—for example, prayer for the Hindu, rather than petition and pleading, as in Abrahamic traditions, is more about chanting the sacred mantra, linked with the search for *darsana* in the divine presence. There is also what can be called "ritual enhancement," that is, a devotional practice that "aims at sustaining or improving the circumstances of the worshiper," whether that

---

57. Ward, *Religion and Community*, 82–84, 96–99.

58. Arvind Sharma, "A Hindu Perspective," in *OHRD*, 309–20.

59. Kewal Ahluwalia, "Shudhi Movement: 85th Shardhanand Shudhi Divas—December 23rd," accessed March 19, 2019, http://www.aryasamaj.com/enews/2012/jan/4.htm.

means practical life situations like sickness or business or family concerns, or the spiritual aims of liberation and release.[60] This is of course also a common feature of Abrahamic traditions.

A foundational difference has to do with another common theme throughout Hindu devotional life, namely, "negotiation or exchange, in which devotional performances become occasions for giving human resources of food, gifts, and devotion to supernatural entities and powers in exchange for human well-being, which is understood to flow from those persons and powers as a consequence of the rite."[61] Although this kind of exchange mentality is not unknown in Christian spirituality, theologically it is a foreign concept.

Religious Diversity: Connections and Disconnections

As has become clear, Hinduism exhibits internal diversity unlike any other living faith tradition, and its relation to the religious other is also more open and complex than in Abrahamic faiths. Hinduism's tendency to assimilate others under itself, believing itself to be the "original" and perhaps best revelation, makes it in some real sense a counterpart to Roman Catholicism. At the same time, the Hindu attitude toward Christian faith is more complicated than that. Consider the well-known spokespersons of Hinduism in the West, Swami Vivekananda, India's delegate to the World Parliament of Religions meeting in Chicago in 1893, and Sarvepalli Radhakrishnan, the former president of India. Known for tolerance and religious coexistence, they are also critics of Christianity.[62]

Indeed, there is no standard, universal Hindu response to the religious other.[63] In light of this complexity, recall that the roots of Hindu-Christian engagement and coexistence go far back in history. It is probable that there was a Christian presence in India as early as the first century. Syrian Christianity is believed to have been present beginning in the fourth century.[64] Although

---

60. Courtright, "Worship and Devotional Life," 9820.

61. Courtright, "Worship and Devotional Life," 9820.

62. Lowell D. Streiker, "The Hindu Attitude toward Other Religions," *Journal of Religious Thought* 23, no. 1 (1966/1967): 75–90.

63. P. S. Daniel, *Hindu Response to Religious Pluralism* (Delhi: Kant Publications, 2000), 233–36.

64. Anantanand Rambachan, "Hindu-Christian Dialogue," in *The Wiley-Blackwell Companion to Inter-Religious Dialogue*, ed. Catherine Cornille (Chichester, UK: Wiley & Sons, 2013), 325–45.

Western colonialism helped poison mutual relations in later history between Hindus and Christians in a number of ways, it is significant that, beginning from the end of the nineteenth century, a new wave of interpretations of Christ related to the so-called Indian renaissance or neo-Hindu reform emerged, testing affinities between the two traditions.

These and related experiences in the past both speak to the complexity of relations between the two traditions and open up some possibilities for continuing mutual exploration of common themes and concerns. It is promising to hear from a Hindu scholar that "the dialogue initiative has come to stay in India."[65]

The Buddhist *Sangha* and the Pursuit of Enlightenment

The Rise of Sangha *and Rapid Proliferation of* Dhamma

Differently from the parent religion of Hinduism, Buddhism (like Christianity) has a founder, Siddhartha Gautama. Although the historical details of Gautama's life are very scarce,[66] the religion- and community-forming narrative is based on the enlightenment experience of this former noble prince and renouncer. The teaching of the emerging new religion, similarly to Hinduism, is not centered on faith as much as on commitment to pursuing release from attachment to the world of impermanence and resulting *dukkha* (see chap. 8 above).

The enlightened Sakyamuni (Gautama) established the *sangha* (also *samgha*) community, with five initial disciples. Originally it was an inclusive community, open to both male monks and female nuns. The nuns lived separately from the men but belonged to the community. That inclusive vision, however, came to be limited through the centuries, and it is normal (particularly in Theravada contexts) to have only male monks.

Soon after the founding of the *sangha*, Buddha began to send the enlightened monks (*arahants*, "worthy ones") out on missionary trips to preach the *dhamma*, the Buddha's teachings. So, unlike Hinduism, but like Christian and Muslim traditions, Buddhism is a missionary religion,[67] and one can find

65. Anand Amaladass, "Viewpoints: Dialogue in India," *Journal of Hindu-Christian Dialogue* 1, no. 7 (June 1988): 7–8.

66. Gajin Nagao, "The Life of the Buddha: An Interpretation," *Eastern Buddhist*, n.s., 20, no. 2 (1987): 1–31.

67. Jonathan S. Walter, "Missions: Buddhist Missions," in *ER* 9:6077–82.

scriptural commissioning for it. Particularly during the founding centuries, the missionary vision was fervent. Similarly to Christianity, the new religion also proliferated through merchants and other travelers.[68]

Following Buddha's *parinirvana* (complete liberation at death), the First Ecumenical Council was summoned, gathering together five hundred *arahants* to whom Buddha's *dhamma* was entrusted, comprising Tipitaka, the "Three Baskets" of teachings, the middle one of which (Vinaya Pitaka) contains all instructions and teachings for the life of the *sangha*. Subsequently, the Second Council, one hundred years later, brought to the surface disagreements and strife. A number of other councils followed, along with deep disagreements and splits.

Around the beginning of the common era, the most significant split occurred, giving birth to the Mahayana school.[69] It made a foundational claim to Buddha's own teaching, believed to be hidden for a while and then rediscovered. Mahayana advocates a much more open access to the pursuit of nirvana for all men and women, not only to a few religious. It also adopted a more theistically oriented cosmology and highlighted the importance of notions of grace and mercy, particularly in its later developments having to do with the Pure Land and related movements. Mahayana has also developed a growing tradition of spiritual exercises in pursuit of liberative insight.

The third major strand is commonly called Vajrayana ("Diamond Vehicle") or Tantrism and can be found in Tibet. Broadly related to Mahayana, it has also contextualized itself in rich Tibetan folk religiosity and mysticism with a focus on diverse rituals, mantras, and esoteric rites.

Devotion and Liturgy

Differently from Jewish-Christian tradition but in keeping with Hindu traditions, initiatory rites are not usually necessary to join the religion (whereas joining the *sangha* takes a long period of discipline and teaching, culminating in "ordination" by a legitimate leader). Instead of an initiatory act, it is (almost) universally taught among Buddhists that taking refuge in Buddha,

---

68. Linda Learman, ed., *Buddhist Missionaries in the Era of Globalization* (Honolulu: University of Hawaii Press, 2005).

69. Whereas Theravada is dominant in Thailand, Myanmar, and Sri Lanka, Mahayana is currently present in India, Vietnam, Tibet (mainly in the form of Tantric Buddhism or Vajrayana), China, Taiwan, Korea, and Japan, among other locations. That tradition is also the most familiar form of Buddhism in the Global North.

dhamma, and *sangha* constitutes becoming a Buddhist. It normally entails intending to adhere to the five precepts of abstaining from killing, stealing, adultery, lying, and drinking. At the same time, one commits oneself to the pursuit of liberation from *dukkha* following the Noble Eightfold Path. Although in Theravada the releasing enlightenment is typically thought to be attained only by the monks, and even among them, by few, Gautama included in the sphere of the *sangha* also laypersons, regardless of their profession.

Sanghas are supposed to be located near the rest of the society, distinct from society but not so separated as to be isolated. Monks go out every morning to collect gifts and donations, and they also serve the people in the temples and homes in religious rituals.

While in principle no rituals or rites are mandatory, Buddhist lands are filled with most elaborate devotional and worship acts and patterns, liturgy at the center.[70] Furthermore, all denominations, astonishingly even Theravada, are highly "animistic": in everyday religiosity, spirits and spirituality are alive and well.

Furthermore, not unlike most religions, "many Buddhists believe that ritual and devotion are also instrumental in bringing about blessings in life and even inner spiritual transformation."[71] Indeed, notwithstanding wide and deep variety in the Buddhist world, rites related to giving or offering in worship form the basic structure. Giving with the right attitude is the key, and only then meritorious. To the honoring posture toward Buddha belongs the use of candles, water, food, flowers, and so forth.

Yet another defining feature across the varied Buddhist world is meditation, whose aim is to bring about "a state of perfect mental health, equilibrium and tranquility." Unlike in many other contexts, Buddhist meditation is not an exit from ordinary life but, on the contrary, is deeply embedded in it. Its core has to do with mindfulness, an aptitude and skill to be developed throughout one's life.[72]

Because of the nontheistic orientation and nondivine status of Buddha, strictly speaking there is no prayer in original Buddhist devotion; "it is only a way of paying homage to the memory of the Master who showed the way."[73]

---

70. Peter Skilling, "Worship and Devotional Life: Buddhist Devotional Life in Southeast Asia," in *ER* 14:9826–34.

71. Ludwig, *The Sacred Paths*, 158.

72. Martine Batchelor, "Meditation and Mindfulness," *Contemporary Buddhism* 12, no. 1 (May 2011): 157–64.

73. Walpola Rahula, *What the Buddha Taught*, rev. ed. (New York: Grove, 1974), 81. See

Similarly, the scriptures—as much as they are honored and venerated in many forms of liturgy (particularly Mahayana)—are not looked upon as divine revelation but rather as guides to human effort. Furthermore, Buddhist devotion, similarly to Islamic religious life, particularly in folk spirituality, has elevated the founder to a (semi)divine status.

Similarly to all other religions, Buddhism embraces daily rituals and worship patterns as well as holy days and festivals, including rites of passage from birth, to initiation into (young) adulthood, to death.[74] Counterintuitively, all over the Buddhist world the worship patterns, rituals, and rites seem to be similar to those of theistic faiths, with a strong focus on devotion.

The Religious Other

Similarly to Hinduism, the proper perspective on investigating the discerning of the religious other among Buddhists embraces both intra- and interfaith dimensions. Yet another shared feature is that it is typical for Buddhist movements to consider other Buddhist movements through the lens of "hierarchical inclusivism." Here is also a resemblance to Roman Catholicism. All these three traditions consider their own movement as the "fulfillment," while others are at a lower level and yet belong to the same family. An aspect of that tolerance of sectarian diversity is to lift up one's own scriptures as superior to the sister movements' scriptures.

Encounter with the non-Buddhist religious other is not new to the tradition; on the contrary, during Buddhism's rise in India, along with emerging Jainism, it had to negotiate its identity not only in relation to Hinduism and other local religions but also (when moving outside India) in relation to Taoism, Confucianism, Shintoism, and others.[75] Although Buddhism's past—or present life—is not without conflicts with the other, occasional campaigns of coercion, and other forms of religious colonialism, by and large Buddhism has sought peaceful coexistence. The inclusivist paradigm

---

also Rita M. Gross, "Meditation and Prayer: A Comparative Inquiry," *Buddhist-Christian Studies* 22 (2002): 77–86.

74. Ludwig, *The Sacred Paths*, 159–63.

75. Masao Abe, *Buddhism and Interfaith Dialogue*, ed. Steven Heine (Honolulu: University of Hawaii Press, 1995); D. W. Chappell, "Buddhist Interreligious Dialogue: To Build a Global Community," in *The Sound of Liberating Truth: Buddhist-Christian Dialogues in Honor of Frederick J. Streng*, ed. S. B. King and P. O. Ingam (Richmond, UK: Curzon, 1999), 3–35.

has also applied at times at least to its closest cousin faiths.[76] That said, as can be said of Hinduism, it is difficult to find many clear examples of what we Westerners call religious pluralism.[77] Only recently have a growing number of Buddhists, many of them scholars from or residing in the Global North, begun more systematic work toward Buddhist comparative theology and interfaith engagement.[78]

The Church and Buddhists

The Slow Emergence of Buddhist and Christian Engagement

In contrast to Christianity's interaction with Judaism and Islam, Christian and Buddhist theologies do not have a history of dialogue and mutual engagement; indeed, until the nineteenth century, very little exchange took place, although from the sixth to the eighth centuries, Nestorian Christians had some meaningful encounters with Buddhists in India and China. The best-chronicled friendship-based and intimate knowledge of Buddhism among Christians comes from the sixteenth-century Jesuit Francis Xavier.[79]

Similarly to all other faith traditions, Buddhism in the contemporary world faces massive challenges, and many of those have to do with relations to Christianity and the intertwined colonialist burden. The effects of modernization are named by D. L. McMahan as "detraditionalization" and "demythologization." Well known also in post-Enlightenment Christianity, they seek to highlight the importance of reason and critique over traditional beliefs and authorities.[80] Part of this process is the coming of Buddhism into the Global North in new contextualized forms, from Zen Buddhism to Buddhist theosophical societies, among others.

76. Kristin Beise Kiblinger, *Buddhist Inclusivism: Attitudes toward Religious Others* (Burlington, VT: Ashgate, 2005).

77. David Burton, "A Buddhist Perspective," in *OHRD*, 324–26.

78. E.g., Alexander Berzin, "A Buddhist View of Islam," in *Islam and Inter-Faith Relations*, ed. P. Schmidt-Leukel and L. Ridgeon (London: SCM, 2007), 225–51.

79. See Hans Küng, "A Christian Response [to Heinz Bechert: Buddhist Perspectives]," in *Christianity and the World Religions: Paths to Dialogue with Islam, Hinduism, and Buddhism*, by Hans Küng, with Josef van Ess, Heinrich von Stietencron, and Heinz Bechert, trans. Peter Heinegg (New York: Doubleday, 1986), 307–8.

80. David L. McMahan, *The Making of Buddhist Modernism* (New York: Oxford University Press, 2008), chap. 2.

Discerning Differences and Potential Common Concerns

For the sake of continuing dialogue, let us register some foundational differences between Christian and Buddhist "ecclesiologies" and theological orientations:

- Although the *sangha* is an important part of Buddhist pursuit of spiritual liberation, as in Hinduism, spiritual liberation is ultimately a matter of each individual's effort. Hence, Buddhism is not, ecclesiologically speaking, a religion of "communion."
- Although not atheistic in the Western sense, god(s) is marginal to Buddhists. One's salvation depends on one's own effort.
- Although Buddhism does not lack a social ethic or noble examples of working toward peace, reconciliation, and improvement of the society and world, as a religious-ethical system it is not optimistic about some future consummation. Ultimately, with Hinduism, it is a religion of renouncement.

Despite these radical differences of orientation, what is common to both traditions is their missionary nature.[81] That said, Buddhism's missional nature is nothing like the Christian tradition, whose mission is anchored in the sending God. The *sangha's* mission is to spread the knowledge of the liberating insight of the Buddha for the sake of men and women pursuing a similar path and for the well-being and benefit of all.

Concerning the related topic of women's status in religion and the religious community, the Christian church may be in a position to inspire and instruct the Buddhist community. Despite the inclusive vision of Buddha discussed above, almost as a rule throughout the Buddhist world females are either completely banned from the highest religious calling—full monastic life—or relegated to lower monastic levels. Religious authority is kept firmly in men's hands.[82]

81. Lisbet Mikaelsson, "Missional Religion—with Special Emphasis on Buddhism, Christianity and Islam," *Swedish Missiological Themes* 92 (2004): 523–38.

82. Suat Yan Lai, "Engendering Buddhism: Female Ordination and Women's 'Voices' in Thailand" (PhD diss., Claremont Graduate University, 2011).

10 | Eschatological Visions and Symbols among Religions

Eschatology in Christian Tradition and among Religions

Christian Eschatological Vision

In traditional theology, eschatology included the doctrine of "the four last things": death, judgment, hell, and heaven (including limbo and purgatory). In contemporary theology, issues related to the resurrection of the body, the "intermediate state" (that is, the "interval" between the personal death and final eschatological consummation, if any), and the fate and destiny of our planet and the whole cosmos are also in view.

The "end" that eschatology speaks of is a notoriously polyvalent word, as the term "end" can mean both completion (that is, coming or bringing to an end) and fulfillment (as in the Greek term *telos*). Both meanings are present in the Christian eschatological expectation. When put in the wider context of religions, "in its broadest sense the term 'eschatology' includes all concepts of life beyond death and everything connected with it such as heaven and hell, paradise and immortality, resurrection and transmigration of the soul, rebirth and reincarnation, and last judgment and doomsday."[1] Although the equivalent of the term "eschatology," the Latin *de novissimis* (the last things), was used much earlier, only at the time of Protestant orthodoxy was the term itself established.

At the center of Christian eschatology is the hope for the bodily resurrection in the new creation, a hope that keeps in dynamic tension continuity and

1. Hans Schwarz, *Eschatology* (Grand Rapids: Eerdmans, 2000), 26.

discontinuity between this life and life eternal. For any kind of future embodied life in personal communion with God and other human beings to make sense, it needs some kind of correspondence with the conditions of current embodied life. Two other Abrahamic faiths by and large also share some kind of idea of the resurrection of the body, but it hardly stands at the center. What also makes Christian eschatology distinctive among religions is that it encompasses all of creation, not only humans, nor merely Earth—but the whole vast cosmos. That said, it took a long time for Christian theology to consider the many implications of this wide horizon. Understandably, in early Christian theology personal (and "human") eschatology became the focus of the Christian hope.

Similarly to the issues of origins (doctrine of creation), contemporary Christian eschatology has to take into consideration the conjectures of natural sciences concerning the fate of our planet, life, and the cosmos. This also creates a tension because, according to the predictions of the sciences, all life and matter will ultimately come to an end and finally lead to nil, whereas in theological eschatology God is bringing about the "new heaven and new earth." Another key issue for contemporary doctrine of last things is to negotiate the identity of personhood in the context of the hope of resurrection: How is it guaranteed that the person who dies is the same person to be resurrected at the end in the new creation?

Eschatology among Religions?

Although the Christian theologian has to be careful when speaking of "eschatology" as a pan-religious theme, it is true that all world religions express a concern over mortality,[2] and all of them also envision "some form of life after death."[3] Furthermore, religions embrace beliefs not only about origins but also about the "end" (or at least cycles of beginning and ending) of the whole of the cosmos.[4] As diverse as these beliefs and symbols may be, it is clear that some kind of common denominator exists.

That said, insofar as eschatology is "the study of the final end of things, the ultimate resolution of the entire creation," it applies much more easily to "theistic religions that hold to a doctrine of creation and a linear view of his-

---

2. See John Hick, *Death and Eternal Life*, with a new preface by the author (Louisville: Westminster John Knox, 1994 [1976]), 21.

3. Paul Badham and Linda Badham, "Death and Immortality in the Religions of the World: An Editorial Survey," in *DIRW*, 1.

4. R. J. Zwi Werblowsky, "Eschatology: An Overview," in *ER* 4:2833-34.

tory and that believe that creation will come to a final end than to nontheistic traditions, particularly Buddhism."[5] Recall that "Buddhist scriptures regularly refer to 'beginningless *saṁsāra*,' a cycle of birth and death of the universe (as well as of the individual) for which no starting point can be discerned. Nor is there an end, for Buddhists share with members of other Indian religions (notably the Hindus and the Jains) the idea that the universe passes through an unending series of cycles of manifestation and nonmanifestation."[6] This kind of vision could perhaps be named a "relative eschatology."[7] Buddhism is a grand example; yet this principle applies also to Hinduism.[8]

This textbook is supported by the vision expressed by the editors of *Death and Immortality in the Religions of the World*, Paul and Linda Badham— one an atheist and the other a naturalist "atheist": "We remain hopeful that a global perspective on the issues of death and immortality may indeed emerge and present a coherent and intelligible account of a possible future hope, which will draw insights from both the religious and the secular experience of the human race." They go on to note that an important asset in this search is the "unanimous testimony of the world religions that belief in an eternal destiny is necessary to any concept of human life serving any larger purpose than the fulfillment of the immediate aspirations we set ourselves."[9]

The investigation begins with Jewish and Islamic traditions and proceeds to study symbols and visions of the "end" in Hindu and Buddhist theologies. The discussion in this chapter refrains from making comparisons with Christian views in order to allow for authentic Jewish, Muslim, Hindu, and Buddhist eschatologies to be presented. The rest of the discussion of eschatology will engage sympathetically and critically specific beliefs and proposals of these traditions.

Jewish Eschatology

The Gradual Emergence of Eschatological Consciousness

No Old Testament books are devoted to death or afterlife; indeed, the theme is marginal. The Old Testament worldview is very much this-worldly (although

5. Jerry L. Walls, introduction to *OHE*, 4.
6. Jan Nattier, "Buddhist Eschatology," in *OHE*, 151.
7. Werblowsky, "Eschatology," 2834.
8. See Robin Boyd, "The End of Eschatology? Questions on the Future of Interfaith Relations—Part 1," *Expository Times* 123, no. 5 (February 2012): 209–17.
9. Badham and Badham, "Death and Immortality," 6.

it is deeply *theo*logical, God-driven). When eschatological themes appear occasionally, they pertain less to individual and much more to national hope and to Yahweh's intervention in the world. This-worldly blessings from Yahweh stand at the center of the Israelite religion. Yahweh's role as judge is also envisioned in relation to earthly affairs, particularly the establishment of justice and righteousness.[10]

The Old Testament describes the condition of the dead as some sort of shadowy existence (Isa. 38:18). The gradual rise of an eschatological consciousness in the Old Testament is just that, *gradual.* The hope for an afterlife in terms of resurrection evolved slowly toward the end of the Old Testament, although intimations and anticipations appear here and there (Job 19:25-26; Pss. 49:15; 73:24; Isa. 26:19). Daniel 12:2 is widely taken as the summit of that development: "And many of those who sleep in the dust of the earth shall awake, some to everlasting life, and some to shame and everlasting contempt."

Only during the postexilic period did intimations of life beyond slowly emerge.[11] The outlook changes radically in the theology of rabbinic Judaism, the formative Jewish tradition. The Talmud and related writings delve deeply and widely into eschatological and apocalyptic speculations. Eschatology becomes a defining feature, and against that background it can be said "that no significant movement in the course of Jewish history had lacked an eschatology."[12] Whence the rise of an eschatological orientation? The standard scholarly response is that it had to do with the question of suffering and theodicy: Why is the believer in Yahweh suffering?

With the rise of the eschatological impulse (beginning in the second century BCE), the hope for the afterlife also became more defined, as death was no longer looked upon as the end. Although the communal orientation still was dominant, under these categories one can see also hope for the individual.

Broadly stated, Jews came to believe that, at the end of days, the dead will be resurrected and come before God to account for their lives on earth; the righteous will be rewarded and the evildoers punished; Jews, free from the yoke of the exile, will return to their homeland, rebuild it, and become masters of their own destiny; they will rebuild the temple and reinstitute

10. Walter Brueggemann, *Theology of the Old Testament: Testimony, Dispute, Advocacy* (Minneapolis: Augsburg Fortress, 1997), 233-50.

11. George W. E. Nickelsburg, *Resurrection, Immortality, and Eternal Life in Intertestamental Judaism* (Cambridge, MA: Harvard University Press, 1972).

12. Neil Gillman, *The Death of Death: Resurrection and Immortality in Jewish Thought* (Woodstock, VT: Jewish Lights, 1997), 12.

the temple cult; the nations of the world will flock to study Torah with the Jewish people; peace and justice will rule; and all people will come to know and worship the God of Israel. This entire scenario will be brought to pass through the initiative of the Messiah.[13]

Like younger sister faiths, postbiblical Judaism also knows apocalypticism, which is escapist.[14] A defining feature of apocalypticism has to do with a changing understanding of history. Not only Israel's enemies (as in the Old Testament) but all powers, including cosmic and heavenly powers, would be destroyed.

Salvation and Condemnation—Heaven and Hell

Who will inherit salvation in the Jewish vision? Whereas, generally speaking, all those who follow the Torah (and consequently, do good deeds) will be saved, rabbinic theology mentions a number of types of people who might end up in hell, including those who deny resurrection or Torah's heavenly origin, or heretics, or those who abuse the divine name.[15]

What about the gentiles? Notwithstanding long-standing debates among various schools, this much can be said: while the Christian type of "no salvation outside the church" principle was often held as the normal opinion, there is also undoubtedly a strong prophetic tradition in the Old Testament that envisions some kind of "universal scope of salvation." Rather than leading to ultimate destruction and annihilation, Yahweh's judgment will have shalom as the final word (Amos 9:11–15; Isa. 2:2–4). But even then, no unanimity exists about whether "nations" (as opposed to the "people" of Yahweh) are being included in this salvation, which also encompasses nature and the whole world.

Broadly speaking, until modernity, the core rabbinic belief in two destinies stood intact. In contrast, the majority of modern and contemporary Jews have left it behind or at least qualified it significantly. This is possible because the Torah, as is well known, explains quite little about the nature of judgment and blessedness beyond this world. As in Christian theology, particularly difficult for contemporary Jewish theologians is the affirmation of hell.

---

13. Gillman, *The Death of Death*, 22.

14. John J. Collins, "Apocalyptic Eschatology in the Ancient World," in *OHE*, 40–55.

15. David Novak, "Jewish Eschatology," in *OHE*, 117.

The Resurrection of the Body

Although the doctrinal solidification took centuries, the resurrection of the dead is a central belief in classical Judaism. Indeed, condemned are those who deny the centrality of this belief. Briefly stated, resurrection and the authority of Torah "are the two dogmas the rabbis required, minimally, that no Jew deny and, maximally, that every Jew affirm."[16] That said, there were of course dissenting voices within Jewish orthodoxy: while the Pharisees fully endorsed the doctrine, the Sadducees did not.[17]

For rabbinic theology, it was not enough to merely affirm immortality; a *bodily* resurrection was to be affirmed. A robust affirmation of embodiment comports well with Jewish anthropology and its holistic orientation (chap. 4). Somewhat similarly to the New Testament, in their attempts to imagine the nature of the bodily resurrection, the Jewish sources use various metaphors, from awakening from sleep, to nature metaphors of morning dew and plants sprouting, to being clothed, and so forth.

Afterlife, Resurrection, and Immortality
in Contemporary Jewish Theology

By and large, modern/contemporary Jewish theologies have not paid much attention to end times. While there might be many reasons, certainly the experience of Auschwitz stands among them. On the other end of the spectrum are radical millenarian and apocalyptic expressions similar to those of other Abrahamic faiths.[18]

Contemporary Jewish eschatologies, similarly to Christianity, follow the ordinary lines of distinction on the continuum from most traditional/conservative to reconstructionist views, and are ultimately reactions to modernity. Significant in this regard was the Reform movements' reworking of key doctrines beginning in the early nineteenth century. Resurrection as a doctrine came to be replaced by the idea of immortality. Along with resurrection went the classic doctrines of hell and heaven.[19]

16. Novak, "Jewish Eschatology," 123.
17. Gillman, *The Death of Death*, 115–22.
18. Yaakov Ariel, "Radical Millennial Movements in Contemporary Judaism in Israel," in *OHM*, 1–15.
19. Gillman, *The Death of Death*, 196–204.

Understandably, opposition arose among the conservatives. However, even Conservative Judaism of the early twentieth century did not necessarily demand a return to resurrection; rather, it insisted on a sort of spiritual immortality. In other words, by the mid-twentieth century, immortality had been adopted as the mainstream Jewish opinion. With the Reconstructionist movement headed by Mordecai Kaplan, a radically new paradigm was offered. His religious naturalism sought to reformulate radically old eschatological beliefs to stick with modern science. On the other end of the spectrum remained Orthodox Judaism, which firmly continued to uphold the doctrine of the resurrection of the body.[20] At the same time, some other leading contemporary Jewish thinkers have been persuaded of the necessity for belief in the bodily resurrection, as difficult as that may be for the modern mind.[21]

A Christian Comment on Jewish Vision

It is easy to discern that the mainstream Jewish and Christian eschatological visions share a common basis, particularly when it comes to rabbinic Judaism. These include the reality and finality of physical death as the end of life, though not the ultimate "end," as there is the hope for bodily resurrection. The doctrine of two religious ends is traditionally affirmed.

Regarding the nature of eschatological consummation, the Christian vision is typically more "otherworldly," even though, with the Jewish tradition, it also intuits some kind of continuity with the current state of affairs due to belief in bodily resurrection. Modern/contemporary Christian theology displays a similar kind of wide variety of orientations typical of the Jewish tradition.

What about the youngest Abrahamic tradition and its vision of the "end"?

---

20. Gillman, *The Death of Death*, 205–13.

21. Arthur A. Cohen, "Resurrection of the Dead," in *20th Century Religious Thought: Original Essays on Critical Concepts, Movements, and Beliefs*, ed. Arthur A. Cohen and Paul Mendes-Flohr (Philadelphia: Jewish Publication Society, 2009), 807–13.

Islamic Eschatology

The Significance of Eschatology in Islam

Eschatology plays an extraordinary role in Islam. Recall that the Prophet's first and continuing message was about coming judgment and the need for submission to Allah to avoid the hell of judgment. The Qur'an and particularly Hadith texts discuss the afterlife at great length.[22]

Generally speaking, contemporary Muslims tend to take the traditional teaching on eschatology much more seriously than do most Jews and Christians. The "eschatological narrative" lays claim on everything in the Muslim's faith and life. Similarly to Judaism and Christianity, a rich tradition of apocalypticism can be found in Islam, including radical millenarian and jihadist movements.[23]

On Discerning the Signs of the "Hour"

As in Christian tradition, in Islam the (final) hour is unknown to all but God (Q 31:34). As the Prophet stated, "Knowledge thereof lies only with God—and what do you know, perhaps the Hour is near" (33:63). Differently from Hadith and apocalyptic traditions, the Qur'an is reticent to talk about signs. That said, eschatological undergirding lies beneath a number of suras such as "The Hour" (22), "The Smoke" (45), and "The Darkened Sun" (82).

Understandably, Muslims have not stopped looking for signs. Books, blogs, and talks on "signs of the hour" abound.[24] The search for the signs is fueled by the presence in the Hadith of detailed lists of signs. "Geological, moral, social, and cosmic signs . . . [as well as] the erosion of the earth, the spread of immorality, the loss of trust among the people, and the administration of unjust rulers [are perceived] as some signs of the Hour." In distinction from these "minor" signs, the Hadith lists as "major" ones the "emergence of the Antichrist, the descent of Jesus, and the rising of the sun in the west," which all point to the imminence of the end. Quite similarly to the descriptions in the

22. William C. Chittick, "Muslim Eschatology," in *OHE*, 132–50.

23. David Cook, "Early Islamic and Classical Sunni and Shi'ite Apocalyptic Movements," in *OHM*, 267–83; Jeffrey T. Kenney, "Millennialism and Radical Islamist Movements," in *OHM*, 688–716.

24. Mehmood Alam, "Signs of Hour," Darussalem, July 23, 2014, https://blog.darussalam publishers.com/signs-of-hour/.

book of Revelation, trumpets, archangels, and cataclysmic changes on earth, including earthquakes, play a role in the final consummation (81:1–14; 99:1–4; 39:67–69); there will also be intense suffering by the unfaithful. The rise of the mysterious nations of Gog and Magog also plays a role in the eschatological scheme of Islam.[25]

Mahdi, Jesus, and the Antichrist: The Major End-Time Figures

Muslim eschatology widely embraces the figure of the Mahdi, whose task is to defeat the antichrist and bring justice and peace to the world, as well as lead people to truth. An ordinary human being rather than a divine figure, the Mahdi is endowed supernaturally to accomplish his task. Affirmed by all major denominations, the Mahdi's role is particularly important among the Shi'ites. Yet, he is unknown not only in the Qur'an but also in the two main Hadith traditions, that of Bukhari and that of Muslim.

Debate persists about a number of issues related to the Mahdi, not least as to whether there is one Mahdi or more than one, as well as the related question of pseudo- (or anti-) Mahdi. Not surprisingly, various Mahdist movements throughout history have tended to identify a specific person. Whatever else the Mahdi tradition may mean to Islamic eschatology, it is linked closely with the yearning for justice and righteousness in a world of evil.

The relationship between the Mahdi and Jesus is close yet somewhat undefined. While the Qur'an does not directly mention Jesus's "descent" to earth, it is widely attested in the Hadith.[26] According to the standard Islamic interpretation, Jesus of Nazareth was not killed on the cross but was instead "taken up" by Allah to heaven to wait for the return. Then he will fight alongside the Mahdi against the antichrist and defeat him.[27] Jesus will slaughter pigs, tear down crosses, and destroy churches and synagogues; most probably he will also kill Christians unwilling to embrace Islamic faith.

The picture of the antichrist is not radically different from that in Christianity. Obviously an archenemy of Jesus, the antichrist can be seen as the personification of evil (similarly to Satan and Iblis). Although the term itself (al-Dajjal) does not appear in the Qur'an, there is wide agreement in Islamic tradition that it contains allusions and indirect references,

25. Zeri Saritoprak, *Islam's Jesus* (Gainesville: University Press of Florida, 2014), 58–59.
26. Saritoprak, *Islam's Jesus*, chap. 4.
27. Q 4:156–58; 3:55; see chap. 5 above.

including the saying attributed to Jesus: "Nay, but verily man is [wont to be] rebellious" (96:6).[28]

Understandably, the Hadith traditions greatly expand and elaborate on the description and influence of the antichrist: "The antichrist is short, hen-toed, woolly-haired, one-eyed, an eye-sightless, and neither protruding nor deep-seated. If you are confused about him, know that your Lord is not one-eyed."[29] The antichrist will fight against the unbelievers until the Mahdi and Jesus come and help defeat his power.

Death and Resurrection

For the Muslim, life on this earth is but preparation for eternity, at the core of which is obedience to and desire to please Allah. Hence, death should be properly kept in mind (Q 23:15; 3:185). There is given a "fixed" time, a stated life span (6:2).

Although the Qur'an provides precious few details about what happens between death and resurrection, later traditions have produced fairly detailed accounts. As in Christian tradition, the body decays but the "soul" (or "spirit") continues to exist (see Q 39:42). According to major Muslim tradition, the deceased person meets two angels—named Munkar and Nakir—who test the faith of the person and help determine the final destiny. In all Muslim accounts of the afterlife, there is thus an intermediate state that, according to some Muslim theologians, approaches the Roman Catholic idea of purgatory.[30] Muslims also believe in the resurrection of the body as well as (eternal) retribution (sura 75; 36:77–79; among others).

The main theological debate about the resurrection is whether it entails a total annihilation of the person before re-creation or a reconstitution and renewal. The lack of unanimity is understandable in light of two directions in scripture itself. Just compare 28:88 ("Everything will perish except His Countenance"), which clearly assumes the annihilationist view, with 10:4: "To Him is the return of all of you. . . . Truly He originates creation, then recreates it," which teaches the other option.

28. Bernard McGinn, *Antichrist: Two Thousand Years of the Human Fascination with Evil* (New York: Columbia University Press, 2000), 111.

29. Abu Dawud, bk. 37 ("Battles"), #4306.

30. Asma Afsaruddin, "Death, Resurrection, and Human Destiny in Islamic Tradition," in *Death, Resurrection, and Human Destiny: Christian and Muslim Perspectives*, ed. David Marshall and Lucinda Mosher (Washington, DC: Georgetown University Press, 2014), 46.

Heaven and Hell—Salvation and Judgment

Consider that a typical list of the basic beliefs of Islam includes "belief in one God, His messengers, His books, His angels, and the day of judgement."[31] The final accounting happens when in the hereafter men and women "return" to their God (Q 32:7–11). Almost every chapter of the Qur'an speaks of or refers to the theme of judgment.[32] Similarly to the New Testament, even the evil spirits (jinn) will be judged.

The general picture of the day of judgment is very similar to that given in the Bible. Great earthquakes will rock the earth, setting mountains in motion (sura 99). The sky will split open and heaven will be "stripped off," rolled up like a parchment scroll. The sun will cease to shine; the stars will be scattered and fall upon the earth. The oceans will boil over. Graves will be opened, the earth bringing forth its burdens (82). All will bow, willingly or not, before God. After resurrection, each human person is given a "book" that indicates the final destiny (18:49), either heaven or hell.

A debated issue among the Muslim schools is the lot of the (gravely) sinning believer, and no agreement has been reached. A related debate asks how the person's good and bad deeds account for the final judgment received. Common to all opinions is the centrality of obedience to Allah or lack thereof; furthermore, it has been widely agreed that only grave sins bring about judgment (4:31).

What about non-Muslims? It seems like the Qur'an teaches a fairly inclusive view of salvation: "Surely those who believe, and those of Jewry, and the Christians, and the Sabaeans,[33] whoever believes in God and the Last Day, and performs righteous deeds—their wage is with their Lord, and no fear shall befall them, neither shall they grieve" (2:62). The implications of this passage are of course widely debated among historical and contemporary Muslim scholars. Echoing the biblical view for those who have never heard the gospel, the Qur'an teaches that "We do not punish unless We send a messenger" (17:15, Marmude Pickthall translation).

What is not debated is that there are two destinies, as taught in the scripture (9:100–102; 7:37–51; and so forth). Hell is a place of great pain and

---

31. Muhammad Abdel Haleem, "Qur'an and Hadith," in *CCCIT*, 25.

32. Allen Fromherz, "Judgment, Final," in *The Oxford Encyclopedia of the Islamic World*, ed. John L. Esposito (Oxford: Oxford University Press, 2009), http://www.oxfordislamicstudies.com/article/opr/t236/e1107.

33. The Sabaeans (or Sabeans, Sabians; also in 5:69) are an obscure, little-known (Old) Arabic-speaking tribe, also mentioned in the Old Testament (Joel 3:8; Isa. 45:14).

torture. What about heaven? Often depicted in the Qur'an with garden images (sura 37), paradise is a place of great enjoyment, peace, and reunion. The Qur'an offers sensual descriptions, including the pleasures of exquisitely delicious food and drink, as well as sexual relations with divine maidens (often interpreted metaphorically). Particularly splendid and elaborate accounts of paradise ("Garden") can be found in the Hadith. Similarly to the Bible, there are also various levels of rewards for the blessed ones.

A Short Christian Comment on Islamic Eschatology

Similarly to Judaism, Islam's eschatological vision shares similar core beliefs. Indeed, there is more similarity between Christian and Muslim visions than there is between the Muslim and Jewish visions, particularly with the important role played by Jesus Christ in the end-time events.

That said, Jesus's role in Islamic eschatology is vastly different from his role in the Christian tradition. This issue is closely linked with the most distinctive Islamic conception, namely, the mysterious figure of the Mahdi. Subordinate and subservient to Mahdi, Jesus plays a role in Islam more like that of a deputy, as opposed to Christian eschatology's assigning to him the main role in ushering in God's kingdom.

Although the belief in resurrection is affirmed in Islam, it seems like its end-time vision is more otherworldly than that of the other two Abrahamic visions. That said, typical garden and city metaphors are also found, coupled with earthly types of pleasures, at least to the chosen ones, the martyrs.

All in all, eschatology plays a significantly more prominent role in Islam than in the two elder sister faiths. No wonder its contemporary apocalypticism and millenarianism are also fervent and at times even violent.

After having engaged the Semitic faiths' end-time visions, it is time to turn to the two Asiatic traditions.

"End-Time" Visions and Symbols in Hindu Traditions

In Search of a Distinctive Hindu Vision of the "End"

Unlike Abrahamic traditions with a linear and historical view of history, "Hinduism has no last day or end time, nor any completion of history, resurrection of the dead, and universal last judgment."[34] The focus lies rather on "the deliverance of the individual from the unreal realm of the empirical and temporal to the timeless realm of the spirit"[35] as opposed to the perspective in the Abrahamic faiths. Even the role of the deities is ambiguous, as a number of them undergo death and even rebirth in another form.[36]

"Cosmic eschatology" is usually described in terms of *kalpas*. Each *kalpa* encompasses the life span of the cosmos from origination to dissolution.[37] At the end of a *kalpa*, a great dissolution occurs, "which coincides with the end of the life of Brahma. The world will be reabsorbed into Brahma by involution and remain in that state until the hatching of a new cosmic age."[38] And so on *ad infinitum*.

Are there any millennial elements in various Hindu traditions? Only with the rise of anticolonialist movements in the nineteenth century did millennial groups emerge. At the same time, various types of self-made gurus appeared, and in their activities millennial features were present.[39]

Death, Rebirth, and Karmic Samsara

The last two books (ninth and tenth) of the oldest Vedic scripture, Rig Veda, speak extensively of death. The Funeral Hymn (10.14), dedicated to Yama, the god of death—the first one to die and show the remainder of mortals the way to go—speaks of death in terms of meeting Yama and the "Fathers" (the honored ancestors). Yama is assisted by two messenger dogs, the guardians of death's pathway. Yama and the "Fathers" prepare a wonderful place for the deceased (10.14.8–11). The last part of the Vedas, the Upanishads, further develops the view of death and afterlife.

The most innovative and theologically significant Upanishadic development has to do with the evolvement of the doctrines of karma and transmigration of the soul (rebirth). The soul continues its afterlife journey from

---

34. David M. Knipe, "Hindu Eschatology," in *OHE*, 171.

35. Mariasusai Dhavamony, "Death and Immortality in Hinduism," in *DIRW*, 100–101 (100).

36. Wendy Doniger, *On Hinduism*, online ed. (Oxford: Oxford University Press, 2014), 97–103.

37. Arvind Sharma, *Classical Hindu Thought: An Introduction* (Oxford: Oxford University Press, 2000), chap. 13.

38. Dhavamony, "Death and Immortality," 100–101 (101).

39. Hugh B. Urban, "Millenarian Elements in the Hindu Religious Traditions," in *OHM*, 369–81.

one state to another conditioned by the deeds of one's lifetime. Until one is ready to be absorbed into "Reality" (*satya*), the migration continues. Belief in these continuous rebirths, known as karmic samsara, is held by all Hindu movements, both theistic and otherwise. It is essential to note that samsara is a "universal" law concerning "the conditioned and ever changing universe as contrasted to an unconditioned, eternal, and transcendent state (*moksa* or *nirvāna*)." The liberated one is no longer under karma.[40]

Karma evolves from moral and immoral actions from past lives to their consequences and one's actions in subsequent lives. While personal, both good and bad karma may also be transferred to another person. At death, "the various component parts of . . . [the deceased person's] body unite with [his] corresponding counterparts in nature, while the sum total of his karma remains attached to his self (*atman*). The force of this karma decides the nature of his next birth where he reaps the fruit of what he merits."[41]

That teaching helps put death in a different perspective: as aversive as it may appear to human desire to cling to life, it is not the ultimate reality and has only relative significance. Death is an "earthly" matter and hence belongs to the "appearance" part of reality. "The knowing (Self) is not born, it dies not; it sprang from nothing, nothing sprang from it. The Ancient is unborn, eternal, everlasting; he is not killed, though the body is killed."[42] That said, however, reverence for the dead and the obligation of the relatives of the deceased form an integral part of Hindu cultures, and sophisticated funeral rites have evolved to help start the journey in the afterlife.

Bhagavad Gita affirms the basic Upanishadic teachings: the inevitability of death, its transitory nature because of transmigration, and two destinies (at least as long as one has not yet achieved the ultimate goal). The Gita pays special attention to one's last thoughts, that is, whether one is totally devoted to one's deity or to some earthly goal.[43]

Avidya *and* Moksa: *"Ignorance" and "Salvation"*

Similarly to the doctrine of resurrection, rebirth raises the question of the constitution of human nature and the corollary question of what continues

---

40. Brian K. Smith, "Samsāra," in *ER* 12:8098.

41. Dhavamony, "Death and Immortality," 94.

42. Katha Upanishad 1.2.18; so also Bhagavad Gita, see 2.12.

43. Bhagavad Gita 8.

beyond physical death. Although the Vedanta Hindu philosophical schools do not typically lean toward the Hellenistic type of body-soul dualism (or if they do, they frame it differently), there is instead a dualism of "true" (real) and "not-self." As long as one does not grasp the single most important insight that "Self [atman] is indeed Brahman [the eternal Self],"[44] one is distanced from the real self.[45] Only with the removal of "ignorance" (avidya) can the effects of karma be overcome and final release (moksa) be achieved (see chap. 4).

Heaven and hell are only vaguely intuited in the Vedic literature. A fairly clearly defined picture of them does not appear until the great epics, particularly the Mahabharata.[46] Because of rebirth, their meaning is obviously different from those of Abrahamic traditions. Neither heaven nor hell is the ultimate destiny.

Because of the vast differences between Abrahamic and Asiatic end-time visions, it is necessary and worthwhile to devote a much more extensive dialogical engagement to the differences between Hindu and Christian eschatologies, as well as to discussion in relation to the Buddhist view.

A Christian Engagement of the Hindu Vision

Much older than the belief in bodily resurrection is the belief in immortality and reincarnation (rebirth) among ancient and living faith traditions. With all their differences, the Greek and Hindu versions of immortality share some common beliefs that differ significantly from those of the Abrahamic faiths. First, rather than the soul possessing inherent powers out of itself, in the Abrahamic view life eternal is a gift from God. Second, rather than the soul being the person itself, let alone the "true" person, the resurrection doctrine considers the whole human being as the human person. Third, rather than the soul having its endless journey and history through incarnations, the person, after a once-for-all earthly life, looks forward to eternal life in communion with the Creator.[47] Finally, for Abrahamic faiths, each human life and human personality (individuality) is unique and nonrepeatable.

With the Abrahamic faiths' doctrine of bodily resurrection, Asiatic

44. Brihadaranyaka Upanishad 4.4.5.
45. R. Balasubramanian, "The Advaita View of Death and Immortality," in *DIRW*, 110–17.
46. Alf Hiltebeitel, "The 'Mahābhārata,' and Hindu Eschatology," *History of Religions* 12, no. 2 (1972): 95–135.
47. Pannenberg, *ST* 3:571–73.

faiths' teaching on reincarnation/transmigration shares the problem of identity constitution, though in the latter that is of course differently framed, that is, How is the identity of the soul preserved in the mutability of the forms that the soul assumes? The problem of identity continuation from one human life to another is a huge challenge. But it becomes hugely more challenging when we think of a sequence of lives from human to animal and back to human. Is the "soul" still the carrier of the identity?[48]

A common and persistent misunderstanding among Christian observers of Hinduism is that rebirth signifies a "second chance." That is a fatal mistake. Belief in rebirth has nothing to do with yet another potential opportunity to fix one's life. Rebirth is rather the result of the karmic law of cause and effect. Even gods cannot break the power of karma. As a result, Hinduism (and Buddhism) at large seeks a way to defeat the possibility of having to be born again. Rather than a positive offer, rebirth is more like a curse.

The Christian notion of grace differs significantly from the ironclad power of karma. In it God acts "contingently and historically," continuously interrupting "the chain of act and destiny," which means the repelling of karma. That is of course what forgiveness does: while not doing away with punishment—because it does not deny the "sowing and reaping" principle taught in the Bible (Gal. 6:7; Jer. 31:29)—it opens up the possibility of being saved without being destroyed or consumed by the consequences. That is truly a second chance in life.

A standard question to Hindu (as well as Buddhist) eschatology has to do with the assignment of this-worldly fortunes or ills to previous lives. Morally, it seems highly questionable to refer the sufferings of the poor, sick, handicapped, and other unfortunate people to their past deeds. Nor does it seem morally fair to count the fortunes of the rich, famous, and healthy as their own accomplishments. Rather, in our kind of world evil and good seem to be mixed together.[49]

Provided (for the sake of the argument) that the karmic cause-and-effect logic were to work, a problem arises with regard to memory. How many persons recall their former lives in order to see the logic and learn from those lives? Hindu philosophy has so far failed to offer a reasonable explanation. It is merely assumed that things are allegedly recalled from past lives, and they are believed to guide in some way or another one's life choices. But even if those

---

48. Jürgen Moltmann, *The Coming of God: Christian Eschatology*, trans. Margaret Kohl (Minneapolis: Fortress, 1996), 112–13.

49. Keith Ward, *Religion and Human Nature* (Oxford: Clarendon, 1998), 60–62.

memories do not appear, the person is claimed to have lived his or her life in the "shadow" of past lives' experiences and memories.

An even more difficult question has to do with the capacities of the "soul" of nonhuman entities in the samsaric cycle. Rebirth (or transmigration) of course assumes some kind of "animating principle, however defined, from one more or less physical, terrestrial body to another."[50] Now, believing that karma may lead the human being not only upward but also downward in the evolutionary tree results in a highly problematic assumption: all souls must know and understand, make choices; in other words, they must have self-consciousness and high-level intellectual skills. While that is not a problem with most humans— unless they die as infants or are mentally impaired—with subhuman entities it is a problem, beginning from even the highest animals. For example: How could the "soul" of the insect or dog have these capacities in its way "upward" in the cycle of rebirths? Again, no satisfactory reasonable account is available.

To the outsider, belief in reincarnation seems highly individualistic. Obviously, it neglects the effects on each person's behavior and attitudes of environmental, social, cultural, sociopolitical, and economic factors, to name a few. However, we know that much of what we are is the result of effects from the milieu in which we evolve and live. Of course, the counterargument could be that we are put in this place of suffering because of our previous deeds, but even then, the effects of the community and human relatedness are not properly addressed. A corollary problem is that if another person—or even a divine being—seeks to alleviate my suffering, then it must lead to the postponement of my final release. Is that charitable act then really charitable, or rather an unintentional way of adding to my suffering?[51]

Hindu and Buddhist visions of afterlife also seem to defeat any permanent meaning of embodiment, and this is a major difference from Abrahamic faith traditions' focus on the resurrection of the body. In Asiatic faiths, final release is understood in terms of liberation *from* all bodily life, not a renewal. Early Christian theology rightly rejected Gnosticism, which could not embrace an eschatological vision related to bodily and earthly realities because it "shared the conviction that the present, embodied condition of human consciousness is not a natural or ideal state, but is itself the sign of a fallen world."[52]

The last eschatology to be engaged here is Buddhist.

---

50. Robert P. Goldman, "Karma, Guilt, and Buried Memories: Public Fantasy and Private Reality in Traditional India," *Journal of the American Oriental Society* 105, no. 3 (1985): 414.

51. Ward, *Religion and Human Nature*, 66–67.

52. Brian E. Daley, "Eschatology in the Early Church Fathers," in *OHE*, 94.

Buddhist Visions of End and "Release"

In Search of an Eschatological Vision in Buddhist Traditions

Although Buddhism, like Hinduism, does not know any final closure—and therefore we should speak of "relative" eschatology[53]—already during the time of Gautama himself a diversity of views of the "end" of human life had emerged. That said, as mentioned repeatedly, Buddha showed great reticence toward speculations into the metaphysical questions of the end (and origin) because he considered them "unbeneficial" in the pursuit of final release.

When entering into speculations concerning the "end," somewhat similarly to Hindu tradition, Buddhism speaks of the "history" of the cosmos in terms of exceedingly long ages—called "great eons" (*mahakalpa*)—and divides them into four periods, beginning with the destruction of the cosmos and extending to various times of renovation when the universe again reemerges. Within each period a number of subperiods can be discerned in which the quality of human life and the level of morality vary.[54]

As discussed, rather than a doctrine of creation, Buddha taught the principle of "dependent origination," also called "causal interdependence." Not surprisingly, then, "everything formed is in a constant process of change"[55] except for *nibbana* (which is not "conditioned").[56] The conditioned nature of all reality is of course due to the foundational analysis of the *dukkha* nature of all reality. This conditioned *dukkha* existence persists as long as one is in the circle of life and death, samsara, an endless series of rebirths.

Keeping in mind these foundational assumptions about the nature of the cosmos and life, we can begin to investigate the distinctive nature of the Buddhist analysis of how to achieve release from the "mass of suffering" and endless cycle of samsara. As is well known, Buddhism joins Indian traditions in affirming the doctrine of rebirth. That said, because of its distinctive analysis of human nature, known as *anatta*, "no-self," that doctrine is affirmed in a radically different manner from Hinduism. To that investigation we devote the bulk of this section on Buddhist eschatology.

53. Werblowsky, "Eschatology," 2834.

54. Nattier, "Buddhist Eschatology," 152–53.

55. Lily de Silva, "The Buddhist Attitude towards Nature," *Access to Insight*, June 5, 2010, n.p., http://www.accesstoinsight.org/lib/authors/desilva/attitude.html. The Pali term *anicca* is routinely used to describe this principle.

56. For details, see Nattier, "Buddhist Eschatology," 154–55.

"No-Self," Kamma, and Rebirth

As discussed, Buddhism's most distinctive doctrine is the denial of a constitutive permanent self, persisting personhood, "no-self," as it is often rendered. This is but a result of the codependent origination and impermanence as well as the *dukkha* nature of all conditioned phenomena. Calling the person a "self" is just an elusive, conventional way of referring to that fleeting combination of elements.[57] There is no "doer" of the deed, as the familiar Buddhist saying goes.

To be liberated from the illusion of being permanent and hence clinging to anything conditioned, one needs the "salvific" insight into the true nature of reality and being (release from samsara, the cycle of rebirths). Otherwise, the ongoing process of rebirth continues due to *kamma*; those who "engage in bad actions . . . generate unwholesome kamma that leads them to rebirth into lower states of existence," including pain and suffering.[58]

Lest one conceive of the karmic samsara cycle of rebirths along the lines of Hinduism—and common sense—that is, that the deceased self will be reborn, the doctrine of *anatta* should be remembered: "Rebirth, in the Buddhist conception, is not the transmigration of a self or soul but the continuation of a process, a flux of becoming in which successive lives are linked together by causal transmission of influence rather than by substantial identity."[59]

What, then, is the Buddhist final release, *nibbana*? What is its nature? Who will achieve it? Because the Buddha, as mentioned, was not interested in metaphysical speculations but rather in "putting an end to suffering and stress,"[60] he did not encourage speculation; rather, he set out to teach the path to liberation; doing so, he began to sketch some idea of its nature.

57. An authoritative study is Steven Collins, *Selfless Persons: Imagery and Thought in Theravada Buddhism* (Cambridge: Cambridge University Press, 1982).

58. Bhikkhu Ñānamoli and Bhikku Bodhi, introduction to *The Middle Length Discourses of the Buddha*, trans. Bhikkhu Ñānamoli and Bhikku Bodhi (Kandy, Sri Lanka: Buddhist Publication Society, 1995), 45; available at http://lirs.ru/lib/sutra/The_Middle_Length_Discourses (Majjhima_Nikaya),Nanamoli,Bodhi,1995.pdf.

59. Ñānamoli and Bodhi, introduction to *Middle Length Discourses*, 45.

60. Alagaddupama Sutta: The WaterSnake Simile of Majjhima Nikaya 22.38 (*Middle Length Discourses*, 234).

Nirvana and the Cessation of "Desire"

The goal of the Buddhist pursuit is to achieve the enlightening insight into the nature of *dukkha* in order to overcome the desire to cling to it. Behind the (misplaced) craving is ignorance. No wonder the very first step in the Eightfold Path of skillful means is rightful knowledge. Recall that even Buddha is not the savior; each person is one's own "savior." The road to enlightenment is long and tedious.

What, if anything, can then be said of the nature of *nibbana*? Recall that this is the only nonconditioned aspect of reality and therefore free from change and decay. In *nibbana*, there is "neither dimension of the infinitude of space, nor dimension of the infinitude of consciousness, nor dimension of nothingness, nor dimension of neither perception nor non-perception; neither this world, nor the next world. . . . This, just this, is the end of stress."[61]

The main logical challenge to such a vision is well known among both Buddhists and its critics: If everything is nonpermanent, how can nirvana then be the "final" goal? I am not aware of satisfactory solutions.[62] How helpful is this Buddhist explanation: "Thou dost not vanish in Nirvana, nor is Nirvana abiding in thee; for it transcends the duality of knowing and known and of being and non-being"?[63]

The end result of reaching *nibbana* in the Theravada tradition is the *arahant*, derived from the "worthy" (also rendered as "accomplished"). That enlightened one is the person, "with taints destroyed, who has lived the holy life, done what had to be done, laid down the burden, reached the true goal, destroyed the fetters of being, and is completely liberated through final knowledge."[64] At the time of the emergence of the Mahayana tradition, this original concept of *arahant* was revised into Boddhisattva, the Enlightened One who for the sake of others postpones the stepping into *nibbana*.

---

61. "Nibbana Sutta: Total Unbinding (1)" (Udana 8.1). For an important contemporary discussion, see Gunapala Dharmasiri, *A Buddhist Critique of the Christian Concept of God: A Critique of the Concept of God in Contemporary Christian Theology and Philosophy of Religion from the Point of View of Early Buddhism* (Colombo, Sri Lanka: Lake House Investments, 1974), 177–214.

62. See also Keith Ward, *Images of Eternity: Concepts of God in Five Religious Traditions* (London: Darton, Longman & Todd, 1987), 61–62.

63. The Lankavatara Sutra: A Mahayana Text 2.1.7; http://lirs.ru/do/lanka_eng/lanka-nondiacritical.htm.

64. Majjhima Nikaya 35.25 (p. 327); for details, see Ñānamoli and Bodhi, introduction to *Middle Length Discourses*, 43–45.

A Christian Engagement of the Buddhist Vision

As mentioned, by far the biggest problem for Abrahamic traditions is Buddhist denial of individuality ("self"). It seems to the Christian (and other Abrahamic faith adherents) that this doctrine fails to properly affirm individuality and the individual's relation to others. A related issue wonders how to affirm the dignity of human personhood if there is nothing "permanent."

With regard to our topic, the main question is simply this: "Who" (or "what") is the one who clings to life due to desire, suffers from the effects of karma, and particularly comes to the enlightening realization? And how should we conceive of the principle of *kamma* in the absence of the "self" whose destiny it should determine?

In the absence of a permanent self, it is difficult to imagine a deeply grounded desire to work for the betterment of this world—particularly following the doctrinal system in which it seems to be better not to try to intervene with other sentient creatures' destiny. This is not to deny the presence of social service initiatives among Buddhists; it is merely to look for a scriptural-theological grounding (or lack thereof) in this tradition.

Similarly to the Hindu vision, it seems from a Christian perspective that the Buddhist end-time goal is highly individualistic and has little or nothing to contribute to the communal destiny. This is particularly pertinent to Theravada, in which each and every enlightened one "steps in the river" as soon as the liberating insight has occurred. Even Mahayana's allowance for postponing one's own liberation in the hopes of assisting others relates ultimately only to each individual's "salvation."

Furthermore, it seems that the Buddhist vision—no more than the Hindu one—does not intuit any kind of consummation that would encompass the whole of the cosmos, or even our own planet. If there is such a vision, I have not found scriptural or traditional teaching on it.

Finally, with regard to both Hindu and Buddhist "relative" eschatologies, a radical difference in relation to the Abrahamic family of faiths has to do with the refusal to allow for a final "end." Reemergence and dissipation *ad infinitum* of the cosmos point in a radically different direction from the final consummation.

Epilogue:
In Search of a "Proper Confidence"

This short primer on comparative theology has provided a number of detailed case studies on key theological-philosophical-religious topics among living faith traditions. This book approaches the comparative task unabashedly and unapologetically from the perspective and resources of Christian theology. Christian theology, indeed, has been on the forefront of developing this comparative approach. It would be a great gain not only to other faith traditions but also to Christian tradition to see the blossoming of comparative theological efforts among Jewish, Islamic, Hindu, Buddhist, and other faiths.

As discussed in the introduction, comparative theology is not a "neutral," noncommittal exercise. It is confessional in that a believer in a particular faith tradition also seeks to advance a reasonable and compelling argument on behalf of that tradition in a critical and sympathetic dialogue with others. Even though this kind of confessional comparative work is neither dogmatic nor closed-minded—indeed, it functions best in a hospitable spirit—it also raises the question of truth. Otherwise, any serious comparative work would appear to be quite meaningless.

In this respect, I find highly useful the musings of the famed Austrian philosopher of the early twentieth century, Ludwig Wittgenstein. In his last year, Wittgenstein penned the work *On Certainty*, in which he reflects on the possibility of finding some confidence in one's beliefs and claims.[1] He won-

---

1. I was inspired to investigate this piece of Wittgenstein by Keith Ward (*Religion and Revelation: A Theology of Revelation in the World's Religions* [Oxford: Clarendon, 1994], 8–10), although my own reading goes in somewhat different directions from his.

ders if there are any certain "foundations" on which to build one's certainty. Complex and nuanced argumentation aside, I wish to lift from his profound insights only this one: that "at the foundation of well-founded belief lies belief that is not founded."[2]

In other words, the mature Wittgenstein is reminding us that in the final analysis, our basic, most "foundational" beliefs cannot be fully justified by neutral, noncommittal reasoning. Rather, these basic beliefs are partially given; we are drawn to them; they are based on something given; and they form some kind of "system" that supports us as much, or more, than we can support them. Furthermore, these beliefs, far from being merely answers to intellectual curiosity, have everything to do with our way of life, our practice.[3]

Indeed, when it comes to religion and faith, the basic beliefs support not only our search for the good life in this age but also in the life to come, and they are answers to questions of life and death. Belief in God/deities emerges out of and is based on these deepest beliefs and convictions—as well as questions and doubts.[4] The best that the theologian has to be willing to live by is a "proper confidence" (to borrow Lesslie Newbigin's book title). There is always the possibility of misplacing one's trust. Recall the nagging acknowledgment by Thomas Hobbes in his 1661 *Leviathan* that "to say God hath spoken to him [a man] in a dream, is not more than to say he dreamed that God spoke to him."[5]

So, what kind of certainty can be expected of religious claims? As mentioned above, in light of the diversity of religions of our age and the advent of modernity's principle of doubt, "it is useless to say that God makes his revelation self-authenticating."[6] If it was self-authenticating, then not only all who trust scientific reasoning but also believers in different faith traditions would be persuaded, perhaps even honest agnostics! On the other hand, this acknowledgment does not mean that there is no place for certainty and confidence in religion, but its specific nature and quality have to be assessed anew

---

2. Ludwig Wittgenstein, *On Certainty*, ed. G. E. M. Anscombe and G. H. von Wright, trans. Denis Paul and G. E. M. Anscombe (New York: Harper & Row, 1969), ##253–54; available as a pdf copy at https://prawfsblawg.blogs.com/files/wittgenstein-on-certainty.pdf.

3. It seems to me that Ward (*Religion and Revelation*, 9) is materially agreeing with this general conclusion.

4. For an important discussion of belief in God in this kind of framework, see Keith Ward, *The Concept of God* (Oxford: Basil Blackwell, 1974).

5. Thomas Hobbes, *The Leviathan (Or the Matter, Forme & Power of a Commonwealth, Ecclesiastical and Civil)*, ed. A. R. Waller, Cambridge English Classics (Cambridge: Cambridge University Press, 1904 [1651]), part 3, chap. 32; 271.

6. Ward, *Religion and Revelation*, 7.

in the intellectual and religious milieu of each age. According to Keith Ward, "such certainty cannot be a matter of simple self-evidence (available when the denial of a proposition is self-contradictory); or of immediate intuition (possible only for immediately experienced noninferential truths); or of universally agreed and testable observation."[7] If it is of any consolation to comparative theologians, the Cartesian "indubitable certainty" hardly is available in any other humanistic disciplines and intellectual pursuits, including history, philosophy, and arts. This does not have to mean there is therefore no difference between an ideological presentation of a nation's history and a careful, scholarly pursuit. There is certainly a difference, but it is a matter of degree of objectivity. Furthermore, with regard to philosophy, some opinions command more respect and hold greater validity and interest than others.[8]

While theology is intellectually rigorous in its pursuit, the certainty in theology—as in other disciplines in the humanities—readily acknowledges its relatedness to a wide and comprehensive network of basic beliefs that sustains our thinking. It is situated and fallible in nature and aims at "proper confidence." It is always tentative and suggestive. It is deeply value-driven and has to do with the deepest and most ultimate questions of death and life. On the other hand, as an academic discipline, comparative theology's claims also have to be subjected to proper critical scrutiny and debate. To theology, as well as philosophy and similar fields, disagreements and different viewpoints belong as an essential part of the inquiry. That is simply because religious "views are extremely wide-ranging beliefs about the nature of things in general; they aim at unrestricted generality and comprehensiveness."[9] These kinds of statements are not easy to formulate and verbalize, and they can be understood in so many ways.

While faith and reason should not be juxtaposed, ultimately theological convictions and beliefs are just that: *convictions* and beliefs. They are person-related. The American philosopher William James's classic essay "The Will to Believe" sets forth some characteristics of a commitment to believe when one is faced with a lack of conclusive evidence. The three basic conditions James outlines are, first, that the decision to believe does not leave any choices ("belief is forced") because of its urgency; second, that it makes a vital difference in life; and third, that it presents itself as a plausible or realistic option.[10] It is

---

7. Ward, *Religion and Revelation*, 7.

8. See further, Ward, *Religion and Revelation*, 8.

9. Ward, *Religion and Revelation*, 12.

10. William James, "The Will to Believe," in *"The Will to Believe" and Other Essays in*

easy to see the application of James's reasoning to the discussion of certainty with regard to religion and theology. Although there is no conclusive evidence available—and in this sense, to quote Kierkegaard, the believer lives in "objective uncertainty"—the religions' claim comes to one's life as a total call for surrender. Even when intellectual and rational homework is done, that alone will persuade no one to surrender to any particular faith tradition. In his discussion, James refers to French philosopher Blaise Pascal's famous wager metaphor, which introduces the concept of risk as well—but risk worth taking. Advises the French philosopher: "Let us weigh the gain and the loss in wagering that God is. Let us estimate these two chances. If you gain, you gain all; if you lose, you lose nothing. Wager, then, without hesitation that He is."[11] This is the recommendation of this short primer as well!

The title of Christian theologian Jürgen Moltmann's wittily titled popular exposition of eschatology, *In the End—the Beginning*,[12] aptly expresses my sentiments with regard to the emerging and quickly progressing enterprise of Christian comparative theology. The completion of this little help for students and practitioners is but another step in the beginning of a long journey.

Popular Philosophy [1897] *and Human Immortality* [1898] (Mineola, NY: Dover Publications, 1956), 1–31 (see esp. 1–4 for a brief presentation and discussion of these conditions). I am indebted to Ward (*Religion and Revelation*, 26–27) for turning my attention to this essay for the consideration of this topic.

11. Blaise Pascal, "Of the Necessity of the Wager," in *Pensées*, trans. W. F. Trotter (1944 [1690]), section 3, citation in #233, ccel.org.

12. With the subtitle *The Life of Hope*.

Bibliography

Abdalla, Mohamad. "Ibn Khaldūn on the Fate of Islamic Science after the 11th Century." In *ISHCP* 3:29–38.

Abd-Allah, Umar F. "Do Christians and Muslims Worship the Same God?" *Christian Century* 121, no. 17 (August 24, 2004).

'Abduh, Muhammad. *The Theology of Unity*. Translated by Ishaq Musa'ad and Kenneth Cragg. London: Allen & Unwin, 1966.

Abdulaziz, Daftari. "Mulla Sadra and the Mind-Body Problem: A Critical Assessment of Sadra's Approach to the Dichotomy of Soul and Spirit." PhD diss., Durham University, 2010. http://etheses.dur.ac.uk/506/.

Abe, Masao. *Buddhism and Interfaith Dialogue*. Edited by Steven Heine. Honolulu: University of Hawaii Press, 1995.

———. "Kenotic God and Dynamic Sunyata." In *DEHF*, 25–90.

Abelson, Joshua. *The Immanence of God in Rabbinical Literature*. London: Macmillan, 1912.

Abhedananda, Swami. *Vedanta Philosophy*. Kolkata: Ramakrishna Vedanta Math, 1959.

Abrahams, Israel, Jacob Haberman, and Charles Manekin. "Belief." In *EJ* 3:290–94.

Adiswarananda, Swami. "Hinduism." Part 2. Ramakrishna-Vivekananda Center of New York, 1996. http://www.ramakrishna.org/activities/message/message15.htm.

Afsaruddin, Asma. "Death, Resurrection, and Human Destiny in Islamic Tradition." In *Death, Resurrection, and Human Destiny: Christian and Muslim Perspectives*, edited by David Marshall and Lucinda Mosher, 43–60. Washington, DC: Georgetown University Press, 2014.

Ahluwalia, Kewal. "Shudhi Movement: 85th Shardhanand Shudhi Divas—December 23rd." Accessed March 19, 2019. http://www.aryasamaj.com/enews/2012/jan/4.htm.

Alam, Mehmood. "Signs of Hour." Darussalam. July 23, 2014. https://blog.darussalam publishers.com/signs-of-hour/.

Amaladass, Anand. "Viewpoints: Dialogue in India." *Journal of Hindu-Christian Dialogue* 1, no. 7 (June 1988): 7–8.

Anees, Munawar A. "Salvation and Suicide: What Does Islamic Theology Say?" *Dialog* 45, no. 3 (Fall 2006): 275–76.

Anguttara Nikaya. In *The Book of the Gradual Sayings (Anguttara Nikaya) or More-Numbered-Suttas*. Edited and translated by F. L. Woodward. Oxford: Pali Text Society, 1992.

Ariel, Yaakov. "Radical Millennial Movements in Contemporary Judaism in Israel." In *OHM*, 1–15.

Asoka. *The Edicts of Asoka*. Edited and translated by N. A. Nikam and Richard McKeon. Chicago: University of Chicago Press, 1959.

Asvaghosa. *Açvaghosha's Discourse on the Awakening of Faith in the Mahâyâna*. Translated by Teitaro Suzuki (1900). http://sacred-texts.com/bud/taf/index.htm.

Attwood, Jayarava Michael. "Did King Ajātasattu Confess to the Buddha, and Did the Buddha Forgive Him?" *Journal of Buddhist Ethics*, n.d., 279–307. http://blogs.dickinson.edu/buddhistethics/files/2010/05/attwood-article.pdf.

Aune, David E. "Repentance." In *ER* 11:7755–60.

Avicenna's Psychology [*De Anima*; *The Treatise on the Soul*]. Translated and edited by Fazlur Rahman. Oxford: Oxford University Press, 1952.

Ayoub, [Mahmud] Mahmoud [Mustafa]. "Creation or Evolution? The Reception of Darwinism in Modern Arab Thought." Chapter 11 in *SRPW*.

———. "Jesus the Son of God: A Study of the Terms *Ibn* and *Walad* in the Qur'ān and *Tafsīr* Tradition." In *Christian-Muslim Encounters*, edited by Y. Y. Haddad and W. Z. Haddad. Gainesville: University of Florida Press, 1995.

———. *The Qur'an and Its Interpreters*. Vol. 1. Albany: State University of New York Press, 1984.

———. "Repentance in the Islamic Tradition." In *RCP*, 96–121.

———. "Trinity Day Lectures." *Trinity Seminary Review* 32 (Winter–Spring 2011): 7–18.

———. "The Word of God in Islam." In *Orthodox Christians and Muslims*, edited by Nomikos Michael Vaporis, 69–78. Brookline, MA: Holy Cross Orthodox Press, 1986.

Badham, Paul, and Linda Badham. "Death and Immortality in the Religions of the World: An Editorial Survey." In *DIRW*, 1–8.

Balasubramanian, R. "The Advaita View of Death and Immortality." In *DIRW*, 109–27.

Balić, Smail. "The Image of Jesus in Contemporary Islamic Theology." In *We Believe in One God*, edited by A. M. Schimmel and Abdoldjavad Falaturi. London: Burns & Oates, 1979.

Bar, Shmuel. "Sunnis and Shiites: Between Rapprochement and Conflict." In *Current Trends in Islamist Ideology*, edited by Hillel Fradkin et al., 2:87–96. Washington, DC: Center on Islam, Democracy, and the Future of the Muslim World, Hudson Institute, 2005.

Barker, Gregory A. "Buddhist Perceptions of Jesus: Key Issues." In *JBC*, 217–22.

Barker, Gregory A., and Stephen E. Gregg. "Muslim Perceptions of Jesus: Key Issues." In *JBC*, 83–86.

Barnes, Michel René. "The Beginning and End of Early Christian Pneumatology." *Augustinian Studies* 39, no. 2 (2008): 169–86.

Baron, Salo W. *A Social and Religious History of the Jews.* Vol. 1. New York: Columbia University Press, 1951.

Barua, Ankur. "The Dialectic of Divine 'Grace' and 'Justice' in St. Augustine and Sri-Vaisnavism." *Religions of South Asia* 4, no. 1 (2010): 45–65.

Bassis, Kinrei. "Forgiveness." Berkeley Buddhist Priory, accessed February 25, 2019. https://berkeleybuddhistpriory.org/?page_id=832.

Batchelor, Martine. "Meditation and Mindfulness." *Contemporary Buddhism* 12, no. 1 (May 2011): 157–64.

Batchelor, Martine, and Kerry Brown, eds. *Buddhism and Ecology.* London: Cassell, 1992.

Bayly, Susan. *Saints, Goddesses, and Kings: Muslims and Christians in South Indian Society, 1700–1900.* Cambridge: Cambridge University Press, 1990.

Beck, Guy L. "Fire in the Ātman: Repentance in Hinduism." In *RCP*, 76–95.

Becker, Adam H., and Annette Yoshiko Reed, eds. *The Ways That Never Parted: Jews and Christians in Late Antiquity and the Early Middle Ages.* Tübingen: Mohr Siebeck, 2003.

Ben-Chorin, Schalom. *Die Antwort des Jona, zum Gestaltwandel Israels.* Hamburg: n.p., 1956.

Bennett, Clinton. *Understanding Christian-Muslim Relations: Past and Present.* London: Continuum, 2008.

Bergen, Jeremy M. "The Holy Spirit in the World." *Vision: A Journal for Church and Theology* 13, no. 1 (Spring 2012): 84–92.

Berkhof, Louis. *Systematic Theology.* Grand Rapids: Eerdmans, 1996.

Berzin, Alexander. "A Buddhist View of Islam." In *Islam and Inter-Faith Relations*, edited by P. Schmidt-Leukel and L. Ridgeon, 225–51. London: SCM, 2007.

Bharat, Sandy. "Hindu Perspectives on Jesus." In *The Blackwell Companion to Jesus*, edited by Delbert Burkett. Oxford: Wiley-Blackwell, 2011.

Bharathi, B. S. "Spirit Possession and Healing Practices in a South Indian Fishing Community." *Man in India* 73, no. 4 (1968): 343–52.

Birch, C., W. Eaking, and J. B. McDaniel, eds. *Liberating Life: Contemporary Approaches to Ecological Theology.* Maryknoll, NY: Orbis, 1990.

Birnbaum, Raoul. *The Healing Buddha.* Boulder, CO: Shambhala, 1989.

Bizri, Nader, -el. "God: Essence and Attributes." In *CCCIT*.

Bloch, Maurice. *Prey into Hunter: The Politics of Religious Experience.* Cambridge: Cambridge University Press, 1992.

Bloesch, Donald G. *The Last Things: Resurrection, Judgment, Glory.* Downers Grove, IL: InterVarsity Press, 2004.

Bloom, Alfred. "Jesus in the Pure Land." Chapter 3 in *JWF*.

―――. *Shinran's Gospel of Pure Grace.* Association for Asian Studies Monographs 20. Tucson: University of Arizona Press, 1965.

Boonyakiat, Satanun. "A Christian Theology of Suffering in the Context of Theravada Buddhism in Thailand." PhD diss., School of Theology, Fuller Theological Seminary, 2009.

Boyd, Gregory A. *God at War: The Bible & Spiritual Conflict*. Downers Grove, IL: Inter-Varsity Press, 1997.

Boyd, Robin H. S. "The End of Eschatology? Questions on the Future of Interfaith Relations—Part 1." *Expository Times* 123, no. 5 (February 2012): 209–17.

———. *An Introduction to Indian Christian Theology*. Madras: Christian Literature Society, 1969.

Braaten, Carl E. "Introduction: The Resurrection in Jewish-Christian Dialogue." In *The Resurrection of Jesus: A Jewish Perspective*, by Pinchas Lapide. Minneapolis: Augsburg, 1983.

Braswell, George W., Jr. *Islam: Its Prophet, Peoples, Politics, and Power*. Nashville: Broadman & Holman, 1996.

Brekke, Torkel. "Conversion in Buddhism?" In *Religious Conversion in India*, edited by Rowena Robinson and Sathianathan Clarke, 181–91. New York: Oxford University Press, 2007.

Brill, Alan. *Judaism and Other Religions: Models of Understanding*. New York: Palgrave Macmillan, 2010.

Brinner, William M., and Devin J. Stewart. "Conversion." In *The Oxford Encyclopedia of the Islamic World*, edited by John L. Esposito. Oxford: Oxford University Press, 2009. Oxford Islamic Studies Online. http://www.oxfordislamicstudies.com /article/opr/t236/e0165.

Brockington, John. *Hinduism and Christianity*. New York: St. Martin's, 1992.

Brown, Michael L. *Israel's Divine Healer*. Grand Rapids: Zondervan, 1995.

Brown, Raymond E. *The Death of the Messiah: From Gethsemane to the Grave*. Vol. 1. New York: Doubleday, 1994.

———. *An Introduction to the New Testament*. New York: Doubleday, 1997.

Brueggemann, Walter. *The Covenanted Self: Explorations in Law and Covenant*. Minneapolis: Augsburg Fortress, 1999.

———. *Theology of the Old Testament: Testimony, Dispute, Advocacy*. Minneapolis: Augsburg Fortress, 1997.

Brunn, Stanley D., ed. *The Changing World Religion Map: Sacred Places, Identities, Practices, and Politics*. 5 vols. Dordrecht and New York: Springer, 2015.

Buber, Martin. *Der Jude und Sein Judentum: Gesammelte Aufsätze und Reden*. Cologne: n.p., 1963.

———. "The Two Foci of the Jewish Soul." In *Israel and the World: Essays in a Time of Crisis*. New York: Schocken Books, 1963.

Buddhagosa. *Visuddhimagga, the Path of Purification: The Classic Manual of Buddhist Doctrine and Meditation*. Translated by Bikkhu Nanamoli. Kandy, Sri Lanka: Buddhist Publication Society, 2011. http://www.accesstoinsight.org/lib/authors /nanamoli/PathofPurification2011.pdf.

Burrell, David B. "Freedom and Creation in the Abrahamic Traditions." *International Philosophical Quarterly* 40 (2000): 161–71.

Burton, David. "A Buddhist Perspective." In *OHRD*, 321–36.

Cabezón, José Ignacio. "Buddhism and Science: On the Nature of the Dialogue." In *Bud-

dhism and Science: Breaking New Ground, edited by B. Alan Wallace, 35–68. New York: Columbia University Press, 2003.

———. "Buddhist Views of Jesus." Chapter 1 in *JWF*.

Candasiri, Sister Ajahn. "Jesus: A Theravadan Perspective." Chapter 2 in *JWF*.

Cantor, Geoffrey, and Marc Swetlitz, eds. *Jewish Tradition and the Challenge of Darwinism.* Chicago: University of Chicago Press, 2006.

Carman, John B. *Majesty and Meekness: A Comparative Study of Contrast and Harmony in the Concept of God.* Grand Rapids: Eerdmans, 1994.

Chandngarm, Saeng. *Arriyasatsee* [Four Noble Truths]. Bangkok: Sangsan Books, 2001.

Chappell, D. W. "Buddhist Interreligious Dialogue: To Build a Global Community." In *The Sound of Liberating Truth: Buddhist-Christian Dialogues in Honor of Frederick J. Streng*, edited by S. B. King and P. O. Ingam, 3–35. Richmond, UK: Curzon, 1999.

Chapple, Christopher. "Asceticism and the Environment: Jainism, Buddhism, and Yoga." *CrossCurrents* 57, no. 4 (2008): 514–25.

Chatterjee, Susmita. "Acharya Jagadish Chandra Bose: Looking beyond the Idiom." In *Science, Spirituality, and the Modernization of India*, edited by Makarand Paranjape. Anthem South Asian Studies. London: Anthem, 2008.

Cheetham, David, Ulrich Winkler, Oddbjørn Leirvik, and Judith Gruber, eds. *Interreligious Hermeneutics in Pluralistic Europe: Between Texts and People.* Amsterdam and New York: Rodopi, 2011.

Chemparathy, George. "The Veda as Revelation." *Journal of Dharma* 7, no. 3 (1982): 253–74.

Chishti, Saadia Khawar Khan. "*Fiṭra*: An Islamic Model for Humans and the Environment." In *I&E*, 67–82.

Chittick, William C. "The Anthropocosmic Vision in Islamic Thought." In *God, Life, and the Cosmos: Christian and Islamic Perspectives*, edited by Ted Peters, Muzaffar Iqbal, and Syed Nomanul Haq, 125–52. Surrey, UK: Ashgate, 2002.

———. "Muslim Eschatology." In *OHE*, 132–50.

Chopra, Deepak. *Journey into Healing: Awakening the Wisdom within You.* London: Ebury, 2010.

Choudhury, Masudul Alam. "The 'Tawhidi' Precept in the Sciences." In *ISHCP* 1:243–67.

Chung, Paul S. *Martin Luther and Buddhism: Aesthetics of Suffering.* 2nd ed. Portland, OR: Pickwick, 2008.

Cleary, J. C. "Trikaya and Trinity: The Mediation of the Absolute." *Buddhist-Christian Studies* 6 (1986): 63–78.

Clifford, Anne M. "Creation." In *Systematic Theology: Roman Catholic Perspectives*, edited by Francis Schüssler Fiorenza and John P. Galvin, 1:193–248. Minneapolis: Fortress, 1991.

Clooney, Francis X., SJ. *Comparative Theology: Deep Learning across Religious Borders.* West Sussex, UK: Wiley-Blackwell, 2010.

———. *Hindu God, Christian God: How Reason Helps Break Down the Boundaries between Religions.* Oxford: Oxford University Press, 2001.

———. "Trinity and Hinduism." In *Cambridge Companion to the Trinity*, edited by Peter C. Phan, 309–24. Cambridge: Cambridge University Press, 2011.

Clouse, Robert G. "Fundamentalist Eschatology." In *OHE*, 263–77.

Cohen, Arthur A. "Resurrection of the Dead." In *20th Century Religious Thought: Original Essays on Critical Concepts, Movements, and Beliefs*, edited by Arthur A. Cohen and Paul Mendes-Flohr, 807–13. Philadelphia: Jewish Publication Society, 2009.

Cohen, Charles L., and Ronald L. Numbers, eds. *Gods in America: Religious Pluralism in the United States*. New York: Oxford University Press, 2013.

Cohen, Hermann. *Religion of Reason: Out of the Sources of Judaism*. Translation and introduction by Simon Kaplan. 2nd rev. ed. New York: Frederick Ungar, 1972 [1919].

Cohn-Sherbok, Daniel. *The Crucified Jew*. London: HarperCollins, 1992.

Cohon, Samuel S. *Essays in Jewish Theology*. Cincinnati: Hebrew Union College Press, 1987.

———. *Jewish Theology: A Historical and Systematic Interpretation of Judaism and Its Foundations*. Assen, the Netherlands: van Gorcum, 1971.

Collins, John J. "Apocalyptic Eschatology in the Ancient World." In *OHE*, 40–55.

Collins, Steven. *Selfless Persons: Imagery and Thought in Theravada Buddhism*. Cambridge: Cambridge University Press, 1982.

Conradie, Ernst M. *Hope for the Earth: Vistas for a New Century*. Eugene, OR: Wipf & Stock, 2005.

Cook, David. "Early Islamic and Classical Sunni and Shi'ite Apocalyptic Movements." In *OHM*, 267–83.

Cook, Michael J. "Jewish Perspectives on Jesus." In *The Blackwell Companion to Jesus*, edited by Delbert Burkett. Oxford: Wiley-Blackwell, 2011.

Cornell, Vincent. "Listening to God through the Qur'an." In *Scriptures in Dialogue: Christians and Muslims Studying the Bible and the Qur'an Together*, edited by Michael Ipgrave, 36–62. London: Church House Publishing, 2004.

Corrigan, John, Frederick M. Denny, Carlos M. N. Eire, and Martin S. Jaffee. *Jews, Christians, Muslims: A Comparative Introduction to Monotheistic Religions*. 2nd ed. Upper Saddle River, NJ: Prentice Hall, 2012.

Courtright, Paul B. "Worship and Devotional Life: Hindu Devotional Life." In *ER* 14:9820–26.

Coward, Harold. Introduction to *Experiencing Scripture in World Religions*, edited by H. Coward, 1–14. Maryknoll, NY: Orbis, 2000.

———. *Pluralism: Challenge to World Religions*. Maryknoll, NY: Orbis, 1985.

———. *Sacred Word and Sacred Text: Scripture in World Religions*. Maryknoll, NY: Orbis, 1988.

———. *Sin and Salvation in the World Religions: A Short Introduction*. Oxford: Oneworld, 2003.

Cragg, Kenneth. "Al-Rahman al-Rahim." *Muslim World* 43 (1953): 235–36.

———. *The Call of the Minaret*. Rev. ed. Maryknoll, NY: Orbis, 1985 [1956].

———. "God and Salvation (an Islamic Study)." *Studia Missionalia* 29 (1980): 154–66.

———. *Jesus and the Muslim: An Exploration*. London: Allen & Unwin, 1985; Oxford: Oneworld, 1999.

———. *The Privilege of Man: A Theme in Judaism, Islam, and Christianity*. London: Athlone Press, 1968.

Crollius, Arya Roest. "Salvation in the Qur'an." *Studia Missionalia* 29 (1980): 125–39.

Daley, Brian E. "Eschatology in the Early Church Fathers." In *OHE*, 91–109.

Danan, Julie Hilton. "The Divine Voice in Scripture: *Ruah ha-Kodesh* in Rabbinic Literature." PhD diss., University of Texas at Austin, 2009. http://repositories.lib.utexas.edu/bitstream/handle/2152/17297/dananj31973.pdf?sequence=2.

Daniel, P. S. *Hindu Response to Religious Pluralism.* Delhi: Kant Publications, 2000.

Darroll, Bryant M., and Christopher Lamb, eds. *Religious Conversion: Contemporary Practices and Controversies.* New York: Cassell, 1999.

Dasgupta, Surendranath. *A History of Indian Philosophy.* Cambridge: Cambridge University Press, 1922.

Davary, Bahar. "Forgiveness in Islam: Is It an Ultimate Reality?" *Ultimate Reality and Meaning: Interdisciplinary Studies in the Philosophy of Understanding* 27, no. 2 (2004): 127–41.

Davies, Steven L. *Jesus the Healer: Possession, Trance, and the Origins of Christianity.* New York: Continuum, 1995.

Davis, John R. *Poles Apart: Contextualizing the Gospel in Asia.* Bangalore: Theological Book Trust, 1998.

Davis, Stephen T. "Karma or Grace." In *The Redemption: An Interdisciplinary Symposium on Christ as Redeemer,* edited by Stephen T. Davis, Daniel Kendall, SJ, and Gerald O'Collins, SJ, 237–38. Oxford: Oxford University Press, 2004.

Deane-Drummond, Celia. *Eco-Theology.* London: Darton, Longman & Todd, 2008.

Deedat, Ahmed. *Crucifixion or Cruci-fiction?* Durban: Islamic Propagation Centre International, 1984.

De Lange, Nicholas. *An Introduction to Judaism.* Cambridge: Cambridge University Press, 2000.

Denffer, Ahmad von. *Ulūm al-Qur'ān: An Introduction to the Sciences of the Qur'an.* Leicester: Islamic Foundation, 1983.

Denny, Frederick Mathewson. *An Introduction to Islam.* 2nd ed. New York: Macmillan, 1994.

———. "The Meaning of Ummah in the Qur'ān." *History of Religions* 15, no. 1 (1975): 34–70.

———. "The Qur'anic Vocabulary of Repentance: Orientations and Attitudes." *Journal of the American Academy of Religion* 47, no. 4 (1979): 649–64.

———. "Salvation in the Qur'an." In *In Quest of an Islamic Humanism,* edited by A. H. Green. Cairo: American University in Cairo Press, 1984.

Desai, Prakash N. *Health and Medicine in the Hindu Tradition: Continuity and Cohesion.* New York: Crossroad, 1989.

Dharmaraj, Jacob S. "Sin and Salvation: Christianity and Islam." *Bangalore Theological Forum* 30 (1998): 45–67.

Dharmasiri, Gunapala. *A Buddhist Critique of the Christian Concept of God: A Critique of the Concept of God in Contemporary Christian Theology and Philosophy of Religion from the Point of View of Early Buddhism.* Colombo, Sri Lanka: Lake House Investments, 1974.

Dhavamony, Mariasusai. "Death and Immortality in Hinduism." In *DIRW*, 93–108.

Dobkowski, Michael. "'A Time for War and Time for Peace': Teaching Religion and Violence in the Jewish Tradition." Chapter 2 in *TRV*.

Doniger, Wendy. *On Hinduism*. Online ed. Oxford: Oxford University Press, 2014.

Dwivedi, O. P. "Classical India." In *A Companion to Environmental Philosophy*, edited by Dale Jamieson, 37–51. Oxford: Blackwell, 2001.

———. "Dharmic Ecology." In *Hinduism and Ecology: The Intersection of Earth, Sky, and Water*, edited by Christopher Key Chapple and Mary Evelyn Tucker, 3–22. Religions of the World and Ecology. Cambridge, MA: Harvard University Press, 2000.

Eckel, Malcolm David. "Buddhism." In *Eastern Religions: Origins, Beliefs, Practices, Holy Texts, Sacred Places*, edited by Michael D. Coogan. Oxford: Oxford University Press, 2005.

———. "A Buddhist Approach to Repentance." In *Repentance: A Comparative Perspective*, edited by Amitai Etzioni and David E. Carney, 122–42. Lanham, MD: Rowman & Littlefield, 1997.

Eckel, Malcolm David, with John J. Thatamanil. "Beginningless Ignorance: A Buddhist View of the Human Condition." In *The Human Condition: A Volume in the Comparative Ideas Project*, edited by Robert Cummings Neville, 49–72. Albany: State University of New York Press, 2001.

Efron, Noah J. *Judaism and Science: A Historical Introduction*. Westport, CT: Greenwood, 2007.

Ellis, Marc H. *Toward a Jewish Theology of Liberation: The Challenge of the 21st Century*. 3rd expanded ed. Waco, TX: Baylor University Press, 2004.

Epste, Isidore. *Judaism*. New York: Penguin Books, 1987.

Federman, Asaf. "What Kind of Free Will Did the Buddha Teach?" *Philosophy East & West* 60, no. 1 (2010): 1–19.

Flannery, Edward H. *The Anguish of the Jews: Twenty-Three Centuries of Antisemitism*. Rev. ed. New York: Paulist, 1985 [1971].

Flood, Gavin D. *An Introduction to Hinduism*. Cambridge: Cambridge University Press, 1996.

———. "Jesus in Hinduism: Closing Reflection." In *JBC*.

Foltz, Richard C. "Islamic Environmentalism: A Matter of Interpretation." In *I&E*, 249–79.

Ford, David F. "An Interfaith Wisdom: Scriptural Reasoning between Jews, Christians and Muslims." *Modern Theology* 22, no. 3 (2006): 345–66.

Ford, David F., and C. C. Pecknold, eds. *The Promise of Scriptural Reasoning*. Oxford: Blackwell, 2006.

Frank, Richard M. *Beings and Their Attributes: The Teachings of the Basrian School of the Mu'tazila in the Classical Period*. Albany: State University of New York Press, 1978.

Fredericks, James. "A Universal Religious Experience? Comparative Theology as an Alternative to a Theology of Religions." *Horizons* 22, no. 1 (1995): 67–87.

Freeman, David L., and Judith Z. Abrams, eds. *Illness and Health in the Jewish Tradition: Writings from the Bible to Today*. Philadelphia: Jewish Publication Society, 1999.

Friedmann, Yohanan. *Tolerance and Coercion in Islam: Interfaith Relations in the Muslim Tradition*. New York: Cambridge University Press, 2003, 2006.

Fromherz, Allen. "Judgment, Final." In *The Oxford Encyclopedia of Islam*, edited by

John L. Esposito. Oxford: Oxford University Press, 2009. http://www.oxford
islamicstudies.com/article/opr/t236/e1107.

Fuller, Steve. "Humanity as an Endangered Species in Science and Religion." In *SRPW*,
3–26.

"Furqan, al-." In *The Oxford Dictionary of Islam*, edited by John L. Esposito. *Oxford Islamic
Studies Online*, April 7, 2014. http://www.oxfordislamicstudies.com/article/opr
/t125/e684.

Gadamer, Hans-Georg. *Truth and Method*. Translated by Joel Weinsheimer and Donald G. Marshall. 2nd rev. ed. New York: Continuum, 2006 [1960].

Gandhi, Mohandas K. *The Bhagavad Gita according to Gandhi*. Blacksburg, VA: Wilder
Publications, 2011.

———. *Hind Swaraj and Indian Home Rule*. Online version available at https://www
.mkgandhi.org/ebks/hind_swaraj.pdf.

———. *The Message of Jesus Christ*. Bombay: Bharatiya Vidya Bhavan, 1963 [1940].

Gardet, Louis. "Allāh." In *The Encyclopedia of Islam*. Edited by H. A. R. Gibb et al. Vol. 1.
New. ed. Leiden: Brill, 1979.

Gaudium et Spes: Pastoral Constitution on the Church in the Modern World (Vatican II).
Available at www.vatican.va.

Gertel, Elliot B. "The Holy Spirit in the Zohar." *CCAR Journal: A Reform Jewish Quarterly*
56, no. 4 (2009): 80–102.

Ghazali [Ghazzali], [Abu Hamid Muhammad] al-. *The Alchemy of Happiness*. Translated
by Henry A. Homes. Albany, NY: Munsell, 1853.

———. *Al-Ghazzali on Repentance*. Translated by M. S. Stern. New Delhi: Sterling Publishers, 1990. Available at pub.flowpaper.com/docs/http://www.en.islamic-sources
.com/download/E-Books/Intellectual/philosophy/Al-Ghazali-on-Repentance.pdf.

———. *The Incoherence of the Philosophers*. Provo, UT: Brigham Young University Press,
1997.

———. *The Niche for Lights [Mishkat al-Anwarâ]*. Translated by W. H. T. Gairdner. 1924.
Available at sacred-texts.com.

Gier, Nicholas F., and Paul Kjellberg. "Buddhism and the Freedom of the Will: Pali and
Mahayanist Responses." In *Freedom and Determinism*, edited by Joseph Keim
Campbell, Michael O'Rourke, and David Shier. Cambridge, MA: MIT Press, 2004.

Gillman, Neil. "Creation in the Bible and in the Liturgy." In *Judaism and Ecology: Created
World and Revealed Word*, edited by Hava Tirosh-Samuelson, 133–54. Cambridge,
MA: Harvard University Press, 2002.

———. *The Death of Death: Resurrection and Immortality in Jewish Thought*. Woodstock,
VT: Jewish Lights, 1997.

Gnanakan, Chris. "The Manthiravadi: A South Indian Wounded Warrior-Healer." Chapter 7 in *A&D*.

Goldman, Robert P. "Karma, Guilt, and Buried Memories: Public Fantasy and Private
Reality in Traditional India." *Journal of the American Oriental Society* 105, no. 3
(1985): 413–25.

Golshani, Mehdi. "Does Science Offer Evidence of a Transcendent Reality and Purpose?"
In *ISHCP* 2:95–108.

―――. "Islam and the Sciences of Nature: Some Fundamental Questions." In *ISHCP* 1:67–79.

Gordon, Haim, and Leonard Grob. *Education for Peace: Testimonies from World Religions.* Maryknoll, NY: Orbis, 1987.

Gosling, David L. "Darwin and the Hindu Tradition: 'Does What Goes Around Come Around?'" *Zygon* 46, no. 2 (June 2011): 345–69.

Grant, Sara, RSCJ. *Towards an Alternative Theology: Confessions of a Non-dualist Christian.* With introduction by Bradley J. Malkovsky. Notre Dame: University of Notre Dame Press, 2002.

Greear, J. D. "Theosis and Muslim Evangelism: How the Recovery of a Patristic Understanding of Salvation Can Aid Evangelical Missionaries in the Evangelization of Islamic Peoples." PhD diss., Southeastern Baptist Theological Seminary, 2003.

Gregorios, Paulos Mar. *Religion and Dialogue.* Kottayam, India: ISPCK, 2000.

Gross, Rita M. "Meditating on Jesus." In *Buddhists Talk about Jesus, Christians Talk about the Buddha,* edited by Rita M. Gross and Terry C. Muck. New York: Continuum, 2000.

―――. "Meditation and Prayer: A Comparative Inquiry." *Buddhist-Christian Studies* 22 (2002): 77–86.

Guessoum, Nidhal. *Islam's Quantum Question: Reconciling Muslim Tradition and Modern Science.* London: I. B. Tauris, 2011.

Gupta, Sanjukta. "Jivanmukti." In *ER* 7:4925–26.

Gurmann, Joseph, and Steven Fine. "Synagogue." In *ER* 13:8920–26.

Guruge, Ananda W. P. "The Buddha's Encounters with Mara the Tempter: Their Representation in Literature and Art." *Access to Insight,* November 30, 2013. http://www.accesstoinsight.org/lib/authors/guruge/wheel419.html.

Habito, Ruben L. F. "Environment or Earth Sangha: Buddhist Perspectives on Our Global Ecological Well-Being." *Contemporary Buddhism* 8, no. 2 (2007): 131–47.

Hagner, Donald A. *The Jewish Reclamation of Jesus: An Analysis and Critique of the Modern Jewish Study of Jesus.* Grand Rapids: Zondervan, 1984.

Haider, Najam. *Shī'ī Islam.* Cambridge: Cambridge University Press, 2014.

Haleem, Muhammad [A. S.] Abdel. "Qur'an and Hadith." In *CCCIT*, 19–32.

Hall, Douglas John. *Thinking the Faith: Christian Theology in a North American Context.* Minneapolis: Fortress, 1991.

Hammond, Robert. *The Philosophy of Alfarabi and Its Influence on Medieval Thought.* New York: Hobson Book Press, 1947.

Hamza, Feras. "Unity and Disunity in the Life of the Muslim Community." In *The Community of Believers,* edited by Lucinda Mosher and David Marshall, 65–80. Washington, DC: Georgetown University Press, 2015.

Henriksen, Jan-Olav. *Desire, Gift, and Recognition: Christology and Postmodern Philosophy.* Grand Rapids: Eerdmans, 2009.

Heschel, Susannah. *Abraham Geiger and the Jewish Jesus.* Chicago: University of Chicago Press, 1998.

―――. "Jewish Views of Jesus." In *JWF*, 149–51.

Hick, John. *Death and Eternal Life*. With a new preface by the author. Louisville: Westminster John Knox, 1994 [1976].

Hiebert, Paul G. "Conversion in Hinduism and Buddhism." In *HRC*, 9–21.

———. "Discerning the Work of God." In *Charismatic Experiences in History*, edited by Cecil M. Robeck, 147–63. Peabody, MA: Hendrickson, 1985.

Hiltebeitel, Alf. "The 'Mahābhārata,' and Hindu Eschatology." *History of Religions* 12, no. 2 (1972): 95–135.

Historic Creeds and Confessions. Edited by Rick Brannan. Available at www.ccel.org.

Hobbes, Thomas. *The Leviathan (Or the Matter, Forme & Power of a Commonwealth, Ecclesiastical and Civil)*. Edited by A. R. Waller. Cambridge English Classics. Cambridge: Cambridge University Press, 1904 [1651]. https://archive.org/details /leviathanormatto2hobbgoog.

Hussain, Amir. "Confronting Misoislamia: Teaching Religion and Violence in Courses on Islam." Chapter 5 in *TRV*.

Ibn Taymiyyah. *Ibn Taymiyyah Expounds on Islam: Selected Writings of Shaykh al-Islam Taqi ad-Din Ibn Taymiyyah on Islamic Faith, Life, and Society*. Compiled and translated by Muhammad ʿAbdul-Haqq Ansari. Fairfax, VA: Institute of Islamic and Arabic Sciences in America, 2007. http://ahlehadith.files.wordpress.com/2010/07 /expounds-on-islam.pdf.

Idinopulos, Thomas A. "Christianity and the Holocaust." *CrossCurrents* 28, no. 3 (Fall 1978): 257–67.

Idinopulos, Thomas A., and Roy Bowen Ward. "Is Christology Inherently Anti-Semitic? A Critical Review of Rosemary Ruether's *Faith and Fratricide*." *Journal of the American Academy of Religions* 45, no. 2 (1977): 193–214.

Imbach, Josef. *Three Faces of Jesus: How Jews, Christians, and Muslims See Him*. Translated by Jane Wilde. Springfield, IL: Templegate Publishers, 1992.

Inagaki, Hisao. *The Three Pure Land Sutras*. Kyoto: Nagata Bunshodo, 1994.

Iqbal, Muhammad. *The Reconstruction of Religious Thought in Islam*. Lahore: Ashraf, 1960.

Iqbal, Muzaffar. *Islam and Science*. Aldershot, UK: Ashgate, 2002.

Jacobs, Louis. *A Jewish Theology*. London: Darton, Longman & Todd, 1973.

Jacobs, Mark X. "Jewish Environmentalism: Past Accomplishments and Future Challenges." In *Judaism and Ecology: Created World and Revealed Word*, edited by Hava Tirosh-Samuelson, 449–80. Cambridge, MA: Harvard University Press, 2002.

James, William. "The Will to Believe." In *"The Will to Believe" and Other Essays in Popular Philosophy* [1897] *and Human Immortality* [1898], 1–31. Mineola, NY: Dover Publications, 1956.

Jeffery, Arthur. *The Foreign Vocabulary of the Qurʾān*. Leiden: Brill, 2007.

Johnson, Luke T. "The New Testament's Anti-Jewish Slander and the Conventions of Ancient Polemic." *Journal of Biblical Literature* 108 (1989): 419–41.

Joseph, P. V. *Indian Interpretation of the Holy Spirit*. Delhi: ISPCK, 2007.

Juergensmeyer, Mark. *Terror in the Mind of God: The Global Rise of Religious Violence*. 3rd rev. ed. Berkeley: University of California Press, 2003.

Kabbani, Rana. *A Letter to Christendom*. London: Virago, 2003.

Karingadayil, Santhosh Thomas. *From Darkness to Light: The Concept of Salvation in the Perspectives of Thomas Aquinas and Sankara*. Frankfurt am Main: Lang, 2011.

Kärkkäinen, Veli-Matti. "The Church in the Post-Christian Society between Modernity and Late Modernity: L. Newbigin's Post-Critical Missional Ecclesiology." In *Theology in Missionary Perspective: Lesslie Newbigin's Legacy*, edited by Mark T. B. Laing and Paul Weston, 125–54. Eugene, OR: Pickwick, 2013.

———. *Creation and Humanity*. Vol. 3 of A Constructive Christian Theology for the Church in the Pluralistic World. Grand Rapids: Eerdmans, 2016.

———. "'How to Speak of the Spirit among Religions': Trinitarian 'Rules' for a Pneumatological Theology of Religions." *International Bulletin of Missionary Research* 30, no. 3 (July 2006): 121–27.

———. *An Introduction to the Theology of Religions: Biblical, Historical, and Contemporary Perspectives*. Downers Grove, IL: InterVarsity Press, 2003.

———. *Trinity and Revelation*. Vol. 2 of A Constructive Christian Theology for the Church in the Pluralistic World. Grand Rapids: Eerdmans, 2014.

Kassis, Hanna. "The Qur'an." In *Experiencing Scripture in World Religions*, edited by H. Coward, 63–84. Maryknoll, NY: Orbis, 2000.

Kateregga, Badru D., and David W. Shenk. *Islam and Christianity: A Muslim and a Christian in Dialogue*. Ibadan, Nigeria: Daystar, 1985.

Kavunkal, Jacob. "The Mystery of God in and through Hinduism." In *Christian Theology in Asia*, edited by Sebastian C. H. Kim, 22–40. Cambridge: Cambridge University Press, 2008.

Kelly, John G. "The Cross, the Church, and the Jewish People." In *Atonement Today*, edited by John Goldingay, 166–84. London: SPCK, 1995.

Kenney, Jeffrey T. "Millennialism and Radical Islamist Movements." In *OHM*, 688–716.

Kepnes, Steven. "A Handbook for Scriptural Reasoning." *Modern Theology* 22, no. 3 (2006): 367–83.

———. "'Turn Us to You and We Shall Return': Original Sin, Atonement, and Redemption in Jewish Terms." In *Christianity in Jewish Terms*, edited by Tikva Frymer-Kensky et al., 293–319. Boulder, CO: Westview, 2000.

Kepnes, Steven, and Basit Bilal Koshul, eds. *Scripture, Reason, and the Contemporary Islam-West Encounter: Studying the "Other," Understanding the "Self."* Hampshire, UK: Palgrave Macmillan, 2007.

Kerr, Hugh T., and John M. Mulder, eds. *Conversions: The Christian Experience*. Grand Rapids: Eerdmans, 1983; republished as *Famous Conversions: The Christian Experience*. 1994.

Kessler, Edward. *An Introduction to Jewish-Christian Relations*. Cambridge: Cambridge University Press, 2010.

Kessler, Edward, and Neil Wenborn, eds. *A Dictionary of Jewish-Christian Relations*. Cambridge: Cambridge University Press, 2005.

Keyes, Charles F. "Communist Revolution and the Buddhist Past in Cambodia." In *Asian Vision of Authority: Religion and the Modern States of East and Southeast Asia*, edited by Charles F. Keyes, Laurel Kendall, and Helen Hardacre, 43–73. Honolulu: University of Hawaii Press, 1994.

————. "Monks, Guns, and Peace." In *Belief and Bloodshed: Religion and Violence across Time and Tradition*, edited by James K. Wellman Jr., 145–63. Lanham, MD: Rowman & Littlefield, 2007.

Khalidi, Tarif. *The Muslim Jesus: Sayings and Stories in Islamic Literature*. Cambridge, MA: Harvard University Press, 2000.

Khalil, Atif. "Early Sufi Approaches to *Tawba*: From the Qur'ān to Abū Ṭālib al-Makkī." PhD diss., University of Toronto, 2009.

Khan, Benjamin. *The Concept of Dharma in Valmiki Ramayana*. 2nd ed. New Delhi: Munshiram Mannoharlal Publishers, 1983.

Khatami, Mahmoud. "On the Transcendental Element of Life: A Recapitulation of Human Spirituality in Islamic Philosophical Psychology." *Journal of Shi'a Islamic Studies* 2, no. 2 (2009): 121–40.

Kiblinger, Kristin Beise. *Buddhist Inclusivism: Attitudes toward Religious Others*. Burlington, VT: Ashgate, 2005.

Kim, Kirsteen. "The Holy Spirit in Mission in India: Indian Contribution to Contemporary Mission Pneumatology." A Presentation at Overseas Christian Missionary Society, April 6, 2004. http://www.ocms.ac.uk/docs/TUESDAY%20LECTURES_Kirsteen.pdf.

Kim, Sebastian C. H. *In Search of Identity: Debates on Religious Conversion in India*. Oxford: Oxford University Press, 2003.

Kinsley, David. *Health, Healing, and Religion: A Cross-Cultural Perspective*. Upper Saddle River, NJ: Prentice Hall, 1996.

Klein, C. *Anti-Judaism in Christian Theology*. Translated by Edward Quinn. Philadelphia: Fortress, 1978.

Kloetzli, W. Randolph. *Buddhist Cosmology: Science and Theology in the Images of Motion and Light*. Delhi: Motilal Banarsidass Publishers, 1989.

Klostermaier, Klaus. *A Survey of Hinduism*. 3rd ed. Albany: State University of New York Press, 2010.

Knipe, David M. "Hindu Eschatology." In *OHE*, 170–90.

Köchler, Hans, ed. *The Concept of Monotheism in Islam and Christianity*. Vienna: Wilhelm Braumüller, 1982.

Kogan, Michael S. *Opening the Covenant: A Jewish Theology of Christianity*. Oxford: Oxford University Press, 2008.

Koshul, Basit. "Affirming the Self through Accepting the Other." In *Scriptures in Dialogue: Christians and Muslims Studying the Bible and the Qur'an Together*, edited by Michael Ipgrave. London: Church House Publishing, 2004.

Krishnananda, Swami. *The Philosophy of the Bhagavadgita*. Rishikesh, India: Divine Life Society Sivananda Ashram, n.d. https://www.swami-krishnananda.org/gita_00.html.

Kritzeck, James. "Holy Spirit in Islam." In *Perspectives on Charismatic Renewal*, edited by Edward D. O'Connor, 101–11. Notre Dame: University of Notre Dame Press, 1975.

Kulandran, Sabapathy. *Grace in Christianity and Hinduism*. Cambridge: James Clarke, 2000 [1964].

Kumar, B. J. Christie. "An Indian Appreciation of the Doctrine of the Holy Spirit: A Search into the Religious Heritage of the Indian Christian." *Indian Journal of Theology* 30 (1981): 29–35.

Küng, Hans. "A Christian Response [to Heinz Bechert: Buddhist Perspectives]," in *Christianity and the World Religions: Paths to Dialogue with Islam, Hinduism, and Buddhism*, by Hans Küng, with Josef van Ess, Heinrich von Stietencron, and Heinz Bechert, translated by Peter Heinegg, 306–28. New York: Doubleday, 1986.

————. "A Christian Response [to Josef van Ess: Islamic Perspectives]," in *Christianity and the World Religions: Paths to Dialogue with Islam, Hinduism, and Buddhism*, by Hans Küng, with Josef van Ess, Heinrich von Stietencron, and Heinz Bechert, translated by Peter Heinegg, 109–30. New York: Doubleday, 1986.

————. "God's Self-Renunciation and Buddhist Self-Emptiness: A Christian Response to Masao Abe." In *DEHF*, 207–23.

Lai, Suat Yan. "Engendering Buddhism: Female Ordination and Women's 'Voices' in Thailand." PhD diss., Claremont Graduate University, 2011.

Lamm, Norman. "Ecology in Jewish Law and Theology." In *Faith and Doubt: Studies in Traditional Jewish Thought*, by N. Lamm. New York: Ktav, 1972.

Lancaster, Lewis. "Buddhist Literature: Its Canon, Scribes, and Editors." In *The Critical Study of Sacred Texts*, edited by Wendy Doniger O'Flaherty. Berkeley Religious Studies Series 2. Berkeley, CA: Graduate Theological Union, 1979.

Langer, Ruth. "Worship and Devotional Life: Jewish Worship." In *ER* 14:9805–9.

Lapide, Pinchas. *Israelis, Jews, and Jesus*. Translated by Peter Heinegg. Garden City, NY: Doubleday, 1979.

————. *The Resurrection of Jesus: A Jewish Perspective*. Minneapolis: Augsburg, 1983.

Lapide, Pinchas, and Jürgen Moltmann. *Jewish Monotheism and Christian Trinitarian Doctrine: A Dialogue by Pinchas Lapide and Jürgen Moltmann*. Translated by Leonard Swidler. Philadelphia: Fortress, 1981.

Largen, Kristin Johnston. *Baby Krishna, Infant Christ: A Comparative Theology of Salvation*. Maryknoll, NY: Orbis, 2011.

————. *What Christians Can Learn from Buddhism: Rethinking Salvation*. Minneapolis: Fortress, 2009.

Learman, Linda, ed. *Buddhist Missionaries in the Era of Globalization*. Honolulu: University of Hawaii Press, 2005.

Lee, Jung Young. *The Theology of Change: A Christian Concept of God in an Eastern Perspective*. Maryknoll, NY: Orbis, 1979.

Lefebure, Leo D. *The Buddha and the Christ: Explorations in Buddhist and Christian Dialogue*. Maryknoll, NY: Orbis, 1993.

Leirvik, Oddbjørn. *Images of Jesus Christ in Islam*. 2nd ed. New York: Continuum, 2010.

Leslie, Donald Daniel, David Flusser, Alvin J. Reines, Gershom Scholem, and Michael J. Graetz. "Redemption." In *EJ* 17:151–55.

Levenson, Jon D. "Do Christians and Muslims Worship the Same God?" *Christian Century* 121, no. 8 (April 20, 2004).

Lewis, Bernard. *Islam and the West*. Oxford: Oxford University Press, 1993.

Lienhard, Joseph T. "On 'Discernment of Spirits' in the Early Church." *Theological Studies* 4 (1980): 505–29.

Lipner, Julius J. *The Face of Truth: A Study of Meaning and Metaphysics in the Vedāntic Theology of Rāmanujā*. London: Macmillan, 1986.

———. *Hindus: Their Religious Beliefs and Practices*. London: Routledge, 1994.

Locklin, Reid B. "A More Comparative Ecclesiology? Bringing Comparative Theology to the Ecclesiological Table." In *Comparative Ecclesiology: Critical Investigations*, edited by Gerard Mannion, 125–49. London: T&T Clark, 2008.

Löfstedt, Torsten. "The Creation and Fall of Adam: A Comparison of the Qur'anic and Biblical Accounts." *Swedish Missiological Themes* 93, no. 4 (2005): 453–77.

Lopez, Donald S. *Buddhism and Science: A Guide for the Perplexed*. Chicago: University of Chicago Press, 2008.

Ludwig, Theodore M. *The Sacred Paths: Understanding the Religions of the World*. 4th ed. Upper Saddle River, NJ: Pearson, 2006.

Luther, Martin. *The Large Catechism*. Translated by F. Bente and W. H. T. Dau. St. Louis: Concordia, 1921.

Lyden, John C. "Atonement in Judaism and Christianity: Towards a Rapprochement." *Journal of Ecumenical Studies* 29, no. 1 (Winter 1992): 47–54.

MacDonald, Duncan B. *Development of Muslim Theology, Jurisprudence, and Constitutional Theory*. New York: Scribner's Sons, 1903. www.sacred-texts.com.

———. "The Development of the Idea of Spirit in Islam: I" and "The Development of the Idea of Spirit in Islam: II." *Moslem World* 22, nos. 1 and 2 (1932): 25–42, 153–68.

Maguire, Daniel. *The Moral Core of Judaism and Christianity: Reclaiming the Revolution*. Philadelphia: Fortress, 1993.

Mahmutcehagic, Rusmir. *The Mosque: The Heart of Submission*. New York: Fordham University Press, 2007.

Maimonides, Moses. *The Eight Chapters of Maimonides on Ethics (Shemonah Perakim)*. Translated and edited by Joseph I. Gorfinkle. New York: Columbia University Press, 1912. http://archive.org/stream/eightchaptersofmoomaim#page/n9/mode/2up.

———. *The Guide for the Perplexed*. Translated by M. Friedländer. 1903. http://www.sacred-texts.com/jud/gfp/index.htm#contents.

Majjhima Nikaya Sutta. In *The Middle Length Discourses of the Buddha*. A new translation of Majjhima Nikaya. Translated by Bhikkhu Ñānamoli and Bhikku Bodhi. Kandy, Sri Lanka: Buddhist Publication Society, 1995.

Majumdar, A. K. *Bhakti Renaissance*. Bombay: Bharatiya Vidya Bhavan, 1965.

Makransky, John J. "Buddhist Analogues of Sin and Grace: A Dialogue with Augustine." Presentation at 2001 Thagaste Symposium, Merrimack College, 2001. http://www.johnmakransky.org/article_12.html.

Malek, Sobhi. "Islam Encountering Spiritual Power." In *Called and Empowered: Global Mission in Pentecostal Perspective*, edited by Murray W. Dempster, Byron D. Klaus, and Douglas Petersen, 180–97. Peabody, MA: Hendrickson, 1991.

Malkovsky, Bradley J. *The Role of Divine Grace in the Soteriology of Śaṃkarācārya*. Leiden: Brill, 2001.

Marcoulesco, Ileana. "Free Will and Determinism." In *ER* 5:3199–3202.

Markham, Ian S. *Against Atheism: Why Dawkins, Hitchens, and Harris Are Fundamentally Wrong*. Oxford: Wiley-Blackwell, 2010.

Martin, F. "Discernment of Spirits, Gift of." In *The New International Dictionary of Pentecostal and Charismatic Movements*, edited by Stanley M. Burgess and Eduard M. van der Maas, 582–84. Rev. and expanded ed. Grand Rapids: Zondervan, 2002.

Martin, Raymond, and John Barresi. *The Rise and Fall of Soul and Self: An Intellectual History of Personal Identity*. New York: Columbia University Press, 2006.

Martindale, Paul. "A Muslim-Christian Dialogue on Salvation: The Role of Works." *Evangelical Missions Quarterly* 46, no. 1 (2010): 69–71.

Martinson, Paul. "Explorations in Lutheran Perspectives on People of Other Faiths: Toward a Christian Theology of Religions." In *Theological Perspectives on Other Faiths: Toward a Christian Theology of Religions*, edited by Hance A. O. Mwakabana. LWF Documentation 41. Geneva: Lutheran World Federation, 1997.

Marty, Martin E. *When Faiths Collide*. Malden, MA: Blackwell, 2005.

May, Peter. "The Trinity and Saccidananda." *Indian Journal of Theology* 7, no. 3 (1958): 92–98.

McGinn, Bernard. *Antichrist: Two Thousand Years of the Human Fascination with Evil.* New York: Columbia University Press, 2000.

McMahan, David L. *The Making of Buddhist Modernism*. New York: Oxford University Press, 2008.

McNamara, Patrick, and Wesley Wildman, eds. *Science and the World's Religions*. Vol. 1, *Origins and Destinies*. Vol. 2, *Persons and Groups*. Vol. 3, *Religions and Controversies*. Santa Barbara, CA: Praeger, 2012.

Mendelssohn, Moses. *Jerusalem; or, On Religious Power and Judaism*. Translated by Allan Arkush. Hanover, NH: University Press of New England, 1983.

Merad, M. A. "Christ according to the Qur'an." *Encounter* (Rome) 69 (1980): 14, 15.

Merrill, John E. "John of Damascus on Islam." *Muslim World* 41 (1951): 88–89. www .answering-islam.org/Books/MW/john_d.htm.

Meshal, Reem A., and M. Reza Pirbhai. "Islamic Perspectives on Jesus." In *The Blackwell Companion to Jesus*, edited by Delbert Burkett. Oxford: Wiley-Blackwell, 2011.

Michael, S. M. *Anthropology of Conversion in India*. Mumbai: Institute of Indian Culture, 1998.

Mikaelsson, Lisbet. "Missional Religion—with Special Emphasis on Buddhism, Christianity and Islam." *Swedish Missiological Themes* 92 (2004): 523–38.

Miller, Jeanine. *The Vision of Cosmic Order in the Vedas*. London: Routledge & Kegan Paul, 1985.

Miller, Roland. "The Muslim Doctrine of Salvation." *Bulletin of Christian Institutes of Islamic Studies* 3, nos. 1–4 (1980): 142–96.

Miller, William D. "Da'wah." In *ER* 4:2225–26.

Mohamed, Yasien. *Fitrah: The Islamic Concept of Human Nature*. London: Ta-Ha Publishers, 1996.

Moltmann, Jürgen. *The Coming of God: Christian Eschatology*. Translated by Margaret Kohl. Minneapolis: Fortress, 1996.

———. *The Way of Jesus Christ: Christology in Messianic Dimensions*. Translated by Margaret Kohl. Minneapolis: Fortress, 1993 [1989].

Momen, Moojan. *An Introduction to Shi'i Islam*. New Haven: Yale University Press, 1985.

Montefiore, C. G. "Rabbinic Conceptions of Repentance." *Jewish Quarterly Review* 16, no. 2 (January 1904): 209–57.

Morris, Henry M. *Beginning of the World*. Denver: Accent Books, 1977.

Mosher, Lucinda, and David Marshall, eds. *Monotheism and Its Complexities: Christian and Muslim Perspectives*. Washington, DC: Georgetown University Press, 2018.

Muhammad, Sayyid. *A Compendium of Muslim Theology and Jurisprudence*. Translated by Saifuddin Annif-Doray. Sri Lanka: A. S. Nordeen, 1963.

Musk, Bill A. "Angels and Demons in Folk Islam." Chapter 10 in *A&D*.

Nagao, Gajin. "The Life of the Buddha: An Interpretation." *Eastern Buddhist*, n.s., 20, no. 2 (1987): 1–31.

Ñānamoli, Bhikkhu, and Bhikku Bodhi. Introduction to *The Middle Length Discourses of the Buddha*. A new translation of Majjhima Nikaya. Translated by Bhikkhu Ñānamoli and Bhikku Bodhi. Kandy, Sri Lanka: Buddhist Publication Society, 1995.

Nanda, Meera. "Vedic Science and Hindu Nationalism: Arguments against a Premature Synthesis of Religion and Science." Chapter 2 in *SRPW*.

Narayanan, Vasudha. "Hinduism." In *Eastern Religions: Origins, Beliefs, Practices, Holy Texts, Sacred Places*, edited by Michael D. Coogan. Oxford: Oxford University Press, 2005.

———. "Karma, Bhakti Yoga and Grace in the Srivaisnava Tradition: Ramaniya and Karattabvan." In *Of Human Bondage and Divine Grace: A Global Testimony*, edited by John Ross Carter, 57–94. La Salle, IL: Open Court, 1992.

Nasr, Seyyed Hossein. "Islam and Science." In *OHRS*, 71–86.

———. *Man and Nature: The Spiritual Crisis in Modern Man*. Rev. ed. Chicago: Kazi Publishers, 1997 [1967].

———. *The Need for a Sacred Science*. Suny Series in Religious Studies. Albany: State University of New York Press, 1993.

———. "The Prayer of the Heart in Hesychasm and Sufism." *Greek Orthodox Theological Review* 31 (1986): 195–203.

———. "The Question of Cosmogenesis: The Cosmos as a Subject of Scientific Study." In *ISHCP* 1:171–87.

———. "Response to Hans Küng's Paper on Christian-Muslim Dialogue." *Muslim World* 77 (1987): 96–105.

———. "The Word of God: The Bridge between Him, You, and Us." In *A Common Word: Muslims and Christians on Loving God and Neighbor*, edited by Miroslav Volf and Prince Ghazi bin Muhammad bin Talal, 110–17. Grand Rapids: Eerdmans, 2010.

Nattier, Jan. "Buddhist Eschatology." In *OHE*, 151–69.

Nazir-Ali, Michael. *Frontiers in Muslim-Christian Encounter*. Oxford: Regnum, 1987.

Nelson-Pallmeyer, Jack. *Is Religion Killing Us? Violence in the Bible and the Quran*. Harrisburg, PA: Trinity, 2003.

Netland, Harold A. *Christianity and Religious Diversity: Clarifying Christian Commitments in a Globalizing Age*. Grand Rapids: Baker Academic, 2015.

———. *Encountering Religious Pluralism: The Challenge to Christian Faith and Mission*. Downers Grove, IL: InterVarsity Press, 2001.

Neufeldt, R. "Hindu Views of Christ." In *Hindu-Christian Dialogue: Perspectives and Encounters*, edited by Harold Coward, 162–75. Maryknoll, NY: Orbis, 1990.

Neumaier, Eva K. "The Dilemma of Authoritative Utterance in Buddhism." In *Experiencing Scripture in World Religions*, edited by H. Coward, 138–67. Maryknoll, NY: Orbis, 2000.

Neusner, Jacob. "Repentance in Judaism." In *RCP*, 60–75.

———. *The Way of Torah: Introduction to Judaism*. Encino, CA: Dickenson, 1970.

Newbigin, Lesslie. *The Light Has Come: An Exposition of the Fourth Gospel*. Edinburgh: Handsel, 1982.

Newby, Gordon D. "Angels" and "Jinn." In *The Oxford Encyclopedia of the Modern Islamic World*, edited by John L. Esposito. Oxford: Oxford University Press, 1995. *Oxford Islamic Studies Online*, http://www.oxfordislamicstudies.com/Public/book_oemiw .html.

Newlands, George, and Allen Smith. *Hospitable God: The Transformative Dream*. Surrey, UK: Ashgate, 2010.

Newman, N. A., ed. *The Early Christian-Muslim Dialogue: A Collection of Documents from the First Three Islamic Centuries (632–900 A.D.); Translations with Commentary*. Hatfield, PA: Interdisciplinary Biblical Research Institute, 1993.

Nicholas of Cusa. *De Pace Fidei and Cribratio Alkorani: Translation and Analysis*. Edited and translated by Jasper Hopkins. 2nd ed. Minneapolis: Arthur J. Banning, 1994. http://jasper-hopkins.info/DePace12-2000.pdf.

———. *Selected Spiritual Writings*. Translated by H. Lawrence Bond. Mahwah, NJ: Paulist, 1997.

Nickel, Gordon. "Islam and Salvation: Some On-Site Observations." *Direction* 23, no. 1 (Spring 1994): 3–16.

Nickelsburg, George W. E. *Resurrection, Immortality, and Eternal Life in Intertestamental Judaism*. Cambridge, MA: Harvard University Press, 1972.

Nostra Aetate: Declaration on the Relation of the Church to Non-Christian Religions (Vatican II, October 28, 1965). http://www.vatican.va/archive/hist_councils/ii _vatican_council/documents/vat-ii_decl_19651028_nostra-aetate_en.html.

Novak, David. "Jewish Eschatology." In *OHE*, 113–31.

"Nurturing Peace, Overcoming Violence: In the Way of Christ for the Sake of the World." World Council of Churches, January 1, 2001. https://www.oikoumene.org/en /resources/documents/commissions/faith-and-order/x-other-documents-from -conferences-and-meetings/theological-reflection-on-peace/nurturing-peace -overcoming-violence-in-the-way-of-christ-for-the-sake-of-the-world.

Oddie, Geoffrey A. "India: Missionaries, Conversion, and Change." In *The Church Mission Society and World Christianity, 1799–1999*, edited by Kevin Ward and Brian Stanley, 228–53. Grand Rapids: Eerdmans, 2000.

Olcott, Henry S. *The Buddhist Catechism*. 2nd ed. London: Theosophical Publishing Society, 1903. Available at www.sacredtexts.com.

Opler, Morris E. "Spirit Possession in a Rural Area of Northern India." In *Reader in Comparative Religion: An Anthropological Approach*, edited by William A. Lessa and Evon Z. Vogt, 553–66. Evanston, IL: Row, Peterson & Co., 1958.

O'Shaughnessy, Thomas J. *The Development of the Meaning of Spirit in the Koran*. Rome: Pont. Institutum Orientalium Studiorum, 1953.

Ott, Heinrich. "The Convergence: Sunyata as a Dynamic Event." In *DEHF*, 127–35.

Özdemir, İbrahim. "Towards an Understanding of Environmental Ethics from a Qur'anic Perspective." In *I&E*, 3–37.

Painadath, Sebastian. "The Integrated Spirituality of the Bhagavad Gita—an Insight for Christians: A Contribution to the Hindu-Christian Dialogue." *Journal of Ecumenical Studies* 39, no. 3–4 (2002): 305–24.

Panikkar, Raimundo. *The Unknown Christ of Hinduism: Towards an Ecumenical Christophany*. Rev. ed. Maryknoll, NY: Orbis, 1981, 1991.

Pannenberg, Wolfhart. "Contributions from Systematic Theology." In *OHRS*, 359–71.

———. "God's Love and the Kenosis of the Son: A Response to Masao Abe." In *DEHF*, 244–50.

Parekh, Bhikhu. *Colonialism, Tradition, and Reform: An Analysis of Gandhi's Political Discourse*. New Delhi: Sage Publications, 1989.

Parrinder, Geoffrey. *Jesus in the Qur'an*. London: Sheldon; Oxford: Oneworld, 1995.

Pascal, Blaise. "Of the Necessity of the Wager." In *Pensées*, translated by W. F. Trotter, section 3. 1944 [1690]. Available at ccel.org.

Pathrapankal, Joseph. "Editorial." *Journal of Dharma* 33, no. 3 (1998): 299–302.

Payutto, P. A. [Venerable Phra Dammapitaka]. *Dependent Origination: The Buddhist Law of Conditionality*. Translated by Bruce Evans. Bangkok: Buddhadhamma Foundation, 1995. http://www.dhammatalks.net/Books3/Payutto_Bhikkhu_Dependent_Origination.htm.

Pearson, Birger. "I Thessalonians 2:13–16: A Deutero-Pauline Interpolation." *Harvard Theological Review* 64 (1971): 79–94.

Pennington, Brian K. "Striking the Delicate Balance: Teaching Violence and Hinduism." In *TRV*, 19–46.

Pew Research Center. *The Global Religious Landscape*. December 18, 2012. http://www.pewforum.org/2012/12/18/global-religious-landscape-exec/.

———. *U.S. Religious Landscape Survey*. June 1, 2008. http://www.pewforum.org/2008/06/01/u-s-religious-landscape-survey-religious-beliefs-and-practices/.

Prabhupāda, A. C. Bhaktivedanta Swami. *Bhagavad-Gita as It Is*. Abridged version. Los Angeles: Bhaktivedanta Book Trust, 1976.

Radhakrishnan, Sir Sarvepalli. *The Hindu View of Life*. London: Allen & Unwin, 1961 [1927].

———. *Indian Philosophy*. Vol. 2. New York: Macmillan; London: Allen & Unwin, 1958 [1927].

———. "The Nature of Hinduism." In *The Ways of Religion*, edited by Roger Eastman, 10–22. New York: Harper & Row, 1975.

Rahman, Fazlur. *Health and Medicine in the Islamic Tradition*. New York: Kazi Publications, 1998.

———. "Some Key Ethical Concepts of the Qur'an." *Journal of Religious Ethics* 11, no. 2 (1983): 170–85.

Rahula, Walpola. *What the Buddha Taught*. Rev. ed. New York: Grove, 1974.

Räisänen, Heikki. "The Portrait of Jesus in the Qur'an: Reflections of a Biblical Scholar." *Muslim World* 70 (1980): 122–33.

Ramakrishna, Sri. *The Gospel of Sri Ramakrishna: Translated into English with an Introduction by Swami Nikhilananda.* New York: Ramakrishna-Vivekananda Center, 1984 [1942]; reproduced in *JBC*.

Rambachan, Anantanand. "Hindu-Christian Dialogue." In *The Wiley-Blackwell Companion to Inter-Religious Dialogue,* edited by Catherine Cornille, 325–45. Chichester, UK: Wiley & Sons, 2013.

———. "Hinduism." In *Experiencing Scripture in World Religions,* edited by H. Coward, 85–112. Maryknoll, NY: Orbis, 2000.

Ram-Prasad, Chakravarthi. "Hindu Views of Jesus." Chapter 9 in *JWF.*

Rauf, M. A. "The Qur'ān and the Free Will [I]" and "The Qur'ān and the Free Will [II]." *Muslim World* 60, nos. 3 and 4 (1970): 205–17 and 289–99.

Rezazadeh, Reza. "Thomas Aquinas and Mulla Sadrá on the Soul-Body Problem: A Comparative Investigation." *Journal of Shi'a Islamic Studies* 4, no. 4 (Autumn 2011): 415–28.

Riddell, Peter G. "How Allah Communicates: Islamic Angels, Devils and the 2004 Tsunami." Chapter 8 in *A&D.*

Rippin, Andrew, and Jan Knappert. *Textual Sources for the Study of Islam.* Totowa, NJ: Barnes & Noble Books, 1986.

Rivera, Mayra. *The Touch of Transcendence: A Postcolonial Theology of God.* Louisville: Westminster John Knox, 2007.

Roberts, Nancy. "Trinity vs. Monotheism: A False Dichotomy?" *Muslim World* 101 (January 2011): 73–93.

Robinson, Neil. *Christ in Islam and Christianity.* New York: State University of New York Press, 1991.

Robinson, Richard H., and Willard L. Johnson. *The Buddhist Religion: An Historical Introduction.* Belmont, CA: Wadsworth, 1997.

Robson, James. "Aspects of the Qur'anic Doctrine of Salvation." In *Man and His Salvation: Studies in Memory of S. G. F. Brandon,* edited by Eric J. Sharpe and John R. Hinnells, 205–19. Manchester: Manchester University Press, 1973.

Rosenbaum, Jonathan. "Judaism: Torah and Tradition." In *The Holy Book in Comparative Perspective,* edited by Frederick M. Denny and Rodney L. Taylor, 10–35. Columbia: University of South Carolina Press, 1985.

Roy, Raja Ram Mohun. *The English Works of Raja Ram Mohun Roy.* Vol. 3, *The Precepts of Jesus—a Guide to Peace and Happiness; Extracted from the Books of the New Testament Ascribed to the Four Evangelists with Translations into Sungscit and Bengalee.* Calcutta: Baptist Mission Press, 1820. [Part I, pp. 172–75, reproduced in *JBC,* 162–64.]

Rubenstein, Richard L., and John K. Roth. *Approaches to Auschwitz: The Holocaust and Its Legacy.* Atlanta: John Knox, 1987.

Ruether, Rosemary Radford. *Faith and Fratricide: The Theological Roots of Anti-Semitism.* New York: Seabury, 1974.

————. *To Change the World: Christology and Cultural Criticism*. New York: Crossroad, 1981.

Russell, Robert J. *Cosmology: From Alpha to Omega; The Creative Mutual Interaction of Theology and Science*. Minneapolis: Fortress, 2008.

Sachedina, Abdulaziz Abdulhussein. *The Islamic Roots of Democratic Pluralism*. New York: Oxford University Press, 2001.

Sadakata, Akira. *Buddhist Cosmology: Philosophy and Origins*. Translated by Gaynor Sekimori. Tokyo: Kōsei, 1997.

Saeed, Abdullah. "The Nature and Purpose of the Community (Ummah) in the Qur'ān." In *The Community of Believers: Christian and Muslim Perspectives*, edited by Lucinda Mosher and David Marshall, 15–28. Washington, DC: Georgetown University Press, 2015.

Samartha, Stanley J. *Between Two Cultures: Ecumenical Ministry in a Pluralist World*. Geneva: WCC Publications, 1996.

————. *Courage for Dialogue: Ecumenical Issues in Inter-Religious Relationships*. Geneva: WCC Publications, 1981; Maryknoll, NY: Orbis, 1982.

————. "The Holy Spirit and People of Other Faiths." *Ecumenical Review* 42, nos. 3–4 (July 1990): 250–63.

Samuel, Reda. "The Incarnation in Arabic Christian Theology from the Beginnings to the Mid-Eleventh Centuries." PhD tutorial, Fuller Theological Seminary, School of Intercultural Studies, Spring 2010.

Sanneh, Lamin. "Do Christians and Muslims Worship the Same God?" *Christian Century* 121, no. 9 (May 4, 2004): 35.

Saritoprak, Zeri. *Islam's Jesus*. Gainesville: University Press of Florida, 2014.

Schmidt-Leukel, Perry. "Buddha and Christ as Mediators of the Transcendent: A Christian Perspective." In *Buddhism and Christianity in Dialogue*, edited by Perry Schmidt-Leukel, 151–75. Gerald Weisfeld Lectures 2004. London: SCM, 2005.

Schofer, Jonathan. "The Image of God: A Study of an Ancient Sensibility." *Journal of the Society for Textual Reasoning* 4, no. 3 (May 2006).

Scholem, Gershom. "Zum Verständnis der messianischen Idee." *Judaica* 1. Frankfurt: n.p., 1963.

Schubel, Vernon James. "Worship and Devotional Life: Muslim Worship." In *ER* 14:9815–20.

Schumm, Darla, and Michael Stoltzfus. "Chronic Illness and Disability: Narratives of Suffering and Healing in Buddhism and Christianity." In *Disability and Religious Diversity*, edited by Darla Schumm and Michael Stoltzfus, 159–75. New York: Palgrave, 2011.

Schüssler Fiorenza, Elisabeth, and David Tracy, eds. *The Holocaust as Interruption*. Concilium 175. Edinburgh: T&T Clark, 1984.

Schwarz, Hans. *Eschatology*. Grand Rapids: Eerdmans, 2000.

Schweizer, Eduard. "On Distinguishing between Spirits." *Ecumenical Review* 41 (July 1989): 406–15.

Segal, Eliezer. "Judaism." In *Experiencing Scripture in World Religions*, edited by H. Coward, 15–33. Maryknoll, NY: Orbis, 2000.

Sen, Keshub Chunder. *Jesus: The Ideal Son; Keshub Chunder Sen's Lectures in India*. 2nd ed. Calcutta: Brahmo Tract Society, 1886.

Sharma, Arvind. *Classical Hindu Thought: An Introduction*. Oxford: Oxford University Press, 2000.

———. "A Hindu Perspective." In *OHRD*, 309–20.

Shatz, David. "A Jewish Perspective." In *OHRD*, 365–80.

Shehadeh, Imad N. "Do Muslims and Christians Believe in the Same God?" *Bibliotheca Sacra* 161 (January–March 2004): 14–26.

Shokek, Simon. *Kabbalah and the Art of Being: The Smithsonian Lectures*. London: Routledge, 2001.

Siddiqui, Mona. "Being Human in Islam." In *Humanity: Texts and Context; Christian and Muslim Perspectives*, edited by Michael Ipgrave and David Marshall, 15–21. Washington, DC: Georgetown University Press, 2011.

Silva, Lily de. "The Buddhist Attitude towards Nature." *Access to Insight*, June 5, 2010. http://www.accesstoinsight.org/lib/authors/desilva/attitude.html.

Sivaraman, K. "The Meaning of *Moksha* in Contemporary Hindu Thought and Life." In *Living Faiths and Ultimate Goals: Salvation and World Religions*, edited by S. J. Samartha, 2–11. Maryknoll, NY: Orbis, 1974.

Skilling, Peter. "Worship and Devotional Life: Buddhist Devotional Life in Southeast Asia." In *ER* 14:9826–34.

Smith, Brian K. "*Saṃsāra*." In *ER* 12:8097–99.

Smith, David Whitten, and Elizabeth Geraldine Burr. *Understanding World Religions: A Road Map for Justice and Peace*. Lanham, MD: Rowman & Littlefield, 2007.

Soskice, Janet M. "*Creatio Ex Nihilo*: Its Jewish and Christian Foundations." In *Creation and the God of Abraham*, edited by David B. Burrell et al., 24–39. Cambridge: Cambridge University Press, 2011.

Stephens, Walter. "Demons: An Overview." In *ER* 4:2275–82.

Streiker, Lowell D. "The Hindu Attitude toward Other Religions." *Journal of Religious Thought* 23, no. 1 (1966/1967): 75–90.

Sutton, Kristin Johnston. "Salvation after Nagarjuna: A Reevaluation of Wolfhart Pannenberg's Soteriology in Light of a Buddhist Cosmology." PhD diss., Graduate Theological Union, 2002.

Tennent, Timothy C. *Theology in the Context of World Christianity: How the Global Church Is Influencing the Way We Think about and Discuss Theology*. Grand Rapids: Zondervan, 2007.

Thatamanil, John J. *The Immanent Divine: God, Creation, and the Human Predicament; An East-West Conversation*. Minneapolis: Fortress, 2006.

Thomas, David. "The Miracles of Jesus in Early Islamic Polemic." *Journal of Semitic Studies* 39, no. 2 (1994): 221–43.

Thomas, M. M. "The Holy Spirit and the Spirituality for Political Struggles." *Ecumenical Review* 42, nos. 3–4 (1990): 216–24.

Tilakaratne, Asanga. "The Buddhist View on Religious Conversion." *Dialogue* (Colombo, Sri Lanka) 32–33 (2005–2006): 58–82.

Timoner, Rachel. *Breath of Life: God as Spirit in Judaism*. Brewster, MA: Paraclete, 2011.

Tirosh-Samuelson, Hava. "Introduction: Judaism and the Natural World." In *Judaism and Ecology: Created World and Revealed Word*, edited by Hava Tirosh-Samuelson, xxxiii–lxii. Cambridge, MA: Harvard University Press, 2002.

Trigg, Roger. *Rationality and Religion: Does Faith Need Reason?* Oxford: Blackwell, 1998.

———. *Religious Diversity: Philosophical and Political Dimensions*. Cambridge: Cambridge University Press, 2014.

Troll, C. W., H. Reifeld, and C. T. R. Hewer, eds. *We Have Justice in Common: Christian and Muslim Voices from Asia and Africa*. Berlin: Konrad-Adenauer-Stiftung, 2010.

Twelftree, Graham H. *Jesus the Exorcist: A Contribution to the Study of the Historical Jesus*. Tübingen: Mohr-Siebeck, 1993.

Umansky, Ellen M. "Election." In *ER* 4:2744–49.

Urban, Hugh B. "Millenarian Elements in the Hindu Religious Traditions." In *OHM*, 369–81.

Van Huyssteen, J. Wentzel. *Alone in the World? Human Uniqueness in Science and Theology*. Grand Rapids: Eerdmans, 2006.

Vargas-O'Bryan, Ivette. "Keeping It All in Balance: Teaching Asian Religions through Illness and Healing." Chapter 4 in *Teaching Religion and Healing*, edited by Linda L. Barnes and Inés Talamantez. New York: Oxford University Press, 2006.

Vattimo, Gianni. *A Farewell to Truth*. Translated by William McCuaig. New York: Columbia University Press, 2011.

Victoria, Brian Daizen. "Teaching Buddhism and Violence." In *TRC*, 74–93.

Vivekananda. *The Complete Works of Vivekananda*. Calcutta: Advaita Ashrama, 12th impr., 1999. [Vol. 8, pp. 159–60 reproduced in *JBC*, 177–79.] http://www.ramakrishnavivekananda.info/vivekananda/complete_works.htm.

———. "Is Vedanta the Future Religion?" In *The Complete Works of Vivekananda*, vol. 8, n.p. http://www.ramakrishnavivekananda.info/vivekananda/complete_works.htm.

Volf, Miroslav. *Allah: A Christian Response*. New York: HarperCollins, 2011.

———. *Exclusion and Embrace: A Theological Exploration of Identity, Otherness, and Reconciliation*. Nashville: Abingdon, 1996.

Vroom, Hendrik. *No Other Gods: Christian Belief in Dialogue with Buddhism, Hinduism, and Islam*. Grand Rapids: Eerdmans, 1996.

Wallace, B. Alan. "A Buddhist View of Free Will: Beyond Determinism and Indeterminism." *Journal of Consciousness Studies* 18 (2011): 217–33.

Wallace, Dewey D. "Free Will and Predestination: Christian Concepts." In *ER* 5:3202–6.

Walls, Jerry L. Introduction to *OHE*, 3–18.

Walter, Jonathan S. "Missions: Buddhist Missions." In *ER* 9:6077–82.

Ward, Keith. *The Concept of God*. Oxford: Basil Blackwell, 1974.

———. *Images of Eternity: Concepts of God in Five Religious Traditions*. London: Darton, Longman & Todd, 1987. Reissued as *Concepts of God: Images of the Divine in Five Religious Traditions*. Oxford: Oneworld, 1998.

———. *Is Religion Dangerous?* Grand Rapids: Eerdmans, 2006.

———. *Religion and Community*. Oxford: Oxford University Press, 1999.

———. *Religion and Creation*. Oxford: Clarendon, 1996.

———. *Religion and Human Nature*. Oxford: Clarendon, 1998.

———. *Religion and Revelation: A Theology of Revelation in the World's Religions.* Oxford: Clarendon, 1994.

Waskow, Arthur. "Is the Earth a Jewish Issue?" *Tikkun* 7, no. 5 (1992): 35–37.

Watt, William Montgomery. "His Name Is Ahmad." *Muslim World* 43, no. 2 (1953): 110–17.

———. *Islam and Christianity Today: A Contribution to Dialogue.* London: Routledge & Kegan Paul, 1983.

———. *Islamic Philosophy and Theology: An Extended Survey.* Edinburgh: Edinburgh University Press, 1962.

———. *Muslim-Christian Encounters: Perceptions and Misperceptions.* London: Routledge, 1991.

Watt, William Montgomery, and Asma Afsaruddin. "Free Will and Predestination: Islamic Concepts." In *ER* 5:3209–13.

Weiming, Tu. "The Ecological Turn in New Confucian Humanism: Implications for China and the World." *Daedalus: Journal of the American Academy of Arts and Sciences* 130, no. 4 (2001): 243–64.

Werblowsky, R. J. Zwi. "Eschatology: An Overview." In *ER* 4:2833–40.

Wheeler, Brannon. "Ummah." In *ER* 14:9446–48.

White, Lynn, Jr. "The Historical Roots of Our Ecological Crisis." *Science* 155, no. 3767 (March 10, 1967): 1203–7. http://www.drexel.edu/~/media/Files/greatworks/pdf_fall09/HistoricalRoots_of_EcologicalCrisis.ashx.

Williamson, Clark. *A Guest in the House of Israel: Post-Holocaust Church Theology.* Louisville: Westminster John Knox, 1993.

Winkler, Lewis E. *Contemporary Muslim and Christian Responses to Religious Plurality: Wolfhart Pannenberg in Dialogue with Abdulaziz Sachedina.* Eugene, OR: Pickwick, 2011.

Wittgenstein, Ludwig. *On Certainty.* Edited by G. E. M. Anscombe and G. H. von Wright. Translated by Denis Paul and G. E. M. Anscombe. New York: Harper & Row, 1969.

Witzel, Michael. "Vedas and Upanisads." In *The Blackwell Companion to Hinduism*, edited by Gavin Flood, 68–98. Oxford: Blackwell, 2003.

Wolfson, Elliot R. "Judaism and Incarnation: The Imaginal Body of God." In *Christianity in Jewish Terms*, edited by Tikva Frymer-Kensky et al., 239–54. Boulder, CO: Westview, 2000.

Woodberry, J. Dudley. "Conversion in Islam." In *HRC*, 22–41.

———. "The Kingdom of God in Islam and the Gospel." In *Anabaptists Meeting Muslims: A Calling for Presence in the Way of Christ*, edited by James R. Krabill, David W. Shenk, and Linford Stutzman, 48–58. Scottdale, PA: Herald, 2005.

Yogananda, Paramahansa. *Man's Eternal Quest.* Los Angeles: Self-Realization Fellowship, 1975.

Yong, Amos. *The Cosmic Breath: Spirit and Nature in the Christianity-Buddhism-Science Trialogue.* Leiden: Brill, 2012.

———. "Discernment; Discerning the Spirits." In *Global Dictionary of Theology*, edited by Veli-Matti Kärkkäinen and William Dyrness; assistant editors, Simon Chan and Juan Martínez, 232–35. Downers Grove, IL: InterVarsity Press, 2008.

———. "The Holy Spirit and the World Religions: On the Christian Discernment of Spirit(s) 'after' Buddhism." *Buddhist-Christian Studies* 24 (2004): 191–207.

———. *Pneumatology and the Christian-Buddhist Dialogue: Does the Spirit Blow through the Middle Way?* Leiden: Brill Academic, 2012.

Yuketswar, Swami. *The Holy Science.* Los Angeles: Self-Realization Fellowship, 1972.

Zaehner, R. C. *Mysticism, Sacred and Profane.* Oxford: Clarendon, 1957.

Zayd, Abu. *Al-Ghazali on Divine Predicates and Their Properties.* Lahore: Sh. Muhammad Ashraft, 1970. http://www.ghazali.org/books/abu-zayd.pdf.

Zebiri, Kare. *Muslims and Christians Face to Face.* Oxford: Oneworld, 1997.

Zwemer, Samuel M. *The Moslem Doctrine of God: An Essay on the Character and Attributes of Allah according to the Koran and Orthodox Tradition.* New York: American Tract Society, 1905.

Index of Authors

Index of Subjects

Abraham/Abram, 50, 54, 137, 210, 222, 236, 242; faith of, 112n3; God of, 57, 67, 79; and Islam, 80–81, 143, 147–48, 166
Acts, book of, 227
Adam, 112–13, 124, 144, 176, 190n6; and Eve, 121, 123; fall of, 120, 122; historic, 89–90
adharma, 125–26, 157, 197
Aditi, 72
advaita, 18n5, 21, 100–102, 111, 118, 198–99, 201, 208
Agni, 72
agnostic/agnosticism, 58, 71, 276
ahimsa, 81, 155
ahsan, 194
Ali, 45, 237, 239
Allah, 80, 107, 112–13, 115, 144, 146, 182, 193–94, 210, 213, 216, 224, 240; and Jesus, 166–67; Qur'an and, 48, 142; spirit of, 176; submission to, 210, 223, 238, 261, 263–64; and Trinity, 59–70
Amidah, 191, 232
Amman, 67
amr, 176
Ananda (disciple), 36
Ananda ("bliss"), 74, 179
ancestor(s), 266; rites, 244
angel(s), 42, 44, 49, 112–15, 124, 134, 174,

176, 194, 263–64; archangels, 262; and demons, 172, 181–83
Anglican, Anglicanism, 121, 188, 221, 228
antaryamin, 178
anthropological concept, 109
anti-Christian, 141, 146, 166n18
anti-Semitism, 54, 131–32, 134, 233
Apocalypse, book of. *See* Revelation, book of
apocalyptic: expressions, 259; speculation, 257; traditions, 261
apocalypticism, 258, 261, 265
apostles, 12, 42
Apostles' Creed, 127n1
Araddha, 38
arahant, 33n50, 168, 205, 248–49, 273
Aranyakas, 18, 21
Arianism, 65
Arjuna, 19, 200, 203
Aryans, 28
Arya Samaj, 246
Asharites, 64, 211
Askari, Hasan ibn Ali al-, 237
atheism, 58, 71, 230
atman, 26, 72, 75, 99–100, 117–18, 267–68; and the Holy Spirit, 178–79
atonement, 161–70, 208; and Christian tradition, 214, 224; and Christology, 11,

Index of Scripture: Christian and Other Traditions